A LUIS LEAL READER

A LUIS LEAL
READER

Edited and with an introduction
by Ilan Stavans

LATINO
VOICES

Northwestern University Press
Evanston, Illinois

Northwestern University Press
www.nupress.northwestern.edu

Printed in the United States of America

10 9 8 7 6 5 4 3 2 1

Library of Congress Cataloging-in-Publication Data

Leal, Luis, 1907–
    A Luis Leal reader / edited and with an introduction by Ilan Stavans.
        p. cm. — (Latino voices)
    Includes index.
    ISBN-13: 978-0-8101-2418-9 (cloth : alk. paper)
    ISBN-10: 0-8101-2418-1 (cloth : alk. paper)
    1. Mexican literature—History and criticism. 2. American literature—Mexican
American authors—History and criticism. I. Stavans, Ilan. II. Title. III. Series.
PQ7114.L43 2007
810.9′86872—dc22

                                                                2007012848

Contents

Introduction: The Day I Was Luis Leal

ILAN STAVANS

The first time I met Luis Leal was at the end of 2003, in the restaurant of a hotel in New York City where the annual meeting of the Modern Language Association was taking place. I am not prone to visit such professional gatherings, which in my view resemble a flock of peacocks. I have made it my code of honor to avoid them as best as possible. But Leal was in town, and after years of correspondence, I did not want to miss the opportunity. Considered to be the doyen of Chicano studies and arguably the most prominent Mexican American literary critic of the twentieth century, he was already ninety-six at the time. I feared his fragile health might not allow me a second chance.

Since his first publication in 1942, Leal has likely done more than any other writer or scholar to foster the critical appreciation of Mexican and Chicano literature and was instrumental in establishing Mexican literary studies in the United States. His earliest work is on such Mexican classics as José Joaquín Fernández de Lizardi, regarded as the first modern novelist in the Americas, and Domingo Faustino Sarmiento, author of *Civilization and Barbarism* and president of Argentina in the nineteenth century. His books on Mariano Azuela's *The Underdogs* and Juan Rulfo's sparse fiction in *The Burning Plain* and *Pedro Páramo* were still sought after when I was a graduate student at Columbia University. And his *Breve historia de la literatura hispanoamericana,* published by Knopf in 1971, which is neither brief nor a single-sided history of south-of-the-border letters, appeared just as so-called El Boom was starting to make noise. It belongs to a time when academics like Seymour Mentor and Jean Franco composed encyclopedic histories, encompassing either the entire hemispheric literature or focusing on a particular genre. Leal concentrated on the short story, in Spanish *el cuento corto*, which, in the fifties and sixties, before the translation of novels such as Julio Cortázar's *Hopscotch* and Gabriel García Márquez's *One Hundred Years of Solitude*, was, as a genre, the Trojan horse of Spanish-language literature. Prior to it, in 1956, Leal, at that time in Mississippi, produced his *Breve historia del cuento mexicano*, in which he highlighted examples from pre-Columbian times (from Mayan, Quiché, Toltec, Aztec, and Tarasco civilizations), as well as those from colonial times, when Mexico was known as the kingdom of New Spain, and then showcased romantic, nationalist, *modernista*, realist, positivist, expressionist, and contemporary stories by such authors as Fray Servando Teresa de Mier, Manuel Gutiérrez Nájera, Martín Luis Guzmán, and Agustín Yáñez. And in 1966, while in Illinois, Leal published the *Historia del cuento hispanoamericano*, an early copy of which I also have in my private collection.

Yet as I told Leal when I sent him a fan e-mail in the late nineties, it was in his brief essays, dispersed in periodicals over a period of six decades, where I found him at his best: ambitious in scope, wide-ranging in knowledge, succinct and crystalline in style, and methodical as well as impartial in judgment. His critical appraisals of Pedro Henríquez Ureña, Amado Nervo, and Rudolfo Anaya, on magic realism and the myth of Aztlán, are a map to the often-tense, fragile relations between the societies that live on both sides of the Rio Grande. When he launched his career, in the early fifties, Chicano studies did not have a place in American academia. Along with Américo Paredes, Leal is deemed a pioneer who placed the discipline on solid ground. His essays on Aztlán, on the mythical figure of La Malinche, and on individual Chicano authors such as Sandra Cisneros, María Cristina Mena, Rolando Hinojosa, and Tomás Rivera fastened the field and allowed others to follow suit.

I expected a fragile, irritable caballero, not quite of this world, and was surprised by his jovial demeanor. It took me a few minutes during breakfast—María Herrera-Sobek and Francisco Lomelí also joined us—to recognize Leal's youthfulness. We discussed comedians like Cantinflas and La India María, the autobiographies of Richard Rodríguez, the debate on immigration. Not long before, Leal had reacted enthusiastically to a meditation I had written on Octavio Paz, and our conversation centered on the controversial first chapter of Paz's, *The Labyrinth of Solitude*, about which Leal wrote an essay in 1977. The aftertaste of our tête-à-tête still lingers in my mind. Ironically, there was an added element to it I did not foresee at the beginning, one that will inevitably color my memory of Leal for good. As a result of it, I ended up becoming Leal for a couple of hours. Since I was already at the MLA, I told an editor and friend of mine I would stop by to say hello an hour after my meeting with Leal. But I did not make the proper arrangements beforehand. As it happens at these types of gatherings, I needed a tag to pass through security and enter the conference. Upon recognizing my dilemma, Leal graciously offered to lend me his, and so, for about half an hour, I became him.

In some sense, it was as if I had suddenly been caught inside a Hollywood movie. There is an age difference of approximately sixty years between the two of us. And our complexions are light years apart. In his early forties, he must have been noticeably taller than I am, and he wears large glasses and is far more ceremonial—formal suit, tie, polished black shoes—in the way he dresses. Leal immigrated to the United States in his late twenties (he was born in Linares, Nuevo León, in the northern part of Mexico, a day after Independence Day, on September 17, 1907), whereas I moved to New York in 1985, in my early twenties—he to enroll in college, I to work as a newspaper correspondent. Consequently, his worldview is less alien and confrontational, more sedate. In an electronic exchange he and I engaged in in June 2003 (titled "Critic at Large," it was collected in *Conversations with Ilan Stavans* [2005]), I asked him what in his opinion is the function of criticism in democracy. "Without general criticism democracy could not survive," he replied. "Or rather, without the liberty to criticize, democracy would be impossible." He then talked about the penurious times when in Latin America dictators like Juan Manuel de Rosas in Argentina, Porfirio Díaz in Mexico, and Augusto Pinochet in Chile silenced, tortured, and exiled dissenters, and thus the right to oppose the status quo, as a way to perpetuate themselves in command. I also probed him on criticism and tenure, suggesting that the comfort of academia has a similar effect: it eradicates disagreement.

I agree with his propositions but believe the critic also to be a thermometer of cultural heat. His responsibility is to ponder ideas big and small, to speak truth to power, to reach out into different disciplines, to be a fearless generalist, to make his message through various genres (the essay, translation, fiction, poetry, political speeches), to engage in media (television, radio, film, Internet), and to leave a record for future generations of the changes under way in his own time. To me, by definition, the literary critic needs to become a cultural commentator. This is because literature no longer holds a privileged place in society. It has been replaced by more nervous media: television, movies, Internet. The critic's duty is to be always on the move, to be an *arriviste*. And since that approach forces him to constantly reinvent himself, to borrow interpreting tools from others, he is also an impostor and an interloper.

Leal is an exemplar of the term *hispanista*. Leal did not receive his bachelor's degree in Spanish and Portuguese until he was thirty-three. Before serving in World War II, already a U.S. citizen, he enrolled in graduate school—the number of Mexican students at the time was insignificant—and in 1950 he received a doctorate from the University of Chicago. He held positions at, among other places, the University of Mississippi, Emory University, the University of Illinois, and finally at the University of California, Santa Barbara, where a Luis Leal endowed chair was established in 1995. (María Herrera-Sobek was its first holder.) As teacher and adviser, Leal has trained a battalion of professionals whose influence is felt nationwide. Among the awards he has received are the Distinguished Scholarly Award from the National Association of Chicano Studies, in recognition of his lifetime achievements; the National Humanities Medal, awarded to him by President Bill Clinton; and the Aztec Eagle, the highest award granted to foreign citizens by the Mexican government. Yet is it accurate to describe Leal as a "foreign citizen" in Mexico? In my eyes, his most significant contribution lies in erasing *la frontera*, the divide between Mexico and the United States. He has spent sixty years of his life building a bookshelf of studies of myth, history, and culture by emphasizing a nonrestrictive, binational identity. Azuela, for instance, a medic during the Mexican Revolution, spent time north of the Rio Grande, as did, at several points, José Vasconcelos, the brothers Flores Magón, the poet Juan José Tablada, Carlos Fuentes, and José Emilio Pacheco, among scores of others.

The two countries are so inextricably connected, Leal's oeuvre shows, as to suggest a single, bifurcated collective self.

For him criticism is almost exclusively preoccupied with community. As Leal stated in "Critic at Large," in Mexico, literature seeks to register people's memory, and among Chicano writers the objective is to use words to legitimize the history and presence of their ethnic minority. For Leal, the critic in the Spanish-speaking world is a heroic debater of ideas. Yet unlike me, Leal has never been a political animal. In our correspondence we have talked about figures like José Enrique Rodó, author of *Ariel*, an invective against materialism released in 1900, at the apex of *modernismo*, and also a subtle attack on U.S. intervention in the Americas. About Amado Alonso, a Spanish philologist, legendary intellectual, and forerunner of contemporary *hispanismo*, who taught at the Instituto de Filología in Buenos Aires, founded the *Nueva Revista de Filología Hispánica* in Mexico, and spent the last period of his life at Harvard. (Leal was his student in Chicago.) And about Alfonso Reyes, a diplomat, classicist, and polymath whose complete works span a total of twenty-two hefty volumes published by Fondo de Cultura Económica. My closeness to Leal has allowed me over time not only to feel connected to him but to claim him as an ancestor. This became apparent as I borrowed his tag at the MLA and momentarily became Luis Leal. Names are not just words; they impose an attitude, a task, a path for us. The exercise was less about superimposed identities—people recognized me okay and a tag at a conference is not read by anyone; it is just a certificate of membership—than about a sense of continuity. Latino culture in the United States is regularly portrayed as light, transient, uprooted. Being Luis Leal for a short time confirmed in me a commitment: to foster intellectual dialogue beyond borders and across languages. I felt a duty toward him. He and I had just met, yet I realized he was my teacher, my link to a tradition I admire but somehow feel alien to.

Regrettably, my trajectory through graduate school was uninspiring. The professors I had at the Casa Hispánica, on Broadway and 116th Street, with the exception of Gonzalo Sobejano, a specialist in Francisco de Quevedo, Leopoldo Alas "Clarín," Camilo José Cela, and Miguel Delibes, were *asalariados* without much passion. When considering Leal's path, one cannot help but feel nostalgic about the noun *philologist*, unfortunately out of fashion today. The *Oxford English Dictionary* defines it thus: "One devoted to learning and literature." And *philology:* "Love of learning and literature; the study of literature, in the wide sense, including grammar, literary criticism, and interpretation, the relation of literature and written records to history, etc.; literary or classical scholarship; polite learning." Since World War II, graduate training in literature has slowly shifted its concentration from language and culture as intertwined organisms in constant change to obtuse French systems of analysis, as well as the countless posts, isms, and other fanciful viewpoints, from structuralism to postcolonialism—all forms of superstition arrogantly reducing literature to forms of oppression. In spite of his drive to catalog knowledge, Leal is the antithesis of hyperintellectualization. Even in the sixties and seventies, when the trend among Chicano students was to denounce, he took a relaxed, contemplative slant. And in the nineties, as the culture wars gave place to a fractured atlas of hemispheric culture, he persisted in looking at texts as bridges between past and present and conduits of straightforward, nonideological information. Indeed, if his career might be said to have a common denominator, it is his rejection of grandiloquence and the need to invariably understand an artist in his proper context.

Among the reasons I wanted to meet Leal was to propose an omnibus of his essays that could serve as a compass to his centripetal awareness. I was convinced such an anthology would help consolidate a field still perceived as incomplete and illegitimate, in part because its critics are tentative about their own standing in the intellectual world. With me I had a file of clippings that included articles in journals and encyclopedias, prefaces, and chapters in books, and proceedings from conferences. They date back to the seventies, when Leal was in his sixties. The majority of the samples were in English. Their date and language more than define their *cosmovisión;* they also announce the way Leal presented himself to the world. Up until the Chicano movement, which stands as a significant chapter of the civil rights era, he fashioned himself as a Mexican in the United States. But the upheaval of the sixties transformed him forever. He no longer was an outsider. For more than three decades he had benefited from the freedom and stability of an academic life. But his students were not foreigners like him. They were bred in barrios across the Southwest and were angry about their living conditions when compared to those of mainstream Americans. Was Leal still an outsider? Until then his writing for newspapers and magazines, and in books, had been predominantly in Spanish. Yet the market forces were changing. There was a desire among English-speaking readers to understand the dilemmas Chicanos experienced. It was then, largely in response to the political and cultural changes that surrounded him, that Leal progressively switched to English. He has never abandoned Cervantes's tongue as a means of expression; still, the majority of his scholarly articles from that period have been in Shakespeare's language. In e-mails and during a subsequent encounter in Santa Barbara, Leal repeated to me that the transition was not easy. He said one always feels more authentic, less restricted, in one's native tongue. But after more than half a life in another country—in another linguistic environment—the primacy of the native starts to crumble and our feelings toward it become conflicted.

All the while I was inside the conference that fateful December, wearing his tag, Leal waited patiently for me in the lobby, far from the hoopla. When I finally came back, he smiled. I thanked him profusely and said the editor I had just visited was eager to publish the omnibus of essays we had discussed.

"Magnífico," Leal said. "Pero . . . ¿será mío o suyo?"

He immediately offered to supplement my sampling with material I might not have seen, some still unpublished. Over the next several months the themes announced themselves, begging to be organized chronologically. I recommended to Leal that the anthology start with an overview of Aztlán, that it include several profiles of figures from colonial times to the age of independence such as Bernardo de Balbuena,

Gaspar Pérez de Villagrá, and Félix Varela, then concentrate on *mexicanos* and Chicanos like Carlos Fuentes and José A. Montoya, and finally conclude with disquisitions on the African influence on Mexican letters, the student massacre of Tlatelolco in 1968, and the ugly American personified by Ernest Hemingway.

Seen in perspective, these thirty-seven pieces deliver an admirably complete picture of *lo mexicano*. (Footnotes have been organically integrated to the narrative and titles have been slightly modified for the sake of coherence. Otherwise, the material appears intact.) The book's title, *A Luis Leal Reader*, was chosen not only to convey the albumlike quality of the book but to underscore Leal's prevalent activity since he was an undergraduate: *la lectura*, the art of reading. These essays, thus, are the memos he himself has compiled over the years, a display of his affinities. Obviously reading for him is not a passive act. It is an act of love that requires discipline. No one should be surprised when coming across repetitions and even a handful of contradictory statements. In collections of this kind, it cannot be otherwise. Plus, intellectuals who profess to sustain a congruous line of thought throughout their lifetime are lying. The life of the mind is filled with paradoxes, ambiguities, and outright inconsistencies. We are not meant to know what we think with any certainty at all times. In fact, a sudden change of heart is often more remarkable than an argument made only to prove consistency of thought.

As this book goes to press, Leal is about to celebrate his centennial birthday. Longevity can be a double-edged sword. In his case, it has enabled him to become a witness to an astonishing array of changes. He came to the world in a preindustrial country, where universal suffrage was not even an idea. An airplane had yet to cross the Atlantic. As Leal moved to the United States, the number of Mexicans like him in El Norte was less than a million. Today the overall Latino population is close to forty-five million. Yes, Mexicans are in the process of becoming Latinos, another component of a minority made of dwellers from various parts of the Americas. He is a role model among Chicanos—Mario T. García and Victor Fuentes produced volumes of interviews with him, published in 1998 and 2000, respectively—but multicultural critics from other disciplines and persuasions do not know him, or else reject him for being fixated on myth and legend. What impact will he have on future generations?

For is there a critic worth the attention who does not invent a tradition?

A LUIS LEAL READER

THEORIZING
AZTLÁN

1

IN SEARCH OF AZTLÁN

One of the functions of the critic is to discover and analyze literary symbols with the object of broadening the perception that one has of a certain social or national group, or of humanity in general. In the case of Chicano literature, a literature that has emerged as a consequence of the fight for social and human rights, most of the symbols have been taken from the surrounding social environment.

For that reason, Chicano literary symbolism cannot be separated from Chicano cultural background. In order to study this symbolism, it is necessary to see it in context with the social ideas that predominate in Chicano contemporary thought. Therefore, we must consult the large bibliography that already exists and pertains to the social, racial, linguistic, and educational problems that the Chicano has confronted since 1848. The social and literary symbols, as we shall see, are the same. Their origin is found in the sociopolitical struggle, from where they have passed on to literature.

The symbols that have served to give unity to the Chicano movement and that appear in literature are many: Aztlán, the black eagle of the farmworkers; the Virgin of Guadalupe; *la huelga* (the strike); the expression *¡Viva la raza!;* and the characteristic handshake, the latter, of course, being outside of the literary field. The greatest part of these

Translated by Gladys Leal. First published in *Aztlán: Essays on the Chicano Homeland,* ed. Rudolfo A. Anaya and Francisco Lomelí (Albuquerque, N. Mex.: Academia/El Norte Publications, 1989), 6–13.

symbols, which give form to the concept of Chicanismo, are of recent origin; they were born with the political and social movement that was initiated with the strike in Delano, California, in 1965. But they have their roots in Mexico's historic past. The Virgin of Guadalupe was one of the symbols that helped to create Mexican nationality and political independence, her image having been hoisted by Father Miguel Hidalgo in 1810. The eagle the farmworkers used has an older origin, dating back to the foundation of Tenochtitlán by the Aztecs in 1325, where the people from Aztlán found on an island an eagle sitting on a nopal devouring a serpent. César Chávez, the creator of this Chicano symbol, said to *Ramparts* magazine:

> I wanted desperately to get some color into the movement, to give people something they could identify with, like a flag. I was reading some books about how various leaders discovered what colors contrasted and stood out the best. The Egyptians had found that a red field with a white circle and a black emblem in the center crashed into your eyes like nothing else. I wanted to use the Aztec eagle in the center, as on the Mexican flag. So I told my cousin Manuel, "Draw an Aztec Eagle." Manuel had a little trouble with it, so we modified the eagle to make it easier for people to draw.

According to accepted definitions, the symbol is a sensory image, which represents a concept or an emotion that cannot be expressed in its totality by any other method. The symbol expresses, with that sensory image, the significance of the spiritual. The image that we see reveals to us or makes us aware of the existence of something beyond the material. In other words, the sensory image, or symbol, is associated with a concept or an emotion (the symbolized thing). Therefore, it is necessary to interpret the symbol (the thing expressed) in terms of what is not expressed. Since the symbol can be social and not necessarily archetypal or mythical, it often has significance only for the group that has produced it and, frequently, only for the artist who has created it.

As a visual symbol, and not a literary one, the black eagle in the white circle over a red background symbolized for the Chicano the triumph

over economic injustice by means of the farmworkers' union, whose aim
is to obtain a better standard of living and also cultural identity. For
those who are not Chicanos, the symbol loses its significance. Nevertheless, since the colors red, black, and white have a universal symbolic
meaning, the image has a broad emotional significance, although not
necessarily the same for all as the one that the Chicano understands. At
the same time, the use of the eagle from the Mexican flag and of the
colors red and white has a symbolic meaning for the *mexicano*, since it
reminds him or her of the national flag. The eagle, Aztlán, the Quinto
Sol, and other Chicano symbols of Mexican origin form a part of a
mythic system, a characteristic often attributed to the symbol. An excellent example of the symbolic use of colors is the creation of Haiti's flag
by the former slave Jean-Jacques Dessalines, who ripped the white color
out of the French flag and sewed together the red and blue, symbolizing
the expulsion of the white people from the country.

Aztlán, which we propose to examine in this study, is as much symbol as it is myth. As a symbol, it conveys the image of the cave (or
sometimes a hill) representative of the origin of man; and as a myth, it
symbolizes the existence of a paradisiacal region where injustice, evil,
sickness, old age, poverty, and misery do not exist. As a Chicano symbol, Aztlán has two meanings: first, it represents the geographic region
known as the Southwest of the United States, composed of the territory
that Mexico ceded in 1848 with the Treaty of Guadalupe Hidalgo; second, and more important, Aztlán symbolizes the spiritual union of the
Chicanos, something that is carried within the heart, no matter where
they may live or where they may find themselves.

As a region in mythical geography, Aztlán has a long history. According to the Nahuatlan myth, the Aztecs were the last remaining tribe
of seven, and they were advised by their god Huitzilopochtli to leave
Aztlán in search of the Promised Land, which they would know by an
eagle sitting on a nopal devouring a serpent. Later, the Aztecs, whose
name is derived from Aztlán, remembered the region of their origin as an
earthly paradise. During the fifteenth century, Moctezuma Ilhuicamina
(1440–49) sent his priests in search of Aztlán. The historian Fray Diego
Durán, in his *Historia de las Indias de Nueva España e Islas de Tierra*

Firme, a work finished in 1581, says that Moctezuma I, desiring to know where the Aztecs' ancestors had lived, what form those seven caves had, and the relation between the people's history and their memory of it, sent for Cuauhcóatl, the royal historian, who told him:

> O mighty lord, I, your unworthy servant, can answer you. . . . Our forebears dwelt in that blissful, happy place called Aztlán, which means "Whiteness." In that place there is a great hill in the midst of the waters, and it is called Culhuacan because its summit is twisted; this is the Twisted Hill. On its slopes were caves or grottos where our fathers and grandfathers lived for many years. There they lived in leisure, when they were called Mexitin and Azteca. There they had at their disposal great flocks of ducks of different kinds, herons, waterfowl, and cranes. Our ancestors loved the song and melody of the little birds with red and yellow heads. They also possessed many kinds of large beautiful fish.
>
> They had the freshness of groves of trees along the edge of the waters. They had springs surrounded by willows, evergreens, and alders, all of them tall and comely. Our ancestors went about in canoes and made floating gardens upon which they sowed maize, chili, tomatoes, amaranth, beans, and all kinds of seeds which we now eat and which were brought here from there.
>
> However, after they came to the mainland and abandoned that delightful place, everything turned against them. The weeds began to bite, the stones became sharp, the fields were filled with thistles and spines. They encountered brambles and thorns that were difficult to pass through. There was no place to sit, there was no place to rest; everything became filled with vipers, snakes, poisonous little animals, jaguars, and wildcats and other ferocious beasts. And this is what our ancestors forsook. I have found it painted in our ancient books. And this, O powerful king, is the answer I can give you to what you ask of me.

Moctezuma I called for all of his sorcerers and magicians and sent them in search of Aztlán and of Coatlicue, the mother of Huitzilopochtli.

The sorcerers in Coatepec, a province of Tula, transformed themselves through the art of magic into birds, tigers, lions, jackals, and wildcats, and in this way arrived at that lagoon in the middle of which is the hill of Culhuacan. They again took the form of humans and asked for Coatlicue "and the place which their ancestors left, which was called Chicomostoc [seven caves]."

The emissaries were taken in canoes to the island of Aztlán, where the hill is. "They say," relates Durán, "that the top half of the hill is made up of a very fine sand." There they found Coatlicue, who demonstrated to them that in Aztlán men never become old. She tells them:

> "Stop so that you can see how men never become old in this country! Do you see my old servant? Watch him climb down the hill! By the time he reaches you he will be a young man."
>
> The old man descended and as he ran he became younger and younger. When he reached the Aztec wizards, he appeared to be about twenty years old. Said he, "Behold, my sons, the virtue of this hill; the old man who seeks youth can climb to the point on the hill that he wishes and there he will acquire the age that he seeks."

The emissaries again transformed themselves into animals in order to make the return trip, which many of them did not succeed in completing because of having been eaten by wild beasts on the way. That is the Aztlán of the Aztec myth, the Aztlán that, like the mythical Atlantis, has never been pinpointed in geography. The search for it, like that for the fountain of youth, has never ceased. Cecilio Robelo, the Mexican historian of Nahuatlan mythology, tells us, "It's generally believed that Aztlán was located to the north of the Gulf of California." But not even that conjecture is accepted, since later he adds, "The inexorable question, then, of the place where the Mexica came from, still remains." And the inexorable question still stands, in spite of the efforts of erudite historians, whether they be Mexican, European, or American, such as Clavijero, Humboldt, Prescott, Orozco y Berra, Eustaquio Buelna, Chavero, Fernando Ramírez, Lapham, Wickersham, or Seler. There was even a book published in 1933 by S. A. Barrett titled *Ancient Aztalan,* which tried to prove that Aztlán can be found in the lakes of Wisconsin. Others have said that it was in Florida; others believe that it was in New Mexico; and still others in California. It was even said that Aztlán was to be found in China. The historian of Santa Barbara, California, Russell A. Ruíz, in a pamphlet published during the summer of 1969 that treats of the passing of the expedition of Portolá through the region, tells us that when the governor arrived on August 20, 1769, at what is today Goleta, California, he baptized the land with the name Pueblos de la Isla, which Father Crespí, who accompanied him, called Santa Margarita de Cortona, and to which the soldiers gave the name Mescaltitlán, believing that they had found themselves in the legendary place of origin of the Aztecs. In a few words, Ruiz says, "Mescaltitlán was another name for Aztlán, the legendary place of origin of the Aztecs or Mexican people. The Aztecs described it as a terrestrial paradise."

What interests us is not determining where Aztlán is found, but documenting the rebirth of the myth in Chicano thought. It is necessary to point out the fact that before March 1969, the date of the First National Chicano Liberation Youth Conference in Denver, no one mentioned Aztlán in writing. In fact, the first time that it was mentioned in a Chicano document was in "El plan espiritual de Aztlán" ("The Spiritual Plan of Aztlán"), which was presented in Denver at that time. Apparently, the rebirth of Aztlán owes its creation to the poet Alurista who already, in autumn 1968, had spoken about Aztlán in a class about Chicano culture held at San Diego State University.

"El plan espiritual de Aztlán" is important because in it the Chicano recognizes his Aztec origins ("We, the Chicano inhabitants and civilizers of the northern land of Aztlán, from whence came our forefathers"); because it established that Aztlán is the Mexican territory ceded to the United States in 1848; and because, following one of the basic ideas of the Mexican Revolution, it recognizes that the land belongs to those who work it ("Aztlán belongs to those that plant the seeds, water the fields, and gather the crops"); and finally, it identifies the Chicano with Aztlán ("We are a nation, we are a union of free pueblos, we are *Aztlán*").

Those words were published in March 1969. Beginning with that date, Aztlán has become the symbol most used by Chicano authors who write about the history, the culture, or the destiny of their people; and the same thing occurs among those who write poetic novels or short stories. During the spring of the following year, 1970, the first number of the journal *Aztlán* was published, and in it the plan was reproduced in both English and Spanish. The prologue consists of a poem by Alurista called "Poem in Lieu of Preface," which united the mythical Aztec past with the present:

it is said
       that MOTECUHZOMA ILHUICAMINA
  SENT
        AN expedition
        looking for the NortherN
  mYthical land
  wherefrom the AZTECS CAME
        la TIERRA
  dE
  AztlÁN
  mYthical land for those
       who dream of roses and
       swallow thorns
       or for those who swallow thorns
    in powdered milk
    feeling guilty about smelling flowers
 about looking for AztlÁN

In the following year, Alurista published the anthology *El ombligo de Aztlán* (*Aztlán's Navel*), and a year later his *Nationchild Plumaroja* appeared, published in San Diego by Toltecas de Aztlán. The title *Nationchild* refers, of course, to the Chicanos of Aztlán. From here on, books in whose title the word *Aztlán* appears would multiply.

    In fiction also, especially in the novel, the symbol has been utilized with advantage for artistic creation. The novels of Méndez, *Peregrinos de Aztlán* (*Pilgrims of Aztlán*, 1974), and of Anaya, *Heart of Aztlán* (1976), are works representative of that tendency. It is fitting to point out that both works have antecedents in Mexican narrative. Gregorio López y Fuentes published in 1944 his novel *Los peregrinos inmóviles* (*Motherless Pilgrims*), and in 1949 María de Lourdes Hernández printed hers, *En el nuevo Aztlán* (*In the New Aztlán*). There is no direct influence between these Mexican and Chicano novels. Nevertheless, the elements that they have in common are significant and permit us to make a comparison. The theme of *Los peregrinos inmóviles* is the search for the Promised Land; in that novel, López y Fuentes re-creates the mythical pilgrimage of the Aztecs. In *Peregrinos de Aztlán* the theme is identical, only that the pilgrimage is in reverse. We read in Méndez's novel: "My imagination got the best of me and I saw a pilgrimage of many Indian people who were being trod upon by the torture of hunger and the humiliation of despoilment, running back through ancient roads in search of their remote origin." López y Fuentes had already written: "We walked all afternoon and part of the night. . . . We were going to the land of abundance: that was the message of the eagle, and we were on the right track."

Another important incidence is that in both works the narrator is an old Indian who remembers the history of his village. For the old Yaqui Loreto Maldonado, in Tijuana, the memories of his fallen and abused people torment him; and for the old Marcos, the memory of the original pilgrimage gives him courage to guide his own people. The first part of *Los peregrinos inmóviles* is titled "Heart of the World." And years later, Rudolfo Anaya would publish his novel with the title *Heart of Aztlán*, in which there is also a pilgrimage that the protagonist makes in search of Aztlán in a vision. Here he has the help of a magic stone instead of the eagle.

A greater similarity exists between *Heart of Aztlán* and *En el nuevo Aztlán*. In both novels the theme is the search for Aztlán, the lost paradise. In the work of Hernández, a group of Aztecs, immediately after the fall of Cuauhtémoc, takes refuge in a secret valley to which they can travel only by means of a mysterious river, which runs inside the grottos of Cacahuamilpa. In that valley, they founded a kind of Shangri-la, a perfect society. In the novel of Anaya, which develops in Barelas, a barrio in Albuquerque, the protagonist Clemente Chávez, not an old man but a man of some years, goes to the mountains, guided by the blind minstrel Crispín, in search of Aztlán on a truly imaginary pilgrimage: "They moved north, and there Aztlán was a woman fringed with snow and ice; they moved west, and there she was a mermaid singing by the sea. . . . They walked to the land where the sun rises, and . . . they found new signs, and the signs pointed them back to the center, back to Aztlán."

It is here where they find out that Aztlán symbolizes the center: "Time stood still, and in that enduring moment he felt the rhythm of the heart of Aztlán beat to the measure of his own heart. Dreams and visions became reality, and reality was but the thin substance of myth and legends. A joyful power coursed from the dark womb-heart of the earth into his soul and he cried out *I am Aztlán!*"

The search, for Clemente, has ended. And that is the way it must be for all Chicanos: whosoever wants to find Aztlán, let him or her look for it, not on the maps, but in the most intimate part of his being.

2

A HISTORICAL PERSPECTIVE

Mexican American literature of all genres is being written, published, and appraised at a striking rate. In addition to established journals such as *El Grito, Aztlán,* and *Con Safos,* new periodicals dedicated to the dissemination of Chicano culture continue to appear. In 1970, at its meeting in New York City, the Modern Language Association included a workshop on Chicano studies; at its meeting in Detroit in 1971, the Midwest Modern Language Association accepted a paper on Chicano literature; and in December of that same year, the American Association of Teachers of Spanish and Portuguese, meeting in Chicago, dedicated an entire section of its program to the examination of Mexican American literature. This condition of affairs has been aptly called by Philip D. Ortego a "Chicano Renaissance."

It is our belief that an effort should be made to trace the historical development of Mexican American literature now that it has been recognized as a subject worthy of serious study. It has not yet been determined, however, whether Mexican American literature should be considered as an entity in itself, as a part of American literature, or even, perhaps, as a part of Mexican literature. It has been pointed out that since Chicanos are Americans, their literature should not be separated from American literature. On the other hand, since a large part of

First published in *Revista Chicano-Riqueña* 1, no. 1 (1973): 32–44. Reprinted in *Modern Chicano Writers: A Collection of Critical Essays,* ed. Joseph Sommers and Tomás Ybarra-Frausto (Englewood Cliffs, N.J.: Prentice Hall, 1979), 18–30.

Mexican American literature is written in Spanish, or is bilingual, its study has often been assigned to critics and professors of Spanish American literature, primarily those acquainted with Mexican literature, for Chicano literature is a living organism: its roots are to be found in the long literary tradition of Mexico, while its flowers grow for the English or bilingual reader, and especially for the Chicanos who form part of that reading public. Though the use of a dual language poses a problem for critics, excellent contributions of criticism and analysis have already been made by specialists in both English and Spanish American studies, such as Philip D. Ortego, Gerald Haslam, Robert Blauner, Edward Simmen, Octavio Ignacio Romano-V., Herminio Ríos C., Tomás Rivera, and José R. Reyna. The training of Chicano specialists conversant not only with American literature but also with Mexican letters and Chicano culture will accelerate the formation of a tradition in Chicano literary criticism. Better still would be the training of Chicanos themselves to evaluate their own artistic productions. In regard to this, Teresa McKenna has said, "The Chicano must not only address himself to the creation of a distinct literature emergent from his own reality, he must also contribute to the further richness of his art through the development of a body of criticism that approaches Chicano literature from a Chicano perspective."

To consider Chicano literature as a part of American literature is an object too idealistic, at least for the time being, for socially Chicanos are considered a group apart. The rejection of the Mexican American in the United States is well documented. One of the best studies is that of Carey McWilliams, who, in 1949, published *North from Mexico,* one of the first books to explore the plight of the Chicano in the United States with a sympathetic attitude.

The rejection of the Chicano is also reflected in literature, as demonstrated by Cecil Robinson in *With the Ears of Strangers: The Mexican in American Literature* and in the short stories collected by Simmen in his anthology *The Chicano: From Caricature to Self-Portrait.*

Neither can we say that Chicano literature is a branch of Mexican literature, even though it has, as we have said, its roots there and still derives inspiration and a model from it. That the Chicano is rejected in the United States does not mean that he or she has always been accepted in Mexico, or even by Mexicans visiting the United States. Amado Nervo, passing through the United States in 1900 on his way to Europe, wrote: "Walking the streets of San Antonio, Texas, I come across one or another type of Mexican, but all so distasteful that I dare not approach them, because I know that from their lips I can expect only gutter sentences, and I do not wish to witness the profanation of the harmonious treasure of my old Latin language." In more recent years, walking down the streets of Los Angeles, another American city with a large Chicano population, the poet Octavio Paz had this to say: "Something similar occurs with the Mexicans whom one meets in the street; although they have lived there for many years, they still wear the same clothing, speak the same language, and are ashamed of their origins. No one would confuse them with authentic North Americans." The same point is made from a different direction by José Vasconcelos in defining *pocho:* "A word that is used in California to designate the outcast who rejects Mexican culture although he has it in his blood, and who attempts to adjust all his actions imitatively to those of the present rulers of the region."

This attitude is not confined to writers alone. The new immigrant, too, often considered himself superior to the conforming Mexican American. The sociologist Manuel Gamio, in 1931, collected this testimony from Anastacio Torres, of León, Guanajuato: "I don't have anything against the *pochos,* but the truth is that although they are Mexicans, for they are of our own blood because their parents were Mexicans, they pretend that they are Americans. They also want to talk in English and they speak Spanish very badly. That is why I don't like them." In recent years, of course, this attitude has changed in Mexico mainly as a result of the Chicanos' struggle for civil rights. The Chicanos and their problems are now viewed with sympathy, and an effort is being made to understand them, as is evidenced by recent articles in the weekly review *Siempre!,* in the important *Cuadernos Americanos,* and in books such as those written by Gilberto López y Rivas and Hernán Solís Garza.

If the Chicano was rejected by both the Anglo-American and the Mexican national, he himself rejected both groups. The pachuco, says

Paz, "does not wish to return to his Mexican origin; nor it would seem does he wish to blend into North American life." This desire to establish an identity has resulted in the creation of a unique literature that reflects Chicano culture and possesses characteristics that differentiate it from Anglo-American as well as Mexican literature.

Before the word *Chicano* became naturalized, no one spoke of a Mexican American literature or a Mexican American art. On this account, some critics have tended to identify Chicano literature with that written during the last decade by militants. Simmen, in the introduction to his collection of short stories, claims that Chicano literature did not exist before our own days. To explain its absence, he argues that Chicano society did not permit the appearance of the Chicano writer. The rich, educated minority were not interested in writing, and the poor were not trained to do so. The emerging middle class, the so-called *vendidos*, was not concerned, Simmen holds, to preserve their way of life, and therefore had no will to give it expression in literary works. To prove his theory, Simmen cites his own bibliography of Chicano literature, in which the earliest Chicano work dates from 1947. But this is argument by fiat. For Simmen, a Chicano can only be an American of Mexican descent who has liberal or radical ideas about the social and economic order. Necessarily, then, Chicano literature is of recent origin, appearing at the same time as the social and economic movement called El Movimiento.

A less restrictive definition is that of Luis Dávila. He holds that Chicano literature is literature written by Americans of Mexican descent "regardless of what they might prefer to call themselves." If it is of recent origin this is because "the bicultural Mexican-American writer of yesteryear often found himself in awkward relation to the supposedly monolithic cultures of the United States and Mexico. For this reason he virtually did not exist." For a definition still less restrictive, one may point to Herminio Ríos C., who identifies Mexican American (or Chicano) literature as that written by the Spanish-speaking inhabitants of the Southwest since 1848.

During the 1930s and before, Americans of Mexican descent and "Americanized" Mexicans were called *pochos* by the recent immigrants. In return, the *pochos* called the immigrants Chicanos (short for *mexicanos*).

The terms *Chicano* and *Mexican American* thus came to be used interchangeably. The review *El Grito,* founded by Chicanos and a stout defender of Chicanismo, calls itself in its subtitle "A Journal of Contemporary Mexican American Thought."

On these grounds, we shall consider Chicano literature here to be that literature written by Mexicans and their descendants living or having lived in what is now the United States. We shall consider works, especially those dating before 1821, written by the inhabitants of this region with a Spanish background, to belong to an early stage of Chicano literature. We are not overlooking the fact that before 1848 Mexican Americans legally did not exist as a group; they have, however, a long uninterrupted literary tradition. Though in 1848 English became the official language of the Mexican territory annexed to the United States, and for this reason affected the development of the literature of the region, it did not interrupt the tradition.

Accepting this definition of *Chicano,* we can say that Chicano literature had its origin when the Southwest was settled by the inhabitants of Mexico during colonial times and continues uninterrupted to the present. We shall divide its course into five literary periods and cite a few representative authors of each. A great deal of research must yet be done to give Mexican American literature the attention it deserves. Here we can only hint at the possibilities.

The Hispanic Period (to 1821)

This first period is characterized by prose writings of a historical or semi-historical nature, including many descriptions left behind by explorers of the region where the majority of Chicanos now live. Among them we find the *relaciones* of Álvar Núñez Cabeza de Vaca, Fray Marcos de Niza (*Relación del descubrimiento de las Siete Ciudades*), and Fray Francisco Palou; the *diarios* of Juan Bautista de Anza, Miguel Costansó, Fray Juan Crespí, Fray Tomás de la Peña, Gaspar de Portolá, and Fray Junípero Serra; also, a number of *historias, memorias, recuerdos, anales,* and *apuntes.* More significant, perhaps, is the *Historia de la Nueva México,* a rhymed history of the conquest of New Mexico in thirty-four cantos, by Gaspar Pérez de Villagrá.

Essentially, these works do *not* belong to the history of Spanish literature. In the words of Federico de Onís, "The originality of Spanish American literature exists from the very beginning, from the very moment at which America itself commences to exist. . . . 'Originality' derives from 'origin,' and American originality lies in the fact of being America and not Europe." Somewhat earlier, another critic, Menéndez y Pelayo, recognized that Spanish American writers, even those born in Spain, confronted a new environment that modified their attitudes. Spanish American literature had its origins, he said, "in the contemplation of a new world, in the very elements of its landscape, in the modification of human beings by the environment, and in the energetic style of life which they created, first in the effort of colonization and conquest, later in the wars of separation, and finally in their periods of civil strife."

Philip D. Ortego, in his article "Chicano Poetry: Roots and Writers," mentions Ercilla's *La Araucana* and calls it "the first modern epic in the New World dealing with an American theme." Pérez de Villagrá's poem, if incomparably less artistic than Ercilla's, also deals with a distinctly American theme. If *La Araucana* belongs to Chilean literature, why can the *Historia de la Nueva México* not be a part of the literature of Aztlán? As Ray Padilla has said, "all works prior to 1848 can be treated as pre-Chicano Aztlanense materials."

Popular literature brought to the Southwest by early settlers from Mexico resembles the popular literature of Mexico in all its aspects. The many *romances*, corridos, folktales, and religious plays are often difficult to assign to a place of origin with any assurance. In 1600, for example, Juan de la Peña wrote a religious play, *Las cuatro apariciones de la Virgen de Guadalupe*. Since nothing is known about the author, we cannot determine if the play belongs to Mexico or New Mexico. We do know, however, that it was very popular in New Mexico and that it is not mentioned by the historians of the Mexican theater. With another play, a *pastorela*, we are more fortunate. We know that it was written in California in 1820 by Fray Francisco Ibáñez of Soledad Mission.

The corrido, a typical poetic form of the Mexican populace, is very common in the Southwest and wherever Chicanos live. Apparently derived from the Spanish *romance,* it expresses brilliantly the oral impulse that runs deep in Chicano literary culture and, as a "form of the people, has served that culture as a primary vehicle toward self-understanding and self-definition."

No less important than the corrido is the folktale, where we often find modified forms reflecting the psychology not only of the Mexican Indian, but also of the American Indian. The folktale, it is well known, is one of the popular forms that can most easily adopt cultural motives to give expression to the desires and aspirations of the people. Aurora Lucero, who has collected popular literature in her native state of New Mexico, has said of those who brought this literature to the region, "They recited her prayers, they retold her stories, they sang her songs, they reenacted her plays. The fervor that went into the doing, the reciting, the telling and the acting was of such nature as to result in a tradition that was to take roots in the soil, roots that flowered into a pattern that has constituted the basis for living in the Hispanic New World, and a tradition that still endures."

The Mexican Period (1821–1848)

When Mexico's independence was finally achieved from Spain in 1821, the northern provinces, the land now called Aztlán by the Chicanos, became part of the Republic of Mexico. This second period, although short-lived and unstable—it ended in 1848 with the Treaty of Guadalupe Hidalgo—represents an important link in the development of Mexican American literature, since it was during this period that the Hispanic Mexican inhabitants of the region had to decide if they were to remain loyal to Mexico or fight for their own independence. This spiritual struggle gives uniqueness to the literature produced during these years. The clashes with the Mexican authorities began almost immediately. In 1830, while celebrating the independence on September 16 in the house of the governor of California, a violent fight occurred between some young *californios* and "los de la otra banda." In another incident, a certain José Castro was imprisoned for posting derogatory remarks about the Mexicans. According to the memoirs of Governor Alvarado, Castro later beat up the Mexican Rodrigo del Pliego because he had insulted *californios* by calling them ill-bred.

The case of the writer Lorenzo de Zavala is instructive. Having defended the independence of Texas, he lost his Mexican citizenship and was ostracized in his own country. His *Viaje a los Estados Unidos de Norte America* (Paris, 1834) definitely belongs to this period of Mexican American literature. Typical of the poetry of the time are the verses of Joaquín Buelna, who in California between 1836 and 1840 wrote compositions dedicated to the native rancheros. Histories, memoirs, and diaries are represented by José Arnaz, Juan Bandini, and Juan Bautista Alvarado. An interest in the cultures of the native Indians also appears. Gerónimo Boscana (1776–1831) wrote a historical account of the origin, customs, and traditions of the Indians of the Mission of San Juan Capistrano under the title *Chinigehinieh.* Popular literature continues to offer the familiar genres. There are several religious plays, among them a *Pastorela en dos actos* dated from 1828 and signed with the initials M. A. de la C. In New Mexico this popular play was performed regularly. An *Auto pastoral,* of Mexican origin, was performed in Taos, New Mexico, as early as 1840.

Transition Period (1848–1910)

The third period begins in 1848 and ends in 1910, the year of the Mexican Revolution. It is a period during which Mexican American literature lays the basis from which Chicano literature is to develop; a period in which Mexicans living on the land taken over by the United States had to make up their minds if they wished to return to Mexico or stay and become American citizens with all the accompanying requirements of learning a new language and going to new schools. Most decided to stay but to remain at the same time faithful to their Mexican traditions and language. In this way they became trapped, forming, politically, a part of a society that socially rejected them. Poised between two cultural worlds, they developed ambivalent attitudes that were to mold their way of thinking for some time and expressed themselves in the literature of the period, often by use of both languages, Spanish and English. But there were times when the new citizens were able to break through the rigid social barriers and pass on to become part of Anglo-American society. Such was the case of Miguel A. Otero, who was appointed governor of the territory of New Mexico in 1897. How this transition from the use of Spanish to English takes place in Mexican American literature is an area not yet sufficiently investigated. Naturally, writers using Spanish still predominate at this time. As an example we shall mention the works of Francisco Palou, the biographer of Fray Junípero Serra.

Popular literature was perhaps the least affected by the political change. The people continued to produce corridos, *romances, pastorelas,* and *cuentos.* Nevertheless, even here, subject matter was expanded to include events related to non-Mexicans, such as the corrido "Muerte del afamado Bilito" ("Death of Famous Bilito"), in which the death of Billy the Kid is related:

El Bilito mentado
por penas bien merecidas
fue en Santa Fe encarcelado
deudor de veinte en la vida
de Santa Fe a la Mesilla.

This well-known Billy the Kid
for punishment he well deserved
was jailed in Santa Fe
for he owed twenty people their lives
from Santa Fe to la Mesilla.

Another corrido ("La voz de mi conciencia") is significant because it introduces the theme of social protest. This corrido corroborates Romano's theory that the Mexican American was not a passive, resigned person expecting all salvation from without. The *corridista* says:

Treintitres días de cárcel
injustamente he sufrido
por un falso testimonio
de un crimen no cometido.
Cuando el juez nos sentenció
fue cosa de reír
al culpable casi libre
y al inocente a sufrir.

Thirty-three days in jail
unjustly have I suffered
because of a false witness
of a crime I did not commit.
When the judge handed down his sentence
it almost made me laugh
the guilty one would go free
while the innocent was left to suffer.

Still another writer of this period, mentioned by H. Herminio Ríos C., is León Calvillo-Ponce.

Interaction Period (1910–1942)

Immigration from Mexico to the United States between 1848 and 1910 was negligible. After 1910, a large influx of immigrants crossed the border in search of security and work in the green fields of Texas, New Mexico, and California, as well as in the factories of more remote states. Most of these immigrants never returned to their native land (except during the Depression years of the 1930s), and their sons and daughters became American citizens by birth, although still attached to the way of life of their parents. The new immigrants brought new blood into the Mexican American community and reinforced the Mexican traditions. The same thing occurred in intellectual circles with the interchange of ideas among writers such as José Vasconcelos, Martín Luis Guzmán,

Mariano Azuela, Ricardo Flores Magón, and others who lived in the United States.

This period, which comes to an end with World War II, is characterized by the appearance among Mexican Americans of a group consciousness that manifests itself in the formation of societies whose purpose is mutual help and protection of the needy. Some of these associations became politically oriented and spearheaded the struggle for equal rights. Their periodicals, as well as the many newspapers that sprang up during the period, included poetry, short stories, and scholarly articles as well as news. The pages of *LULAC News*, *Alianza*, and others are a good source for the literary production of this period. Ortego, in his study of Chicano poetry, has brought to light the names of some of the poets who published in these periodicals. He also discusses the poetry of Vicente Bernal and Fray Angélico Chávez, the former the author of an early book of poems, *Las primicias* (1916), and the latter a representative of the mystic tradition in three works, *New Mexico Triptych* (1940), *Eleven Lady-Lyrics and Other Poems* (1945), and *The Single Rose* (1948).

As a consequence of the revolution, Mariano Azuela published his famous novel, *Los de abajo*, in the pages of the newspaper *El Paso del Norte*, of El Paso, Texas, in November 1915. Later, in 1935, Teodoro Torres, who lived nine years in the United States and was editor of *La Prensa* of San Antonio, Texas, published *La patria perdida*, a novel whose first part takes place in the United States and deals with life among Mexican Americans. Another Mexican, Alberto Rembao, who lived in New York and edited the review *La Nueva Democracia*, published novels with Mexican themes and settings. In general, the novel and short story of this period need study. Research will undoubtedly uncover many novels written by Mexican Americans, both in English and Spanish.

The corrido continues at this time to be a popular form of expression, with social protest and politics entering more prominently into its content. In 1936, a corrido was written about some Gallup, New Mexico, coal miners who had been subdued with gunfire by the sheriff and his men during a strike. Senator Bronson Cutting's defense of the lawmen elicited a protest poem that ended with the following lines:

Usted se come sus coles
Con su pan y mantequilla
Y yo me como mis frijoles
Con un pedazo de tortilla.

You eat your cabbages
With your bread and butter
And I eat mine with beans
And with a bit of tortilla.

During this period, serious scholarship and literary criticism begin to appear with the works of Carlos Castañeda, Juan B. Rael, George Sánchez, Arthur L. Campa, and Aurelio M. Espinosa.

Chicano Period (1943–Present)

June 1943 marks the beginning of a new period in the history of the Mexican American. The so-called zoot suit riots, which took place in Los Angeles that month, began an open confrontation that was to be intensified during the postwar years by the presence of thousands of returning Mexican American veterans. A new type of literature emerges animated by a rebellious spirit often inspired by the revolutionary leaders of Mexico, such as Villa and Zapata. Characteristic of this writing is the Chicano's search for identity, often probing for the roots of his being in the Indian past. This quest is found in the poetry of Luis Omar Salinas, Miguel Ponce, Alurista, Sergio Elizondo, and Rodolfo "Corky" Gonzales, the last of whom expresses this sentiment in *I Am Joaquín* (1967):

I am Cuauhtémoc,
Proud and noble
leader of men

I am the Maya Prince.
I am Nezahualcóyotl,
Great leader of the Chichimecas

25

I am the Eagle and Serpent of
the Aztec civilization.

In his metaphoric prose "Tata Casehua," Miguel Méndez M. goes back
to more recent, but timeless Indian ancestry. He dedicates his story, "To
My Indian Ancestors, nailed to the sign of Omega, and to their tragic
Fate."

Other writers find inspiration for their poetry and prose from their
barrio experiences. Sometimes the language is that of the barrio, and
almost always there is the use of Spanish and English in a juxtaposition
that is often startling in effect. We find this in the tender poem of José
Montoya, "La jefita," about a barrio mother.

Several anthologies of Mexican American literature have already
been published. In addition to *El Espejo*, which contains prose and poetry, we have Ed Ludwig and James Santibáñez (eds.), *The Chicanos:
Mexican-American Voices* (1971); Antonia Castañeda Shular, Tomás
Ybarra-Frausto, and Joseph Sommers (eds.), *Chicano Literature: Text
and Context* (1972); Luis Valdez and Stan Steiner (eds.), *Aztlán: An
Anthology of Mexican American Literature* (1972); Philip D. Ortego (ed.),
We Are Chicanos (1973); and Luis Omar Salinas and Lillian Faderman
(comps.), *From the Barrio: A Chicano Anthology* (1973); and many
others.

Three novels—*Tattoo the Wicked Cross* (1967), by Floyd Salas; *The
Plum Plum Pickers* (1969), by Raymond Barrio; and *Chicano* (1970),
by Richard Vásquez—are reviewed by Teresa McKenna in her article
"Three Novels: An Analysis." An earlier novel, *Pocho*, by José Antonio
Villarreal, was first published in 1959. *Barrio Boy*, by Ernesto Galarza,
appeared in 1971, and *Bless Me, Ultima*, by Rudolfo A. Anaya in 1972.
The book . . .*Y no se lo tragó la tierra* (1971), by Tomás Rivera, is an
artistically written collection of stories. Other short fiction has appeared
in periodicals and anthologies.

The possibilities of the drama have not yet been explored, though El
Teatro Campesino has carried on its traditions under the directorship
of Luis Valdez. The corrido, the most enduring of the popular genres,
is still being composed and sung by Chicanos, especially the *huelguistas;*

unfortunately, very few have been written down. One is "The Corrido of César Chávez," in English, which in part says:

> On March seventeenth,
> First Thursday morning of Lent
> César walked from Delano,
> Taking with him his faith.

> When we arrive in Fresno
> All the people shout:
> Long live César Chávez,
> And all who follow him.

In conclusion, it may be reemphasized that Mexican American literature is not just a by-product of the struggle for civil rights. By this I do not mean to minimize the efforts of the Chicano movement or to underestimate the new energy that it has sparked. The very term *Chicano*, whatever connotation it may eventually receive, has spurred the production of literature. Even so, it is only when we look at Mexican American literature from a historical perspective that we understand its true nature. From Mexican literature it has derived its forms, both erudite and popular, as well as its spirit of rebellion. And although the more recent phase of it may emphasize social protest or a search for Chicano identity, its roots reach far back to poets like Vicente Bernal who write simply about mystic experience or other universal themes.

3

THE PROBLEM OF IDENTIFYING
CHICANO LITERATURE

The simplest but also the narrowest way of defining Chicano literature is to say that it is the literature written by Chicanos. This definition, although neat and precise, presents us with at least two problems. It is difficult to identify a particular author as being Chicano, and it focuses the attention of the critic on the origin of the writer rather than on the work itself. The reader must be familiar with the author's life, especially if he has a non-Spanish name as in the case of John Rechy. There may be such Chicano writers publishing literary works whose origins we are not aware of. It may be equally difficult to identify as Chicanos those writers with Spanish names, as, for instance, Amado Muro and Silvio Villavicencio. Muro was an American named Chester Seltzer married to a Mexican woman and using her maiden name, Amado Muro, as a pseudonym. Villavicencio, on the other hand, is a young writer from Central America now living in Guadalajara, Mexico, who, as far as we know, has never been to the United States. Two of his stories appeared in the anthology *El Espejo* (*The Mirror*), considered as representative of Chicano writing.

No less important is the fact that there is no consensus of opinion as to who is a Chicano. To show how rapidly the meaning of Chicano has changed, I shall quote the two definitions given by Edward Simmen and published a year apart. In 1971, he defined the Chicano as "a dissat-

First published in *The Identification and Analysis of Chicano Literature,* ed. Francisco Jiménez (New York: Bilingual Press/Editorial Bilingüe, 1979), 2–6.

isfied American of Mexican descent whose ideas regarding his position in the social and economic order are, in general, considered to be liberal or radical and whose statements and actions are often extreme and sometimes violent." One year later he defined as Chicano "an American of Mexican descent who attempts through peaceful, reasonable, and responsible means to correct the image of the Mexican-American and to improve the position of this minority in the American social structure." Other definitions of the Chicano are extremely limited, as to both time and social philosophy.

If we define the Chicano as this socially oriented person, then only that literature written by him, but especially that in support of the social movement called *la causa*, initiated during the early 1960s, is Chicano literature. The best example of this would be the plays of Luis Valdez, performed by El Teatro Campesino. Are we to say, then, that such works as Rudolfo Anaya's novel *Bless Me, Ultima,* Estela Portillo's drama *The Day of the Swallows,* and others not dealing with social protest do not belong to Chicano literature? A broader definition is definitely in order, so that we may be able to include all aspects of that literature. The definition should be broad enough to cover not only the plays of Luis Valdez but also other works not dealing with social themes.

Those critics who are aware of the difficulty of reaching agreement as to who is a Chicano have turned to a different approach, the identification of Chicano literature by its intrinsic characteristics. This approach is more satisfying to the humanist, since he feels that defining the Chicano is a task for the social scientist and not for the literary critic. As we said before, this approach has the advantage of focusing the critic's attention upon itself. But, here again, the characteristics of Chicano literature most often mentioned by critics give us an extremely narrow concept of that literature. Most of them apply to what is considered to be realistic literature. For instance, subject matter, it is said, must reflect the Chicano experience and deal with Chicano themes. It is for this reason that some critics exclude Floyd Salas's novel *Tattoo the Wicked Cross* from being classified purely as a Chicano novel. Why should the Chicano experience be limited to the campesino struggle, the description of life in the barrio, or the social confrontation with the majority culture? Why can it not go beyond to include the universal nature of man?

Another often-mentioned characteristic of Chicano literature is its sympathetic attitude toward Chicanismo. One of the accomplishments of Chicano literature has indeed been the creation of a new image for the Mexican American. The Chicano, as revealed by that literature, is not the stereotyped creature portrayed by the mass media. The danger here is that, in order to avoid a negative presentation of the Chicano, the writer often falls into the trap of Manichaeism and the lack of ambiguity. What Carlos Fuentes said about the Spanish American novel written before 1940 can very well be applied to Chicano literature. For him that novel was "caught in the net of the reality close at hand and can only reflect it. That surrounding reality demands a struggle in order to be changed, and that struggle demands an epic simplification: the exploited man, because he is exploited, is good; the exploiter, also intrinsically, is evil. This primitive gallery of heroes and villains, what literature has not had it?" Manichaeism, of course, can be avoided. Corky Gonzales does it by identifying the hero of his poem not only with Cuauhtémoc, Juárez, and Madero, but also with Cortés, Maximiliano, and Huerta. "Writing *I Am Joaquín*," he says in the introduction to the poem,

> was a journey back through history, a painful self-evaluation, a wandering search for the people and, most of all, for my own identity. The totality of all social inequities and injustices had to come to the surface. All the while, the truth about our own flaws—the villains and the heroes had to ride together—in order to draw an honest, clear conclusion of what we were, who we are, and where we are going. *I Am Joaquín* became a historical essay, a social statement, a conclusion of our *mestizaje,* a welding of the oppressor (e.g., Spaniard) and the oppressed (e.g., Indian).

Chicano literature, like all other literatures, can give expression to the universal through the regional. Over and above the social problems with which he is at present preoccupied, the Chicano is a human being facing the concerns of all humanity. And he is giving expression to this in an original style. By writing in a combination of English and Spanish he is creating new images. And the creation of a new image is precisely the problem that confronts the Chicano writer, for it is not easy to give universality to the regional or particular if the writer does not go beyond his immediate circumstance. The Chicano has to create a new synthesis out of history, tradition, and his everyday confrontation with the ever-changing culture in which he lives. But he cannot do so unless he creates mythical images. And that is just what the Chicano writer has been do-ing, as we can see in Rivera's ... *Y no se lo tragó la tierra* (... *And the Earth Did Not Part*), Méndez's *Peregrinos de Aztlán*, Anaya's *Bless Me, Ultima*, and other representative Chicano creations. Méndez's pilgrims inhabit a mythical Aztlán. With Aztlán, Alurista, Méndez, and others have cre-ated a mythical place as important as the descriptions of the barrios that we find in Mario Suárez's short stories. The Chicano can identify as easily with Aztlán as he can with Señor Garza's barbershop or Hinojosa-Smith's Klail City. This can be so because the myth of Aztlán was born out of history, having been the place where the Aztecs originated. And since the Chicano identifies readily with the pre-Hispanic cultures of Mexico, the myth took hold of the people's imagination.

For these reasons, the new definitions of Chicano literature, which are not restricted only to social, realistic works, are much more satisfying and can account not only for Chicano literature as it exists today, but also for what is to be written in the future. A broad definition is necessary even to account for socially oriented Chicano literature where mythical and legendary elements are frequent. Otherwise, how can we analyze, in their totality, such poems as Alurista's "La Llorona" and Omar Salinas's "Aztec Angel," or even poems of the barrio, such as Raul Salinas's "A Trip Through the Mind Jail," where we find this stanza:

Neighborhood of Zaragoza Park
where scary stories interspersed with
inherited superstitions were exchanged
waiting for midnight and the haunting
lament of La Llorona—the weeping lady

of our myth and folklore, who wept nightly,
along the banks of Boggy Creek . . .

In a very brief article published in *Mester* in 1973, Gustavo Segade says, "Chicano literature, then, refers to the historical, cultural, and mythical dialectic of the Chicano people. In its historical and cultural sense, Chicano literature is specific and unique; in its mythical sense, it's general and universal." And Bruce-Novoa, with his original and challenging theory about the spatial nature of Chicano literature, has presented us with a significant definition worthy of consideration.

We can see, then, that in a relatively short time, Chicano literature not only has established itself as a significant part of minority literatures in the United States, and, at the same time, of literature in general, but also has produced a criticism that has kept up with the rapid change taking place. In a few years, the identification of Chicano literature has progressed from the narrow, sociological definition to the broad, humanistic, and universal approach. Chicano literature, by lifting the regional to a universal level, has emerged from the barrio to take its place alongside the literatures of the world.

4

INTO THE LABYRINTH

As a rule, theories are not formulated before there is a body of materials the nature of which has to be explained. This is true of Chicano literature, in existence before it became a subject of formal study, but neglected by mainstream criticism and theory. It is for this reason that Chicano literary theories are of recent origin. It was not until the first decades of the twentieth century before critics began to manifest a desire to collect the literary production of the Mexican American people. The first to do this was Aurelio M. Espinosa, who began collecting, in his native state of Colorado and in New Mexico, and publishing, in the *Journal of American Folklore,* all types of popular literature, which we now call Chicano, especially *romances, décimas,* and folktales. When he was appointed professor of romance languages at Stanford University, he did the same thing for the oral production existing in California.

Early Theories of Chicano Literature

Espinosa formulated the first theory of Mexican American literature but limited it to popular manifestations. According to his Hispanist theory, Mexican American folk literature had been brought to the Southwest directly from Spain. In the short introduction to his article

First published in *Aztlán* 22, no. 2 (Fall 1997): 107–19.

"Folklore de California" (1932), Espinosa says that he is now publishing "folklore materials of old Spanish California, where you can still find today, everywhere, eloquent living vestiges of the traditions, culture, and the same blood of Spain." In his study "Los romances tradicionales en California," he argues that the *romance* tradition in California, when compared to that of New Mexico, "turns out to be very poor, almost decadent." Not only that, but he excludes from his study everything south of Santa Barbara, which includes Los Angeles, and north of San José, which includes San Francisco. For him, "the true Californios are found today mainly between Santa Barbara and San Jose." However, Espinosa admitted, as he stated in his article "Trovos del viejo Vilmas," that some poetic forms are of Mexican origin: "Indeed," he wrote, "the suspicion arises that the New-Mexican compositions may be versions of compositions of Mexican origin." This and other statements indicate that a revision of Espinosa's position vis-à-vis his *españolismo* is in order. A better designation would be, perhaps, his *criollismo*.

Espinosa's theory was first rejected by Arthur Campa, although he did not propose a substitute theory, as did Américo Paredes later, arguing that Southwestern Chicano folklore did not come directly from Spain, but through Mexico. "Genetically," Paredes wrote, "we are *mestizos;* culturally, we belong to a generalized Mexican culture." Paredes also rejected Vicente T. Mendoza's theory about the origin of the corrido, that is, the idea that it was brought from Michoacán to the Southwest by the Mexican immigrants who came searching for work in the fields. Paredes argued that the corrido had not been brought from central Mexico, but had originated along the border, having been the result of the conflicts between Mexicans and Americans in 1836, first when Texas became independent, and later in 1846–48, when Mexico lost half its territory. This theory, attributing the origin of Chicano literature to racial and cultural confrontations, has been very influential among some young followers of Paredes, among them Ramón Saldívar, who finds the origin of Chicano narrative in border corridos.

Paredes was also the first critic who published a book, *With His Pistol in His Hand* (1958), dedicated totally to the study of a Chicano literary subject, the *Corrido de Gregorio Cortez*. This book, based on the theory that literature should be studied in a social context, has served Chicano scholars as a methodological model for analyzing a poem in its historical context and for carrying out research projects. On the other hand, what can be considered as the first, although not well formulated, regionalist literary theory, is to be found in the brief pamphlet *Breve reseña de la literatura hispana de Nuevo México y Colorado,* by José Timoteo López, Edgardo Núñez, and Roberto Lara Vialpando, published in Ciudad Juárez in 1959. This work had no influence upon the development of literary theory, as it was too regional, its scope too limited.

Indigenismo versus *criollismo*

It was not until the 1960s, the decade of El Movimiento, when an interest in Chicano culture, education, literature, and the arts was awakened. Also, at the same time, a theory of cultural nationalism was formulated simultaneously by Luis Valdez and his followers, and in Berkeley where, on September 1967, Nick C. Vaca, Octavio Romano, and other Chicanos at the University of California, published *El Grito: A Journal of Contemporary Mexican-American Thought*. This periodical was instrumental in spreading cultural nationalism, one element of which was the great importance its advocates gave to the Indian cultures of Mexico. This belated *indigenismo* was the result of the influence that the Mexican philosopher José Vasconcelos had upon early Chicano intellectuals. Although Vasconcelos had criticized the Chicanos, or *pochos,* as he called them, he attracted the attention of the *indigenistas* with his books *La raza cósmica* (1925) and *Indología* (1926), as well as with his creation of the National University of Mexico's motto, "Por mi raza hablará el espíritu." In 1969, Mario García published a short article in *El Grito* comparing the meanings of the word *raza* as used by both Vasconcelos and Chicano writers. Although García believes that Vasconcelos's theory of a cosmic race is too idealistic, he ends his article by saying that "Chicanos should keep in mind the idealistic views of José Vasconcelos."

As late as 1993, José Antonio Burciaga wrote: "Vasconcelos' theory of *La Raza Cósmica* has more validity in this country with the Chicano than with the Mexicano."

In his essay "The Historical and Intellectual Presence of Mexican-Americans" (1969), Romano adds other propositions to Paredes's historical confrontation theory. Romano says: "The ideas that were and are present wherever people of Mexican descent live involve the Indianist philosophy, Historical Confrontation, and Cultural Nationalism. Now, to the three currents of thought manifested historically there was added a fourth, The Immigrant Experience." According to Romano, although *indigenismo* was important as a literary device, it "has never been a focus or a rallying cry for action among Mexican Americans." He concedes that it permeates barrio culture, in the use of names, murals, dances, legends, and poetry. "The Indian," he says, "is root and origin, past and present, virtually timeless in his barrio manifestations." As late as 1992, the Chicano poet Francisco X. Alarcón joined the *indigenistas* with his book *Snake Poems: An Aztec Invocation,* a translation of 104 Aztec beliefs collected by Hernando Ruíz de Alarcón in Mexico in 1629. In the introduction, Alfred Arteaga, however, interprets these poems not as a manifestation of *indigenismo,* but of *mestizaje,* a derivative theory. He says: "Read these poems as expressions of life, as a celebration of the Native heritage of Mestizo America."

At about the same time the poet Alurista, in San Diego, was also speaking about *indigenismo.* He re-created for the Chicanos the mythical nation of Aztlán, thus given concreteness to the nationalist theory. *Indigenismo,* however, was severely criticized by several social thinkers, who thought that glorifying the Indian past and forgetting the problems of the present day Indians was contrary to the principles of cultural nationalism. As a theory, *indigenismo* was also criticized by those who believed that Chicano literature should be interpreted from a historical-dialectical perspective.

Opposed to *indigenismo,* but a view held by only a small number of critics, was the theory of *criollismo,* based on the belief that Mexican culture is European. Samuel Ramos, the Mexican philosopher, says, "We must recognize the fact that our cultural perspectives are European by definition. Culture is not a matter of choice, like the brand of a hat. We have European blood, our language is European, our customs and morality are European, and the sum of our vices and virtues is a legacy of the Spanish race." According to Ramos, some of the elements that characterize this culture are the result of the people's fervent religious nature. "Church art," Ramos says, "emerged as Mexico's first expression of Creole culture." The principal contributions of Mexican *criollismo* to Chicano culture are in the fields of religion, language, literature, and social philosophy.

Another Mexican thinker who has influenced Chicano literary theory is Octavio Paz, who was popular among Chicano intellectuals during the 1950s as the author of the seminal book *El laberinto de la soledad* (*The Labyrinth of Solitude*), in which he included a chapter on the pachuco. His theories were rejected by Carlos Blanco Aguinaga, Arturo Madrid, and others. In his article "In Search of the Authentic Pachuco" (1973), Madrid argues that Paz presents the pachuco as a character without a history.

Mestizaje

Although *indigenismo* was very important in Chicano thought, as seen also by the influence of Mayan thinking in Luis Valdez, in his work *Pensamiento serpentino*, this trend did not endure, nor did *criollismo*. The synthesis of both, cultural *mestizaje*, is the theory that has predominated. The roots of this theory can be found in Paredes's study "Mexican Legendry and the Rise of the Mestizo: A Survey" (1971), in which he applies the theory of *mestizaje* directly to the analysis of literary works. He considers to be mestizo any Mexican, and therefore Chicano, legend (and this can be said of any other genre) retold from a European perspective. As an example, he makes reference to the interpretation that Bernal Díaz del Castillo gives to the meeting of La Malinche and her mother and brother. According to Díaz del Castillo, the relationship of Doña Marina to her family "seems to me to indicate what happened in Egypt to Joseph with his brothers; they came under his power during the business of the wheat. This is what happened and not what they told Gómara."

The best expression of the *mestizaje* theory in Chicano literature is to be found in Gloria Anzaldúa's book *Borderlands/La Frontera: The New Mestiza* (1987). According to her theory, the new mestizo and mestiza consciousness will be spiritual, not racial. Her theory is reflected in the structure of her book, made up of several genres. Regarding literary theory she has said, "Theory doesn't have to be written in an abstract and convoluted language. Writers like myself are considered low theorists, and writings like *Borderlands* are considered 'low theory' . . . because it's accessible. People can understand it. It's got narrative, it's got poetry and I did the unforgivable—I mix genres."

Establishing a New Chronology

Early Chicano literary theories had to be based on a very limited body of works. In 1973, at Indiana University, Luis Dávila and Nicolás Kanellos were preparing to publish the *Revista Chicano-Riqueña,* and they asked me to write an article for the first number. It was then that I began to think about establishing a chronology of Chicano literature. Inspired by Ríos's words about Chicano literature existing before 1848, I began to do research about writers not only during the Mexican period but also since the first explorers and settlers came to the Southwest during the sixteenth century, writers who had contributed to the literature of the region. I titled my study "Mexican American Literature: A Historical Perspective," and it appeared in the first number of *Revista* in the spring of 1973.

In that first study, I did not make an attempt to delve deeply into the nature of Chicano literature, but I did include some of the topics suggested by Ríos, such as literary currents; the fact that artistic sentiment was no longer totally Mexican but consciously reflecting a Mexican American reality; and the presence of a rich oral tradition, the only aspect of that literature that had been previously studied by Chicano pioneer critics.

In 1971, an important year in the development of Chicano literary historiography, the first doctoral dissertations dealing with the history of Chicano literature were accepted at leading universities. Philip D. Ortego presented for his doctorate a well-researched "Background of Mexican American Literature," in which for the first time an extraordinary amount of information on Chicano literature in the nineteenth century was collected. However, he placed the birth of Chicano literature in 1848. I argued that it began in the sixteenth century.

The literature of the Mexican people living in the northern provinces of New Spain was somewhat different from that of central Mexico. In this literature we already find a new sensibility, due mainly to the presence of different environmental factors, such as a new landscape and a different climate, as well as the nature of the cultures of the native people, unlike those of central Mexico. Not less important is the fact that during this colonial period, the settlers from central Mexico established the bases upon which Chicano culture was to develop. The institutions and the cultural elements that were brought to the Southwest from Mexico helped to shape Chicano culture and therefore its literature. This tradition was strengthened after 1821, when Mexico received its independence from Spain. During this short period, the printing presses were introduced, important in the development of periodical literature. All these political and cultural changes, however, did not affect popular literature, whose uninterrupted existence from colonial days to the present attests to its durable nature. This theory, that Chicano literature had its beginning during the sixteenth century, was influential in the establishment in 1990 at the University of Houston, with a generous grant from several foundations, of the ambitious project "Recovering the U.S. Hispanic Literary Heritage."

Recent Theories

Tomás Rivera is well known as a novelist, but his literary theories have been neglected. In 1971, he argued that Chicano literature should be able to help the reader or the listener understand himself. This essay was first written in Spanish with the title "Literatura chicana: Vida en busca de forma," for he wanted to give emphasis to the idea that Chicano literature was a literature still experimenting with forms. We must keep in mind that when the essay was written, his idea of the search for a form had to be based on the works that had been published between 1959 and 1971. This search for a form is difficult, according to Rivera, because the writer has two models, the American and the Mexican. In a later essay, "Chicano Literature: The Establishment of Community" (1982), Rivera argues that during the 1970s, Chicano literature "reflected the urge and desire to establish such elements [community, myth, language] of the Chicano ethnic group."

Since the space attributed to Chicano literature has expanded, and recent production has exploded, literary theories have had to be revised to accommodate it. In 1977, Joseph Sommers published his essay "From the Central Premise to the Product: Critical Modes and Their Application to a Chicano Literary Text," in which he discusses three theories, the formalist, the culturalist, and the historical-dialectical. He demonstrates how each approach functions when applied to a narrative text, such as Tomás Rivera's novel . . . *Y no se lo tragó la tierra*. He rejects the formalist theory of literature because it undervalues oral literature; assumes that the most important value in a text is the aesthetic quality; and praises unity, complexity, and universality. Cultural criticism is rejected because it is antihistorical, believing that a distant, mythical past controls the present, "regardless of social and historical development"; besides, it "places primacy on the distinctive ethnic origins of Chicano culture, setting it apart from other cultures and indeed from other nations. Here the stress is on racial fusion, on Indian and Mexican constituent elements with occasional references to a Hispano component. There is frequent harking back to José Vasconcelos' 'la raza cósmica,' and to *mestizaje* as being the distinctive feature characterizing the Chicano experience." However, recent studies of Chicano literature using the cultural approach have been very successful, such as the one by Guillermo Hernández titled *Chicano Satire: A Study in Literary Culture* (1991). In the preface we read: "I have opted to provide an intertextual approach to the examination of Chicano literary works—from various regions, perspectives, and genres—by placing them within a larger cultural framework." In an earlier study, "On the Theoretical Bases of Chicano Literature," Hernández had already stated that "the analysis of Chicano texts must be framed within the social and cultural history of the Chicano."

The critical theory preferred by Sommers for the study of Chicano literature is the historical-dialectical, since with its application the text can be studied "in the light of an understanding of social structures." Its analysis includes intertextuality and the response to literary tradition. Sommers also proposes that the critic should account for interactions "with both Mexican and North American middle classical popular literary traditions."

To the historical-dialectical approach proposed by Sommers, Ramón Saldívar, also focusing on the novel, adds another theory, that of difference, a theory based on the tenet of deconstructionism, as discussed in his article "A Dialectic of Difference: Towards a Theory of the Chicano Novel" (1979) and in his book *Chicano Narrative: The Dialectics of Difference* (1990). While Saldívar has focused on narrative, Bruce-Novoa has concentrated on poetry, considering it as a response to chaos. His book *Chicano Poetry: A Response to Chaos* (1982) is a formalist analysis of the poetry of the principal Chicano poets, from Alurista to Gary Soto.

One of the latest Chicano theories proposed, one that goes beyond literature, is the feminist, as practiced by Rosaura Sánchez, Norma Alarcón, María Herrera-Sobek, Tey Diana Rebolledo, Erlinda Gonzales-Berry, Cordelia Candelaria, Angie Chabram, and others. Other theories are those of Manuel de Jesús Hernández-Gutiérrez, who, in his book *El colonialismo interno en la narrativa chicana: Barrio, el anti-barrio y el exterior* (1994), considers Chicano literature as being the product of members of an internal colony. José David Saldívar, on the other hand, argues in his book *The Dialectics of Our America* (1991) that Chicano literary criticism should move beyond ethnicity and culturalism to a global and interactive plane. And finally, Héctor Calderón, coeditor with José David Saldívar of the book *Criticism in the Borderlands* (1991), has approached Chicano literature through the theory of reader response, a theory also used by Manuel M. Martín Rodríguez to analyze Rolando

Hinojosa-Smith's Klail City Death Trip series in his book *Rolando Hinojosa y su "cronicón" chicano: Una novela del lector* (1993). Other critics, of course, are eclectic, making use of combined aspects of several theories, including the mythical.

Summarizing, we could say that the discipline of Chicano literary criticism, born during the 1960s, has achieved maturity in a short period. The first theories, dominated by the political trend toward nationalism and *indigenismo*, dealt mainly with the problems of its nature and its identity, in books like Francisco Jiménez's *The Identification and Analysis of Chicano Literature* (1979); from there it went to explore other theories, such as the formalist, the culturalist, the historical-dialectical, and the mythical; and finally, it has experimented with feminist theories, and with the latest European theories, such as poststructuralism, deconstructionism, reader response, and postmodernity. The last one has been studied by Rosaura Sánchez in her article "Postmodernism and Chicano Literature" (1987), in which she comes to the conclusion that Chicano literature, "albeit within the cultural dominant of postmodernism, will be only tangentially postmodernist."

What do we foresee for the future? Since more and more Chicano critics are coming from the English departments of the universities, the tendency to follow mainstream literary theories probably will continue. Perhaps in the future critics may be able to develop a literary theory that is derived from the Chicano text itself. Are Chicano literary theorists out of the labyrinth? We agree with Tomás Rivera, who told us that the important thing is not whether we can get out of the labyrinth or reach its center, but the search in itself.

5

TRUTH-TELLING TONGUES

On February 2, 1848, the Republic of Mexico and the United States signed the Treaty of Guadalupe Hidalgo, and one year later, according to Article 8 of that treaty, the Mexican people who decided to remain in the ceded lands, a region today known as the Southwest, became American citizens and were therefore threatened with the loss of their culture and their native language. That did not happen, however, as Spanish has survived as the spoken language of the people, due mainly to the constant influx of immigrants from Mexico and other Spanish-speaking countries of the Americas and Spain. Spanish also survived in their literature, which kept their language alive over the years, due to a desire to maintain a cultural tradition established when Mexico's northern provinces were colonized.

The purpose of this study is to document the uninterrupted tradition that has existed in the writing of poetry in Spanish—the same could be done with other genres—by Americans of Mexican descent, and to examine the nature of that poetry, giving attention to the practice of using two languages in the same poetic construct, the presence of old and new popular forms, and thematic preferences. The emphasis of my study will fall upon the poetry produced between 1848 and 1910, although one immediate difficulty is that not all of this poetry is known, since most of it was published in Spanish-language newspapers, many of which have

First published in *Recovering the U.S.-Hispanic Literary Heritage*, ed. Ramón Gutiérrez and Genaro Padilla (Houston, Tex.: Arte Público Press, 1993), 91–105.

yet to be examined. What has been collected by such literary historians as Aurelio M. Espinosa, Arthur L. Campa, Américo Paredes, Anselmo F. Arellano, Francisco Lomelí, Luis Torres, Reynaldo Ruiz, and others is sufficient, however, to make it possible to observe its influence. A second difficulty hindering the study of this poetry, and this applies to other genres as well, has been the problem of determining whether the poems published were written by native composers or copied from Spanish or Latin American books or periodical publications. Although the appearance of poems by non-Chicanos demonstrates an interest in Hispanic literature in general on the part of the Spanish-speaking public residing in the Southwest, care must be taken to see that they are not included in studies or anthologies of the genre. In his manuscript, Luis Torres includes "Don Dinero," a poem published anonymously in the *Gaceta de Santa Bárbara* (California) in 1881, which happens to be by the seventeenth-century Spanish writer Francisco de Quevedo; and in Reynaldo Ruiz's collection of poems published in the Spanish-language newspapers of Los Angeles between 1850 and 1900 there are some by such Latin American poets as José Joaquín Pesado, Luis Maneiro, Rosa Espino, and others.

The preceding observations indicate that today no study about early Chicano literature can yet be called definitive. However, it is our belief that a study of what we already know could be useful in the understanding of what will be discovered in the future. Today we can already examine the nineteenth-century poetry of New Mexico in Arellano's book *Los nuevomexicanos y su poesía, 1889–1950,* and the archives of Francisco Lomelí, who has been collecting the poetry of New Mexico not included in Arellano's book; and that of California in the collections of Luis Torres and Reynaldo Ruíz. I myself have an unpublished manuscript of the poetry found in the *Gaceta de Santa Bárbara* (California) published between 1879 and 1881. However, much more research must be undertaken in order to have a complete picture of nineteenth-century Chicano poetry.

The main formal characteristic of contemporary Chicano poetry is the artistic use of two languages in the same poetic construct. Although this rhetorical device acquired legitimacy only recently, especially with the poetry of Alurista, Ricardo Sánchez, José Montoya, Tino Villanueva, and other contemporary poets, its practice has deep roots in the Chicano literary tradition, since as long ago as the sixteenth century poets in Mexico were already using Spanish and Nahuatl in the same composition. The best example of this practice, but not necessarily the first or only one, is the poetry of Mateo Rosas de Oquendo (1559?–1621?), who used native words in his Spanish poems to satirize the customs of the emerging society he found in Mexico. The poetic device he used in some of the verses of his *Sátira que hizo un galán a una dama criolla que le alababa mucho a México* (*Satire Composed by a Young Man to a* criolla [woman of Spanish parents born in Mexico] *Who Unduly Praised Mexico to Him*) consists in closing the verse line with a native word, either in its original form or as modified by the Spaniards:

Por la salsa tienen chile
por velas queman ocote
las damas mascan copal
y es su fruta el epazote.

For dressing they use *chile* [chili]
instead of candles, *ocote* [torch-pine],
the ladies chew *copal* [transparent resin]
and their [favorite] fruit is the *epazote* [sapodilla].

Or by enumerating the native products, as those used in the making of chocolate during the sixteenth century:

[*El chocolate*] *es hecho de cacao*
de patastle y de achiote,
con súchil, suchicatlaste,
con su chipatleo y atole.

Chocolate is made with cocoa
with *patastle* and achiote,
with *súchil* and *suchicatlaste*,
and with *chiplateo* and *atole*.

The use of Nahuatl words related to food products, some of them still used in Mexico and by Chicanos today (and even more widely), has the function of demeaning the nature of Mexican cooking, unconscious of the fact that in Spain the process had been the same, with the introduction of Arabian words to designate certain foods and condiments. Although Oquendo used the two languages to satirize Mexican society in general, the most acerbic poems in which he employed this device were directed at the Indians.

The use of the two languages continued in Mexico during the seventeenth century by Sor Juana Inés de la Cruz, especially in her *villancicos,* or Christmas plays, in which often other languages and dialects also appear, as Latin by students or the language spoken by the blacks of Puerto Rico. In the *villancicos* that she composed in 1677 in honor of San Pedro Nolasco, there is a "Villancico de la ensaladilla," where the word *ensaladilla* (hodgepodge) refers to the use of assorted languages spoken by characters of different nationalities, a mixture that reflects the composition of the society for whom Sor Juana wrote her *villancicos.* The Indian in the play sings and dances a "Tocotín mestizo," a mestizo song in which we find not only isolated Nahuatl words, as used by Oquendo, but phrases and even complete sentences:

> *Huel ni machicahuac*
> *no soy hablador*
> *no teco qui mati,*
> *que soy valentón.*

> I may forget, [but]
> I'm not a liar,
> my master knows
> I'm a brave man.

Unlike Oquendo, Sor Juana does not demean the indigenous culture; on the contrary, she presents in her poem an individual ready to fight to defend his rights.

The trend continued during the eighteenth century. In the *Entremés para las posadas,* a short Christmas play presented in Mexico City in 1790, there are several Indian characters who speak Spanish intercalating Nahuatl phrases. Even the *monigote* (lay brother), who is perhaps a criollo or a mestizo, uses this type of discourse. It is assumed that the public still understood the Nahuatl language; otherwise, the rhetorical device would have had only a humorous function on the part of the criollos and the mestizos, since it made fun of the Indians.

Even after Mexico obtained its political independence from Spain in 1821, satirical poets continued to use Nahuatl in their compositions not to denigrate the Indians, but to ridicule those persons of Indian origin who had attained high positions in the government, especially those who sided with Maximilian when he was emperor of Mexico from 1864 to 1867. Juan Nepomuseno Almonte, a general who had fought with Santa Anna at the Alamo and was made prisoner at San Jacinto (1836), and who was later instrumental in bringing Maximilian to Mexico, became the butt of many anonymous satirical poets. In "Glorias de Juan Pamuceno" (1862), the writer satirizes a fiesta Almonte gave for his powerful French friends, among them generals Forey and Saligny. In this poem, Almonte answers a question raised by his French friends, "los señores de rango" (the high-ranking gentlemen): he calls Forey *Teutli* [god], the name given by the Aztecs to the Spaniards, whom they considered to be gods. The rhetorical device utilized by the anonymous poet is the same as that introduced by Oquendo:

Estuvo el Teutli Forey
con nosotros muy contento
comió pipián y tamalli,
tlemolito con xumiles,
y se hartó de mextlapiles
en sus tacos de tlaxcalli.
Saligny, no hay que decir,
se bebió muchos tzacoallis
de neutli, y en los comallis
quiso su almuerzo engullir.

Teutli (God) Forey was there
in our company very happy
he ate *pipián* (chicken stew) and tamales,
tlemolito (stew) with *xumiles* (insects),
and stuffed himself with *mextlapiles* (fish tamales)
in his tacos of *tlaxcalli* (corn tortillas).
Saligny, why say it,
drank many *tzacoallis* (gourdfuls)
of *neutli* (pulque); and from the *comallis* (griddles)
his lunch he gulped down.

The poets living in the Southwest after 1848 were familiar with this use of two languages for rhetorical purposes. The substitution of one language for the other (English instead of Nahuatl) was an easy matter, since the syntactical structure was not altered. This substitution occurred first in Mexico, during the years of the Mexican-American War (1846–48), when English became popular due to the presence of the American soldiers, who did not know Spanish. As early as 1847, songs and corridos where English words appear became popular. In "De las Margaritas," the composer criticizes the Mexican girls who associated with the American invaders:

Ya las Margaritas
hablan el inglés,
les dicen: —Me quieres?
y responden: —Yes.
   Mi entiende de monis,
mucho güeno está.

The girls called Margaritas
have learned to speak English,
they are asked: "Do you like me?"
and they answer: "Yes."
   Me know about money,
which is very good.

In the poetry appearing in the Spanish-language newspapers of the Southwest published after 1848, the use of interpolated English words and phrases was also common. The device was used in New Mexico by an anonymous poet to criticize the Mexican women who had become *agringadas,* that is, who had adapted gringo culture and refused to speak Spanish. In the *romance* "A una niña de este país" ("To a Young Girl of This Country"), collected by Professor Espinosa in New Mexico before the 1930s but not published until 1953, a dialogue is established between a Mexican with a limited knowledge of English and an *agringada:*

> *A una niña de este país [sic]*
> *yo le hablaba una vez;*
> *yo le hablaba en español,*
> *y ella me hablaba en inglés.*
> > *Le dije: —¿Será mi amada*
> *y mi corazón también?*
> > *Y me dijo la agringada:*
> > *—Me no like Mexican men.*
> > *Le empecé a hacer cariñitos*
> *en sus dientes de marfil,*
> *y me dijo con modito:*
> > *—I tell you, you keep still.*
> *Le escribí un papel por nota;*
> *le dije: —Entérese de él*
> > *Y me dijo la ingratota:*
> > *—I tell you, you go to hell.*
> > *—I tell you, te voy a decir,*
> *I'll tell you, yo te diré,*
> *si tú me quieres a mí,*
> *es todo el inglés que sé.*

> To a girl of this country
> I was talking once;
> I spoke to her in Spanish
> and in English she would answer.

I said to her: "Will you be my beloved
and my sweetheart too?"
    And the Americanized girl answered:
    "Me no like Mexican men."
I began to praise her marble-like teeth,
and she said with affectation:
    "I tell you, you keep still."
I wrote her a brief note;
I told her: "Please take notice."
And the ungrateful one said,
    "I tell you, you go to hell."
    "I tell you, *te voy a decir.*
I'll tell you, *yo te diré,*
    If you love me,
That's all the English I know."

Similar compositions were collected by Professor Américo Paredes in southern Texas, one in the form of a song and the other as part of a zarzuela (musical comedy). In the first, "Los mexicanos que hablan inglés" ("English-Speaking Mexicans"), the *pochos,* the sons of Mexicans born in the United States, are criticized for refusing to speak Spanish (the translation is by Paredes):

En Texas es terrible
por la revoltura que hay,
no hay quien diga "hasta mañana,"
nomás puro good-bye.
Y jau-dididu mai fren,
en ayl si yu tumora,
para decir "diez reales"
dicen dola yene cuora.

In Texas it is terrible
how things are all mixed up;
no one says "hasta mañana,"

it's nothing but "goodbye."
And "howdy-dee-do, my friend,"
and "I'll see you tomorrow";
when they want to say "diez reales"
they say "dollar and a quarter."

The formula was so popular that it was used on the stage for other purposes. In the fragment of a zarzuela reproduced by Paredes, English is used not to ridicule, but to produce a humorous effect (again, the translation is by Paredes):

Como estamos en Texas
el inglés hay que aprender,
para que con nuestros primos [Americans]
nos podamos entender.

Y venderles charamuscas
en la lengua del Tío Sam:
—Mucho bueno palanquetas,
piloncillo very fine.

—One cent the merengues,
one cent the pastel,
one cent the turrones,
and todo one cent.

"What is it you want, Mister?"

Since we are in Texas,
we must learn the English language,
so that we can make ourselves
understood to our cousins.

So that we can sell them *charamuscas* [candy twists]
in the language of Uncle Sam:
the honeyed popcorn is very good
the brown sugar loaves are very fine.

"One cent the *merengues* [sugarplums],
one cent the pie,
one cent the nougats,
and everything one cent.

"What is it you want, Mister?"

In California some of the earliest Chicano poems appeared in *La Estrella* (1851), the Spanish-language supplement of the *Los Angeles Star*. About its director, Manuel Clemente Rojo, who published several poems, Antonio Blanco S. has said, "Rojo was not only editor and translator, but also a man of letters. We have collected a large number of the poems published under his name, which seem to us to be the product of a skillful poet. He deserves to be studied." The second Spanish-language newspaper in California, and one of the most important, was *El Clamor Público* (1855–59), edited by Francisco P. Ramírez, who also wrote poetry.

Neither Rojo nor Ramírez used English in their poems. The earliest poem published in a California newspaper using the bilingual (in this case trilingual) device that has come to our attention is "El cura aprendiendo inglés" ("The Priest Learning English"), published in *El Nuevo Mundo* of San Francisco, on July 29, 1864, by a poet signing with the pseudonym "El Cura de Tamajona." The contents of this *letrilla* (festive poem in verses of less than eight syllables) are ambiguous, since there are motifs belonging to two historical periods in the history of Mexico, the American invasion of 1846 and the French invasion of 1862, as well as the use of English and French words and phrases:

Reste sans cu
Abajo . . . y dancen
Zi Yankee dul.

Reste sans cu[*llotes*]
Down . . . and dance
The Yankee dul[doodle].

This poem was probably published in Mexican newspapers first, and then reprinted in *El Nuevo Mundo*. By 1864, the stereotype of the American, as a man having a large frame, big feet, and being unable to speak Spanish correctly, was well established in Mexico; that is the way the Yankee appears in the poem, exaggeration making him even more grotesque (Torres's translation):

—*Yo no te entende,*
dijo el atún
(que era un Yankazo
como un abedul,
con cada pata
como un almud) . . .

"I don't understand you,"
said the idiot.
(He was a big Yankee,
big as a birch tree,
with each foot
like half an acre) . . .

The purpose of this satirical poem, and others in which the American is presented as a grotesque individual, was, of course, to instill pride in the Mexican people by demeaning the appearance of the invaders. The generalization about Americans having big feet was born during the invasion of 1846. As early as 1847, in the anonymous poem already cited, "De las Margaritas," they are referred to as "gringos patones."

In California, *El Clamor Público* was the first Spanish-language newspaper that accepted social protest poems, a theme that was to remain a constant in Chicano literature. As early as 1856, that newspaper published the anonymous poem "Justicia" ("Justice"), in which the Supreme Court is criticized for being biased against Chicanos ("el Tribunal/No nos considera igual," "this Tribunal/Does not consider us as equals), for favoring the rich, and for other injustices. The use of English and Spanish in social protest and political poems comes much later. It is not until the last decade of the nineteenth century that this literary device was utilized for this purpose. One of the earliest examples of this type of bilingual composition, which was to become so popular with contemporary Chicano poets, is "Lo que dirá," a political poem published in *El Hispano Americano* of Las Vegas, New Mexico, October 15, 1892, and signed with the pseudonym "T. A. Tornillo" (*Te atornillo* [I'll fix you!]). In this type of truly bilingual construct, the poet alternates the use of the two languages not only within the same sentence but also between sentences. The poem is directed to the voters, telling them not to elect a certain candidate:

> *Y que el pueblo vea*
> That T. B. Catron don't get there.
> *El 8 de noviembre lo dirá*
> *Si al pueblo, Catron, mancillará.*
> *El pueblo* on that day will blare
> *Que el panzón* never got there.

> And let the people see to it
> That T. B. Catron don't get there.
> November eighth will tell
> If by Catron the people will be blemished
> The people on that day will blare
> That the potbellied never got there.

According to the poem, candidate Catron, apparently selected to run for office by the dominant Anglo politicians, should be rejected by the Hispanic voters because, as a banker, he has robbed the sheepherders. And no matter how much he will shout to the people in his political speeches, he will not be able to deceive them, nor silence the poet, who speaks the truth:

> For his bursting lungs
> Can't silence truth-telling tongues.

Although political subject matter proliferated during the last decade of the nineteenth century, some poets kept writing about traditional themes and in traditional forms. Representative of this so-called learned poetry are the poems of José Escobar, a Mexican expatriate living in New Mexico who edited several Spanish-language newspapers between 1891 and 1898. His style follows the trend established by the early *modernista* Mexican poets, whom he often imitated. Doris L. Meyer, who has collected and studied his poetry and that of others publishing in New Mexico during the last decades of the century, sees Escobar's contributions "as evidence of a 'learned' literature in New Mexico which, because it's less apparent than New Mexico's folk culture in Spanish, has been neglected by literary historians."

Why have critics neglected the study of nineteenth-century learned poetry? It is true that most studies have been dedicated to the popular aspects of early Chicano poetry. Lately, however, Arellano, Ruíz, and Torres, in addition to Meyer, have been collecting and studying learned poetry. There is no question that this poetry is less representative of Chicano society than popular poetry. It is less representative because learned poets insisted on using standard Spanish to address a society that was rapidly becoming bilingual; on writing about traditional subjects indistinguishable from those treated by most Latin American and Spanish authors; and on rejecting the influence of popular forms, which have the greatest appeal for most newspaper readers, the medium in which the learned poems were published.

There is no question that early Chicano poetry was very close to the people, being generally influenced by traditional popular forms and popular themes, some of them having originated in colonial Mexico, and others going further back to medieval Spain. The oldest forms are found in New Mexico, the region that has the oldest poetic tradition, both popular and learned. The most common forms found there are the *trovo*, the *romance*, the *décima*, the *memoria*, and the corrido. Verse is also found in most of the popular religious forms, as the *pastorela*, the *auto*, the *villancico*, and even in secular plays. As observed by Tomás Ybarra-Frausto, "these rhymed dramas have rarely been examined as popular poetry. As examples of people's verse, they document the process of oral transmission and collective improvisation."

The *décima* and the *trovo* are two of the oldest forms used during the nineteenth century by Chicano folk poets, or *puetas*, as they were called by the people. The *décima* consists of four ten-line stanzas introduced by a quatrain, which is glossed, a reason why the name *glosa* is often given to this form. Its origin was traced by Professor Campa to sixteenth-century Spain, in the poetry of an obscure writer, Gregorio Silvestre. The form, which became very popular in New Mexico, was derived, however, directly from Mexico, where it was very common. In both regions it was used for political diatribes, as can be seen in those collected by Rubén M. Campos in Mexico and Campa in New Mexico.

The other form, the *trovo*, a dialogic poetic composition, was very popular in nineteenth-century Hispanic poetry, both popular and semi-popular. It is found in the *poesía gauchesca* of Uruguay and Argentina, as well as in Mexico, although not necessarily with the name *trovo*, a name derived from *trovar*. Its oral form consists in a contest between two *puetas*, who, accompanied by the guitar, challenge each other by asking difficult questions in octosyllabic verses grouped in stanzas of four, eight, or ten lines, that is, quatrains, octaves, or *décimas*. The second *pueta* must answer the query beginning with the last rhyme of the previous strophe, that is, *debe trovar el verso* (must rhyme the verse). In Mexico, this form was made popular by the folk poet José Vasconcelos, "El Negrito Poeta," a semimythical character to whom *trovos* were attributed. José Joaquín Fernández de Lizardi, in his novel *El periquillo sarniento* (*The Itching Parrot*, 1816), refers to him as being a contemporary of Sor Juana Inés de la Cruz, who was unable to rhyme a verse ending in the preposition *de*, a challenge that El Negrito had mastered.

In New Mexico the most famous *pueta* composer of *trovos* was El Viejo Vilmas, whose compositions were studied by Professor Espinosa in his article "Los trovos del viejo Vilmas" (1914), in which he infers that according to his New Mexican friends, Vilmas was a native *pueta*. However, he adds, "but there is no proof of it." El Negrito Poeta appears in Vilma's *trovos* as one of several *puetas* challenging him and, of course, losing the contest:

Oy' [oye], afamado Negrito,
ti [te] advierto que no soy pudiente;
tú pensarás cai [caer] parado
pero vas a cai de frente.

Listen here, famous Negrito,
I'm warning you I'm not powerful;
you think you're going to land on your feet,
but you're going to land flat on your face.

The presence of these poetic forms, both popular and learned, in early Chicano poetry indicates an adherence to a long-established literary tradition, a tendency that often prevented poets from writing original compositions. This has been observed by Professor Campa, who wrote, "As a rule, the metrical structure of the *décima* is too confining to allow much originality and spontaneity to the composer. The subordination of content to form makes the type of composition a bit stiff and unnatural. . . . This lack of lyricism may be accounted for by the fact that *décimas* are no longer used as folksongs in New Mexico."

Another reason for the abandonment of the *décima* and all other restrictive popular forms may be the popularity of the corrido, which has survived to the present. The corrido, as a narrative form, has a greater appeal than the *décima*, which was limited to expressing lyrical or philosophical themes. The desire to overcome the confining nature of the traditional poetic structures led also to the creation of new forms, and eventually to free verse in all its ramifications, as observed in the multiform works of contemporary Chicano poets.

In conclusion, it can be said that Chicano poetry has deep roots; that it is the product of a long, uninterrupted literary tradition; and that its study can help the reader to better appreciate contemporary Chicano poetry, where some of the same characteristics may be found. From a historical perspective, it can be observed that some of the devices utilized by contemporary Chicano poets have their origin in the poetry of the nineteenth century, while others can be found in earlier periods of Mexican literature. The linguistic alternation of English and Spanish that the reader admires in the poetry of Alurista, José Montoya, Tino Villanueva, and others, had been used by earlier poets, although they did it for purposes other than aesthetic, as is done today. Perhaps that is the greatest difference between early and contemporary Chicano poetry.

During the nineteenth century, the use of both Spanish and English served mainly to provide social information, reveal cultural values, and expose the clash that had existed between the two cultures; it was also used to reflect the importance that interpersonal relationships have among the people of Mexican origin. In contemporary poetry, on the other hand, the extensive use of English and Spanish is not limited to the above purposes but is used as well for the aesthetic values derived from the combination of the two languages, a procedure that has reached a distinctive equilibrium today.

The study of nineteenth-century poetry also helps the critic and the linguist to trace other changes that have taken place in the use of the two languages by poets utilizing this literary device. Up to almost the end of the century, all poets used Spanish as the basic language, introducing English words only when referring to the culture of the other or to ridicule those who had partially accepted the foreign culture, especially if they were women. In most contemporary poetry, on the other hand, English is the basic language, and Spanish is used most often to establish a relationship with the mother culture, and for aesthetic purposes.

Although there are some studies dedicated to the analysis of code switching in contemporary Chicano literature, especially in poetry, there are hardly any studies examining its historical development. The study of early Chicano poetry is in need of further development, not only in the collection of materials but also in its analysis. We must establish the significance of the use of the two languages in the same poem and even in the same phrase, as well as the origins and uses of other changes throughout the history of this aspect of Chicano literary expression. This is important because poetry was the best means for the people to give vent to their thoughts and emotions, since poetry was easier to publish at that time in the newspapers available in their communities. Their poetry was first written in Spanish and then, as the change from

Spanish to English took place, in both languages. The development of this process should be thoroughly documented, as it will substantiate that here has existed a tradition that has continued to the present. It will also lend testimony to the fact that the people of Mexican descent living in the United States have not been voiceless and expressionless, as portrayed until recently in sociological and historical studies.

6

LO REAL MARAVILLOSO IN NUEVO MÉXICO

To Rudolfo Anaya

In spite of what the critic Theo L. D'haen has said about magic realism and postmodernism, that "they now seem almost the only shorthands available to categorize contemporary developments in Western fiction," literary critics, as far as I know, have not claimed that Chicano literature belongs to the magic realist mode or to postmodernism. In the analyses and reviews of the works of several authors, there are, however, passing references stating that the work being discussed belongs to the magic realism mode. There is also an article on the influence of Latin American magic realism on modern Chicano writers, as well as a study of magic realism in Miguel Méndez's novel *El sueño de Santa María de las Piedras*. Some critics have also mentioned the related mode, *lo real maravilloso*. Rosaura Sánchez, in her essay "Postmodernism and Chicano Literature," for example, stated in 1987 that in Chicano literature, "Burlesque realism *à la* García Márquez, is now beginning to appear, as have 'magical' elements, in the Carpentier mode of the 'marvelous real,' common in the works of Rodolfo [*sic*] Anaya, Genaro González, and Alejandro Morales."

In a more recent statement Manuel M. Martín-Rodríguez says that "another narrative trajectory that utilized some of the essential characteristics of Magical Realism and the Latin American *nueva novela*

First published in *Nuevomexicano Cultural Legacy: Forms, Agencies, and Discourses,* ed. Francisco A. Lomelí, Victor A. Sorell, and Genaro M. Padilla (Albuquerque: University of New Mexico Press, 2002), 151–63.

appears to have been more fruitful. *The Road to Tamazunchale* (1975) by the Californian, Ron Arias, is the first example that we have." The phrase "more fruitful" in the quotation refers to what the critic had stated about the failed attempt by Anaya and Estela Portillo Trambley to produce an integrated mythical and social reality. He does, however, acknowledge that Anaya, Portillo Trambley, and Orlando Romero are "the best exponents of this recovery of myth or legends for the purpose of incorporating them in a current context."

It is my purpose in this presentation, which I dedicate to Rudolfo Anaya, to bring to light *lo real maravilloso* and magic realist elements found in *nuevomexicano* narrative, and their contributions to postmodernist American fiction. I will touch upon some of the most important early works in this mode, and then concentrate on two novels, Anaya's *Bless Me, Ultima* and Orlando Romero's *Nambé—Year One*. I would like to argue that the works of Anaya and Romero are earlier examples not only of the mythical approach, as stated by several critics in the case of Anaya, but also of the magic realism approach. But before I do that I want to talk about the relation between magic realism and *lo real maravilloso*. Most recently, both literary modes have been amply studied, but there is still much controversy and misunderstanding about them. I will begin with *magic realism*, since this term is the most important of the two.

Magic Realism

The term *magic realism* was coined by the German art critic Franz Roh in 1925 to refer to the postexpressionist movement that appeared in Europe about that time, a movement that was essentially a return to figurative representation in art, but, according to Roh, from the viewpoint that "doesn't acknowledge that radiation of magic, that spirituality, that lugubrious quality throbbing in the best works of the new mode." Today, the term *magic realism* is applied to a literature (or art) that is nonrealistic, or rather, that is concerned with a reality that is considered to be magical.

Roh's book was translated by Fernando Vela into Spanish and published in abbreviated form in the *Revista de Occidente,* the famous periodical edited in Madrid by José Ortega y Gasset in 1927, and the same year it appeared in book form. The term became popular in Latin America. However, it was not until 1948 that it appeared in literary writing. The first to do this was the Venezuelan novelist Arturo Uslar Pietri, who in 1948 wrote: "What predominated in the short story and left an indelible mark there was the consideration of man as a mystery surrounded by realistic facts. A poetic prediction or a poetic denial of reality. What for lack of another name could be called a magical realism."

In the United States, the first to write about magic realism in Spanish American literature was the Puerto Rican critic Ángel Flores, who in 1955 published an article titled "Magical Realism in Spanish American Fiction." Without mentioning Roh or Uslar Pietri, Flores states that magic realism began with Franz Kafka in Europe and Borges in Latin America. His definition, however, cannot be accepted, since for him magic realist literature is a mode practiced by the elite only. He says that "the magical realists do not cater to a popular taste, rather they address themselves to the sophisticated, those not merely initiated in aesthetic mysteries but versed in subtleties. Often their writings approach closely that art characterized by Ortega y Gasset as 'dehumanized.'" His article, however, was beneficial because he was the first to apply the term to contemporary Spanish American narrative fiction, and this started a controversy, which has not ended yet after almost half a century.

In spite of its novelty, Flores's article did not have an impact on Latin American literary criticism. It was not until 1966 when a student announced that he was writing his dissertation on magic realism in contemporary Argentine literature. Motivated by that announcement, I decided to write an article defining magic realism in a more precise form than what Flores had done. In my study, published in 1967, I mention Roh and Uslar Pietri, consider magic realism to be an attitude toward reality that can be expressed in popular or cultured forms, in elaborate or rustic styles, in closed or open structures, separated from fantastic and oneiric literature and also from surrealism; and I further say that in magic realism "the writer confronts reality and tries to untangle it, to discover what is mysterious in things, in life, in human acts." Since the 1960s, and especially during the 1980s and 1990s, magic realism has gained respectability in American and European mainstream literary criticism, as a component of postmodernism, cultural studies, postcolonial discourse, and has been extended to cover film.

Lo real maravilloso

In order to present a total picture of magic realism, I will point out how it differs from *lo real maravilloso* and give some examples from early *nuevomexicano* narrative. This is necessary because critics often confuse the two modes and often accept them as synonymous. The phrase *lo real maravilloso* was coined by the Cuban novelist Alejo Carpentier. It first appeared in 1949 in the *prólogo* to his novel *El reino de este mundo* (*The Kingdom of This World*). An expanded version of this *prólogo* was published in 1967 in his collection of essays *Tientos y diferencias* (*Approaches and Distinctions*), where the word *americano* appears in the title, which reads: "De lo real maravillosamente americano." In 1943, Carpentier had visited Haiti and was fascinated by what he saw there; that is, "algo que podríamos llamar lo real maravilloso" (something we could call the marvelous real). In the prologue of 1949, he defined the term in these words: "The marvelous begins to be unmistakably marvelous when it arises from an unexpected alteration of reality (the miracle), from a privileged revelation of reality, an unaccustomed insight that is singularly favored by the unexpected richness of reality or an amplification of the scale and categories of reality, perceived with particular intensity by virtue of an exaltation of the spirit that leads it to a kind of extreme state."

A few paragraphs later, however, Carpentier localizes the term, making *lo real maravilloso* a characteristic of Latin American culture. He wrote:

> I thought, the presence and vitality of this marvelous real was not the unique privilege of Haiti, but the heritage of all of America, where we have not yet begun to establish an inventory of our cosmogonies.

The marvelous real is found at every stage in the lives of men who inscribed dates in the history of the continent and who left the names that we still carry: from those who searched for the fountain of eternal youth and the golden city of Manoa to certain early rebels or modern heroes of mythological fame from our wars of independence, such as Colonel Juana de Azurduy.

The difference between *lo real maravilloso* and magic realism can be derived from that quotation. *Lo real maravilloso* is to be found in nature and in men of the Americas who evoke a reaction called "marvelous," that is, causing wonder or astonishment. On the other hand, in magic realism, the important characteristic is the mystery found in men, nature, and objects, a mystery that eludes the understanding of the observer. In *lo real maravilloso* only certain events are considered to be marvelous; in magic realism, all reality is magical.

Abundant examples of *lo real maravilloso*, in New Mexico and other areas of the Southwest, can be found in the chronicles of the explorers who came to the region during the sixteenth and seventeenth centuries, as well as in the many folktales brought by the settlers who came from central Mexico. Famous early *cronistas* whose works are rich in marvelous experiences in New Mexico are those of Cabeza de Vaca, Fray Marcos de Niza, Coronado, Fray Alonso de Benavides, and others. New Mexico is the richest area where this type of literature is found. When Fray Marcos de Niza came in search of the fabulous Seven Cities, of which Cíbola is the most important, he described the homes in superlative terms, saying that "the facades of the principal houses have much turquoise stonework of which there is great abundance." His account of the richness of Cíbola, although not actually observed by him, inspired Coronado's expedition into New Mexico.

Fray Marcos was guided in his expedition by a *real maravilloso* character, the black man Estevanico, companion of Cabeza de Vaca, who found his death in New Mexico. Also known throughout the Southwest is the story of the lady in blue; that is, the Spanish nun Sor María de Agreda (1602–65), who, as retold by Alonso de Benavides, brought the gospel to the natives and preached to them in their native tongues without ever leaving Spain.

Magic Realism and Postmodernism

Wendy L. Faris, Theo D'haen, and other contemporary literary critics have suggested that magic realism is an important component of postmodernism. Faris argues that "magical realism, wherever it may flourish and in whatever style, contributes significantly to postmodernism." Other critics go so far as to say that the two terms are equivalent. For the Canadian critic Geert Lermout they are interchangeable. In his article "Postmodernist Fiction in Canada," he observes that "what is postmodern in the rest of the world used to be called magical realist in South America and still goes by that name in Canada." How the terms *magic realism* and *postmodernism* first came to be associated is not clear. This matter, however, is inconsequential. The real problem is not to prove the relationship, which is now taken for granted, but how it has contributed to shaping postmodernism. As D'haen says: "If magical realism, then, seems firmly established as part of postmodernism, the question remains as to *what* part it plays in this larger current or movement, and where and why." It is not our purpose to answer that question, but to demonstrate how Chicano fiction in New Mexico, in its magic realist aspect, contributes to that movement, keeping in mind that some features of postmodernism apply to Chicano literature and others do not.

Magic Realism and *Nuevomexicano* Fiction

Chicanao literary criticism has identified very few texts that fall within the magic realist mode or have aspects that can be considered as such. The first to refer to some Chicano works as being magic realist were Francisco A. Lomelí and Donald Urioste in their 1976 book *Chicano*

Perspectives in Literature, although their definition of magic realism is not given in the text, but in the glossary, nor do they say why the works designated as magic realist belong to this mode. They define magic realism as "a vision of reality in which true and unbelievable events may be found in the same plane without seeming incongruous. Natural phenomena [are] closely associated to supernatural beliefs, thus creating a magical atmosphere."

Among the New Mexican works they consider magic realist are, of course, Rudolfo Anaya's *Bless Me, Ultima* (1972), which they call "a rich reservoir of myth and legend. Chicano-style magical realism of wizardry and dreams as dimensions of reality that foretell happenings and reveal otherwise unknown occurrences." Unfortunately, they do not explain what is meant by "Chicano-style magical realism." The other work mentioned in this category is Orlando Romero's novel *Nambé—Year One* (1976), which they call "a fascinating work of magical realism." Due to the nature of Lomelí and Urioste's book, whose subtitle is "A Critical and Annotated Bibliography," the authors did not, unfortunately, demonstrate how the magic realism found in the books mentioned is expressed. Catherine Bartlett, in her 1986 article "Magical Realism: The Latin American Influence on Modern Chicano Writers," includes only one *nuevomexicano* author, Orlando Romero, whose novel *Nambé—Year One* she considers to be "a flowery, sugar-coated imitation" of new Latin American techniques.

Earlier *nuevomexicano* texts of magic realism have not yet been identified, although they may exist. For example, the folk play *The Texans,* composed in New Mexico around 1846, although based on a historical event, the invasion of New Mexico by a Texan army in 1846, contains a character, Don Jorge Ramírez, who is believed to have magical powers. According to another character, the Indian, and believed by the Texans McLeod and Navarro, Don Jorge "can take a stone and turn it into gold. He can tear up a piece of cloth and then make it like new. He can turn you into a chicken in the twinkling of an eye." Don Jorge is introduced by means of a literary motif common in magic realist texts, a song in the distance. The Indian says, "The one who is singing is Ramírez," a statement the reader has to accept without objective confirmation.

Another New Mexican early text where critics find magic realism is the novelette *El hijo de la tempestad* (1892), by Eusebio Chacón. According to Lomelí and Urioste, this early fiction "is a combination of folklore beliefs, *novela caballeresca,* adventures and magical realism."

Although these critics do not give any examples of magic realism in the novel, motifs of this nature can be found in the two female characters, the Gypsy girl and her mysterious enemy, Sombra de la Luz. Of interest is this early reference in Chicano literature about the earth that parts and swallows those who are sinful. With the help of her monkey, transformed into the devil, the Gypsy girl conquers her enemy: "Lanzó una carcajada el diablo y la vieja cayó muerta a sus pies, y la tierra se abrió y se la tragó" (The devil busted out laughing and the old lady fell down dead at his feet; the earth opened up and swallowed her).

However, it is during the contemporary period that Chicano fiction has produced several magic realist texts that fall within the definition now accepted as characterizing the mode. Among recent authors producing magic realist texts in New Mexico the following have to be considered: Fray Angélico Chávez, Sabine Ulibarrí, Rudolfo Anaya, Orlando Romero, and Denise Chávez. Even if not born in New Mexico, Ana Castillo has to be included, for she has written a magic realist novel that takes place in New Mexico, *So Far from God* (1993).

In the fiction of Fray Angélico Chávez there is a special kind of magic realism, for he combines it with religious imagery. His magic realist topics and images are usually associated to the figure of the *santero,* as can be seen in "Hunchback Madonna," where Mana Seda, caught in a rainstorm in the forest, finds refuge in the adobe hut of a mysterious *santero,* a fact she attributes to having prayed to the Holy Lady. Religious images are introduced to re-create the legend of the Virgin of Guadalupe. In "The Bell That Sang Again," the death of the rivals Capitán Pelayo and Joaquín, Ysabel's husband, causes the bell to magically lose its silvery tone, which is regained when Ysabel gives birth to her child. The religious imagery here is presented in the context of a hagiographic legend, that of Saint Ysabel, mother of John the Baptist. When Saint Ysabel meets her namesake, the girl Ysabel, who, after her husband's death, is about to commit suicide, she tells her that she heard the movements of the baby she is carrying in her womb and saves her. In the context of *nuevomexicano* religious culture, the opinion of Father Bartolo regarding New Mexico is significant because he believes that New Mexico is like the Holy Land, and that its soil is red because of all the blood spilled from Saint John's head.

Magic realist topics like those mentioned can be found in "The Fiddler and the Angelito," where humor, also present in other stories, is an essential element; the burro's owner has to receive help from the wise little angel to make his beast of burden move. In "The Black Ewe," the girlfriend of the *patrón* is transformed into a ewe. In the story "The Colonel and the Santo," the colonel visits the mother of a soldier to tell her that her son had been killed, but not revealing that he had also been crucified, and is mystified when he sees a painting in her home of a crucified saint dressed as a soldier.

There are in Chávez's stories instances of mysticism. Whether they should be considered as a special aspect of magic realism is a question that has not been resolved. Clark Colahan, in his study of the mystical journey of Sor María Agreda, states that "in view of contemporary Latin American fiction's magical realism, which incorporates much of traditional Hispanic mysticism, perhaps the time has come to argue against the other side of the question."

In his 1964 collection of short stories, *Tierra amarilla,* Sabine Ulibarrí included "Mi caballo mago" ("My Wonder Horse"), which can be classified as a tale of magic realism. This characteristic is found in the attitude of the narrator, a fifteen-year-old young man, toward a wild white horse and the environment wherein he roams. The wonder horse, who filled the boy's imagination, is called mysterious and talismanic. When the boy sees him, nature is suspended: The planet, life, and time itself have stopped in an inexplicable way: "I sit drowsily still, forgetting the cattle in the glade. Suddenly the forest falls silent, a deafening quiet. The afternoon comes to a standstill. The breeze stops blowing, but it vibrates. The sun flares hotly. The planet, life, and time itself have stopped in an inexplicable way. For a moment, I don't understand what is happening. Then my eyes focus. There he is! The Wonder Horse!"

The young man's whole being is fused with that of the horse. "I was going in search of the white light that galloped through my dreams." When he finally faces the horse, he says: "We saw one another at the same time. Together, we turned to stone." When he is able to rope the horse, "The whole earth shakes and shudders." He brings the horse home and lets him roam in the pasture, from where he soon escapes. Before letting him loose in the pasture, the young man had asked him: "What shall I do with you, Mago?" He knows that a magic horse like Mago cannot be kept prisoner, that it belongs to the wild range, that he is part of the landscape.

In his essay "An Author's Reflections: *The Silence of the Llano,*" Rudolfo Anaya refers to the short story "The Village Which the Gods Painted Yellow," whose plot takes place in Mexico, as "that strange tale." He continues, saying that he will return to Yucatán and Guatemala, "armed with magic," and ends by saying that Aztlán is also a land where "power flows through the land and the people, [where] dimensions of reality quickly evaporate under the sun, [and where] the visions and the dreams compel as much as any other force." The two great natural forces are, of course, the llano and the river where the llaneros and the people of the valley live. The stories "The Road to Platero" and "The Silence of the Llano" reflect the mystery of the llano and "The Place of the Swallows" that of the river. Both motifs are given a full treatment in *Bless Me, Ultima.* But the great mystery, of course, is life itself, "the deep sense of the mystery of life which pulsed along the dark green river." The color green seems to be symbolic of mystery.

In *Bless Me, Ultima,* the magic of the color green is precisely what Antonio, through Ultima's power, experiences. He says: "She took my hand, and I felt the power of a whirlwind sweep around me. Her eyes swept the surrounding hills and through them I saw for the first time the wild beauty of our hills and the magic of the green river."

A great novel lends itself to numerous interpretations. And that is what has happened with *Bless Me, Ultima.* The many interpretations that the novel has undergone have been summarized by Roberto Cantú in his article "Apocalypse as an Ideological Construct: The Storyteller's Art in *Bless Me, Ultima.*" To those interpretations I want to add one more, the magic realist perspective, which is based on the sense of mystery present throughout the work. In the opening paragraph, Antonio mentions the two key motifs, the llano and the river, and wraps them around the word *mystery*. "Ultima came to stay with us the summer I was almost seven. When she came the beauty of the llano unfolded before my eyes, and the gurgling waters of the river sang to the hum of the turning earth. The magical time of childhood stood still, and the pulse of the living earth pressed its mystery into my living blood." The reference to the image of the turning earth brings to memory the use of the same image in a magic realist Mexican novel, *Pedro Páramo* (1955), by Juan Rulfo. "As dawn breaks, the day turns, stopping and starting. The rusty gears of the earth are almost audible: the vibration of this ancient earth overturning darkness." For Cantú, the landscape in the opening paragraphs of *Bless Me, Ultima* "is integrally rhetorized in an apocalyptic mode according to the ideal landscape literary tradition." In the following statement, however, Cantú comes close to describing a magic realist experience but attributes it to a different mode: "The revelatory experience undergone by Antonio is extraordinary in the sense that he reaches a peculiar level of cognition better known in apocalyptic literature as a vision trance." An alternative interpretation would be the magic realist one, which can be applied to most of the experiences undergone by Antonio. Throughout the novel, the words *mystery* and *mysterious* recur frequently.

Four years after Anaya's novel appeared, Orlando Romero published *Nambé—Year One*, a novel that has much in common with *Bless Me, Ultima*. Both narratives take place in the same region. The narrators, Antonio and Mateo, are remembering events that began at the magical age of seven years; and, most important, the authors' attitudes toward reality can be called magic realist. In Anaya's novel, Ultima inspires Antonio; in *Nambé—Year One*, it is the green-eyed Gypsy. Unlike Eusebio Chacón's Gypsy in *El hijo de la tempestad*, a mere traditional stereotype, Romero's is idealized and becomes a New Mexican Dulcinea. Some critics have thought that to create his Gypsy girl, Romero was inspired by García Márquez. Most likely it was Cervantes's Preciosa, the young Gypsy with the "ojos de esmeralda" from the novelette *La gitanilla*, the beauty who had also inspired Victor Hugo, who renamed her Esmeralda, the green-eyed beauty.

The landscape in both novels, Anaya's and Romero's, is mysterious and magical, as are the two women. They have hypnotic powers, although emanating from different sources. A bond is established between Antonio and Ultima, as is done between Mateo and the Gypsy girl. The motifs through which these bonds are established are an owl and a golden chain. Both are motifs having magical powers; the owl represents Ultima, and the golden chain transforms feet into wings. Both Antonio and Mateo are strongly attached to the land and the people of their communities. The central magical motif in *Bless Me, Ultima* is the golden carp; the corresponding one in *Nambé—Year One* is a giant salamander. The difference between these two motifs is to be found in the fact that Antonio sees the golden carp. When that magical moment comes, Antonio's reaction is typical of that of a person who experiences *lo real maravilloso*. "'The golden carp,' I whispered in awe. . . . I knew I had witnessed a miraculous thing." The carp looks at Antonio and is cognizant of his presence. On the other hand, the giant salamander appears to Mateo in a vision, talks to him, and advises him never to leave his native land, an advice Mateo accepted without question.

This attachment to the land, for Mateo, is centered on the old house inherited from his great-grandfather, a house that "kept hidden and forgotten secrets within its worn floorboards. Every step taken on them was recorded and memorized. . . . It caught time itself, made it stop, and its haunting memories were left as reminders. Other times as well as these were only echoes, vibrations and waves of energy that, as if by accident, had been thrown into the earth that went to make these walls as well as are physical and spiritual beings."

The source of mystery in Romero's novel is ethnicity and the landscape. The title itself, from the Tewa and meaning "the people of the roundish earth," is expressive of those two elements. Mateo feels that he is the incarnation of his grandfather, "of his wild blood, that hybrid of solar-maize plant blood," and finds his mestizo nature to be a source of mystery, as he says: "There is Indian in us, of ancient forgotten peoples that roamed the world before there was history," a reference to the second part of the title, the year one. Like Antonio, Mateo becomes conscious of this mystery the night he was seven years old, again the magical number. In both novels there are references to La Llorona. In Romero she is a real person called La Bartola. As Nasario García tells us, "La Llorona is very much a part of New Mexico's culture; and physically La Bartola in her old age becomes indistinguishable from the soil." As Mateo says: "She looked like her adobe house." And so does Mateo himself, who is strongly attached to the earth and feels that "the adobe earth, dampened by the street rain," is pulling him. These two novels are perhaps the best examples of magic realism in *nuevomexicano* fiction.

Conclusion

If any literature outside of the Latin American and Caribbean regions lends itself to analysis from the perspective of magic realism, it is *nuevomexicano* literature, for even in the fiction of social realism there are motifs, symbols, and images that can be identified as belonging to the magic realist mode. As stated before, I want to argue that *nuevomexicano* literature is a literature rich in magic realist features, and therefore a contributor of postmodernism, as is evident in the novel *The Milagro Beanfield War* (1974) by John Nichols, as well as in the work of other important novelists. By focusing on these features in *nuevomexicano* letters, it is possible also to consider this literature as belonging to the larger Latin American literary sphere and as an aspect of postmodern American literature. Magic realism offers an alternative theory helpful in analyzing Chicano literature. With magic realism, myth and other aspects of imaginative literature can be considered an aspect of the mode, for it combines the two worlds, the real and the imaginary, both so rich in New Mexican culture.

By analyzing fiction from the perspective of magic realism, it is not necessary to consider structural, genre, or stylistic elements in the text, since it is a mode that can be expressed in any structure, any style, and in any genre. At the same time, it is not necessary to study Chicano or any other Hispanic literature as a separate entity, for magic realism allows the critic to see it in the context of Latin American literature, even if it is written in English. Nor is it necessary to separate popular literature from erudite literature, or dwell on the racial background of the writers or the racial contents of the text. *Y en fin,* magic realism is most appropriate to study Hispanic and indigenous literatures, since it is a methodology born from the American soil, just like the texts to which it is applied.

A final note: with the great advances in the physical sciences, it is possible now to create what is called virtual reality; you can see and feel something that is not there. Is this much different from magic realism?

7

THE SPANISH-LANGUAGE PRESS

The task of documenting the Spanish-language newspapers published in the United States is a formidable one. As early as 1938, *La Prensa* of San Antonio, Texas, published the following *noticia:* "Más de cuatrocientos periódicos en español se han editado en los Estados Unidos" (More than 400 newspapers have been published in the United States). The first listing, of 451 titles, appeared in the pages of *La Prensa* on February 13 of that year, when that venerable newspaper was celebrating its twenty-fifth anniversary. The publication of that list is considered to be the basis for the study of the history of Spanish-language journalism in the United States.

I myself have been able to document, that is, collect the titles and dates of publication, of almost five hundred newspapers. Unfortunately, most of them are known only by title. As is to be expected, the majority have been published in Texas, New Mexico, Colorado, Arizona, and California. But since 1808, when the first newspaper written in Spanish, *El Misisipí,* appeared in New Orleans, Spanish-language newspapers have been published in all regions, and in almost all the large cities, from New York to San Diego, and from San Francisco to Miami. Florida and Louisiana have extensive lists of newspaper publications.

In order to demonstrate the widespread presence of Chicano and Mexicano newspapers in the United States, I will read the following short

First published in *The Americas Review* 17, no. 3–4 (Fall–Winter, 1989): 157–62.

letter that appeared in the *Chicago Daily News* in 1975. It was written by Rubén Torres, a member of the National Association of Mexican Americans.

> In the *Daily News* some time ago was an article entitled "Old countries live in own press here," written by Meg Moritz. I would like to enlighten Ms. Moritz on the Spanish-language newspapers in Chicago.
>
> Since the Mexican-American community has been in Chicago for 66 years, they have the distinction of having the first Spanish-language paper in Chicago. The weekly newspaper was called *Mexico* and was edited in 1922 by the publisher, Francisco Bulnes. Also, in 1922, another Mexican newspaper was *El Correo de México*. Next came *La Chispa* in 1931, there was *La Defensa* with José de la Mora, as editor. This newspaper later became the *ABC* when taken over by the late Armando Almonte.

The same thing can be said of other large American cities. One does not expect, for example, to find Spanish-language newspapers in a Midwestern city like Milwaukee, Wisconsin, famous for its European population and its beer. And yet, during the 1930s, Federico Herrera was publishing there the paper *Sancho Panza,* and between 1947 and 1950 there was *El Mutualista,* one of the few Chicano newspapers we can read in its entirety, for in 1983, Rodolfo Cortina Jr. and Herrera published a facsimile edition, using the only complete copy in existence, which was in the possession of the editor.

My list of Spanish-language newspapers published in the United States is, of course, not complete, as many titles have not come to my attention. However, some Chicano researchers are at present actively undertaking the task of reconstructing the history of Spanish-language journalism in the United States. Among them are Juanita Lawhn in San Antonio; Francisco Lomelí in California, who is working on New Mexico newspapers; Armando Miguélez in Arizona, who has compiled a listing of over four hundred items; Félix Gutiérrez, who has studied the history of Chicano journalism; Guadalupe Castillo and Herminio

Ríos, pioneers in the field; Guillermo Rojas and Rodolfo Cortina, both researching Chicano journalism in the Midwest; and many others.

The reconstruction of the history of Chicano journalism is important not only in itself, but also because newspapers are the best source of information for the study of Chicano history and culture in general. Almost ten years ago, Juan Rodríguez read a paper, at the convention of the American Association of Teachers of Spanish and Portuguese, which met in San Diego, entitled "El periodismo como fuente para la investigación de la historia literaria chicana." He mentioned the periodical *Hispanoamérica,* published in San Francisco between 1914 and 1934, originally called *La Crónica,* as one of the first and best Chicano publications. In its pages, he found Ulica's *Crónicas diabólicas,* later collected and published in the form of a book. Chicano scholars are beginning to make use of the rich source of information available in the pages of Chicano and Mexicano newspapers. Some historians, among them Roberto Sifuentes, Emilio Zamora, and Francisco Rosales, have availed themselves of these materials to study Chicano life and culture, and critics have made excellent use of Spanish-language newspapers to write the history of Chicano literature. Since reconstructing the history of these newspapers is a very complex and difficult task, it should be undertaken by a team of scholars in contact with one another in order to avoid duplicating the same research, as has already been done in the past. And since it is difficult to consult the sources of information, the research could be distributed by states, with one scholar in charge of editing all the materials.

From the very beginning, in the few numbers published in 1808 under the title *El Misisipí,* we find local and world news. This has been, then, the most important function of newspapers, not only those directed to a Spanish-speaking minority, but of newspapers in general. Spanish-speaking readers living in the United States want to be informed about events taking place in the Spanish-speaking world, since they often do not get this information in the English-language press. Most of the early Spanish-language newspapers, however, did not provide the reader with exclusive reports; they generally copied from other sources, and sometimes translated from the English. The front-page story of *El Misisipí* of October 12, 1808, is an account of the war between France and Spain taken from a newspaper in New York (*El Diario de New York*) apparently translated from the English language, since no Spanish-language newspapers have been found earlier than 1808.

After the news, the second function of newspapers is to provide space for advertising. In the Spanish-language newspapers published in the United States, from the very beginning, the ads have been bilingual, since the advertisers want to reach the English-speaking public. In the front page of the October 12, 1808, issue of *El Misisipí* there is an ad by Dn. Juan Rodríguez, Abogado, announcing his new residence. The interesting aspect of the translation is that the first name is also translated, Dn. John Rodríguez.

Chicano newspapers have always had other important functions, such as political and social activism; the promotion of civic duties; the defense of the population against the abuse of the authorities and other organized groups; the sponsoring of national and religious holidays; the provision of an outlet for the public to express their ideas in the form of letters or to express their activity in the form of poems, short stories, essays, and an occasional serialized novel, much of which, as I mentioned before, has been useful in the documentation of a Chicano literary history. Not less important has been the publication of community social news.

The antecedents of the political function of the Chicano press are found in the nineteenth century, in the Mexican newspapers published in the Southwest before that region became a part of the United States. In 1834, in Santa Fe, Ramón Abreu campaigned in his newspaper, *El Crepúsculo de la Libertad,* for the election of deputies to the Mexican Congress.

Social activists have made good use of the press to promote their campaigns against injustices, social evils, and also to propose needed social reforms. In 1834, the missionary priest Antonio Martínez, in Taos, New Mexico, defended the rights of the Indians in the pages of *El Crepúsculo* and fought for a better distribution of land.

After 1848, the Chicano press took up the defense of the dispossessed Mexican inhabitants of the Southwest. The outstanding newspaper in this respect, considered the precursor of the contemporary Chicano militant press, was *El Clamor Público*, published in Los Angeles by a young man, Francisco Ramírez, who had been the editor of the Spanish-language page of the *Los Angeles Star*. For a time, the Chicano historian Félix González tells us, Ramírez was "moderate in tone, campaigning for cooperative work between Anglos and Mexicans. A series of Mexican lynchings by Anglo mobs led to a blistering attack by Ramírez in the editorial pages of *El Clamor Público*." But he also scolded the Mexicans for not standing up against the indignities inflicted on them and even suggested that they return to Mexico. In San Antonio, in 1855, *El Bejareño* (February 13 and March 5) protested the attacks on Chicano and Mexicano *carreteros* (cart drivers) by Anglo teamsters.

Not all of the Spanish-language press, however, followed the same policy. Many sided with the establishment or the so-called educated Mexicans. Nor did they support the same political party. As pointed out by Gutiérrez, heated political debates took place during the late 1850s between the editors of *El Bejareño* (1855–61) and *El Ranchero*.

During the years when Porfirio Díaz was in power, many Mexican intellectuals, some of them owners or editors of newspapers critical of the government, came to the United States as exiles. The Flores Magón brothers were, of course, the most famous, but there were many others. Here they contributed to newspapers already established or founded new ones. They made good use of the pages of these Spanish-language newspapers to fight the Díaz regime, and after 1913 to attack the revolutionary faction, with which they did not agree. This aspect of the problem has been studied by Richard Griswold del Castillo in his article "The Mexican Revolution and the Spanish-Language Press in the Borderlands."

Of course, not all newspapers have the same function. Those published by labor unions, *sociedades mutualistas*, religious organizations, students, and other groups, have a limited function, as they are primarily interested in promoting the interests of their own organizations. In 1880, in Brownsville, Texas, the Sociedad Mutualista Benito Juárez published *El Proletario*, and in 1907, in Phoenix, La Alianza Hispano-Americana published *Alianza*. Among the Catholic publications, the most important was the *Revista Católica*, published from 1875 to 1962, first in Las Vegas, New Mexico, and then in El Paso, Texas. A more recent religious publication is *La Voz Católica*, published in Oakland, California, in 1970. There are also some newspapers dedicated to special fields, such as *El Agricultor Moderno*, published in Bernalillo, New Mexico, in 1916. Of more recent origin are the school and university publications, in which students can express their ideas freely. A study of these specialized publications is yet to be undertaken.

All Spanish-language newspapers published in the United States, however, have had one important function: to preserve the Mexican cultural heritage of the Chicano and to stimulate a sense of identity. Most important, they have contributed to keeping the Spanish written language alive. The critic Anselmo Arellano, who collected poems published in several New Mexico Spanish-language newspapers between 1889 and 1950, and who published them in his book *Los pobladores nuevomexicanos y su poesía*, reproduces the poem "El idioma español," by José María H. Alarid, written in 1889, in which the poet says:

> *Hablaremos a porfía*
> *nuestro idioma primitivo*
> *que siempre, siempre, esté vivo*
> *y exista en el corazón.*

> We shall insist on speaking
> our mother tongue
> that will always, always
> be alive in our hearts.

The Spanish-language newspapers published in the United States, and especially *La Prensa* in San Antonio, have, without question, helped to make this poet's dream a reality.

8

EL PASO Y LA HUELLA

It was customary for the early explorers of the Southwest to write on a stone the inscription *Pasó por aquí,* adding a name and a date. And when they arrived they found that the native peoples living here had left hieroglyphics on cliffs and the walls of caves telling of their accomplishments. If we go back to mythical times, we discover that Quetzalcoatl, during his journey from Tula to Cholula under the name of Huémac, left the imprint of his hand on the stones wherever he stopped to rest. Centuries later, we find that many Chicanos recorded not on stones, as did the explorers, but on the walls of France, Germany, Italy, the Philippines, Korea, and Vietnam, their names and the dates when they had been there. Today, no barrio wall escapes the hands of young Chicanos and their graffiti, as documented by Gusmano Cesaretti in his book *Street Writers: A Guided Tour of Chicano Graffiti,* or the brush of the muralists. All these inscriptions, past and present, express a longing for immortality and are a testimony to a people with a strong will to survive and a desire to record their experiences.

The human desire to leave a permanent *huella* on this earth is not original to Chicanos, although those possessed of a very superficial knowledge of our rich history have claimed otherwise. Chicanos are not any different from other people in their desire to record their *pasos* and

First published in *Estudios Chicanos and the Politics of Community: Selected Proceedings, National Association for Chicano Studies,* ed. Mary Romero and Cordelia Candelaria ([Colorado Springs]: NACS, 1989), 19–30.

leave permanent *huellas*. Their *huellas* have been in existence for a long time, waiting for Chicano scholars to link them together to reconstruct the history of all those who have lived here and who have contributed so much to enrich the culture of this land. Their *huellas* are not simple inscriptions saying *pasó por aquí;* they consist of important oral and written accounts. Although the oral traditions have been the most difficult to preserve due to the fieldwork involved, much progress has been made in collecting them since folklorist Aurelio M. Espinosa initiated this field of research a few decades ago. Researching the written documents, which include diaries, memoirs, letters, autobiographies, essays, monographs, poems, literary and art criticism, novels, and all types of fiction, from the popular to the erudite, has not fared much better.

Why has it been so difficult and why has it taken so long to reconstruct and write a comprehensive history of Chicano culture? Are we to accept the explanations given by some writers who depict Chicanos as a people without a past, without a voice, an illiterate people unable to record their history? According to them, the Chicano has been walking on sand all these years. Not long ago, the metaphors "the invisible minority," "the minority nobody knows," "the voiceless, expressionless minority," and others were still being used by writers to refer to the Chicano people. For his book, Manuel P. Servin chose the title *An Awakening Minority,* which he changed to *An Awakened Minority* in the second edition. As early as 1844, Thomas Jefferson Farnham, a New England attorney who visited California, spoke of the *californios* as being "incapable of reading or writing, and knowing nothing of science and literature." In the introduction to his book *Foreigners in Their Native Land,* David J. Weber states that although more than five million Mexican Americans live in the Southwest, "until recently this sizable ethnic group had been characterized as the 'invisible minority,' 'a minority nobody knows,' or 'the forgotten people.'" As late as 1969, the Chicano scholars Ernesto Galarza, Hernán Gallegos, and Julián Samora were bemoaning "the almost total lack of historical and literary treatment of the Mexican-American in the United States."

According to Edward Simmen, editor of a collection of stories entitled *The Chicano: From Caricature to Self-Portrait,* published in 1971, "the Mexican-American has never, until recently, written about himself." Even the venerable Carey McWilliams, in his pioneer work about Chicanos, *North from Mexico*, states, "In the past, Mexicans have been a more or less anonymous, voiceless, expressionless minority. There has yet to be written, for example, a novel of Southwestern experience by an American-born person of Mexican descent or a significant autobiography by a native-born Mexican." The first edition of McWilliams's book appeared in 1949, two years after Luis Pérez had published his autobiographical novel *El Coyote the Rebel*, which is about the protagonist's experiences in the Southwest. We know now that there are several novels written by Americans of Mexican descent that date back to the nineteenth century, such as *La historia de un caminante* (*Story of a Wanderer*, 1881), by Manuel M. Salazar; *El hijo de la tempestad* (*Son of the Tempest*, 1892), by Eusebio Chacón; and *Silva y sus 40 bandidos* (*Silva and the Forty Thieves*, 1896), by Manuel C. de Baca.

It is not clear whether by "native-born Mexican" McWilliams refers to a Mexican living in Mexico or in the United States. He was evidently not familiar with Mexican literature. If he had been, he would not have denied the existence of Sor Juana's *Respuesta a Sor Filotea*, one of the great autobiographies in the Spanish language; or of Fray Servando Teresa de Mier's *Memorias*, comparable to Franklin's *Autobiography;* or of José Vasconcelos's *Ulises Criollo*, one of the most outstanding contemporary autobiographies.

Many autobiographies have also been written by Mexicans living in this country, although most of them are unknown, due mainly to the fact that their authors have been denied access to the means of publication. Public and university libraries, some private collections, and even Chicano households are the repositories of large numbers of unpublished documents written by Mexicans who lived in the United States before 1848, and by their descendants after that year until the present. Only recently have Chicano scholars and others been discovering them, studying them, and publishing them.

What do these documents contain? Nothing less than the evidence needed to demonstrate that Chicanos have always been interested in recording their life experiences to preserve their history for posterity.

As J. Luz Sáenz says at the beginning of his unpublished autobiography titled *Yo:*

> I undertake the writing of these notes—memories of my activities during the first years of my life—in order to satisfy the precocious curiosity of my son, Eduardo Francisco, who, when he was still a young boy ... asked me unexpectedly: "I would like to know how you were when you were a boy, and everything you did with your friends. ... For you did not know all the things that we know today, nor were there during those days so many towns and so many people, nor did you have airplanes, automobiles, radios, and so many other things that we have today." That is the reason why I have tried to remember, or salvage from the cold ashes of my past, all those events which have not been erased from my mind, in order to describe them according to my poor intelligence and in our vernacular Texas style, a style which, in time, will have to be accepted as a new language, which will be useful to others, no matter how much those who adhere to Castilian or purist rules may regret it.

Sáenz's unpublished autobiography was written in 1944. A decade earlier, that is, in 1935, Miguel Antonio Otero had published the first volume of his autobiographical trilogy, *My Life on the Frontier,* one of the best documentations of life in the Southwest during the last half of the nineteenth century. McWilliams, evidently, was not acquainted with Otero's autobiography, one of the few that had the fortune to be published when it was completed.

These and numerous other documents, published and unpublished, prove that Chicanos have a history, a history whose study had been neglected. When we take time to trace their *huellas* we discover a heritage as rich as that of any other group of people. The discovery of that inheritance had to wait until the Chicano movement produced a new type of scholar who, like an anthropologist reconstructing the early history of mankind, uncovered the buried documents and demonstrated that the cultural history of his people is not of recent origin, that their steps had not been lost, but only covered with the dust of neglect. These scholars have proved that Chicano cultural horizons extend farther back in time than those of any other United States ethnic group. This journey into the past has not ended. It would be much more appropriate to say that it has just begun, but there is no question that it has been made easier by the pioneer work of Chicano scholars who opened several research paths. The scholarly work of George Sánchez in education; of Américo Paredes in anthropology and folklore; of Ernesto Galarza in labor problems; and of Arthur Campa, among others, in popular literature have served as models and have helped scholars to formulate their own original techniques.

Let us briefly review the contributions of these early writers. Chicano scholarship is often said to be a product of the 1960s and 1970s. This notion persists because Chicano scholarship has not been documented. As a matter of fact, Chicano writers began to work soon after 1848. In only one bibliography, that used by Hubert H. Bancroft to write his *History of California* (1884), almost a thousand manuscripts by Spanish-speaking natives of California are listed.

Though McWilliams's book is usually considered to be the study that set the basis for Chicano historical scholarship, his book is, in part, based on the research done by earlier Chicano scholars. In his "Note on Sources," McWilliams lists as his first preference for the study of New Mexico the book *Forgotten People: A Study of New Mexicans* (1940), by George I. Sánchez, which he calls "a most valuable source," and for the study of Texas he made use of Jovita González's unpublished dissertation titled "Social Life in Cameron, Starr, and Zapata Counties" (University of Texas, 1930). He continues, saying that "perhaps the most interesting material on the Spanish-speaking of Colorado is to be found in yet another unpublished dissertation: 'The Spanish Heritage of the San Luis Valley' by Olibama López (University of Denver, 1942)." In his "Chapter Notes," he mentions studies by Arthur Campa and Juan B. Rael; and in the body of his work he refers to Aurelio Espinosa, Manuel Gamio, and Ernesto Galarza.

The question arises: why were the studies of Jovita Gonzáles and Olibama López never published? That has been the fate of Chicano writers in general. Most of their research has not reached the public.

When this is done, it will be evident that Chicanos, past and present, have been self-conscious writers aware of the fact that they are documenting their life experiences for posterity, to satisfy the desires of a community eager to learn about their past. This wish was expressed by the late Tomás Rivera in his essay "Chicano Literature: Fiesta of the Living," in which he observes that at an early age he was already looking for books by his own people, of which he could find very, very few. But then he met Bartolo, the town's itinerant poet. When he first met him he felt "an exaltation brought on by the sudden sensation that my own life had relationships, that my own family had relationships, that the people I lived with had connections beyond those at the conscious level. . . . Bartolo's poetry was my first contact with literature by my own people. To me there is no greater joy than reading a creative work by a Chicano. I like to see my students come to feel this bond and to savor moments of immortality, of the total experience."

The history of Chicano culture first drew the attention of the historians. For example, Donaciano Vigil compiled a history of New Mexico in which he included events up to 1851. And when the *mexicanos* who had chosen to remain here realized that their way of life was changing, they began to document historical events as well as community life as it had existed. The memoirs of José María Amador and Isabel Chacón, the *Recuerdos históricos* of Florencio Serrano, and the *Personal Memoirs* of John N. Seguín are all realistic *testimonios* of that period. There were also the Arcadians, writers who depicted an idealized society. Representative of that period are Nellie Van de Grift Sánchez (*Spanish Arcadia,* 1929) and Nina Otero Warren (*Old Spain in Our Southwest,* 1936).

Alongside the historians, the *memorialistas,* and the Arcadians, we find the scholars interested in other aspects and other interpretations of Chicano culture. First came the linguists and folklorists, spearheaded by Espinosa, Campa, and Rael. In education, George I. Sánchez opened the field in 1932 with his article "Age-Grade Studies of the Rural Child in New Mexico." These scholars were the first to apply a scientific methodology to Chicano studies and to establish a tradition in anthropology, brilliantly continued by Américo Paredes with his theoretical articles and his epoch-making study *With a Pistol in His Hand.* Today that field is represented by younger scholars, among them José Limón, José Reynaldo Reyna, María Herrera-Sobek, David Carrasco, and others.

To the fields of history, folklore, anthropology, and linguistics, other areas of knowledge were added during the 1960s and 1970s, the most important among them being sociology, political science, religious studies, literary criticism, and art criticism. The books of Julián Samora, Albert Camarillo, Mario García, Mario Barrera, Richard Griswold del Castillo, and Jorge A. Huerta, among others, attest to the great progress that has been made during the past two decades. Most recently, feminist criticism has been an important activity. The rest of the fields of knowledge, that is, the physical and biological sciences, as well as mathematics, are less developed. But there are scholars doing research in these fields also, especially biology, health problems, psychology, and educational psychology.

What would desiderata in Chicano studies be for the future? First of all, to write a comprehensive history of Chicano scholarship as it now exists in order to discover gaps that it is necessary to cover. After that, to encourage young graduate students to continue in these endeavors. And, of course, to continue to improve Chicano studies by training doctoral candidates in those fields. Also, the establishment of a national center for the preservation of oral history. I would like to propose to NACS (National Association of Chicano Studies) the establishment of a committee to be in charge of writing the history of Chicano scholarship. Also, the establishment of a scholarly periodical and the publication of important research papers dealing with the condition of the Chicano population would be a worthwhile undertaking.

COLONIALS AND
DECIMONÓNICOS

9

BERNARDO DE BALBUENA

The poet and man of letters Bernardo de Balbuena (sometimes spelled Valbuena) was born in Valdepeñas, Spain, on November 20, 1562, and was brought to Nueva Galicia (the province formed by the present states of Jalisco and Nayarit) at a very early age. In 1585, he went to Mexico City to study theology at the university, where he took part in several poetic contests, having won several prizes. In 1590, ordained as a priest, he was sent to Guadalajara, and from there to San Pedro Lagunillas in Nayarit. Wishing to participate in the life of a more intellectual community, he went back to Mexico City in 1602, and there he published in 1604 his best-known poem, "La grandeza mexicana." Two years later, he went to Spain to study for the doctorate in theology, a degree he received from the University of Sigüenza in 1607. He remained in Spain until the following year, when he was appointed abbot of Jamaica, a position he held from 1610 to 1622. In 1619, he had been named bishop of Puerto Rico, but he did not go there until 1623. Two years later, Dutch pirates burned the city of San Juan and destroyed his library. Balbuena died in that city two years later, on October 11.

Besides "La grandeza mexicana," an epistolary poem in hendecasyllabic tercets written with the purpose of telling Doña Isabel de Tovar y Guzmán (who lived in Culiacán) about the greatness of the capital, he published, in 1608, in the style of the popular *Arcadia* by Jacopo

First published in *Encyclopedia of Mexico,* ed. Michael S. Werner (Chicago: Fitzroy Dearborn Publishers, 1997), 125–26.

Sannazaro, a pastoral novel in verse and prose entitled *Siglo de oro en las selvas de Erífile.* It was not until 1624 that his next important poem appeared, the long epic (forty thousand verses in hendecasyllabic octaves), "El Bernardo o victoria de Roncesvalles," in which he glorified the deeds of the medieval Spanish hero Bernardo del Carpio.

Balbuena can be considered as a poet of transition between the Renaissance and the baroque. In his principal works, he uses Renaissance subjects, motifs, and themes, although baroque images are frequent. The novel *Siglo de oro* and the epic "El Bernardo" belong to the literature of the Renaissance. In the first, a collection of twelve bucolic poems, the mixture of prose and verse as well as the Renaissance forms (eclogues, sonnets, dialogues) predominate. The themes are those typical of the sixteenth century: the golden age, artificial idylls among shepherds, the intervention of gods and goddesses in the affairs of humans, and so on. Yet, a few tercets appear, a strophe seldom used by Renaissance poets.

For his epic poem "El Bernardo," Balbuena selected a Spanish medieval subject, the epic deeds of Bernardo del Carpio. However, he transcends the epic mode. In the poem's twenty-four books there are geographical descriptions, legends, acts of magic, historical references, allegorical fables, and marvelous adventures. In order to integrate the great variety of materials, he had to create a fictitious character, Wizard Malgesí, who, among other fantastic deeds, travels through the air over the American continent, stopping over the capital of New Spain to describe its greatness. In the following self-conscious verses he describes the volcano Xola:

> *El gran volcán Xola, monstruo horrible*
> *del mundo, y sus asombros el más vivo,*
> *que ahora con su roja luz visible*
> *de clara antorcha sirve a lo que escribo.*

> The great Xola volcano, horrible monster
> of the world, with its bright wonders,
> now with its visible red light
> serves as a clear torch for my writing.

Fantastic descriptions abound in "El Bernardo," the most spectacular being those of the fairies Morgana and Galiana. In spite of this lack of unity (a baroque characteristic), the poem is of interest because of its vivid descriptions and the variety of imaginative adventures that it contains.

"El Bernardo" has not attained the popularity conceded to "La grandeza mexicana," Balbuena's most inspired composition. In this descriptive poem in tercets, the author glosses an initial octave in which a synthesis of the contents of the total poem is provided.

> *De la famosa México el asiento,*
> *origen y grandeza de edificios,*
> *caballos, calles, trato, cumplimiento,*
> *letras, virtudes, variedad de oficios,*
> *regalos, ocasiones de contento,*
> *primavera inmortal y sus indicios,*
> *gobierno ilustre, religión, estado,*
> *todo en este discurso está cifrado.*

> Of famous Mexico the seat,
> origin and greatness of its buildings,
> horses, streets, manners, courtesy,
> letters, virtues, variety of occupations,
> gifts, moments of merriment,
> immortal spring and its designs,
> illustrious government, religion, state,
> everything in this discourse is summarized.

Since the poem is just a description of the city as it was in 1604, all historical and archeological information about Mexico is omitted. Balbuena describes what he sees, presenting everything idealized and using a hyperbolic style. The long poem is the richest description of a city founded on an island, as most utopias are. For "La grandeza mexicana," as well as the rest of his poetry, Balbuena will be remembered as a poet of superior imagination and great descriptive ability and fluency.

10

GASPAR PÉREZ DE VILLAGRÁ

One of the salient characteristics of Latin America's colonial literature (of which the American Southwest's colonial heritage is an integral part) is the incipient *mestizaje,* or racial and cultural mixture, that appeared in its forms and, even more significantly, in its thematic content. This is patently evident in Gaspar Pérez de Villagrá's epic poem "Historia de la Nueva México," which I will examine in this essay.

Pérez de Villagrá, a criollo captain born in Puebla de los Ángeles in 1555, actively participated with Juan de Oñate in the conquest of the northern regions of New Spain in 1598. His poem, published in 1610, is a historical account of the conquest of New Mexico written in the characteristic form of epic poetry common in the Renaissance: hendecasyllabic verse separated into cantos; in this case thirty-four cantos.

Villagrá's work was not the first in Hispanic American literature to utilize poetic discourse to narrate a history. The two discourses intertwined in the composition, historical and poetic, are the same we find in Alonso de Ercilla's *Araucana,* whose first part appeared in 1569; in the unfinished epic-historic poem "Nuevo Mundo y conquista," written by the Mexican author Francisco de Terrazas; and in Antonio de Saavedra Guzmán's *El peregrino indiano,* which was published in Madrid in 1599 and describes Hernán Cortés's conquest of Mexico.

Translated by María Herrera-Sobek. First published in *Reconstructing a Chicano/a Literary Heritage,* ed. María Herrera-Sobek (Tucson: University of Arizona Press, 1993), 95–117.

With the possible exception of *La Araucana,* all of these works have been categorized as true historical documents. None, however, has been classified as a "true" poetic composition by those critics who, no doubt inspired by classic literary criteria, demand that the literary work should not violate the concept of unity in all its forms—generic, thematic, or disciplinary—and that verse and prose should not be integrated in the same composition.

The American historian W. H. Prescott asserts that Saavedra Guzmán, author of *El peregrino indiano,* was more of a chronicler than a poet. And regarding the author of *Historia de la Nueva México,* the editor of the 1900 edition, Luis González Obregón, observes: "Of Villagrá may be repeated what is said of the author of *El peregrino indiano,* D. Antonio de Saavedra y Guzmán, that he was a poet-chronicler, but more of a chronicler than a poet." He adds that Villagrá's poem "is a history in rhyme, interesting because of the dates and facts which he gives. It would have been more interesting if, instead of writing in verse, he had written in prose. Unfettered by rhyme, this principal actor and eyewitness of the events he relates might have rendered an invaluable service . . . as did Cortés and Bernal Díaz del Castillo, . . . authors who also wielded the sword and the pen."

An even more acerbic criticism is Alfonso Reyes's dictum published in his *Letras de la Nueva España*: "The Cortesian cycle is initiated by Terrazas. Although lacking in *brío* it does have a certain amount of dignity. Soon—even though intermittently there will be exceptions—it begins to lose its impetus with José de Amizola and with Antonio de Saavedra Guzmán's *El Peregrino Indiano.* The latter was the famous journal of daily operations written in verse, and penned during 'seventy days of navigation with the constant swaying of the ship.' Later the genre barely survives the 'thirty-four mortal cantos' with which Villagrá laboriously stitched the *Historia de la Nueva México.*"

Even though Villagrá, in order to "stitch," as Reyes so indelicately puts it, his *Historia* resorts to metered and rhymed verse, he also interpolates a long passage of prose at the end of the fourteenth canto regarding "how the new land was conquered and taken possession of," which in my view is the least interesting part of the work. This fact contradicts what González Obregón observes; that is, that if Villagrá had written a chronicle in prose instead of writing it in verse, such a work would have been more interesting. I doubt it. The *Historia de la Nueva México* is a literary artifact whose content is as historic as it is poetic, just as Ercilla's *Araucana* is. I should point out that Villagrá was way ahead of his time, for it was not until the nineteenth century that the historical novel appeared in Europe. This subgenre became popular in Europe and in the rest of the Western world as a continuation of the Renaissance taste for historical accounts in poetic form. And it was not until the romantic period that American indigenist literature appeared with the European indigenist literature already present in the works of Ercilla, Villagrá, and numerous other authors. The epic poem was transformed into the historical novel, with the only difference being that the first was written in verse and the second in prose. The historical novel subgenre culminated with such works as *I promessi sposi*, by Alessandro Manzoni, and Leo Tolstoy's *War and Peace*, both of which are frequently referred to by historians. Tolstoy's novel contains a minute description of the Battle of Borodino analogous to the description of the Battle of Ácoma found in Villagrá's work, which has frequently been cited by historians interested in the history of the Southwest.

When the above critics and others, such as the Mexican Francisco Pimentel, speak of the poverty of poetics in Villagrá's *Historia*, they are expressing a personal value judgment regarding the aesthetic merits of the work. They do not, however, deny that the poem encompasses a literary discourse; that is, that it is an epic poem containing thirty-four cantos written in hendecasyllabic verse—be they perfectly rhymed and metered or not. Pimentel states that Villagrá's *Historia* is commendable for the "fidelity in which the historical events are rendered," but that it is "very prosaic, without any poetic fictions to adorn it; and it's written in an 'unstructured' verse, generally quite weak which makes the reading of the work tedious." He sums up by stating that the work "can only be appreciated by erudite scholars who are searching for obscure or hidden data as they would in any other historical chronicle." One cannot deny that there are few poetic images in Villagrá's work. Bur who can categorically affirm that the more poetic images a work contains the better the aesthetic quality of such a work? If such were the case, one would need only to count the number of images in a literary work and in that manner establish its aesthetic value. But that is not the case.

No one can deny that Villagrá's poem contains lively passages encompassing mythic themes such as the one describing the Aztecs' migration from their remote place of origin: "aquella parte donde el norte esconde, / del presuroso Boreas esforzado, / la cóncava caverna desabrida" ("that region where the North lays hidden / from the vigorous north wind, Boreas, / The unpleasant concave cavern") until they arrive at the location indicated by their god:

Vieredes una tuna estar plantada,
y sobre cuyas gruesas y anchas hojas,
una águila caudal bella disforme,
con braveza cebando se estuviera,
en una gran culebra que a sus garras,
veréis que está revuelta y bien asida.

You will see a cactus planted
and upon whose thick and wide leaves
perches an eagle, with beautiful uneven feathers,
fearless she feeds
upon a great serpent in whose talons
she is encoiled and firmly grasped.

There they shall build "la metrópoli alta y generosa, / al cual expresamencemente, / que México Tenochtitlán se ponga" ("a tall and noble metropolis / which [their god] expressly bids / that Mexico Tenochtitlán be called").

During their pilgrimage, they encounter a frightful "demon" in the guise of a woman. The baroque description leads us to believe it was probably Coatlicue, the mother of Huitzilopochtli, the Aztec war god, since Villagrá describes her thus:

En figura de vieja rebozada
cuya espantosa y gran desenvoltura,
daba pavor y miedo imaginarla

El rostro descarnado y macilento,
de fiera y espantosa catadura,
desmesurados pechos, largas tetas,
hambrientas, flacas y fruncidas,

sumidos ojos de color de fuego,
deforme boca desde oreja a oreja,
por cuyos labios secos y desmedidos,
cuatro solos colmillos hacia afuera,
de un largo palmo corvos se mostraban

encima de la fuerte y gran cabeza,
un grave peso casi en forma
de concha de tortuga levantada,
que ochocientos quintales excedia,
de hierro bien macizo y amazado.

In the guise of an old and withered hag
whose horrible great visage
brought fear and fright just to imagine it

The horrid fleshless putrid face,
a fierce and terrifying visage,
overflowing flaccid breast, with monstrous teats,
lean, emaciated, and wrinkled,

her eyes, like glowing coals,
misshapen mouth extends from ear to ear,
from whose parched monstrous lips
four fanglike teeth protrude on either side,
huge as a man's palm and curled they leered

atop her monstrous head she bore
a great object shaped not unlike a tortoise shell;

weighing more than eight hundred quintals,
an enormous mass of solid ore.

Another poetic element of great significance in Villagrá's work is the theme of arms and letters so common in Renaissance literature. When Villagrá wrote the *Historia de la Nueva México,* he was waiting at the Spanish court in hopes of a reward for his participation in Juan de Oñate's conquest of New Mexico in 1598. The *Historia* was well received and produced the desired results, as evidenced by the fact that he was named alcalde *mayor* in a Guatemalan town. Fate decreed that he was not to fill this appointment, for he died during the voyage to Guatemala. While he lived, however, he distinguished himself in the military as well as in literary pursuits, even though Baltasar Gracián's assessment of Cortés can be applied to our author—that he "never would have been a Spanish Alexander or a New World Caesar, the prodigious Marqués del Valle, D. Fernando Cortés, if he had not changed his employment. At the most through his literary endeavors, he might have acquired a mediocre reputation, but through the military he was able to reach the peak of eminence."

In practicing both arms and letters, Captain Gaspar Pérez de Villagrá was the scion of illustrious predecessors. Among the many others who achieved distinction in Hispanic circles were Garcilaso de la Vega, Hernán Cortés, Bernal Díaz del Castillo, Alonso de Ercilla, and, of course, Miguel de Cervantes.

The similarities between Cervantes and Villagrá are particularly interesting: both were engaged in the military and in literature, and their works reflect ideas prevalent during their epoch. As soldiers, they both participated in bloody military encounters, Cervantes in the Battle of Lepanto and Villagrá in the Battle of Ácoma. As authors, both described the total destruction of a town: Cervantes wrote about the destruction of Numancia and Villagrá about Ácoma. And by coincidence, Villagrá's *Historia* was published in Alcalá de Henares, Cervantes's birthplace, five years after the publication of the first part of *Don Quijote* and five years before the publication of the second part. It is precisely in part 1 of *Don Quijote* that we find the well-known speech regarding an individual's engagement in both military and literary endeavors. Did Villagrá read *Don Quijote*, and was Cervantes acquainted with the *Historia de la Nueva México*? We do not have any proof that either was acquainted with the other's work, but we can conjecture that Cervantes read Villagrá, since we do know he was an avid reader. And regarding *Don Quijote*, who could have escaped reading it at that time?

The subject of arms and letters made famous by *Don Quijote* had illustrious antecedents by 1605. As José Antonio Maravall observes: "To compare and contrast the practicing of arms and letters was a frequent theme in humanist thought." I shall cite a few examples from writers who treat the subject; some defend the involvement of arms, while others support the involvement in literary pursuits, and still others praise both disciplines. In Spain, Antonio de Guevara, in his book *Libro áureo de Marco Aurelio*, written during the period between 1518 and 1524, privileges letters above the military. "Few," he states, "have been lost because they practiced the art of writing and even less so those who have been won over by arms." For Guevara, it is literature that brings honor to a nation; all those remembered from antiquity, he asserts, left their imprint and honored their country by distinguishing themselves in letters as opposed to the military.

During the same period Guevara was writing, an author of Italian origin, Baltasar Castiglione, was expressing the same ideas in his famous book *El cortesano*, which he completed in 1524 and published in Venice four years later. In Castiglione's view, literature ennobles gentlemen and courtiers. He specifically criticizes the French, who thought literature detracted from an individual's engagement in arms. For this author, the practice of literary pursuits is far superior to the practice of arms, because without the former, gentlemen could not praise their own merits. True glory, says Castiglione, is that which "is written in the memory of a literary work." And he adds, "But if someone wants to contradict me, I should not want to be brought to task on this and have my opinion obviated since it seems to me some negative effects do accrue in those who practice arms and are engaged in literature." Needless to say, this does not mean that the courtier should not know the art of weaponry; according to Castiglione, he should be deft in its use and practice, excellent at riding and handling horses, and skilled in all areas employing force and speed in running a lance, tournaments, and jousting. Castiglione was speaking from personal experience, as Menéndez y Pelayo indicates in his prologue to Juan Boscán's translation of *El cortesano:* Castiglione "was a man of arms and of the court; he was skilled in all the sports and gentlemanly exercises. . . . He was a lyric and dramatic poet and was the organizer of courtly festivals."

A few years later, in 1546, Fernán Pérez de Oliva wrote his *Diálogo de la dignidad del hombre,* in which he presents two contrasting opinions: Aurelio's and Antonio's. The former is pessimistic; he can see only the drawbacks of both disciplines, while the latter tries to demonstrate the merits of both. Man, according to Aurelio, can only achieve understanding when he is old and near death. "And even then, he suffers a thousand defects when his senses fail him." And with respect to those engaged in warfare, "see them dressed in armor, earning their daily bread through theft, with fears of inflicting death on others and the dread of being killed themselves; constantly on the run, wherever fortune bids them, with constant tasks before them both day and night." Antonio answers, defending both literary and military endeavors and enumerating the positive aspects of each, pointing out that knowledge is "the Queen and Lady of all virtues. . . . It teaches justice and tempers one's vigor"; through her knowledge, "kings and princes govern; and she is the one who founded the laws which rule mankind." Weapons are beneficent and useful because they safeguard all the good found in a republic. "Gentlemen are the mainstay in the safety and security of a town. . . . They dress in armor and suffer hunger and exhaustion in order not to bear the yoke of the enemy."

Cervantes takes up the theme of arms and letters in *Don Quijote* (part 1, chapters 37 and 38), but he seems to favor the practice of arms. Don Quijote begins his second speech by stating: "Quítenseme de delante los que dijeren que las letras hacen ventaja a las armas" ("Be gone from my sight those of you who believe literature is more advantageous than arms"). Those who defend literary endeavors assert that "los trabajos del espíritu exceden a los del cuerpo, y que las armas sólo con el cuerpo se ejercitan" ("the tasks of the spirit exceed those of the body, and the tasks of arms require only the body"). Don Quijote defends the practice of arms by stating that it is not a "career for louts" and that the practice of arms "requieren espíritu, como las letras" ("requires spirit as do literary endeavors"). For Don Quijote, the goal of literature is justice and the goal of arms is peace. But as "el mejor bien que los hombres pueden tener en esta vida" ("the best thing man can have in this life") is peace, and because without arms peace could not be possible, we can deduce that the practice of arms is superior because without arms literature could not exist.

Why did Cervantes defend the practice of arms through Don Quijote's arguments? It is well known that Cervantes, like Villagrá, was first of all a soldier and only later a writer. Perhaps, as his biographer Jaime Fitzmaurice-Kelly states, it was because toward 1585, the year *La galatea* was published, Cervantes "was learning that with respect to earning a living the pen was a weaker tool than the sword: it was a lesson he learned hesitantly and grudgingly." His speech in defense of arms was the result of that bitter lesson. Cervantes's defense of the practice of arms certainly influenced later attitudes. As late as the nineteenth century we see the narrator-captain in Ignacio Manuel Altamirano's novel *La navidad en las montañas* (*Christmas in the Mountains,* 1871), telling a priest who offers him shelter: "I am a soldier, your excellency, and I will find to my liking anything you have to offer me. I am accustomed to hardships and privations. You well know what this difficult profession entails. That is why I will refrain from quoting a speech Don Quijote made in a style that would be impossible for me to imitate."

Villagrá agreed with Cervantes regarding the superiority of the practice of arms. His *Historia de la Nueva México,* as a literary piece and not a historical document, is a paean both to the practice of arms and to the conquerors of the New World, who with their deeds brought glory to Spain. The poem begins with these verses, a distant echo of Virgil's poem (stanza 1, canto 1):

> *Las armas y el varón heroico canto,*
> *el ser, valor, prudencia y alto esfuerzo,*

de aquellos españoles valerosos,
que en la Occidental India remontados,
descubriendo del mundo lo que esconde,
plus ultra con braveza van diciendo.

Of arms and heroic man I sing,
of his wondrous deeds and of his victories won.

I sing of the glory of that mighty band,
who nobly strive in that far distant land,
the world's most hidden regions they defy,
Plus ultra is ever their battle cry.

That Villagrá privileged arms over letters is quite clear in these verses from a later canto:

O soldados que al bélico ejercicio,
sois con gran razón aficionados,
advertir que es grandísima grandeza,
no ser nada muy pródigos en lengua,
y serlo por la espada es cosa noble.

Oh, ye soldiers who with warlike exercise
with good reason are greatly enamored,
be advised that it is of great worth
to know not to be prodigious in tongue
but 'tis noble to be so with the sword.

Oñate named the first town he founded San Juan de los Caballeros, an action that demonstrates his close affiliation (and that of his captains) with the Renaissance world. In the *Historia*, Villagrá presents Oñate as the son of kings, a descendant of Cortés and Moctezuma, representatives of the two cultures that, upon uniting, gave form and spirit to the resultant Mexican nationality. And the same occurs with captains Juan and Vicente Zaldívar, the nephews of Cristóbal de Oñate, the father of the general (Juan de Oñate):

Aquel gran general grande famoso
que Cristóbal de Oñate habemos dicho
que fue su claro nombre, y también tío
de Juan y de Vicente de Zaldívar,
el uno general de Chichimecas
y el otro explorador de aquesta entrada,
y padre de don Juan que fue casado,
con biznieta del rey, hija que he dicho
del buen Marqués, de cuyo tronco nace
don Cristóbal de Oñate descendiente
de todos estos reyes y no reyes.

That great and praiseworthy general
whose name Cristóbal de Oñate I spoke of earlier,
of noble lineage he was,
the uncle of Juan and Vicente Zaldívar,
one was a general of the Chichimeca tribe,
the other an explorer of this region
and the father of Don Juan who was
the husband of the great-granddaughter
of the last Mexican king
and the granddaughter of the Marquis,
from this ancestry Don Cristóbal de Oñate was descended
A son of kings and nonkings.

All of these gentlemen are skilled in both arms and letters, although they prefer the first to the second, as Don Quijote did. In times of respite and in honor of a celebration or fiesta, both skills were practiced in tournaments and festivities:

Unas solemnes fiestas que duraron
una semana entera, donde hubo

juego de cañas, toros y sortijas
y una alegre comedia bien compuesta.

A week of celebration and festivities
where we enjoyed
tilting matches, bullfights, and *sortijas*
and a comedy especially composed for the occasion.

Villagrá is not referring here to the play written by the Sevillian Marcos Farfán de los Godos; he will tell us about Farfán's work in another place. Indeed, Farfán's comedia was presented when the expedition crossed the Rio Grande, and this dramatic piece can thus be considered the first play staged in the United States. Villagrá describes how the dramatic enactment of the comedia came about: "y luego que acabaron los oficios, / representaron una gran comedia, / que el noble capitán Farfán compuso" ("and after all the functions were set aside, / a great and wondrous comedy was enacted, / penned by the noble Captain Farfán").

Perhaps other soldiers who accompanied Oñate also wrote literary compositions. We do not know. However, one of them, Juan Velarde, was appointed secretary: "pues por la pluma, / no menos era noble y bien mirado, / que por la ilustre espada que cenia" ("because of his skill with the pen / he was no less noble and well liked / than for the illustrious sword he sported").

According to Don Quijote, those who practice arms suffer great penalties; they expose their lives to battles and for their troubles receive less recompense than those who practice the art of writing:

> *Alcanzar alguno a ser eminente en letras le cuesta tiempo, vigilias, hambre,*
> *desnudez, vaguidos de cabeza, indigestiones de estómago, y otras cosas . . .*
> *mas llegar uno por sus términos a ser buen soldado le cuesta todo lo que al*
> *estudiante en tanto mayor grado, que no tiene comparación, porque a cada*
> *paso está a pique de perder la vida.*

In order to achieve eminence in literary endeavors one has to spend a lot of time, suffer sleepless nights, hunger, poverty, headaches, stom-

achaches, indigestion, and much more . . . on the other hand, in order
to be a soldier it takes all the sufferings a student must endure and in
greater degree which is really without comparison, because at each
step of the way he is on the verge of losing his life.

Villagrá, likewise, in the twentieth canto tells us "of the excessive
travails soldiers must endure" and of the meager salary they receive for
their pains. In that same verse he complains that his poetry does not do
justice to the great deeds those valiant soldiers accomplished:

De sus muchos quebrantos padecidos,
y por mostrar mejor si son soldados

fuera bien se encargara, y escribiera
sus claros y altos hechos hazañosos,
mas como inculto, bronco y mal limado,
dellos informaré lo que supiere.

Of the great hardships they suffered,
and to better demonstrate their mettle as soldiers

it would be of great value
if their great deeds and valorous actions
were written for their glory, and even though I'm
rough, unpolished, and unlettered,
I shall relate what I have know of them.

Later on, he promises to do so in the second part of the *Historia*, which,
unfortunately, was never published:

Muchos así las vidas escaparon,
temerarias hazañas emprendiendo,
y hechos hazañosos acabando,
cual cantaré, señor si Dios me deja,
ver la segunda parte a luz echada,

donde veréis gran Rey prodigios grandes
de tierras y naciones nunca vistas,
trabajos y aventuras no contadas,
empresas inauditas y desdichas
que a fuerza de fortuna y malos hados,
también nos persiguieron y acosaron.

Many escaped with their lives in such a manner,
blazing their way with great and dangerous deeds
and forging glorious actions
of which I'll sing, if God permits it,
in the second part of this work,
where thou shall see, O Great King, of wonders
of these distant and unknown lands,
and the adventures and travails of valiant men
their prowess, audaciousness and even ill fortune
that through misfortunes and ill luck,
also was wont to follow and inflict us.

Villagrá himself is an excellent example of a man who preferred the practice of arms but also cultivated the art of literature. His *Historia* is a testimonial to his qualities both as a soldier (he spent thirty years in the service of his king) and as a fairly accomplished poet. In the "Canción pindárica en loor del capitán Gaspar de Villagrá, y don Juan de Oñate, descubridor y conquistador de la nueva México," which Luis Tribaldo de Toledo used as a preface to the *Historia*, we read the following:

Vos Villagrá castellano
con la pluma y con la mano
fundáis la gloria española

pues hoy de vos nuevo Ercilla
corre esta voz por Castilla,
que nunca el tiempo consuma,

que en México la moderna,
será vuestra fama eterna,
por la lanza, y por la pluma.

You, Villagrá, noble Castilian,
with your pen and with your sword
Spain's glory have founded.

For throughout Castile today
of you, new Ercilla, we hear,
and let it be known forever
that in modern Mexico the fame
of your pen and your sword,
will remain eternal.

And from the "Canción" dedicated to Don Juan de Oñate and written
by Juan de Valdés Caballero, which also prefaces the work, the following closing verses appear in which Villagrá is praised for having been
equal to the task of using the pen and the sword. Valdés Caballero first
describes the feats of Oñate and afterward directly addresses the poet's
achievements:

Y tu canción humilde que has subido,
a tan heroico y singular sujeto,
basta no desvanescas el sentido,
remite tantas glorias y alabanzas,
y plectro más subido y más perfecto,
vos capitán discreto,
que igualastes la espada con la pluma,
haréis la copia y la sucinta suma,
que llegue altiva al conquistado ocaso,
animaréis vuestro veloz pegaso.

And thy humble paean that elevates to such heights,
and sings of such heroic and singular person,
do not weaken thy voice,

do continue singing of such glories and such praises
a plectrum more exalted and most perfect,
you my most discreet Captain possess,
who has proved equal to the sword and pen,
you shall recount both part and whole,
let it reach the summits of the conquered West,
give loose rein to your fleet-footed Pegasus.

The final canto's description of the destruction of Ácoma is without a doubt the most memorable and most important passage in the *Historia*. It is representative of the Chicano literature to come because it is a literature born in the heat of cultural conflict. In 1938, Mabel Major, one of the first critics to defend the colonial literature of the Southwest in her book *Southwest Heritage,* was ahead of her time in defending the work of Pérez de Villagrá, and one can consider her the first North American critic (who was not a historian) who recognized its literary value. "It's annoying to find American history and letters continually described as a style tradition with its genesis in the *Mayflower* and the Massachusetts Bay Psalm Book. . . .Villagrá's account of the heroic capture of Ácoma by Zaldívar and seventy men bears comparison with the scaling of the heights outside Quebec by Wolfe if one keeps all the circumstances in mind."

Equally valuable are Villagrá's literary descriptions of the Southwest, the first written in poetic discourse. Among those regarding the fauna, his description of the bison is particularly outstanding. In describing this American animal he utilizes the image of the European bull, to which he adds other characteristics specific to the bison. The explorers encountered great herds of these animals as they trekked inland, northward bound.

> *Tanta suma y grandeza de ganados,*
> *que fue cosa espantosa imaginarlos.*
> *Son del cuerpo que toros castellanos*
> *lanudos por extremo, corcobados,*
> *de regalada carne y negros cuernos.*

Such a great and grand herd of cattle,
that it was a horrifying spectacle even to imagine.
They are not unlike Castilian bulls
Quite woolly and humpbacked,
robust flesh and black of horn.

Just as interesting are the descriptions of the great prairies where the
bison roamed. Villagrá here uses a metaphor that Domingo Faustino
Sarmiento later made famous in his description of the Argentine pampas in *Facundo* (1845). "Y gozan de unos llanos tan tendidos, / que por
seiscientas y ochocientas leguas / un sosegado mar parece todo" ("And
they enjoy such a great expanse of land, / that for six or eight hundred
leagues / these plains resemble a sea at calm"). Anyone who loses his way
in such expanses will be without hope: "en medio de la mar sin esperanza" ("in the middle of the ocean without hope"). And it is Villagrá
who provides us with the first description of the vaquero, a person later
to become one of the most popular prototypes of Southwestern culture,
now better known as the cowboy. He also describes for us in anecdotal
form the activity that would come to be known as the rodeo:

Queriendo pues en estos grandes llanos,
el sargento mayor coger algunas
de aquestas vacas sueltas y traerlas
al pueblo de San Juan, porque las viesen,
mandó que una manga se hiciese
de fuerte palizada prolongada,
la cual hicieron con presteza,
y luego que la manga se compuso,
salieron para dar el aventado

Todos en buenas yeguas voladoras.

The sergeant, desirous of capturing some
of these great bulls inhabiting the Great Plains
who roaming loose he wanted to bring

to the town of San Juan, so we could see,
ordered a strong stockade to be built
with the greatest of haste,
and after the stockade was built
they went forward to round them up

All this done on their fleet-footed mares.

The image Villagrá utilizes to describe the bison stampede is most
original:

Y así como la manga descubrieron,
cual poderoso viento arrebatado,
que remata en un grande remolino,
así fue reparando y revolviendo,
la fuerza del ganado levantando.

And as soon as the stockade was discovered,
as a strong gust of powerful wind engulfs
or a raging whirlpool sucks, such was
the force which startled and drove the bison to stampede.

It is interesting to note, since it reveals the mestizo origins of frontier
culture, that Villagrá calls the Indians who were helping in the rodeo
cowboys. The author records how Oñate and his men encountered these
cowboys in the plains:

Gran suma de vaqueros, que a pie matan,
aquestas mismas vacas que decimos
y dellas se sustentan y mantienen

y tienen lindas tiendas por extremo,
y lindos y lucidos pabellones,
del cuero de las vacas, cuyo adobo,
es tan tratable y dócil, que mojado,
aqueste mismo cuero que decimos,

vuelve después de seco más suave
que si fuera de lienzo, o fina holanda.

A great number of cowboys who kill on foot,
these same cattle herds we talked about
and from these they take their sustenance

and they have such beautiful tents
and such splendid canopies
made from the hide of these same cattle,
whose skin is so tender and so malleable
that when wet this same hide
will be as soft as linen
or fine Flemish lace when dried.

It is characteristic of Villagrá's poetic discourse to use aphoristic expressions and sharp commentaries concerning the life and culture he is observing. This indicates that he possessed a well-defined philosophy of life. At the same time, he tries to display his erudition by citing classic authors and famous books or interspersing Latin phrases: "y así dice muy bien el Mantuano/o sacra hambre, de riquezas vanas" ("and thus with such fine phrases Virgil speaks,/Oh those who hunger for vain riches").

Simultaneously, in the introduction of each canto we find passages with both a poetic and a historical content. In the introduction to canto 21, Villagrá utilizes a poetic discourse to express the conflict between Oñate's men and the people of Ácoma—that is to say, the conflict between Europe and America. In the passage below, representative of that type of discourse, there is not a single reference to historical fact.

O mundo instable de miserias lleno,
verdugo atroz de aquel que te conoce,
disimulado engaño no entendido,
prodigiosa tragedia portentosa,
maldito cáncer, solapada peste,

mortal veneno, landre que te encubre,
dime, traidor, aleve, fementido,
cuantas traiciones tienes fabricadas,
cuantos varones tienes consumidos,
de cuanto mal enredo estás cargado,
o mundo vano, o vana y miserable
tantos daños adquirida,
o vanas esperanzas de mortales,
o vanos pensamientos engañosos,
sujetos siempre a míseros temores,
y a mil sucesos tristes y accidentes.

Oh, unstable world, with misery filled,
cruel master to those who know you,
unacknowledged deceit not understood,
prodigious and portentous tragedy,
vile cancer, sly plague,
deadly poison, evil curse which engulfs,
speak up, you traitor, perfidious, treacherous,
how many deceits have you concocted,
how many gentlemen have you consumed,
in what vile deceits are you engaged,
Oh wicked world, Oh vain and miserable
honor with so much pain acquired,
Oh vain hopes of mortal men,
Oh vain and treacherous thoughts,
always subjected to such miserable fears
and to a thousand sad and tragic accidents.

A few metaphors are reiterated consistently throughout the poem. One of these tropes is the ship at sea, symbolic of the flow of history (history being similar to a voyage on the high seas):

Llegados habemos gran señor al punto
y engolfados en alta mar estamos,

la tierra se ha perdido, y solo resta,
el buen gobierno y cuenta de la nave.

Arrived we have, O great king, to that most distant land
and engulfed on the high seas we tarry,
the land's been lost, and all we have,
is the control of our ship afloat.

A literary analysis of Villagrá's *Historia* requires more attention than
can be afforded here in these few pages. The quotes I have mentioned
are only examples of what the poem entails vis-à-vis its literary form
and content; they do not include the historical aspects encompassed
with regard to the conquest of New Mexico. Villagrá, like Cervantes,
was a writer who preferred the practice of arms to that of letters. However, as he was composing the poem, he was conscious that it would
have a niche in the history of Hispanic literature. His presence in the
poem, not as a soldier but as a poet, is clearly manifested in a number
of the cantos. Alfonso Reyes has observed that "the history and epics
regarding the conquest had a practical purpose which was to ask for a
recompense. It sought a false equilibrium between the representation
of reality . . . and a manner in which to exaggerate the debt, i.e., feats
accomplished in the name of the Crown." I must point out that Villagrá
does not ask for a reward for his services, although he believes recompense is due to the soldiers who risked their lives in order to expand
the Spanish Empire in the New World. His primary purpose in writing the poem was to inform the king of the conquest of New Mexico.
The poem is dedicated to His Majesty Felipe III, and the poet assumes
the king is listening to him, is the receptor of the poem. We know that
because in the last canto he addresses the king with these words: "Y
vos Felipe sacro, que escuchando / mi tosca musa habéis estado atento, /
suplico no os canséis, que ya he llegado" ("And O most sacred Felipe,
who listening / to my rough, unpolished muse you've been attentive / I
beg of you not to tire, for I am done").

Doubtless Villagrá had a desire to be remembered as a poet. If this
had not been the case he would not have selected the verse form to

relate the history of the destruction of Ácoma, just as Cervantes previously had done with the Battle of Numancia. Villagrá was conscious of the similarity of the two events, and he refers to it in the last canto:

Sin cuya ayuda dudo, y soy muy cierto,
que aquella gran Numancia trabajosa,
cuando más desdichada y más perdida,
quedara más desierta y despoblada,
que aquesta pobre fuerza ya rendida.

Without whose help I doubt I could have made it,
for that great Numancia,
when it was most unhappy was most lost
and was left deserted and uninhabited,
even more than this my efforts now exhausted.

The laudatory poems written by his friends certainly afforded Villagrá great satisfaction. He died quite young and thus was not able to enjoy the praise granted him by some of his contemporaries. At the same time, he was spared hearing the negative barbs of some critics. In spite of the adverse criticism, though, the poem has survived; it has been republished and translated into English. If as a soldier Villagrá helped in the conquest of New Mexico, as an author he left us the *Historia*, thus planting the seeds of Aztlán's literary heritage. As Gabriel Gómez states in the laudatory *canción* written in the dedicatory pages:

No de otra suerte al nuevo mexicano
libras tú del olvido,
después que valeroso le has vencido.

Salga tu libro al mundo,
admiración de ingenios superiores.
frena de detractores.
Y Marón tenga su lugar segundo,
que si él cantó, tú solo
cantas a Marte y das batalla a Apolo.

And in such a manner you have saved
the New Mexican from oblivion
after you so daringly have vanquished him.

May your book see the world
and be admired by superior minds
who'll stop inferior tongues from wagging.
And Maron will take a second place,
for if he sang, you alone
sing to Mars and battle with Apollo.

Bancroft called Pérez de Villagrá our New Mexican Homer. If the aesthetic value of Villagrá's work is not sufficient to make him deserving of such a distinction, the fact that he was the first to sing in honor and remembrance of the tragedy at Ácoma (just as Homer sung about the Trojan War) should grant him that title. But it really is not necessary to use such comparisons to evaluate Villagrá's work. It is of sufficient merit to have been the founder of a literature, the literature of New Mexico, for, as Luis Tribaldo de Toledo puts it in the preface to the *Historia:*

Long years ago, fate had decreed
That all these annals we should read
From the worthy pen of one
Who knows what happened where
These wondrous deeds were done,
For he himself was there.

11

LA CONQUISTADORA

Fray Angélico Chávez's earliest interest as a writer was poetry. However, in the forties he began to publish history and historical fiction. In his documented study "La Conquistadora Is a Paisana," he wrote: "Three years ago, led by an irresistible fascination, I began to piece together a few known facts about La Conquistadora in an effort to separate fact from fiction." Twenty years later, in 1970, he stated that he "took up history because it's there and makes my writing readable. There was a drama to the colonial life, and I have found its records." His first historical monograph, "Nuestra Señora del Rosario, La Conquistadora," appeared in 1948 in the *New Mexico Historical Review,* and that same year was reprinted in book form by the Historical Society of New Mexico under the title *Our Lady of the Conquest.* Six years later, under the title *La Conquistadora: The Autobiography of an Ancient Statue,* he transformed that documented history into a fictionalized autobiography of this most famous New Mexican statue of the Virgin Mary. In that book, instead of the author as a historian writing a biography, he lets the statue itself relate its life and adventures as if it were a real person. Here, Chávez's focus has changed. Instead of separating fact from fiction, which was his original aim when he took up history, he reverses the process and combines both discourses to produce a very original fictitious autobiography.

First published in *Fray Angélico Chávez: Poet, Priest, and Artist,* ed. Elen McCracken (Albuquerque: University of New Mexico Press, 2000), 37–44.

That La Conquistadora is the same statue brought to New Mexico by Fray Alonso de Benavides in 1625 is the thesis of Fray Angélico's 1948 monograph. Two years later he said, "I discovered seventeenth-century documents about La Conquistadora which supported the conclusions I had previously drawn." During Fray Alonso's time the statue represented the Virgin of the Assumption, as stated by the author in his *Memorial* of 1630; it was much later that she became La Conquistadora. In Chávez's book of 1954, the statue says, "I have been in this country [the United States] for more than three hundred and twenty-five years." In the chapter "Apaches, vaqueros del ganado de Síbola" of the *Memorial,* Benavides says:

> . . . *y habiendo sus Capitanes mayores oído decir que los españoles en la villa de Santa Fe tenían a la Madre de Dios, que era una imagen de bulto del Tránsito de la Virgen nuestra Señora que yo allí había llevado y estaba bien adornada en una capilla, vinieron a verla y le quedaron muy aficionados y le prometieron ser cristianos.*

> . . . and having their principal captains heard that the Spaniards in the village of Santa Fe had the Mother of God, which was a statue of Our Lady the Virgin of the Assumption, which I had brought there and was very well dressed, in a niche, they came to see her and remained very devoted and promised to become Christians.

According to what the statue says, she had been in New Mexico three hundred twenty-five years. This number is apparently derived from Fray Alonso's *Memorial* of 1630, in which he states, "Y el año pasado de 29 fue Dios servido que los redujésemos de paz" ("And last year, [16]29, God was served, for we were able to make peace with them [the Pueblo Indians]"). If 1629 is subtracted from 1954, the year the autobiography of the statue was published, the result is three hundred twenty-five years.

Chavez's sources for the writing of his fictionalized autobiography, as listed in the book's "Bibliography and Historical Comment," are historical in nature. And although all the historical references mentioned by the statue can be documented, the book is often classified as fiction.

Alejandro Morales, in his doctoral dissertation, speaks of *La Conquistadora* as a novel. This is true only in the context of the picaresque novel, which is essentially a fictitious autobiography narrated by the protagonist, a picaro. There are novels in which the narrator is a female picaro, as in Francisco López Úbeda's *La pícara Justina* (1605), Alonso Jerónimo de Salas Barbadillo's *La hija de Celestina* (1612), and Alonso de Castillo Solórzano's *La niña de los embustes, Teresa de Manzanares* (1632). In Mexico, José Joaquín Fernández de Lizardi published *La Quijotita y su prima* in 1818, and in 1969, Elena Poniatowska her novel *Hasta no verte Jesús mío*, in which the protagonist, Jesusa Palancares, relates her life. The difference between these novels and *La Conquistadora* is not found in the form, but in the subject matter and the attitude of the narrator toward life, which is not picaresque but historical and religious in nature. Other antecedents for wooden figures who talk and act are to be found in the popular puppet shows, an excellent example of which is one found in Cervantes's *Don Quijote*, wherein the knight-errant engages the puppets in combat.

The statue of the Virgin Mary brought to New Mexico by Fray Alonso in 1625 did not become La Conquistadora until much later in the century. It was first called, by Benavides, "Tránsito de la Virgen," a name translated by Fray Angélico as "Assumption of the Virgin." In his early book, *Our Lady of the Conquest*, he gives the following reasons to justify his translation: "I have used the word 'Assumption' for 'Tránsito' in the originals [1630 and 1634 editions of Benavides's *Memorial*], which others have translated as the 'death' of the Virgin. Their translation is correct literally, but wrong liturgically. In employing the word 'Tránsito,' Benavides, by metonymy, was merely using one of the three ideas celebrated in the title and feast of the Assumption: The Death or Passing Away of Mary, her Assumption into Heaven, and her Coronation."

In *La Conquistadora* the statue says, "In the beginning I was 'Our Lady of the Assumption,' then for a short time 'The Immaculate Conception,' and finally 'Our lady of the Rosary.' In these titles I was regarded by my people as Queen of New Mexico and of Santa Fe, but all the while, as with a beloved actress, I have been popularly known as

'La Conquistadora.'" The reason why she is called by that name is also stated by the statue: "My name for centuries has been 'La Conquistadora.' This is because I came to the Southwest with the Spanish pioneers who called themselves conquistadores." Historically, however, she was not called La Conquistadora until 1693, the year Diego de Vargas returned the statue to Santa Fe after his reconquest of the Pueblo Indians.

On August 10, 1680, the Pueblo Indians had revolted and set siege to Santa Fe. In spite of a counterattack on August 20, for which the people "invoked my aid with special prayers the night before," they were forced to abandon the city and go south to El Paso. "I myself left Santa Fe clasped in the arms of a young housewife, who pressed her wet and trembling cheek to mine and wept as she trudged along with the rest. Her name was Josefa López Sambrano de Grijalva." The so-called reconquest of Santa Fe was begun by Don Diego de Vargas in 1692, and it was not until December 16, 1693, that he triumphantly entered the city without a single casualty. Although the reconquest was begun under the banner of the Lady of the Remedies, he changed it to the Lady of the Rosary. On January 16, 1693, Vargas wrote to the viceroy in Mexico City, "It's my wish . . . that they should . . . build the church and holy temple, setting up in it before all else the patroness of the said kingdom and villa, who is the one that was saved from the fury of the savages, her title being Our Lady of the Conquest."

The fictitious aspect of the autobiography is to be found in the use of an old narrative technique, that of letting an inanimate object become the narrator. In Latin American fiction this technique is common. In 1930, Francisco Rojas González, in Mexico, published *Historia de un frac,* in which the *frac* (tuxedo) is the narrator and tells about his life. In 1965, the Argentine Marco Denevi published the short story "Apocalipsis," in which a machine is the narrator, a fact the reader does not know until the final phrase.

In *La Conquistadora,* the wooden statue begins to speak about her life since she was carved in Spain from a piece of the trunk of a willow tree. The trip across the ocean to the city of Mexico, where she was brought by an unnamed person, is hardly recollected. She says, "I remember, later on, a journey over water—an ocean, or a lake, it does not matter. Next

I found myself in a different land." In 1623, Fray Alonso saw her and decided to take her to New Mexico, as he had been appointed head of the missions there. His decision to take this statue and not another was based on two reasons, the statue's beauty and her small size.

> It was then that he first saw me and called me beautiful with his eyes.
>
> His heart decided at once that I would go with him to Santa Fe, and there reign in its parish church of the Assumption. Not only did my loveliness captivate Father Alonso, but my small self was just right, since it was impractical to haul large statues, in those early days, on a journey by oxcart that took at least three months over trackless mountains and deserts. And a man like Father Alonso had little trouble in getting my owner to part with me.

If she could not remember her trip across the ocean, her 1,200 mile trip by oxcart from Mexico City to Santa Fe is told with numerous details, such as the places where they stopped (Tepeyac, Zacatecas, Durango, El Paso); the people who accompanied them, like the new governor of New Mexico, Don Francisco Sotelo, and Captain Francisco Gómez, a Portuguese soldier (ancestor of Fray Angélico), and many others. She describes the landscape, the desert, the climate, and other elements. Well packed in a wooden crate, she tells the story of the Virgin of Guadalupe, about whom she says, talking directly to the reader, "Most of you already know about the heavenly painting of Our Lady of Guadalupe. It could be that someone might suspect that I, as a woman, could be jealous of a rival representation of the Mother of God. I am only jesting, of course." Similar statements as this one demonstrate her human nature, a characteristic of the statue very well developed by Fray Angélico. The historical source of the story of the Virgin of Guadalupe is the *Historia de la Virgen de Guadalupe*, published in Mexico City in 1897 by an anonymous Jesuit. Conscious of the fact that this is a very common story, the author has the statue say, again talking to the reader, "If I have bored you by recounting this well-known happening in its every detail, I myself have greatly enjoyed retelling it."

Technically, the statue could only be remembering the story through interior monologue, since she is enclosed in a strong case nailed inside a sturdy wooden box. This observation can be made about all the other references to reality outside the box during the trip. The reader, of course, accepts this omniscient nature of the statue, since from the beginning, like in all fables, he has suspended his credibility when he admits that the statue can talk.

The fictitious element in this book, that is, letting a wooden statue be the narrator, really has the function of an aesthetic frame, in which a novelistic discourse is used in order to make the history of New Mexico, from the early seventeenth century to the middle of the nineteenth, as interesting as possible. There is no question that Fray Angélico's aim is to retell that history, as he did in his earlier works about La Conquistadora. In the fictitious autobiography, he makes use of all the historical sources he used before, beginning with the two versions of Fray Alonso de Benavides's *Memorial* as well as information about Fray Alonso himself. The statue says, "Fray Alonso de Benavides left us when the supply ox train departed for New Spain in the fall of 1629. The following year he wrote a *Memorial* describing the missions of New Mexico, their great problems and greater possibilities. This was presented [by Fray Juan de Santander] to the King of Spain, was printed in Madrid, and soon was being translated and published in various countries of Europe. Three years later he wrote a revision of it at the request of Pope Urban VIII. In both works, Fray Alonso makes special mention of me."

The statue's main interests, when she is not talking about herself, are history, religion, and the biography of Fray Angélico's ancestors, of whom there is a genealogical tree at the beginning of the book. The statue is very skillful about characterizing herself and is not jealous, as she says, of other representations of the Mother of God. Besides the Mexican Virgin of Guadalupe, whom she praises, she relates the lives of the Spanish Virgin of Guadalupe, of Our Lady of the Remedies, of Our Lady of Light, and of Our Lady of Toledo. The Spanish Virgin of Guadalupe has a long history. The medium is the same as that of La Conquistadora: "It's a seated figure of wood, about my own height, representing Mary with her Child on her left arm." She appeared during the thirteenth century to a peasant of Cáceres, Extremadura, who was looking for a stray cow, and told him to dig at the spot, where they would find her image, and build there a shrine for her. "In the year 1340 this Alfonso [Alfonso XI] won a great victory over Albohacen, the ruler of Morocco, after imploring the help of Our Lady of Guadalupe."

In the New World, the first Conquistadora was not New Mexico's Lady of the Assumption, but Our Lady of Remedies, brought by Hernán Cortés to Mexico in 1519. The New Mexico statue recognizes this fact, as she admits that "the first Conquistadora is a small statue of Our Lady of the Angels, known also afterward as Our Lady of Remedies, which Cortés had with him in the conquest of Mexico City."

When La Conquistadora speaks about herself, she gives emphasis to her feminine traits. She does not mind being compared with actresses, for, "like one, I have played the part of Mary in different glorious roles." She is old, but "a lady, even a wooden one, will not tell her exact age." When Father Domínguez speaks of her as being about a yard tall, very old, recently retouched and wearing a wig, she becomes indignant and says, "He somehow insulted me . . . was rather crude in his veracity." She does not hide the fact that she likes men, as she says, "I myself liked the captain, too, knowing that he also would love me."

La Conquistadora is also tolerant as she defends Francisco Gómez Robledo, the son of Francisco Gómez and Ana Robledo, who is accused of being a Jew because his sons were supposed to have tails. Her knowledge of anatomy is revealed when she explains the reason why people think Gómez's sons have tails. "The fact is that one of the sons (some say Juan, others say Francisco) has an abnormal coccyx . . . this tiny bone at the end of the spine stuck out instead of curling inward and out of sight under the skin, as with most people." Of the racial conflict with the Indians, she says, "a passion blinder even than that of the flesh, it seems, is that of race."

Most of the text of *La Conquistadora* is taken up with the history of New Mexico: the exploration and founding of the villages by Juan de Oñate in 1598; the arrival and departure of Fray Alonso de Benavides and Governor Sotero; the short period of Flores as governor and his appointment of Francisco Gómez as acting governor; the 1680 uprising of the Pueblo Indians and the abandonment of Santa Fe by Governor Otermin; the reconquest of Santa Fe by Don Diego de Vargas in 1693 and his imprisonment by Governor Pedro Cuervo in 1697 and Vargas's campaign against the Pueblo Indians in 1706; the defeat of the Utes and Comanches by acting governor Valverde; the long period (1717–65) of Bernardino de Sena ("born in the Valley of Mexico, not far from the shrine of Guadalupe") as mayordomo of the statue's confraternity; the governments of other obscure rulers until 1821, when New Mexico is "no longer a Kingdom but a poor forgotten frontier province"; the Mexican governors and the conquest of New Mexico by General Kerney; and the arrival of Bishop Lamy in 1851.

The other important elements in the book are the references to Fray Angélico's ancestors, beginning with Captain Francisco Gómez and his wife Ana Robledo. In his 1950 article, he included a brief list of his direct ancestors. "I will be brief," he says, "by enumerating them in handy Biblical fashion: Francisco Gómez and Ana Robledo begat Andrés Gómez Robledo, . . . Romualdo Roybal, who begat María Nicolasa Roybal (my mother)." He continues, saying, "This personal genealogy is not proffered here as a claim to any social superiority. In my opinion, the chief virtue of genealogies lies in the invaluable aid that they give to historical and social studies, and not in the vain pretensions for which genealogies are employed everywhere. By simply showing my own direct connection with the original and subsequent Conquistadora devotees I am also demonstrating how all native New Mexicans have been honoring their Queen." From the perspective of La Conquistadora, this interest in genealogy has a different source. She says, "At this particular period my people had become strongly aware of their ancestry, perhaps because there was not much else to boast about."

The autobiography ends with an epilogue in which La Conquistadora invites the reader to visit her in the Cathedral of Saint Francis of Assisi. She then goes on to describe her several dresses, all of them fashioned after those of an ancient Spanish queen. The nature of this most human statue is revealed when she says, "Of course, I know that I myself am not immortal. The day will come when I shall join the rest of the willow by being burned to ashes." Thus, the image of the willow, which appears at the beginning of the autobiography, when the statue relates her birth, reappears at the end of the book, giving this most interesting fictitious autobiography an artistic narrative frame, a frame worthy of the painting of the most famous of statues.

The narrative trend dealing with the author's ancestors is introduced in *La Conquistadora* right after the title, in the form of a genealogical tree of his family, from the early seventeenth century to the time the book was published. Throughout the narrative, these persons appear associated to the activities of La Conquistadora. The founder of the family, Captain Francisco López, was a Portuguese "born in a suburb of Lisbon [Coina, near Lisbon], and after both his parents died, was reared" by a half brother. He was brought to Mexico by a brother of Juan de Oñate, and then came to New Mexico, where he was given an encomienda. Soon he was promoted to *sargento mayor* and became one of the most powerful men in New Mexico. His wife, Ana Robledo, born in San Gabriel, New Mexico, in 1600, was only twenty-five years old when La Conquistadora came to Santa Fe. Ana married Francisco Gómez in that city and had several children, among them Francisco Gómez Robledo, who was later accused of being a Jew by the Inquisition, as was his father. La Conquistadora says about the family, "Ana Robledo lived on for many years, and some of her children also, to be further knitted into my life's story."

Often, fiction and history blend to create a new dimension. In *La Conquistadora*, historical facts are intermingled with the statue's personal observations to give the narrative verisimilitude. When Don Diego de Vargas arrived in El Paso in 1691 (a historical fact about a real person), the statue adds: "he, too, fell in love with me" (a fictitious statement). Like a medieval lady, she has her knights, although they are not wooden, but real: "My chief knight at this period was Don Juan Páez Hurtado." And she also says, "But to me these particular [historical] people were the salt of the earth. Were it not for them I would not be known; perhaps I would not even exist today with a story to tell."

12

FÉLIX VARELA

Félix Varela is the first modern Cuban thinker. Unlike other Cubans, for instance José Martí, Varela is hardly known outside of his own country. Only the Cubans themselves have been concerned enough to read his works and write about his philosophy. His contributions to the development of Latin American liberal thought have been ignored; if the histories of Spanish American philosophy and the histories of the essay are examined, it is discovered that Varela is dismissed with a sentence or two.

Cuban critics, on the other hand, have not forgotten Varela. Rather, they have rediscovered his importance in the history of ideas, not only philosophical but also political. As early as 1878, the Cuban José Ignacio Rodríguez, writing in Washington, D.C., and New York, published the first biography of Varela, reproducing some of his articles, letters, and speeches, which otherwise would have been lost.

A study of the philosophical reforms introduced by Varela cannot be made without mentioning the preparatory work done in Mexico by Juan Bautista Díaz de Gamarra and in Cuba by Varela's own teachers, José Agustín Caballero and Bernardo O'Gaván. These men represent the pioneers in the revolt against Scholasticism in Latin American thought. Gamarra, born in Mexico, received his doctorate at the University of Pisa, where he became acquainted with the new philosophy. Back in

First published in *The Ibero-American Enlightenment*, ed. A. Owen Aldidge (Urbana: University of Illinois Press, 1971), 234–42.

Mexico, he published in 1774 his *Elementa recentioris philosophiae* (*Elements of Modern Philosophy*), in which he declares that the philosopher should eagerly investigate the truth without adhering to any sect, be it that of Aristotle, Plato, Leibniz, or Newton. He should pursue the truth without acknowledging any authority. Antonio Caso, commenting upon this statement of principles, has said: "Here we have the highest devotion to the liberty of thought expressed in the classroom of the Colonial university." In 1781, Gamarra published, under the pseudonym Juan Bendiaga, his *Errores del entendimiento humano* (*Errors of Human Understanding*), and it is known that his works definitely influenced Varela, for in 1840, he wrote to a friend: "I can affirm that when I studied philosophy at the College of San Carlos in Havana I was a *cousiano* [a follower of Cousin], as were all the students of my illustrious teacher José Agustín Caballero, who always defended pure intellectual ideas following in the steps of Jacquier and Gamarra."

It is not known whether Varela actually read Gamarra himself or learned about his ideas through his teacher Caballero, who used Gamarra's book. Caballero represents, in Cuba, the point of transition between Scholasticism and the new philosophy. He did not, however, break away completely from Scholasticism, although the title of his notes, written in 1797, was *Eclect philosophy*. He was, however, the first one to introduce reforms in the teaching of philosophy in Cuban universities.

Caballero's reforms were continued by Bernardo O'Gaván, with whom Varela completed his study of philosophy. O'Gaván rejected Cousin's ideas and praised those of Locke and Condillac. His articles of 1808 in the newspaper *La Aurora,* reproduced by Mexican periodicals, were condemned by the Inquisition. Varela, in the same letter of 1840, says: "Mr. O'Gaván, who succeeded him [Caballero], and with whom I completed my course in philosophy, changed this doctrine [Cousin's doctrine], adopting what today, in fashionable terms, they call *sensualismo,* which I, who succeeded him [O'Gaván], always taught, although without so much *aparato.*"

Varela succeeded O'Gaván in the teaching of philosophy at the university in 1811 and immediately set out to reform the courses by introducing Descartes' ideas and abandoning Scholasticism. His first *Elenco* was printed in 1812, and it served as an outline for the teaching of the subject. This pamphlet has been called "the first essay on modern philosophy by a Cuban writer." The *Elenco*, lost until 1873, when Bachiller y Morales found a copy in New York City, is made up of 226 propositions and is written in Latin. Proposition 13 states that the Cartesian method should always be admitted, and proposition 14 that the best philosophy is the eclectic. In the propositions regarding the physical sciences it is stated that experience and reason are the only sources of knowledge in the sciences.

This *Elenco* served as the basis for the writing of the *Institutiones philosophiae eclecticae* (*Principles of Eclectic Philosophy*), a work in four volumes, the first two, in Latin, having appeared in 1812. The third and fourth volumes, written in Spanish, appeared in 1813 and 1814, respectively. This book gave a deathblow to the teaching of Scholastic philosophy in Cuba. In the academic year 1813–14, Latin was discarded as the language of the classroom. The natural sciences were taught for the first time in Spanish, using the experimental method. Thus, Varela precedes other thinkers in Latin America, as the reforms introduced by Juan Crisóstomo Lafinur in Argentina began in 1819, and the same can be said of other countries.

Varela's first work on philosophy was to be followed by his *Lecciones de filosófica* (*Philosophy Lessons*, 1818) and his *Miscelánea filosófica* (*Philosophical Miscellanea*, 1819), both written in Spanish. In the last one, Varela reaffirms his opposition to Scholasticism and his belief in the experimental sciences. "There is no other way," he says, "except to proceed by observation of the facts, examining with attention the relations, and having great care in forming ideas that contain exact elements, and trying not to alter those ideas while formulating our deductions." It is interesting to note that Varela, like the contemporary behaviorists, believed that in order to think one must make use of signs. He said:

> In the present state of our knowledge, all acquired through sensations, and closely attached to signs, it's impossible to think without their help. No matter what effort we may make to exclude them, we are not able to do it, and experience proves that whenever we think, it seems

to us that we hear ourselves talk, and often we pronounce the words aloud without being conscious of it, and that's why it's said that *we speak to ourselves*. From this it's deducted that to think is the same as to use signs, and to think well is to use signs correctly.

This book also contains an essay on the doctrines of Kant, perhaps the first one on the German philosopher by a Latin American writer. No less interesting is his essay on patriotism, among the finest pages of Varela.

Hernández Travieso has expressed very well the transition in Cuban philosophy from Scholasticism to *sensualismo:* "We shall consider Caballero as the necessary link between Scholasticism and the new ideas, without breaking definitely with tradition, which language he uses in his text, and O'Gaván as the first who broke with the medieval-theological version of Aristotle in a conclusive way, to the point of having defied, in spite of being a clergyman, the powerful Tribunal of the Holy Inquisition. In Varela we see how the early attack of Caballero and the passionate one of O'Gaván upon Scholasticism become a vocation. He will become the philosophy teacher of future Cubans."

It must be observed that although Varela follows, in the formulation of his philosophical concepts, the ideas expressed by Locke in his *Essay Concerning Human Understanding* (1666), Condillac's *Traite des sensations* (*Testimony on the Senses,* 1754), and Testutt de Tracy's *Elements d'ideologie* (*Elements of Ideology,* 1804), he does not follow them as to religious ideas. Varela, an ordained priest, managed to retain his religious beliefs and never broke away from the church. Nevertheless, his philosophy undermined the religious beliefs of his disciples, as they paid no attention to his declarations of faith. At the same time, his ideas prepared the way for political independence. Varela has often been called the precursor of Cuban independence.

Félix Varela, like most of the Latin American *pensadores* of the period of independence, was interested not only in philosophy and science, but also in social and political affairs. His contributions in this aspect of Cuban life are just as important as those in the field of ideas. In Spain, in 1820, General Riego's liberal pronouncement brought about the implementation of the forgotten liberal constitution of 1812. By royal decree, special courses were to be established to teach the people the meaning of the constitution. In Havana, Father Varela was designated to teach this new course; he began his classes in 1821 and had about one hundred students. This class came to be known as "the class of liberty, of the rights of man, of national guarantees and the regeneration of Spain." His notes for the course were published the same year under the title *Observaciones sobre la constitución política de la monarquía española*. In the first observation, titled "Soberanía," Varela says: "To be sure, all men, by nature, have equal rights and equal liberties." His course was so successful that the following year Varela was appointed, with his friends Tomás Gener and Leonardo Santos Suárez, as representative to the Spanish Cortes for the period 1822–23.

Varela's activities in the Cortes during 1823 demonstrated that he was a great patriot and a man of vision. He participated actively in the debates and presented several projects, all of them motivated by his desire to save Spain from disaster. He presented, among others, proposals for the reorganization of the clergy, for the abolition of slavery, and for the reorganization of the American provinces. He was, of course, defeated. Slavery was a profitable, if degrading, business for the Spanish government, and recognizing the independence of the American provinces was, in 1823, out of the question. Defending his thesis for the granting of independence, Varela wrote: "No matter what happens, Spain can only lose what she cannot keep . . . but if she recognizes their independence, she will not lose their friendship. . . . If Spain waits, she can only benefit other countries, as she will forego all cooperation with [Spanish] America." The members of the Cortes decided that there was no reason why they should consider Varela's proposal. Soon Ferdinand VII was to abolish the Cortes, and the liberal members fled to Seville and from there to Cádiz. There, some of them, including Varela, signed a document, proposed by Alcalá Galiano, declaring Ferdinand incapable of governing and replacing him with a *consejo de regencia*. All those who signed the document were condemned to death in absentia. With the help of the English, Varela and others were able to take refuge in Gibraltar. From there they came to the United States, arriving in New

York on December 17, 1823. After a short time, Varela went to Philadelphia, where he was to remain for some time. He was never to leave the United States; he died in St. Augustine, Florida, in 1853.

While in Spain, Varela did not advocate that Cuba be granted independence. Following in the steps of his teacher, Caballero, he was in favor of autonomy for the island, and in 1823 prepared his *Proyecto de gobierno autónomo,* a document that was ignored by the Spanish government. As a result of his experiences in the Cortes, Varela changed his attitude and ideas and became a fervent advocate of independence for Cuba. To promote this cause, he published the periodical *El Habanero* in Philadelphia, considered to be Cuba's first revolutionary paper.

In Philadelphia, Varela was not alone in his fight for Cuban independence. There he found a group of liberals who sympathized with his ideas—the Philadelphia of that time was a center of conspirators. Among others working with Varela, or sympathizing with his ideas, were his two friends Tomás Gener and Leonardo Santos Suárez, who had come with him from Gibraltar; José de la Luz Caballero, nephew of Varela's teacher; the writer Domingo del Monte; the poet José María Heredia; the restless Ecuadorean Vicente Rocafuerte; the Colombian man of letters José Fernández Madrid; the Venezuelan Nicanor Bolet Peraza; and the Argentine José Antonio Miralla. They all published original works or translations into Spanish either in Philadelphia or New York. Varela himself translated Jefferson's *Manual of Parliamentary Practice* and Davy's *Elements of Chemistry Applied to Agriculture.*

Of the seven numbers published of *El Habanero,* three appeared in Philadelphia between 1823 and 1824, and the last four in New York between 1824 and 1826. The last number, without place of publication or date, is unknown, as not a single copy has been found, either in Cuba or the United States. In spite of the severe censorship in the island, Varela managed to put the paper in the hands of his friends in Cuba, where its effect, because it was the first to advocate independence, was sensational. The Spanish government denounced the paper, and a royal order was issued to prohibit its circulation. They even tried to assassinate the publisher, an act that Varela condemned in the strongest terms. In a supplement to the third number of *El Habanero* (1825) he wrote: "In La

Habana the government's only worry seems to be to persecute my poor *Habanero* and to send a man to assassinate its author. I have just heard that as a consequence of the effect caused by the second number they have called for a donation to pay a man to assassinate me. *¡Miserables! ¿Creen destruir la verdad asesinando al que la dice?* [Wretched! They believe they can kill the faith by killing the one who says it?]"

Varela is at his best in the pages of *El Habanero,* fighting for a cause he sincerely believed to be right; expressing his ideals with fervor; and writing in a style that, without being oratorical, is very effective in moving the reader to act in favor of the cause he is advocating. Here are found some of his best essays; from the first, "Máscaras políticas," to the last, "Consecuencias de la rendición del Castillo de San Juan de Ulúa respeto de la Isla de Cuba"; they reflect the author's liberal ideas, humanism, and patriotism. He did not hate Spaniards per se. He hated only those who were against liberty, against human rights, against freedom of expression. With good reason the essays of *El Habanero* have been compared to the tolling of the bells that woke the Cubans from their colonial slumber.

Half a century was to pass before José Martí would take up where Varela left off, also, like Varela, fighting for Cuban independence with that powerful arm, the written word. But the initiator of this chain of events was Félix Varela, whose liberal ideas became an inspiration for later Cuban thinkers.

13

MIGUEL ANTONIO OTERO

Miguel Antonio Otero's three-volume autobiography is one of the best documentations of life on the American frontier during the last half of the nineteenth century. His recollection of his life from his childhood until the end of his term as governor of the territory of New Mexico in 1906 is written in the tradition of chronicles of the Southwest. His aim in writing it, he tells readers, was to provide future generations with a firsthand account of what really happened during that interesting period of his life. No less important, since he knew the subject personally, is his 1936 book on William H. Bonney, "Billy the Kid," which he wrote because, according to him, all the others were "pure fiction, wholly devoid of fact." His, on the other hand, is "based entirely on actual fact."

Born on October 17, 1859, in St. Louis, Missouri, Otero was the son of the famous Miguel Antonio Otero (1829–82), professor of Latin and Greek at Pingree College, Fishkill on the Hudson, for two years (1847–49) and three-time delegate to the United States Congress (1855, 1857, 1859) from the territory of New Mexico. President Lincoln offered him an appointment as minister to Spain, which he refused because he wanted to retire from public life and dedicate himself entirely to his banking business, the firm of Whiting and Otero. He did, however, accept the position of secretary of the territory. In 1857, he married Mary

First published in *Dictionary of Literary Biography: Chicano Writers,* vol. 82, 1st ser., ed. Francisco A. Lomelí and Carl R. Shirley (Detroit: A Bruccoli Clark Layman Book, Gale Research, 1989), 189–93.

Josephine Blackwood, born in New Orleans and brought up in Charleston, South Carolina. The couple raised two boys, Page Blackwood (b. January 4, 1858–d. unknown) and Miguel Antonio, and two girls, Gertrude Vicenta (1865–76) and Mamie Josephine (1867–1928).

The Otero family moved freely in the Midwest and the Southwest, living in Missouri, Kansas, Colorado, Arizona, and New Mexico. In 1866, the two brothers were sent to a boarding school in Topeka, Kansas, where they underwent unpleasant experiences. "The school proved to be a detestable place and its horrors are still fresh in my memory, though nearly seventy years have passed since then. I can only compare my experiences at the frontier boarding school with those which Dickens relates in *Oliver Twist*."

In 1867, the family moved to Ellsworth, Kansas, where Otero's father had a business. Miguel Antonio was introduced to the "rough life of the frontier towns." Later they moved to Hayes City, "a wild and woolly town" whose main street was "almost a solid row of saloons, dance halls, restaurants, barber shops, and houses of prostitution kept by such notorious characters as 'Calamity Jane,' 'Lousy Liz,' 'Stink-Foot Mag,' and 'Steamboat.'" To cope with lawlessness, the city hired as town marshal the famous James Butler "Wild Bill" Hickok, who, according to Otero, was "one of the most perfect specimens of manhood I have ever seen." He met Wild Bill in 1868 and took "a great fancy to him and greatly enjoyed his company. . . . He often took my brother and myself on buffalo hunts." On the other hand, Otero did not have a very high opinion of William Frederick "Buffalo Bill" Cody, whom he considered too cautious to be brave. Nonetheless, Otero called Cody "a gentleman and a good businessman." In spite of his love for life on the frontier, Otero was able to leave it in order to study, first at St. Louis University and then at Notre Dame, where he was trained in business administration.

After returning to the frontier from college, Otero joined his father's firm in the capacity of accountant. In 1886, he was elected probate clerk of San Miguel County, and on December 19, 1888, he married Caroline Virginia Emmett, with whom he had a son in 1891, Miguel Antonio III, who died a few days after birth. The following year, his second son, Miguel Antonio IV, was born. In 1891, Otero represented New Mexico at the Republican National Convention, and there he met the future president, William McKinley, who was to name Otero governor of the territory of New Mexico in 1897. As governor, Otero organized a powerful Republican political machine. His power and influence at the White House continued under President Theodore Roosevelt. Historian Ralph Emerson Twitchell summarized Otero's incumbency with these words: "The political policies and methods advocated and pursued by Governor Otero are susceptible of adverse criticism. This cannot be said of his administration so far as the business interests of New Mexico were involved. Calling to his aid in the conduct of his office the business methods with which he was familiar and in which he had received a thorough education, he accomplished much for the welfare of New Mexico."

Otero's works consist of several reports written during his tenancy as governor; a six-page sketch of Colonel José Francisco Cháves; his autobiography in three volumes; and the biography of Billy the Kid. Otero was a friend and admirer of Colonel Cháves, whom he met in 1872 at his home in Valencia County, New Mexico. Eight years were to pass before he met him again, this time at the twenty-fourth legislative assembly in Santa Fe. From that year (1880) on, they met often, as Cháves was the presiding officer of the territory of New Mexico. While Otero was governor, he named him superintendent of public instruction twice, in 1901 and 1903. The cowardly assassination of the colonel on November 26, 1904, for political reasons moved Otero deeply.

It was not until he had retired that some of his friends asked former governor Otero to write his memoirs. He accepted the advice, and in 1935, he published the first volume of what turned out to be the trilogy. The first part ends with the death of his father, which occurred on May 30, 1882, when the author was twenty-three years old. This volume contains stories his mother had told him about the Old West, observations about life on the frontier as seen first through the eyes of a boy and then of a young man, and descriptions of local types, some of whom, Hickok, Cody, and Bonney, became famous nationally.

Like Bernal Díaz del Castillo, the chronicler of the Conquest of Mexico, Otero had an excellent memory and late in life made use of his early impressions to elaborate the early part of his memoirs. The first volume of his life appeared when the author was already seventy-six years old. The reader, however, is impressed with the vividness of the narration and receives the impression that it was written shortly after the mentioned events took place, a circumstance that leads to the assumption that Otero wrote some of his pages well before publication. He does not, however, rely entirely on memory, as he often quotes the newspapers of the period. His main preoccupation was to confine his writing to actual facts "and adhere strictly to the truth, [and] let the chips fall where they may." This task was difficult to accomplish, since he wanted first of all to hold the attention of the reader. It is for this reason that in his life he gives emphasis to those images of the West that during his youth were already becoming the material out of which the myth of the frontier was to be woven. As George P. Hammond says in the foreword to the 1939 life, "Otero pictures a young, ribald, resourceful, and unregenerate West."

In the first volume of the trilogy, the presence of the popular western heroes predominates. Much space is given to relate the lives of Wild Bill Hickok, Buffalo Bill, and Billy the Kid. To the last one he dedicated an entire book, *The Real Billy the Kid*, published in 1936, between the first and second volumes of *My Life on the Frontier*. To write the biography of the famous western outlaw, Otero collected an enormous amount of material, "both as a youth and then as an official of the State of New Mexico." He also availed himself of all the written information about his subject, especially the books of Sheriff Pat Garrett (the killer of Bonney). Firsthand information collected by Otero came from M. A. (Ash) Upton, a close friend of Bonney's from early youth to the time of his death, and other contemporaries. Otero met Bonney when the outlaw was taken prisoner in December 1880 and conducted to Santa Fe by train. "My brother and I were so much interested that Father permitted us to go along on the train to Santa Fe. On the way we talked to Billy the Kid. . . . In Santa Fe we were allowed to visit the Kid in jail. I was just one month older than Billy. I liked the Kid very much. In looking back to my first meeting with Billy the Kid, my impressions were most favorable and I can honestly say that he was a man more sinned against than sinning."

The second volume of *My Life on the Frontier* covers a period of fifteen years, from 1882 to 1897. In style and content it is very much like the first volume, except that the experiences related are those of a man in his prime. Here and in the last volume he makes greater use of quotations from newspapers and even books, such as that of Twitchell, to document his statements. He gives less emphasis to personal experiences and more to territorial matters: land grants, politics in the late 1890s, and frontier problems. Of particular interest is the chapter dedicated to the political organization known as Partido del Pueblo Unido (The United People's Party), under the leadership of Sheriff Lorenzo López. According to Otero, it was a well-known fact that this organization was supported by two allegedly criminal organizations, the Gorras Blanco [*sic*] (The White Caps) and La Sociedad de Bandidos de Nuevo México (The Society of New Mexican Bandits). There is little mention of individual outlaws, although a chapter is dedicated to "the frontier ruffian" Dick Rogers. Also of interest is the chapter on the secret religious order Los Penitentes.

References to personal happenings, although less frequent, continue to form an important part of the second autobiography, especially those about his trip to Europe, his marriage in the Episcopal church, and an incident typical of life on the frontier: upon his return from Europe some of his many enemies hired Johnnie Carroll, "a reputed killer," to assassinate him. Carroll was sent to the Harvey House saloon, where Otero was playing a game of billiards, "to try his best to get me into an argument and then shoot me." The plot, of course, failed, and Otero lived to become governor of the territory.

The second volume of the autobiography ends with an account of how President McKinley came to name Otero governor of New Mexico in 1897. The president asked him not to mention the fact of his appointment, "not even to your wife, for if it got out I would, perhaps, receive a thousand telegrams advising me not to appoint you." The day the president sent the appointment to the Senate for confirmation,

Senator George L. Shoup of Idaho received the following telegram from a Thomas Brannigan: "Hold up confirmation of Otero for Governor of New Mexico. He is a dangerous and unscrupulous man. Documentary evidence will follow." Shoup gave the telegram to Otero, saying that his committee was not going to consider it. The Senate confirmed Otero's appointment, and he became the first Hispanic to be appointed governor of a southwestern territory.

The last volume of Otero's autobiography is the least interesting. *My Nine Years as Governor of the Territory of New Mexico, 1897–1906* was published in 1940, when the author was eighty-one years old. In it he gives a detailed account of his administration during his two terms as governor (he had been reappointed in 1901, in spite of his political enemies); the part he took in the movement for statehood; and his relations with Theodore Roosevelt, with whom he helped organize the military regiment known as the Rough Riders. When Roosevelt was still governor of New York, he sent Otero the following telegram: "To you, more than any other man, we owe the getting up of the regiment." However, he says, his relations with Roosevelt lacked the kind thoughtfulness for others that always characterized William McKinley.

Not an intellectual but rather a politician and a man of action, Otero was able to leave an autobiography that is vigorous, warm, and full of life. His writings reflect his personality, which was that of a man of strong convictions who did not hesitate to fight those who opposed him or to help his friends. He enjoyed the company of men of strong character and did not veil his sympathy for men who lived outside the law. As Hammond observes in his introduction to the second volume of the trilogy, "not all readers will agree with everything Mr. Otero has written . . . but few will deny that he has drawn a striking picture of that phase of life in New Mexico of which he was a leading actor."

It must be added that Otero was aware of a principle of primary importance in writing for the public, be it in fiction or nonfiction: whatever is related must be interesting. Realizing, however, that it is difficult to write an autobiography of interest "without having an appearance of indulging in much self-adulation," he endeavored, to the best of his ability, to confine himself "wholly to actual happenings." However, some of the events narrated are recorded as being remembered and are often embellished by imagination. Nevertheless, the trilogy remains one of the most important sources of information about life in the Southwest during a critical period. Otero's autobiography is one of the most important and worthy antecedents of a genre that has been a favorite among contemporary Chicano writers.

PROFILES OF THE TWENTIETH CENTURY AND BEYOND

14

MARIANO AZUELA

Mariano Azuela (1873–1952), doctor and novelist, had the opportunity to observe firsthand the unfolding of the Mexican Revolution of 1910. When Francisco I. Madero decided on November 20 of that year to take up arms in order to rid Mexico of the Díaz dictatorship and reestablish a democratic form of government, Azuela was living in his native town of Lagos de Moreno (in the state of Jalisco) practicing medicine and writing novels, although not unaware of the many injustices being committed by the caciques (political bosses) and hacendados (hacienda owners). By then he had already published some short stories and three novels, *María Luisa* (1907), *Los fracasados* (*The Failures*, 1908), and *Mala yerba* (1909; translated by Anita Brenner as *Marcela*, 1932). But it was during the period of the armed conflict when he was to produce his best novels, among them his masterpiece, *Los de abajo* (*The Underdogs*, 1915). The revolution provided him with subject matter for the rest of his life to write over twenty novels and an equal number of short stories. Until his death in 1952, he never stopped transforming the raw materials he collected from direct observation and from readings into prose fiction depicting the changes that the revolution had brought about not only in the social and political structure of the nation but also in the character of its people.

Although Azuela made use of historical characters, facts, and events in his novels, he never forgot that he was writing fiction and not history.

Not previously published.

That he was well aware of their difference can be seen by what he had to say about a contemporary novelist for confusing the two. Of Heriberto Frías, the author of *Tomóchic* (1893), he said, "Entranced with the exact presentation of the facts of which he was an eye witness, he often forgets that he is writing a novel and not history. He therefore fills his text with comments, which distract the reader. For example, he says, 'Lieutenant Cota was later executed in Mexico City for having committed a military transgression.' Or, 'This brave veteran died in Mexico City as a result of this wound.'" This criticism does not mean, of course, that Azuela believed that no historical facts can be used in a novel. On the contrary, he thought that there is a closer relationship between history and the novel than there is between the novel and other disciplines, for he said, "It's possible that I may have learned some history reading novels—, but it has never occurred to me that I could study in them mathematics, philosophy, or religion." It can be inferred that this criticism of Frías was not made because he used historical facts, but rather because he did not integrate them into the context of his novels. Azuela himself constantly introduced historical facts but never forgot to present them as part of the world of the novel, giving them a function in the plot.

In *Los fracasados,* his first full-length novel, Azuela painted life in a small town (his own Lagos de Moreno, disguised under the name of Álamos), giving emphasis to the clash of ideas between the conservatives (the defenders of the Porfirio Díaz regime) and the liberals, made up of those who wanted to uphold Juárez's laws of reform. Both liberals and conservatives are depicted as having failed. The conservatives, represented by the hacendados, the clergy, and the corrupted politicians, cannot be reformed by Reséndez, the idealist lawyer. On the other hand, Father Cabezudo [the name means "stubborn"], who has to fight against the ignorance and stupidity of his parishioners, also fails in his mission. More important than the plot is the criticism that Azuela directs against the social institutions that existed in small Mexican towns during the Díaz era. This criticism is presented through the eyes and minds of the fictitious characters and not of the author, although the point of view is that of the omniscient narrator. Doña Carmelita, Díaz's wife, for instance, was criticized for favoring those who violated the laws of reform as regards the church. To show this criticism, Azuela has one of his characters say while observing a religious procession prohibited by law, "A violation of the Laws of Reform. Long live the diplomacy of conciliation and long live Doña Carmelita." In this way, Azuela is able to allude with sarcasm to a historical person without interrupting the thread of the narrative, as is frequent in Frías's novel.

Mala yerba, Azuela's third novel, is a scathing denunciation of the peonage system as practiced on the Mexican haciendas at the turn of the century. Here he makes use of legal documents rather than historical facts. While serving as a municipal doctor in Lagos, Azuela had the opportunity to become acquainted with numerous legal cases. In an interview granted to the critic Gregorio Ortega in 1925, he made this statement, "As a municipal doctor I was able to find out about all the crimes committed by the hacendados. How astonishing the number of cases. An hacendado could kill a peon under the slightest pretext, or even without one. That, of course, took place during the days of Porfirio Díaz. Things are different now. Oh, how many crimes!" One of these crimes provided the background for his novel. One day, while going over the materials of a murder trial, he became interested in the case and decided to turn it into fiction. It was the story of a rich hacendado who had murdered his stableman and his own young and beautiful wife after accusing her of infidelity. Using a modified version as the core of the novel, he was able to describe life on the haciendas with great realism. Two American critics, Otis W. Coan and Richard G. Lilland, have said that this novel can help the reader to understand the causes of the revolution. They characterize it as "a pathetic story of the life of poor peasants on a large hacienda." And they add, "The terrible treatment of the peons by their overlords helps the reader to see the conditions leading up to the first revolutions of this century. An appealing, tragic picture."

Although the story was taken from real life, and the plight of the peons was drawn from firsthand information, there are in this novel scarcely any historical facts. However, Azuela presents the fictitious Andrade clan, the feudal lords of the province, in a historical frame. "From the Wars of Independence until the triumph of Tuxtepec the Andrade family had considered the province as a private fief." Ernest Gruening, describing the Díaz system of government, says, "The states became fiefs of individuals or families. Chihuahua was controlled by the Terrazas clan. One of the family, so dissolute that he seduced his own niece ... was put into the government to steady him! The Corral-Torres combination controlled Sonora. The small states of Querétaro and Tlaxcala were governed for twenty-six years by Francisco Cosío and Próspero Cahuantzi, respectively. The three Cravioto brothers took over the state of Hidalgo. Occasionally, death would alter the local baronial succession."

It is surprising that Azuela was not punished for having dared to publish these two works that criticize the social conditions under Díaz. Surprising, if we think of what happened to Heriberto Frías, who was condemned to death by a military tribunal for criticizing the federal army in his novel *Tomóchic* (1893). Fortunately, his execution was stayed and he lived to write other novels.

In 1911, Azuela published *Andrés Pérez, maderista,* considered to be the first novel of the Mexican Revolution. In it, the Madero uprising comes to life before our eyes. At the same time, in this work Azuela gives expression to his disillusionment with the results of the revolution, for he saw that the *maderistas* were being outmaneuvered by the followers of Díaz, who now pretended to be in favor of the change. Gruening, analyzing the forces arrayed against Madero, says, "The forces against which Madero had to contend were varied. There was, first, the opposition of the Vázquez Gómez element, incorrectly called 'within his own camp.' This revolutionary element was typical of the support which, for mercenary reasons, had joined Madero and was to function throughout the Revolution. It had never been truly identified with the democratic purposes and ideals of Madero. Second, was the entire Porfirian group: *científicos,* large landowners, clericals, who foresaw in the political change a menace to their long established privileges." It is this second group that Azuela so vividly brings to life in *Andrés Pérez, maderista.*

In this short novel, Azuela reveals the way in which the revolution fell into the hands of the former caciques. Colonel Hernández, the town's political boss under Díaz, and Don Cuco, the newspaperman, both of them dyed-in-the-wool *porfiristas,* jump on the bandwagon as soon as they see that the revolution has triumphed. They immediately put on the uniform of the revolutionaries and are thus able to continue at the helm of the town's government. Colonel Hernández, now a general, "because there is no higher rank," cynically relates how timely the uprising has been, as it has coincided with Díaz's departure to Europe and has therefore saved them their positions.

The novel is based on a personal experience. In 1910, Azuela, following the advice of his friend Becerra, joined Madero's movement and was named political representative in his hometown. He was soon deposed by the intrigues of former *porfiristas* who, in sheep's clothing, were undermining the revolution. "As if to mock the Revolution," Azuela wrote, "I had to transfer the office to the same person from whom I had received it."

That experience, which forms the core of the novel, is supplemented with news items of the period, when Mexico was celebrating its first hundred years of independence from Spain. The novel opens with one of the characters reading to another this newspaper article, "Cereals have reached the highest price ever. The workers survive on corn and beans. While a laborer makes only thirty-seven cents a day, corn is worth seven pesos the hectoliter and beans, fourteen. But the government will spend more than twenty million in the construction of a National Theatre, twenty million to beautify the Capital, twenty million to feast the foreign guests of honor who have been invited to celebrate the first century of our independence. At least the diplomatic corps will be pleased to see the prosperity of the inhabitants of the Mexican Republic."

Soon, Andrés Pérez, the pseudorevolutionary, learns via the newspapers that the revolution has started. He reads the headlines aloud to his friends, "The Puebla incident. Aquiles Serdán's death. Uprisings on the border." Andrés Pérez had left the capital and had taken refuge in a small town with his friend Toño Reyes, a *maderista* and a liberal. In town, Pérez is taken for a secret agent of Madero and is questioned by the townspeople about the oncoming revolution, about Madero, about Pascual Orozco and José de la Luz Blanco. On the other hand, Colonel Hernández, the reactionary cacique, praises those who uphold the Díaz system. To him, Corral is a genius, Pineda a brain. To his friend Don Cuco, the unscrupulous newspaperman, Madero is a madman, Urueta a wretched drug addict, Cabrera an ungrateful cur, and Sánchez Ascona a man who takes bread away from children. These historical characters are mentioned by fictitious persons in the novel with the purpose of giving the work historical authenticity.

Azuela's accurate appraisal of the political situation in *Andrés Pérez, maderista* was soon to be verified by national events. Two years later, Madero was assassinated by the *huertistas,* former followers of Díaz who in real life lived the part of Colonel Hernández and his friends in Azuela's novel. Later, Azuela made the following comment about this event, "All those of us who had our eyes open were expecting Madero's fall at any moment, but not the brutal crime of which he was the victim."

When Villa took Zacatecas on June 24, 1914, Azuela was putting the finishing touches to another novel, *Los caciques,* in which he does for the city what he had done for rural Mexico in *Mala yerba,* that is, to expose how the bosses (businessmen, clergy, politicians) misrule the urban centers. Of this novel, the author said, "I was touching up the last part when isolated groups of federal soldiers began to arrive in the city showing the marks of defeat in their torn clothes, their emaciated faces and their bandaged arms and legs after the combat with Villa in Zacatecas. The Revolution had triumphed!" The rivalries that took place among revolutionaries after Huerta's fall in July 1914 were to affect Azuela for the rest of his life. Through personal sympathy, but also influenced by his friend José Becerra, he joined Villa's forces. Becerra, while serving as attorney in the town of Tequila, in the state of Jalisco, had joined the rebel army of Julián Medina. "When Medina went through Lagos, after the Aguascalientes Convention," says Azuela, "he invited me to collaborate in the formation of a government to substitute that of General Manuel M. Diéguez, who was a close friend of Carranza and whose government was unconstitutional." But Azuela also believed that Villa represented the legal side of the revolution. He wrote, "I found myself on the side of the party of the Convention of Aguascalientes, not only because I sympathized with the cause, but also because, for me, it represented the legal aspect of the Revolution; in the second place, having decided to side with the party and therefore relinquish some of my personal liberties by so doing, I found myself on the side of Villa and his followers."

Toward the end of October 1914, Medina was at Irapuato waiting for the rest of Villa's army. Azuela was appointed head of his medical staff there, with the rank of lieutenant colonel. While in Irapuato, Azuela conceived the idea of writing *Los de abajo* (*The Underdogs*), his most famous novel. Medina, according to Azuela, was fond of telling him his adventures as a revolutionary general, many of which Azuela elaborated and adopted for his novel, of which Medina was to be the hero. Pursued by Carranza's forces, Medina had to withdraw toward Guadalajara, where he arrived in December 1914. Here Azuela continued to write *Los de abajo* and decided to call the hero Demetrio Macías, a fictitious name. At the same time, he gave up the idea of elaborating on the portrayal of Medina in order to give the hero Macías additional traits peculiar to other officers he had met.

Villa's defeat by Obregón in Celaya (April 16, 1915) forced Medina to take refuge in Lagos, where he remained until May when he was forced by Obregón's army to withdraw to the north. Azuela separated from the main body of Medina's troops and remained in Tepatitlán (between Lagos and Guadalajara) to take care of some wounded soldiers. It was there that he became acquainted with a young colonel, Manuel Caloca, who had been wounded in the battle that took place in Tlaquepaque, just outside Guadalajara. As the *carrancistas* were threatening to take the town, Azuela, Caloca, and eighty of their men left Tepatitlán and took refuge in the mountains of Juchipila. There they were overtaken by a group of *carrancistas* at the bottom of the canyon, but Caloca's men were excellent horsemen and were able to defeat the enemy. Azuela, meanwhile, in a cave on the side of the mountain, was taking notes for the final scene of the novel, the defeat and death of the hero, Demetrio Macías. After going through the town of Limón, they reached Aguascalientes, where Azuela took the wounded Caloca to the hospital and operated on him there. From Aguascalientes they went to Chihuahua, and there Caloca remained in the hospital. Later they were reunited in El Paso, Texas. "One night of November 1915," Azuela tells us, "in a hotel room, I was reading a chapter of my novel to a group of expatriates like myself. Among them were Enrique Pérez Arce, Abelardo Medina, Enrique Luna Román, and other professional men, most of them lawyers.

When I came to the passage where Demetrio Macías is being carried on a stretcher through the canyon of Juchipila, Manuel Caloca, who was among those who were listening, recognized himself."

There is no question about the authenticity of *Los de abajo*. Azuela himself tells us who the characters represent: Demetrio Macías was drawn from Caloca, Medina, and other officers; Luis Cervantes, the other important character in the novel, represents Colonel Francisco M. Delgado, Medina's private secretary, or, rather, what others thought Delgado to be. Even El Güero Margarito, the sadist in Macías's army, is drawn from a waiter Azuela met in Ciudad Juárez, in the Café Delmónico, and others.

The novel opens with the defeat of the federals by Macías in the canyon of Juchipila and ends with his death in the same place, two years later. And yet, *Los de abajo* is not a historical novel. Commenting upon the writing of this novel, Azuela said, "The novelist surely takes the elements that go into his novel from reality or from other books. He does not, however, limit himself to the accumulation of the inert materials, but goes on to organize a new world, a world to which he has given its own life, in other words, to the writing of a creative work. The best characters, therefore, are those who are farther removed from the model." Azuela did such an excellent portrayal of his characters that some of them have been considered to be historical. One critic, speaking of Azuela's life, says, "Born in Lagos de Moreno, Jalisco. Died in the Capital of the Republic. Army Doctor. During the Revolution he exercised his profession serving in the *villista* army commanded by Demetrio Macías." Since Luis Cervantes is characterized as a former medical student, and Azuela was a doctor, some critics have concluded that he represents the author, which could not be, as the two are exactly the opposite in moral standards.

Unhappy in El Paso because of the long separation from his family, Azuela decided to return to Mexico. Early in 1916, taking advantage of the confusion caused by the taking of Ciudad Juárez by the *carrancistas*, he crossed the border and returned to Mexico City, where his family later joined him. He settled down in the neighborhood of Santa María la Ribera, where he dedicated the rest of his life to the practice of medicine

and the writing of novels. Between 1917 and 1918, he wrote and published *Las moscas* (*The Flies*), *Domitilo quiere ser diputado* (*Domitilo Wants
to Be a Congressman*), *Las tribulaciones de una familia decente* (*The Trials
of a Respectable Family*), and the short story "De como al fin lloró Juan
Pablo" ("How Juan Pablo Finally Cried"). In these novels, Azuela concentrated on the social upheaval brought about by the revolution. In *Las
moscas* (1918), he wrote about the swarms of government employees and
bureaucrats in search of work, indifferent to the nature of the political
ideas of those able to provide jobs for them. The prevailing humor and
satire in this short novel create a dimension that gives it unity as well as an
artistic touch. It may not be a great novel, but in it Azuela has certainly
preserved an aspect of the revolution. The picture may not be edifying,
but, surely, it was painted with realism and a critical attitude. The last
scene, of Villa in defeat, is a magnificent sketch of that fallen hero.

With *Las tribulaciones de una familia decente* (1918), Azuela closed
the cycle of novels of the revolution. Here he continues to depict the
ill effects of the struggle, relating the events that took place in Mexico
City in 1916 and 1917 under the Carranza administration. Since he was
a sincere man and an eyewitness to the events he described, this work
has value as a historical document; that is, a historical document presenting the facts from the point of view of a chronicler unsympathetic
to Carranza. It cannot be said that the revolution is the theme of *Las
tribulaciones,* although it does serve as a background for the events that
unfold, and the fate of the characters is intrinsically bound to the outcome of the struggle; the real theme is the agony that a family from the
interior of the country must undergo to adapt itself to a new environment after losing all of its properties to the revolutionaries. Azuela does
not here criticize the revolution itself, but the fact that it fell into the
hands of bandits like general Covarrubias, portrayed as a common thief,
who saw in the revolution a rich mine that he could exploit. Azuela, a
strong follower of the Constitutional Party, could not forgive Carranza
for the favoritism he bestowed, in real life, upon such drones as portrayed by the fictitious General Covarrubias. No less interesting are the
scenes in which Azuela describes the ravaging acts of the soldiers, as
seen through the eyes of two of the younger characters, Lulú and César.

This novel has endured as a social document since, in it, Azuela has recorded for posterity the events that took place in Mexico City during those turbulent years when the revolution reached its peak. It is a work that confirms Azuela's often-repeated maxim, "I write what I think and what I feel, without worrying whether my opinions coincide with or differ from those usually accepted. Loyalty and honesty consist, in a writer, of giving his own vision of the world with bravery and sincerity." Azuela may sometimes be wrong in interpreting the facts, but he would never say what he did not think or feel.

In 1931, after publishing his controversial novel *El camarada Pantoja*, in which he criticizes the governments of Álvaro Obregón and Plutarco Elías Calles, Azuela was taken to task for not telling the truth. He was accused of presenting only one side of the situation. Azuela responded calmly and sensibly. Among other things, he said, "Some critics have said that in my novels of the Revolution I have expressed half the truth, and this is perhaps the greatest praise I could have received. But I do not accept it because it's not true. Truth has a thousand faces, and a man can only give reality to that aspect of the truth he has in front of him. It's not half the truth that I have given, but only a very small part of it, my truth, which I have presented with honesty and fidelity." Thus we can see that Azuela, while writing novels based on historical facts, was conscious of the difference between an objectively determined historical event and one presented from the point of view of a single person. For this reason, his novels cannot be used to prove historical facts or to determine the course of history, only as fictions based on events experienced by the author. They are, however, very useful in that they help the reader to see history in a total context, a context often missing in straight historical narrative. Moreover, in the novels of Azuela, the reader finds not only the portrait of a country in transition, but also absorbing stories well told, for Azuela was truly a born novelist. Thus, his novels have a double purpose: to entertain while making us aware of the significance of the Mexican Revolution and other historical events.

15

MARÍA CRISTINA MENA

The first woman of Mexican descent writing fiction in English in the United States, as far as we know, was María Amparo Ruíz de Burton, the author of the novels *Who Would Have Thought?* (1872) and *The Squatter and the Don* (1885), the first having been published anonymously and the second under the name C. Loyal. Before the discovery of these romances just a few years ago, the short stories and novels of María Cristina Mena (1893–1965) were considered by literary historians to be the first. She began to publish under her maiden name and, beginning in 1927, under that of her husband, Henry Kellett Chambers, the dramatic author and journalist who was editor of the *Literary Digest* from 1920 to 1935. Mena's stories, which began to appear in New York in 1913, at first were considered the earliest examples of fiction published in English by a Mexican American writer. Matthew Hoehn, in his short article "María Cristina Chambers," which appeared in 1948 in *Catholic Authors; Contemporary Biographical Sketches, 1930–1947* states: "At the age of 20, María Cristina Chambers became the first woman of Mexican birth to write fiction in English." Burton and Mena were ignored by mainstream literary historians, and therefore it was not until recently that critics interested in reconstructing the history of Chicano literature discovered these two and other pre-Chicana writers. The significance

First published in *Chicano Writers*, 3rd ser., ed. Francisco A. Lomelí and Carl R. Shirley (Detroit: Gale Research, 1999), 88–91.

of these discoveries is that they change the idea that the first novel by a Mexican American was *Pocho* (1959) by José Antonio Villareal.

María Cristina Mena was born in Mexico City, the daughter of a Mexican father and a Spanish mother. In 1907, at the age of fourteen and under circumstances unknown, she came to New York, where she lived most of her life. Although, as stated by Hoehn, she started to write when she was ten years old, it was not until November 1913 that a series of her stories began to appear in *Century Illustrated Monthly Magazine,* the first and most successful being "John of God, the Water-Carrier." The same month she published "The Gold Vanity Set" in *American Magazine.* Until 1940, she continued to publish short stories and articles in *Century, Cosmopolitan,* and *Household* magazines. Between 1942 and 1946, she published four novels, and one more in 1953, all of them about Mexican subjects and directed to young readers. Two of her most successful novels were *The Water-Carrier's Secrets* (1942) and *The Bull-fighter's Son* (1944). About the first one, as quoted by Hoehn, she wrote: "I've written this book—my first juvenile—with 'the hand on the heart' as we say in Mexico. It's my small contribution and very large wish for a better understanding by the youth of the United States—my adopted country—of Mexico—the country of my birth."

After her marriage, sometime before 1927, she began to publish her fiction under the name of Chambers, and therefore her narrative was not integrated into the histories of Chicano literature until recent years, as was that of Ruíz de Burton. According to Ernestina N. Eger, who has made an extensive study of Mena's literary productions as well as her relations with the literary figures of her day, especially with D. H. Lawrence, references to Mena and her works are not very common in mainstream literary criticism. After her marriage to Chambers her first story, "John of God, the Water-Carrier," was reprinted, in 1927, in London by T. S. Eliot in *The Monthly Criterion: A Literary Review* and, the following year, was selected by Edward J. O'Brien to be included in the *Best Short Stories of 1928.*

After 1928, Mena stopped publishing, as far as we know, until 1942, when her first novel, *The Water-Carrier's Secrets,* appeared in London and New York, published by Oxford University Press. In rapid succession, she published three other novels for the same editorial house: *The Two Eagles* (1943), *The Bullfighter's Son* (1944), and *The Three Kings* (1946). In 1953, her last novel, *Boy Heroes of Chapultepec,* appeared in Philadelphia. These juvenile novels by Mena were well received, judging by the number of reviews her five novels received from mainstream critics. It was not until 1969, however, that she was recognized as an ethnic writer; that year she was mentioned in the book *Speaking for Ourselves: American Ethnic Writing,* edited by Lillian Faderman and Barbara Bradshaw. After that, Mena was forgotten until 1978, when Raymund Paredes discovered her early short stories, published under her maiden name. In his survey article "The Evolution of Chicano Literature," he made a brief analysis of her stories, but his negative evaluation did much to prevent others from undertaking an extensive study of her fiction.

Among other things, Paredes criticized Mena's condescending attitude toward the Indians of Mexico, whose presence in her fiction prevails. According to him:

> Mena was a talented storyteller whose sensibility unfortunately tended towards sentimentalism and preciousness. She aimed to portray Mexican culture in a positive light, but with great decorum; as a consequence, her stories seem trivial and condescending. Mena took pride in the aboriginal past of Mexico and she had real sympathy for the downtrodden Indians, but she could not, for the life of her, resist describing how they 'washed their little brown faces . . . and assumed expressions of astonishing intelligence and zeal.' Occasionally, she struck a blow at the pretensions of Mexico's ruling class, but to little effect; Mena's genteelness simply is incapable of warming the reader's blood.

After briefly discussing the story "The Vine Leaf" as an example of how Mena strikes a blow at the ruling class, he adds that Mena "tried to depict her characters within the boundaries of conventional American attitudes about Mexico," and that "she knew what Americans liked to read about Mexico so she gave it to them: quaint and humble *inditos,* passionate señoritas . . . a dashing caballero or two 'with music in their fingers.'"

The interest of Lawrence in Mena and her fiction about Mexican Indians was the result of two unrelated events that took place in 1927. That year Lawrence published, in London and New York, his book *Mornings in Mexico,* which contains the essay "El mozo," about an Indian named Rosalino. In October of that same year, Mena's story "John of God, the Water-Carrier" appeared next to Lawrence's prose "Flowery Tuscany" in *The Criterion.* Mena was delighted with "El mozo" and wrote to Lawrence telling him that she not only knew Rosalino, but that she was his godmother. This exchange of letters between Mena and Lawrence lasted for two years, and led to her visit to him in Italy just before his death. Mena's article, "Afternoons in Italy with D. H. Lawrence" (1964), gives us an excellent description of Lawrence a few months before his death on March 2, 1930. From it, I quote the following excerpt, in which Lawrence's interest in Mexican popular culture is revealed:

> My last evening with Lawrence was one of the most memorable in my life. I didn't see him until dinnertime. He had been "teasing" with the Huxleys, and when he returned he was in a strange mood, very silent, lost in some wretched depression.
>
> * * *
>
> We heard music in the distance. Someone was playing the piano. "It's Aldous," Lawrence said. "He likes only classical music. I like folk songs."
>
> "Do you know the Mexican song 'Cielito Lindo'?" I asked.
>
> Lawrence began to hum it and I began to sing it with him. I had never heard anyone but a Mexican give the perfect turn to the words with the music. But Lawrence did. When he finished he bowed his head over his knees and was silent again.

Mena's interest in the writings of Lawrence lasted all her life. She was interested in them not only for their literary value, but also to have them distributed, especially his novel *Lady Chatterley's Lover,* which had been banned in the United States upon publication in 1928. Apparently she had read the manuscript before publication, for in her "Afternoons in Italy with D. H. Lawrence" she says: "Pino Orioli [Lawrence's friend] had agreed to print *Lady Chatterley's Lover* in Italy, when Lawrence had rewritten the novel three times, still couldn't find a publisher, and had almost decided to burn the manuscript. As for me, I had volunteered to take advance orders from friends and foes in the United States." That Lawrence was interested in distributing his works in the United States is revealed in his letter to Mena dated September 28, 1929, in which he suggests to her that she open a bookstore to sell his books. "I wonder if you could have a tiny bookshop. Or better, if someone would let you be a partner in a shop, and you could have a little section for yourself, to deal only with special authors—say me, Norman Douglas, and others of Pino's connection." That suggestion indicates that Lawrence's interest in Mena was less in her writings and more in her ability to promote his own works. In his letter of November 11, 1927, he praises her story "John of God" but doubts that she wrote it. "And it's so well written too—but perhaps your husband helped you. Or are you so much at ease in English?" What Lawrence did not know was that the story had been published in 1913, before Mena's marriage to Chambers. Three months later, after reading another of her stories, he discouraged her from continuing to write fiction and advised her to try autobiography, "That would probably come more direct and more you, off your pen." His ambivalent attitude toward Mena, as a person, can be appreciated when comparing two of his letters. In one, addressed to Mabel Dodge Luhan, one of their friends, dated March 2, 1929, he says: "Tell María Cristina—yes, I like her too, I like the feeling one has of her." Yet less than a year later, in his letter to Dorothy Brett, dated January 8, 1930, he says: "María Cristina Chambers cabled she would come over in February. Frankly, I don't like her very much but don't say so to anybody, as she seems to slave for me—for my books in New York. Not that much is achieved."

Without knowing how Lawrence really felt about her, Mena kept her admiration of him, both as a person and for his literary works, until her death. However, there seems to be no influence of his style on her own works written after 1927, the year of her first letter to him. Mena, from the very beginning, had created her own style, as can be seen in what she says about writing in the brief note included by Matthew Hoehn in *Catholic Authors:* "I have never read, much less studied, the so-called 'methods' for learning how to write. I do not believe an aspirant for authorship needs any more than to learn from observation and much reading of good authors: that writing is something that is born and grows naturally through much working at it and particularly from one's own original and very personal feeling and thinking."

Lawrence, of course, was included among the good authors that she read. But her own style is unique not only for the treatment of Mexican themes, customs, and characters but also for the use of Spanish, as is the custom with contemporary Chicano authors. The editors of the time, especially those at *The Century,* tried to discourage her from this practice. From the very beginning, when she submitted her first story, "John of God," the editor suggested deleting Spanish words and some passages related to Mexican customs. Writing fiction about Mexico and its indigenous people at the time of the Mexican Revolution and publishing it in prestigious reviews was really an act of courage, whether the characters are called *inditos* or *indígenas.* And yet, that was Mena's priority. As early as 1913, the year when President Francisco I. Madero was assassinated and the forces of Victoriano Huerta usurped the democratically elected government, Mena had stated the purpose of her stories. In a letter to Robert Sterling Yard quoted by Eger, Mena says: "I expect to write more stories of Inditos than of any other class in Mexico. They form the majority; the issue of their rights and wrongs, their aspirations and possibilities, is at the root of the present situation in my unhappy country. . . . I believe that American readers, with their intense interest in Mexico, are ripe for a true picture of a people so near to them, so intrinsically picturesque, so misrepresented in current fiction." When she submitted "John of God" to the editors of *The Century,* they wanted to make radical changes, even cutting it in half. She bitterly complained, although she had to accept the cuts. In a letter to the editor, Robert Sterling Yard, written during the fall of 1913, she told him:

> Please forgive my long delay in writing about the curtailed version of "John of God, the Water Carrier." . . . I was perplexed by discovering in the August *Century* a story very much longer than "John of God."

... Could it be that the water carrier's lowly station in life made him a literary undesirable?

Then what of Maupassant's Norman peasants, Kipling's soldiers and low-caste Hindus, Myra Kelly's tenement children, and many other social nobodies of successful fiction?

Ernestina Eger has come to a different conclusion regarding the nature of Mena's fiction. For her, Mena's writings represent the first examples of the *indigenista* movement in Mexico, which came to fruition in both literature and the arts during the 1920s and 1930s. It must be added that she is the author of perhaps the first short story of the Mexican Revolution. Around 1915, she wrote "The Son of His Master," which was not accepted by the editor of *The Century* but later, in 1931, published in *Household* magazine under the title "A Son of the Tropics." The opinion of Paredes, however, is the one that has predominated in contemporary Chicano literary criticism. In 1982, Charles M. Tatum, in his book *Chicano Literature,* states: "María Cristina Mena is a fine writer whose short stories and sketches appeared early in this century in the *Century* and *American* magazines. Unfortunately, her talents are undermined by her tendency to create obsequious Mexican characters who fit comfortably within the American reader's expectations. This results in trivial and condescending stories." And in 1985, Gloria Treviño, in her doctoral dissertation, gives emphasis to the condescending attitude of Mena toward her *inditos.* In 1988, Carl R. Shirley, in his book *Understanding Chicano Literature,* states: "María Cristina Mena wrote romantic, sentimental, completely idealized and unrealistic stories which she published from 1913 to 1916, principally in the magazine *Century.* It's unfortunate that her work did much to perpetuate among Anglo readers a romanticized stereotype of Mexican-Americans. As Raymund Paredes has noted, Mena's portrayals are 'ultimately obsequious, and if one can appreciate the weight of popular attitudes on Mena's consciousness, one can also say that a braver, more perceptive writer would have confronted the life of her culture more forcefully.'"

One aspect of Mena's contribution to the development of Chicano literature is the use she makes in her fiction of Spanish. Although Ruíz de Burton used this technique in her nineteenth-century novels, Mena's contribution is worthy of study, especially when her editor disagreed about this. In an undated letter accompanying the revised manuscript of her story "The Son of His Master," which Mena sent to Mr. Douglas Zabriskie Doty, the new editor of *Century,* she says that she had to "cut out many of the Spanish words—but I must make a special plea for the few that remain, all of them having a definite value of humor, irony, local color, or what not." This story was never published by *Century.* It did not appear until 1931 in *Household* under the title "A Son of the Tropics."

Another one of her stories, "Doña Rita's Rivals," had better luck. It was published in *Century* in September 1914, in spite of the fact that Mena uses Spanish names, words, and phrases in the English text. The introduction to this story deals with class distinctions in the Mexico of Don Porfirio Díaz: "With her packet of love-letters in her hand, Alegría returned to the roof—Alegría Peralta—, the band-master's daughter, who had committed the error of loving above her. She should have known better than to imagine that she would ever be received into a family of hat, she who was of shawl. . . . The females of a family of shawl—*de tápalo*—do not aspire to decorate their heads with millinery, for the excellent reason that God has not assigned them to the *casta de sombrero.* Their consolation is that they may look down upon those *de rebozo.*"

Sexual distinctions and the preference given to men even in spiritual matters was the norm in the Mexico of Don Porfirio: "Doña Rita wept over this little tragedy of the ordinary, which had slanted so perilously into the orbit of her own existence. Her tears brought relief, and a sense of peace with herself. She was glad for the poor girl's sake that she no longer suffered. But her soul? If a suicide, she had died in mortal sin. *¡Qué audacia e impiedad!* Nevertheless, Doña Rita would have offered a prayer for her soul had she not felt that all her prayers were needed for her son."

It is difficult to explain Doty's attitude regarding the use of Spanish in the stories when, at the same time, he was asking Mena to write about Mexican Americans in some of them. When he was appointed editor of *Century,* he wrote a letter to Mena introducing himself and, at the same time, taking the opportunity to praise her work. In this letter, written September 26, 1914, he says in part: "I know your work and have read several of the stories that have gone into the magazine, but this one, 'The Vine-Leaf,' is by all odds the best you have done. It's an exquisite thing, worthy of Maupassant, both for style and treatment." And most unexpectedly, he adds in a last paragraph, "I am wondering whether you would be interested to consider the idea of transplanting a Spanish character to this country; that is to say, using a Mexican character with an American background." Mena, unfortunately, did not take up the challenge, although she wrote two days later: "Such praise from you is very precious, and your letter has made me happier than I can tell you. Yes, I would be very glad indeed to make some stories of a Spanish or Mexican character with an American background and many thanks to you for the suggestion." However, she never wrote such a story, and if she did, she did not publish it. Commenting upon this exchange of letters about this topic, Ernestina Eger has made the following insightful interpretation (my translation):

> This unexplainable rejection of the primordial situation of Chicano literature—the conflict between two cultures—must surprise the contemporary reader. It might have been that she did not experience personal ethnic prejudice (or refused to acknowledge it), or that, first, her socioeconomic class, and then her literary relations protected her from discrimination, or that she preferred to maintain a conciliatory rather than a conformational attitude; the fact is that Mena, upon confronting Mexican and American characters, never went beyond innocuous encounters among tourists in Mexico in which the American—both in real life and as characters—is eliminated by the cultural relativism of the author.

Mena was not really interested in depicting Mexican Americans in her writings. As stated by Eger, two aspects of her fiction stand out, her desire to interpret Mexico and the Mexican people to the American reader and the plight of the indigenous people of Mexico. This thematic unity, however, does not give her stories and novels a monotonous, repetitive tone, since she can manipulate numerous variations and interpret these limited themes differently, although all her stories may deal with the same subject matter. The only exception in her repertoire is the last story of her first period, "The Soul of Hilda Brunel" (1916), a tale dealing with reincarnation that does not take place in Mexico and the characters are not Mexican.

Except for the unpublished work of Ernestina Eger, in which she reconstructs Mena's bibliography (including her fiction, correspondence, book reviews, and criticism) and analyzes some of her stories, Mena's contributions to the history of Chicano literature have not received the attention they deserve. Aside from what some critics say about her condescending attitude toward the indigenous people of Mexico, her desire to present Mexico in its best light, and her limited thematic repertoire, she should be given credit for her success in a very demanding literary world where her writings were accepted by the most prestigious literary magazines of the period, an accomplishment that few Mexican American writers, of either sex, were able to attain.

In the context of the development of Chicano fiction written in English, Mena can be considered as the link between Amparo Ruíz de Burton and writers like Jovita González, Fabiola Cabeza de Baca, Nina Otero, Nellie Sánchez Van de Grift, and Josefina Niggli. In the field of the Mexican American short story written in English she is a pioneer. Since she did not collect her stories in a book, her influence was minimal. The genre was not to flourish until the 1930s and 1940s, with the short stories of Fray Angélico Chávez and Mario Suárez. More influential were Mena's contemporaries writing in Spanish and publishing in the newspapers, as did Julio G. Arce ("Jorge Ulica"), Benjamín Padilla, Laura de Pereda, Adolfo Carrillo, and others. Among her Mexican American contemporaries, María Cristina Mena stands alone in her production of fiction, in both quantity and quality.

16

JOSÉ RUBÉN ROMERO

Although several semifictional works appeared in Mexico during the colonial period, which lasted three hundred years (1521–1821), it was not until 1816 that the first modern Latin American novel, *El periquillo sarniento* (*The Itching Parrot*), was published in Mexico City by José Joaquín Fernández de Lizardi. That author utilized the picaresque form in order to criticize the unbearable social conditions that existed during the last years of the Spanish presence in Mexico.

The picaresque form represents the revival of a genre created in Spain during the middle of the sixteenth century and considered dead in the Spanish-speaking world one hundred years later. However, in eighteenth-century England and France, the picaresque underwent a revival, which doubtless influenced Lizardi in the selection of the form for his novel. Works such as Alain-René Lesage's *Gil Blas de Santillane* (1715–35) were well known in Mexico, and there are indications that Lizardi was acquainted with them. His example, however, was not imitated by later writers, and it was not until 1938 that another picaresque novel, *La vida inútil de Pito Pérez* (*The Futile Life of Pita Pérez*), by José Rubén Romero, was published. The novel not only made Romero famous but also proved that old literary forms may remain dormant for long periods of time but cannot be considered dead.

First published in *Latin American Writers*, vol. 2, ed. Carlos A. Solé and María Isabel Abreu (New York: Charles Scribner's Sons, 1989), 711–15.

Romero was born in Cotija, in the state of Michoacán, Mexico, on September 25, 1890, the son of Melesio Romero and Refugio González. He attended elementary school in his hometown and as an adolescent lived in Mexico City with his family for six years (1898–1904). There he attended the school of Mr. Barona, where he began to read nineteenth-century Spanish and French fiction and poetry.

When he was offered a position in the government, Romero's father went back to his native state, where he established his home in the town of Ario de Rosales. There Romero and some friends began to publish the periodical *Iris,* in which his first known verses appeared. Two years later, his father was transferred to Pátzcuaro, a larger city in the state of Michoacán, and there Romero published his first prose work, "De invierno" ("Of Winter"). Soon after, his father was transferred once more, this time to the city of Sahuayo, where, at the age of seventeen, Romero accepted his first employment, as administrator of the revenue office. He continued to write poems, which he published in several of the state's newspapers.

Romero's first book of poems, *Fantasías* (*Fantasies*), appeared in 1908. The only copy in existence was for many years in the possession of the author's mother, and no critic has been able to examine it. Although poetry was Romero's main interest, he also wrote portraits of the people of the community and of rural areas. "In my town there were many fools; some roamed the streets begging; some, who were not as foolish as they appeared to be, lived at the expense of relatives."

Meanwhile in Sahuayo, Romero began to court Rosa, the daughter of the richest man in town. Not approving of this relationship, Rosa's father pulled some strings and had Romero's father transferred from Sahuayo to Santa Clara del Cobre near Pátzcuaro. This maneuver put an end to Romero's first love affair.

Romero's residence in Santa Clara turned out to be of great importance in the life of the young writer, for there he met Mariana García, his future wife. There he also met a popular character, Pito Pérez, whose life was later to become the subject of his most famous novel. And there he participated in the revolution, on the side of the rebels. While he was in Pátzcuaro, where he had been sent on a secret mission, the city fell into the hands of the rebels, and Romero had the opportunity to meet and become acquainted with rural revolutionary leaders, among them Pascual Ortiz Rubio, later to be elected president of Mexico. The young writer's revolutionary activities did not prevent him from writing poetry. In 1912, he published three books: *Rimas bohemias* (*Bohemian Rhymes*), *Hojas marchitas* (*Withered Leaves*), and *La musa heroica* (*The Heroic Muse*), the last a collection of patriotic verses mostly about the two best-known heroes of the wars of independence, Miguel Hidalgo and José María Morelos.

In the 1912 elections, the first to be held under the revolutionary government, Don Miguel Silva won his state's governorship and named Romero his private secretary, taking him to Morelia, Michoacán's capital. The counterrevolution led by Victoriano Huerta in 1913, which resulted in the assassination of President Francisco I. Madero, affected Romero's life, because Governor Silva was forced to resign and Romero had to take refuge first in Mexico City and then in Morelia. There he escaped being executed through the intervention of his father and several friends, who assured the new governor that Romero had no intention of joining the armies of Francisco (Pancho) Villa, who had begun to fight against Huerta.

Having had his life saved, Romero settled in the city of Tacámbaro, Michoacán, where he spent the following four years managing the small store of a friend. There he had the opportunity to observe the customs of the people in a small town, but he was not yet ready to transform these observations into works of fiction. He continued to write poetry, and in 1917, the same year he married Mariana García, he published two collections, *La musa loca* (*The Mad Muse*) and *Alma heroica* (*Heroic Soul*).

Humor, the underlying characteristic of Romero's works, was evident at this early stage of his development. The author of the introduction to *La musa loca* said that the poet had written his verses while dispensing lard and beans at the store. Romero responded that the reason his book of poems had sold so well was the highly nutritious nature of the contents. Later he discovered that a woman who secretly loved him had bought most of the books. When she died, the copies were found in a box, "which for my verses was like a coffin made to order."

The tranquillity enjoyed by Romero in Tacámbaro came to a sudden end when the revolutionaries, under the leadership of José Inés Chávez García, devastated the town and the poet had to flee once again. This change, however, was for the good. In Morelia, where he took refuge, Ortiz Rubio, then governor, named Romero as his private secretary. Romero also began to teach literature in the old Colegio de San Nicolás. He held the two positions until 1919, when Ortiz Rubio sent him to Mexico City to serve as his representative. That same year he published his seventh volume of poems, *Sentimental* (*Sentimental Verses*), the publication costs paid for by the governor. The book was ignored by the critics.

In Mexico City from 1920 on, Romero led a rather comfortable life. That year, Álvaro Obregón was elected president of Mexico, and he appointed Romero to a position in the Department of Communications. The following year, Romero advanced to the foreign relations section as chief of the Department of Publicity. There he met prominent writers, among them Genaro Estrada, José Juan Tablada, and Anemio de Valle Arizpe. Tablada, who had lived in Japan for several months in 1900, had introduced the haiku into Mexican poetry. He inspired Romero to write poems in this short form, which Romero collected under the title *Tacámbaro* (1922). The book, unlike his earlier poetic efforts, was very successful, at least among the public. In his following book, however, he went back to earlier forms, which he collected under the appropriate title *Versos viejos* (*Old Verses*, 1930).

In 1930, his friend Ortiz Rubio was elected president of the republic and named Romero consul general to Barcelona, Spain. There, feeling nostalgic, Romero began to write a novel, *Apuntes de un lugareño* (*Notes of a Villager*), which he published in 1932. Up to that time, his only prose writings had been a few sketches of popular characters and a collection of short stories, *Cuentos rurales* (*Rural Stories*, 1915), which apparently was destroyed by the author. The success he obtained with his first novel, however, convinced him to give up poetry and continue writing fiction. The transition was a wise one, for as a poet he could not have obtained the recognition he gained with his novels.

Returning to Mexico, in 1934, he published two more novels, *Desbandada* (*Disbandment*) and *El pueblo inocente* (*Innocent People*). In these two works, as in his first one, Romero made use of his personal experiences in the several towns in which he had lived in his native state of Michoacán. Romero was then appointed a second time to serve as consul general in Barcelona, this time by President Lázaro Cárdenas. He published there, in 1936, the novel *Mi caballo, mi perro y mi rifle* (*My Horse, My Dog, and My Rifle*), which is about the Mexican Revolution. In 1937, Romero was appointed ambassador to Brazil, where he wrote his most famous novel, *The Futile Life of Pito Pérez*. In 1939, he was appointed ambassador to Cuba, where he remained until 1945. During this period, he published two more novels, *Anticipación a la muerte* (*Anticipation of Death*, 1939) and his last, *Rosenda* (1946).

The recognition that Romero had received through his novels won him a chair in the Academia Mexicana de la Lengua, which he occupied in July 1950. During the reception, attended by President Miguel Alemán, Romero proposed a meeting in Mexico City of all the language academies of the Spanish-speaking world. Alemán accepted the proposal, and the first meeting was held the following year, with Romero representing the Mexican academy. He was appointed vice president and treasurer of the permanent committee that was established, a position he held for only a short time, for he died in Mexico City on July 4, 1952.

Although Romero was a popular poet and served with distinction as a diplomat, his fame has resulted mainly from his novels. With the exception of the collection *Tacámbaro,* which has been translated into several European languages, his poetry has been almost forgotten. On the other hand, his novels, very popular and widely read, are reprinted almost yearly.

In his first novels, Romero traces the development of the revolution as it affected the people of his state of Michoacán. Of this group of novels, the most outstanding is *Mi caballo, mi perro y mi rifle;* the author captures the essence of the struggle through the mind of a young revolutionary, as Mariano Azuela had done earlier in *Los de abajo* (*The Underdogs,* 1915). The protagonist, Julián Osorio, becomes disillusioned with the revolutionaries, who seem to be fighting for personal power rather than for the good of the people. The three images of the title become symbols representing the brutal force of those who hold power, the poor and unfortunate, and the violent and arbitrary nature of the revolution. In the third and last part of the novel, the revolutionary leaders are criticized for their lack of sympathy for the poor and their greed for power.

The novel includes a surrealistic scene that seems out of place in a realistic work. Romero lacked the skill of Luis Buñuel, a master at interpolating the surrealistic into the realistic without having it appear to be an external element. In Romero's novel, the protagonist is wounded and loses consciousness; while delirious, he has a vision in which his horse, his dog, and his rifle hold a conversation regarding the nature of the revolution; unfortunately, the scene is not well done.

Julián wakes up to find that he has been saved by some humble campesinos, who represent the good people of Mexico whom the revolutionaries should be helping. Julián believes that when the revolution triumphs, the life of the common people will change for the better. The novel ends, however, with Julián completely disillusioned with the results of the revolution, because nothing has really changed.

In *The Futile Life of Pito Pérez*, Romero was able to blend subject matter, form, and style much more skillfully than in any of his earlier novels. Although he used the traditional picaresque form, he was able to create an original picaro in the person of Pito Pérez, a character taken from real life. Although Pito conforms, in general, to the concept of the picaro (a rogue motivated by hunger but unwilling to work for a living, who therefore passes from master to master), Romero created a character that transcends the stereotype and becomes a real person. He accomplished this by endowing Pito with a personal philosophy, in this case disillusionment with society and with the human race in general.

Pito Pérez is an outcast who blames society for the conditions under which he and those like him have to live. His last will and testament is a strong indictment of society: "Humanity, I know you. I have been one of your victims. As a child, you took school away from me, . . . as a young man, you took love away from me, and in my ripe age, you took faith and confidence in myself away from me. Even my name you took away to convert it into a degrading nickname."

The novel's pessimistic view of society is softened by the presence of a pervading humor, the main characteristic of Romero's literary works. Like the writers of the traditional picaresque novel, Romero makes use of humor to ridicule humanity's frailties. No social class, position, rank, or occupation escapes Pito's scorn; lawyers, doctors, professors, newspapermen, merchants, women, the rich, the clergy, the poor—all receive their share. Sentimentality, present in all of Romero's previous works, has disappeared, and what remains is bitterness toward humanity.

In *Rosenda,* his last novel, Romero makes use of a well-known plot, the education of an untutored woman. The story is given originality by the use of a straightforward style and structure; by the perceptive characterization of Rosenda; and by its setting, a rural area of Mexico. The result is one of Romero's best fictional efforts.

José Rubén Romero's main contribution to Mexican letters was using humor in the novel to criticize society. Equally important was his revival of the picaresque, a form perfectly suited to his purpose. Romero was fortunate, for his friendship with persons in high political office granted him a freedom of expression denied the less fortunate Fernández de Lizardi, who published the first modern Latin American novel.

17

PEDRO HENRÍQUEZ UREÑA

Throughout his life, the Dominican Pedro Henríquez Ureña (1884–1946) manifested a predilection for the study of Latin American literature. From 1900 to the year of his death, not a year passed without his publishing at least one essay about the subject, for which he felt such a passion. It is our purpose here to examine his contributions to Spanish American literary criticism, although it is difficult to separate these from the criticism he dedicated to other literatures and to culture in general, as his approach was not narrow.

His study of Latin American literature reflects a concentration on those countries best known to him. To the literature of the Dominican Republic he dedicated several essays; the first, which appeared in 1900 when he was sixteen years old, is a study of the poetry of José Joaquín Pérez, which appeared in the *Revista Ilustrada* of Santo Domingo. In the essay "Brother and Teacher," his brother Max says that they copied numerous poems, pasted them on handmade scrapbooks, and gave them the title "Poetas dominicanos." Pedro then decided to dedicate his time to a single poet and selected Pérez. At the death of the poet, Ureña's collection of his poems formed the basis for the publication of his complete poems, with a study by Ureña, later reprinted in *Horas de estudio* (1910), Ureña's second book, alongside other essays dedicated to Dominican writers.

First published in *Revista Interamericana de Bibliografía* 27, no. 3 (July–September 1977): 241–53.

From 1901 to 1904, Ureña lived in New York, where he became quite interested in American arts and literature. After a brief visit to Santo Domingo, he went to Cuba. There, in 1905, he published his first book, *Ensayos críticos,* which was very well received in Spain and Latin America, as it contains several important critical essays on *modernismo* in Cuban poetry, José Enrique Rodó's *Ariel,* the ideas of the sociologists José María Hostos and Enrique Lluria, D'Annunzio the poet, Oscar Wilde, Arthur W. Pinero, and Bernard Shaw. The essay on Cuban poetry is helpful in tracing the development of the author as a critic. It is there that he, for the first time, searches for the characteristics that give Latin American literature its identity. *Modernista* poetry, in spite of European influence, he considered to be truly representative of that literature, "because the Hispanic American literary school that calls itself *modernista,* under whose banner militate all the young poets, represents an important and necessary phase of our artistic evolution. In its productions, from which it has not excluded, like French modernism, a single genuinely human element, an American psychological cell predominates. The action of this cell can be discovered even in the Greek, Scandinavian, and French imagery of poets Guillermo Valencia, Leopoldo Lugones, and Ricardo Jaimes Freyre."

From Havana, Ureña went to Mexico in January 1906, where he was to remain until 1914. In exile, his love for his country increased, as is evident in the books and articles he dedicated to its culture. In 1936, he published in Buenos Aires *La cultura y las letras coloniales en Santo Domingo* (*Colonial Culture and Letters in Santo Domingo*), and four years later *El español en Santo Domingo* (*The Spanish Language in Santo Domingo*). His studies were highly praised by the Mexican intellectual Alfonso Reyes in the prologue to the anthology *Pedro Henríquez Ureña: Páginas escogidas* (1946), where he said, "Among his critical essays there are some that are insuperable, as is his 'Juan Ruiz de Alarcón.'... His American syntheses are perfect, as can be seen in his Harvard lectures and his lectures on methodology in his monograph about Dominican culture."

In his second book, *Horas de estudio* (1910), Ureña included an essay dedicated to Rubén Darío's poetry, important for the revelation of his interest in Spanish versification, as the result of having found interesting variants in Darío's work. As he prophesized, "future historians will consecrate Darío as the supreme artist in the field of Spanish versification, if not as the one who has mastered certain typical meters of the Spanish language; indeed the one who used the largest number of different verses. ... Spanish versification seemed to tend fatally towards fixed uniformity until the new Spanish American school came to make popular verses and stanzas rarely used." As he demonstrates in the same essay, Darío is the poet in whose works the evolution of the new versification can best be studied. The conclusion he reached was that the principal innovations achieved by Darío and the other Latin American *modernistas* was the definitive modification of poetic stress. In 1920, Ureña published in Madrid *La versificación irregular en la poesía castellana* (*Irregular Versification in Castilian Poetry*), a book that became a classic in the field. However, he did not limit himself to the exclusive analysis of versification. He also analyzed the relations between form and subject matter. This approach does not disappear from the rest of his criticism, especially when form helps to express some "beauty, harmony of thought, music of the senses, or fantasy creations." The Nicaraguan critic Ernesto Mejía Sánchez pointed out the importance of that credo in the development of Ureña as a critic of Latin American literature. That trend in his criticism began with his essay on Darío's work.

Rubén Darío was not the only Spanish American author Ureña admired. For Hostos, Rodó, Martí, and Varona, he always felt a singular predilection. His attention to Hostos began with a note he dedicated to his memory in 1903, the year the sociologist died; then in his *Ensayos críticos* (1905), he included an analysis of Hostos's sociological principles as expressed in his *Tratado de sociología* (1904). Another study, "La sociología de Hostos," appeared in 1910 in Ureña's second book, *Horas de estudio,* and finally, in 1939, he edited Hostos's *Moral social* for the series Grandes Escritores de América. According to Ureña, Hostos, in his *Sociología,* which was the product of lectures offered at the Escuela Nacional de Santo Domingo, is not deterministic, as he is in his fundamental philosophy, where "he accepts cosmic laws as absolute and necessary." But in sociology he admits liberty as a product of individual life. "Following the ideas of Claude Bernard, he recognizes individuality as the guiding idea of each organism, as irreducible to sociological laws." Ureña rejected his determinism, but not his sociological concepts. It must not be forgotten, however, that Ureña's essay was written in 1905, when antipositivism had not yet appeared in Hispanic America. With that essay about Hostos, Ureña became the precursor of the change in the philosophical ideas that were soon to take place in Hispanic America. His philosophical position in 1905, the year he published *Horas de estudio,* was not, however, as clear-cut as it was in 1909, the year he published, in the *Revista Moderna de México,* the essays "Nietzsche y el pragmatismo" ("Nietzsche and Pragmatism"), "El positivismo de Comte" ("Comte's Positivism"), and "El positivismo independiente" ("Independent-Minded Positivism").

His essay on Rodó's *Ariel* is of a different nature. If in the ones dedicated to Hostos he concentrated, as was to be expected, on content and neglected to talk about form, in the one on *Ariel* he emphasizes the formal values, especially the stylistic ones. For him, Rodó was the most brilliant stylist of his generation. "His prose transformed the Spanish language, for he abandoned the extremes of vulgarity and pomposity and attained a just median and his style became spiritual, subtle, obedient to the most diverse modalities." In a letter to Ureña, Rodó acknowledged his criticism. Among other things he said, "I'm grateful for your book and your judgments, for they reveal a spirit above the level of mediocrity, and because I see in you a true writer, a beautiful promise for our American criticism, so in need of new blood to revive it. . . . I'm pleased with the solid and balanced judgment, the thoughtful seriousness emitted by the tone of your thinking, the thorough analysis and judgment, the clearness and precision of your style."

In that same essay on *Ariel,* he expressed the idea regarding the dichotomy between discontent and promise, but he did not develop it until later. He first complains pessimistically about the lack of faith, hope, enthusiasm, consistency, and vigor among young Latin Americans to carry on with the tremendous job of elevating the cultural level of their nations. That idea embittered him and he came to the conclusion that this spiritual weakness was alarming. Toward the end of the essay, however, his optimism appears: "Faith in the future, credo of all healthy and noble youth, should be our victory banner!" And for the first time also, he unveils his position regarding foreign influences, which he did not reject: "The aim of our communities should be to look for meaningful lessons wherever they may be found. The trend towards cosmopolitanism is a sure sign that no exclusionary tendency will prevail." No less important is the expression of his Americanism: "We are Spanish, but we are Americans first."

His essays about Enrique José Varona and José Martí were not included in his first two books. The one on Martí had appeared in 1905 in the periodical *La Discusión;* it was revised and published once more in 1905, and then in 1931. He also collected several of Martí's essays and edited them under the title *Nuestra América* in the series Grandes Escritores de América. He had also planned to edit another of Martí's books, *La edad de oro* (*The Golden Age*), a collection of stories for children, but the task was never accomplished. Ureña considered Martí's writings to have great value, and his name appears among the few that, according to him, should be included in a history of Spanish American literature, alongside Andrés Bello, Domingo F. Sarmiento, Rubén Darío, and José Enrique Rodó. For him, Martí and Darío were the two "exceptionally great artists." All this indicates that Ureña was conscious of Martí's great contributions to Spanish American literature and of his having initiated the *modernista* movement. In his brief introduction to *Nuestra América,* he says: "His native originality leads him away from the worn out European Romantic poetic forms used in Spain and Spanish America, and that is the reason why his diminutive book, *Ismaelillo* (1882) turns out to be the first book of verse of the innovative movement that spread from América to Spain. His prose, one of the most singular and marvelous innovations in our language, is another contribution of great importance, but of less influence than his poetry." In this same introduction, there is an observation about Martí's literary criticism that can well be applied to Ureña himself. "Martí," he says, "was interested in all America, and was enthusiastic about all its great things, but not without criticism; although his praise of authors and their works is never mean, at the same time it is never excessive, and if there are imperfections, he refers to them indirectly, without stressing them."

It was not until he left Cuba that Ureña wrote about Varona. His first note—a review of Varona's book *Curso de psicología* (*Course in Psychology*)—appeared in Veracruz in 1906 in the *Revista Crítica*. Years were to pass before he returned to him. In his visit to Cuba in 1911, he heard a lecture by Varona that, without question, according to Félix Lizaso, "impressed the young teacher." The result was the essay "Oyendo a Varona" ("Hearing Varona"), published the same year in the periodical *El Fígaro*. In his article Ureña tried to soften Varona's disbelief. As Lizaso observed, Ureña "ended his essay trying to clarify Varona's position, making a reference to his possible contact with William James' pragmatism, and concluding that the purpose of the lecture was not to offer a *discurso del método* but a lesson in faith." In that essay, Ureña anticipated for more than thirty years his thinking about Varona, as expressed in his 1936 essay, "Maestro de América" ("Teacher of America"), later reprinted as "El maestro de América: Enrique José Varona." That year Ureña had, of course, a better example than William James with which to explain Varona's skepticism, that of George Santayana. Varona was, according to Ureña, "a skeptic, but without anorexia, knowing that, no matter what the insolvable of his transcendental dialectics were, his practical reason would choose the good. Years later another intellectual of Hispanic origin, Santayana, accepted a similar position."

It is necessary to keep in mind that in 1911, the year Ureña heard Varona, his thinking had already evolved as a result of his contact with Mexican intellectuals. Upon arriving in Mexico in 1906, he had immediately joined the group of writers who published the *Revista Moderna*, and soon after *Savia Moderna*, edited by Alfonso Cravioto and others who rejected *modernismo* and positivism, the official philosophy of the dictator Porfirio Díaz's advisers, the so-called *científicos*. In Mexico, as observed by Lizaso, Ureña "contributed strongly to the formation of a new literary, artistic, and cultural consciousness, and to prepare for the changes that were predicted." Alfonso Reyes remembers those years with these words: "In private, Ureña's influence was profound. He taught us how to listen, how to see, how to think, and introduced a real reform of our culture. . . . Of all of us he was the only established writer, although not the oldest. There was not among us a better example of spiritual community and enthusiasm as those elicited by him."

While in Mexico, Ureña added a new dimension to his Spanish American literary criticism. Up to that time, his interest had been confined to contemporary letters. As a result of the research tasks that were assigned to him in 1910, that is, the collecting of literary materials and the coediting of the *Antología del centenario* with Luis G. Urbina and Nicolás Rangel, his interest expanded to include first the eighteenth century, and then the seventeenth. He dedicated studies to the literature of the period of Mexican independence, and several to Sor Juana Inés de la Cruz and other colonial figures. In 1913, he delivered the famous lecture about the Mexican characteristics of Juan Ruíz de Alarcón's plays. He became well known for his thesis, which was not superseded until recently. If his desire to recover Ruíz de Alarcón's plays for Mexican literature led him to see in his works certain Mexican characteristics, the search for them made him think about the nature of national literatures and their future, a subject that he was to develop later in his essays and histories dedicated to Spanish American literature. That, however, did not happen until after 1924, the year he left Mexico to join the Instituto Filológico at the University of Buenos Aires.

At the institute, he added to his field of research the study of the Spanish language in the Americas and published several monographs on the subject. He did not, however, abandon literary criticism. Indeed, it was during those years that he produced his best works. In 1925, he published the essay "Caminos de nuestra historia literaria" ("Paths of Our Literary History"), which in 1938 appeared as one of the *Seis ensayos en busca de nuestra expresión*, alongside "El descontento y la promesa" ("Discontent and Promise"), "Hacia el nuevo teatro" ("Toward a New Theater"), "Figuras" ("Profiles"), "Dos apuntes argentinos" ("Two Argentinean Notes"), and "Panorama de la otra América" ("Panorama of the Other America").

In "Caminos de nuestra historia literaria," he continues the search, initiated with his essay on Ruíz de Alarcón, for the originality of Spanish American literature, this time taking into consideration all the available national literatures. He also offered a plan to be used by anyone who may decide to write the complete history of that literature. It is now known that it was he himself who wrote that history later following his own plan, consisting of four concepts: a table of values, nationalities, exuberance, and good and bad (Hispanic) America. The historian who undertakes that task, he thought, has to establish the relative value of each work included. As a negative example he mentions Coester, who gives Rodó's works only four lines, while Samuel Blixen's theater, today totally forgotten, merits a whole page. Finally, he believed that the history of Spanish American literature should be written around a few key authors, an idea that has influenced Spanish American literary historians.

Henríquez Ureña's idea about national literatures is also significant. It is in this essay on Ruíz de Alarcón where he points out that there is an obvious difference between Spanish literature and Spanish American literature. Unfortunately, he does not offer precise information regarding the differences. He only says that they are self-evident; in everyday life, everyone, even those who do not speak Spanish, can distinguish between a Spaniard and a Spanish American person. Therefore, differential traits must exist. And if they do exist, the question arises: is it possible that those personal traits do not exist in the literatures? The answer is, of course, negative: "No. He who may pay attention soon will discover them, and it will be easy to determine if the writer is from the Río de la Plata region, Chile, or Mexico." Farther on he adds, underlining the phrase, "our literature is different from that of Spain *because it cannot be otherwise,* and that difference is known to all observers." Those statements indicate that Ureña accepted the existence of national or regional literatures in Spanish America. The differences, he adds, are not like those existing between England and France, or Italy and Germany, but like those between England and the United States. He ends the essay saying that in the future the differences will perhaps be greater. More than half a century has passed since he expressed that opinion, and his prediction has not come to pass. That may be due, perhaps, to changes in technology he did not foresee, such as television, aviation, the Internet, and other discoveries that have improved communications between countries.

After accepting the existence of national literatures, he goes on to reject, successfully, the idea, prevalent in non-Spanish-speaking countries, that the principal characteristic of Latin American literatures is exuberance. He observes that if exuberance means fecundity, then it is not the patrimony of the best writers. Hispanic Americans are not exuberant, since there is not a Lope de Vega, a Galdós, or even a Tirso de Molina or a Calderón de la Barca. On the other hand, Ruíz de Alarcón wrote little. If exuberance means verbosity, verbosity is not their patrimony either. He finds verbosity in Englishmen (Ruskin, De Quincey), Russians (Andreyev), and Spaniards (Castelar, Zorrilla). He adds: "And besides, in any literature the mediocre author, with poor ideas and little culture tends to be verbose. And this is true of Spanish literature more than of any other." And finally, if exuberance means emphasis, emphatic were Victor Hugo, Byron, and Espronceda. He finishes, saying: "Not all of us have been emphatic, nor is this our greatest active sin. There are countries in Latin America, like Mexico and Peru, where exaltation is exceptional."

In the last part of the essay, "Good and Bad (Spanish) America," he combines the previous two concepts, nationalism and exuberance, to underscore that it cannot be said that there is good literature written in countries with temperate climate and bad literature in tropical countries. "There is a literature of Mexico, of Central America, of the Caribbean, of Venezuela, of Colombia, of the Peruvian region, of Chile, of the Río de la Plata region, but there is not an exuberant and emphatic literature from tropical America and a serious and discreet one from temperate America." However, if the concept of a good and a bad Spanish America is to be applied, it should not depend on climate, but on the degree of political and economic stability. And he concludes that during the twentieth century, literature will flourish in the good countries and become dormant in the bad ones. In general, it can be said that this essay is one of the best in the book. Even the most severe of Ureña's critics, J. I. Jiménez-Grullón, exclaimed, "Here we have a work that reveals depth and sharpness, in spite of its polemical points. . . . Briefly, the essay stimulates meditation and is almost flawless. It will be hard for posterity to forget it."

In his second fundamental essay dedicated to literary criticism, "El descontento y la promesa," which appeared a year after "Caminos," Ureña develops an idea expressed first in the essay on Rodó's *Ariel*. He begins delineating the history of Spanish America since the independence period, the period during which Andrés Bello also declared literary independence in his *Silvas americanas*. The romantic period, he continues, left two works as robust and resistant as the ombu tree, Domingo F. Sarmiento's *Facundo* and José Hernández's *Martín Fierro*. He considered *modernismo* to be a discontent with romanticism, just like thirty years later a new generation manifested discontent with *modernismo*. He adds: "There are now in Spanish America restless young people who get irritated with the old generation and offer to work seriously in search of our genuine expression."

What were those young people complaining about? According to Ureña, their discontent centered on Spanish American authors, imitating of European writers, especially those from France and Spain, and their neglect of the Spanish American world. He concludes that imitating Europe is not an unusual or unforgivable crime, and perhaps it may be better than imitating the blind *criollistas*, with their nationalist preoccupation. The ideal would be a synthesis of tradition and rebellion, a synthesis that cannot take place regarding language, since Spanish is European. "We have not rejected writing in Spanish, and our problem of an original and proper expression begins there." To conquer that initial disadvantage, the writer has to make use of certain *americanista* formulas: nature, the Indian and the Creole, that is, what Spanish America comprises in its native elements. What is important is not the presence of those elements, but to limit, always, the themes to the New World, "in poetry as well as in the novel and the drama, in criticism as well as in history." Those American themes must be expressed in depth; if they are not, it means the sources are secondary; if they are, "then the firm expression of an artistic intuition has been attained and it conveys not only a universal meaning, but the essence of the spirit that possesses it, as well as the flavor of the land that nursed it." Ureña was, however, wise enough to know that you cannot write applying formulas, so he added: "Each great work of art creates its own peculiar means of expression."

He ends the essay with a glance to the future, when there will be in Hispanic America not only great writers but also a demanding reading public interested in literature. He suspected that it may be too late, but he adds that he does not want to close the essay on a pessimistic note: "If arts and letters are not extinguished, we have the right to consider a bright future.... There is no reason to fear the foreign stamp on the language in which we write, because by then, the spiritual axis of the Hispanic world will have moved to the shores on this side of the Atlantic."

With these two essays, Ureña set the basis for his history of Hispanic American literature. Twenty years were to pass before he accomplished his dream. The opportunity to write that history presented itself when he was invited by Harvard University to offer the Charles Eliot Norton lectures, which he delivered in the academic year 1940–41, published in 1943 as the *Literary Currents in Hispanic America,* translated by Joaquín Díez-Canedo in 1945 as *Las corrientes literarias en la América hispana.* Meanwhile, he had published the essay "La América española y su originalidad" ("The Originality of Spanish America"), a study of colonial theater and, for the first time, a study of indigenous literatures. These studies were not, of course, the first he had written about the history of Spanish American letters. In 1937, he had published the outline "Esquema de la historia de la literatura, en especial en la literatura argentina" ("Outline of the History of Literature, Especially Argentinian Literature") and "Bibliografía literaria de la América española"("Literary Bibliography of Spanish America"), the article "Barroco americano" ("American Baroque"), and "Literatura de la América central" ("Central American Literature"). He also published a series of sketches about important Spanish American writers, and edited several classical works by Spanish American authors. With all these materials, he finally dedicated himself to the writing of an organic history. The result was the book *Literary Currents in Hispanic America,* a work now considered as the starting point of a new Spanish American historical literary criticism.

Before 1945, the history of Spanish American literature was still in a formative stage, although by that year national literatures had already abundant bibliographical and critical materials. The first work written from the perspective of all the countries was the anthology *América poética* (*Poetic America*, 1846), by the Argentine Juan María Gutiérrez, whose three volumes were dedicated to poetry only. This work was followed by the three volumes of *Ensayos biográficos y de crítica literaria...* (*Essays on Biography and Literary Criticism . . .*, 1868), by José María Torres-Caicedo. In 1893, the Spaniard Marcelino Menéndez y Pelayo published in Madrid the important four-volume *Antología de poetas hispanoamericanos* (*Anthology of Hispanic-American Poets*), whose critical introductions appeared in 1913 under the title *Historia de la poesía hispanoamericana* (*History of Hispanic-American Poetry*). Although limited to poetry (prose writers are hardly mentioned), this is the first organic history based on the analysis of the works included. The often-quoted judgments expressed, although limited to authors who died before 1892, and often mistaken, were not superseded for several years. Ureña was a great admirer of Menéndez y Pelayo, considering him as "one of the most important critics." He nevertheless warned about imitating his historical method, for he, "with his historical attitude, felt compelled to give the same space to Gracián, who still can teach us, and to Mariana, who has little to tell us today."

Menéndez y Pelayo's example encouraged others to write global histories of Hispanic American literature. No one before Ureña, however, had the vast knowledge, wide erudition, and needed documents to accomplish the task satisfactorily, as can be seen in Juan Valera's *Cartas americanas* (*American Letters*, 1788–1887), Francisco Sosa's *Escritores y poetas sudamericanos* (*South American Writers and Poets*, 1890), Father Manuel Ponce's *Literatura hispanoamericana* (*Hispanic-American Literature*, 1896), Enrique Piñeyro's *Biografías americanas* (1906), or Alfred Coester's *The Literary History of Spanish America* (1916). Since Coester's book was published in the United States, and the Spanish translation did not appear until 1925, it had little influence on the development of Hispanic literary criticism. After Coester, historiography advanced slowly. Most publications were reprints or summaries of early work, as can be seen in the histories of the German Max Leopold Wagner, the French Max Daireaux, and the Spanish Crispín Ayala Duarte. Before Ureña's work appeared, two works by Hispanic Americans were published, Isaac J. Becerra's *Historia de la literatura hispanoamericana*

(*History of Hispanic-American Literature,* 1935), which added nothing new, and Luis Alberto Sánchez's *Historia de la literatura americana* (*History of Pan-American Literature,* 1937), a work which, in spite of its errors in dates and names, introduced the novelty of presenting the subject from the perspective of a well-defined point of view, that of indigenous America. According to the author, the presence of the Indian is what characterizes and defines its literature. This book encouraged literary historians of the following decade, when histories of Hispanic American literature became more discriminating. The Chilean Arturo Torres Ríoseco published in 1945 *La gran literatura iberoamericana,* in which for the first time Brazil is included. In 1946, the year Ureña published his *Literary Currents,* the Argentine Julio A. Leguizamón came out with a two-volume *Historia de la literatura hispanoamericana.*

Except the last two, all those histories, as well as the ones dedicated to national literatures, were at the disposition of Ureña to write his own history, with which he initiated a new trend in Hispanic American historiography. The central idea that guided his work can be found in an early work, his 1925 essay "Caminos de nuestra historia literaria," where he spoke about the necessity of writing a true history. In spite of the fact that Hispanic American literature was four centuries old, he said, "until now the only two attempts to write its complete history have been in foreign languages, one in English almost ten years old (Coester's), and the other in German (Wagner's).... A history covering all the countries does not exist, and we do not have a summary of all the national histories." The most important thing in that essay is the expression of his desire to write his own history. "All of us who in America have an interest in literary history have thought of writing our own." Twenty years were to pass until finally he wrote it. The waiting was worth it, for his *Literary Currents,* published one year before his death, became the model to follow in the writing of that history, a history that he deeply loved.

18

OCTAVIO PAZ

Poet, essayist, critic, and diplomat, Octavio Paz was one of the most brilliant men of letters not only in the Hispanic world, but internationally as well. His prose and poetry have been translated into many languages, and he received the Nobel Prize in Literature in 1990 in recognition of the excellence of his prose and poetic writings. In his numerous essays, he was able to convey a convincing portrayal of the Mexican people and their culture and, as a poet, to express with deep feeling his personal vision of humanity and his own place in the cosmos. His ideas are always expressed in a terse and clear style but elaborated by striking figures of speech.

Octavio Paz was born on March 31, 1914, in Mexico City, the son of Octavio Paz and Josefina Lozano. His paternal grandfather, Ireneo Paz (1836–1924) from Guadalajara, Jalisco, is remembered by the numerous historical novels he wrote and published. Paz said that his grandfather was a well-known journalist and writer who fought against the French intervention and who, at first a supporter of Porfirio Díaz, later opposed the old dictator. Octavio Paz's father, who died in 1934 in a railroad accident, was an attorney, diplomat, and journalist. He represented Emiliano Zapata in the United States in 1916 as his liaison officer and was one of the initiators of the agrarian reform. Paz's mother, of Andalusian parents, was born in Mexico. Except for a short time in Los

First published in *Dictionary of Literary Biography Year Book: 1998* (Detroit: A Bruccoli Clark Layman Book, Gale Research, 1999), 310–17.

Angeles, California, where his father was an exile, Paz spent his childhood and youth in one of Mexico City's southern suburbs, Mixcoac, today an integral part of the metropolis. "As in all Mexican houses at that time," Paz said, "the men of my house weren't very good Catholics, but rather freethinkers, Masons, or liberals. Whereas, the women were devout Catholics."

Paz's primary school studies were all in Mexico City, first in a French school of Marist Brothers; from there he went to Williams English School, where he learned to write clearly and concisely. Among the first books that he read were works by three French writers, the political theorist Jean-Jacques Rousseau, the historian Jules Michelet, and the novelist Victor Hugo, authors recommended by his aunt Amalia (his father's sister), who taught him French. He was also reading other books found in the library of his grandfather. "My grandfather had collected a fine library and I had completely free access to it in my childhood." The library was rich in French literature, in poets, in nineteenth-century Spanish novelists, and in modernist and Mexican writers. Another book that impressed him was the Latin satirist narrative romance *The Golden Ass*.

Paz's secondary studies were done in the Escuela Secundaria Número 5, to which he had to take the streetcar, a forty-five minute ride from Mixcoac to Colonia Juárez, where the school was located on Marsella Street. In 1929, he met there a Spanish student, José Bosh, who later died in the Spanish civil war and to whose death Paz dedicated an elegy, "Elegía a un compañero muerto en el frente de Aragón" ("Elegy to a Friend Who Died at the Aragon Front). Bosh, according to Paz, had influence upon the formation of his political ideas and his attitude toward totalitarian governments and institutions.

At age seventeen, Paz began studying at the National Preparatory School (San Ildefonso), and during his second year—in 1932—he published his first poems in *Barandal*, a review that he founded and directed in cooperation with other poets of his generation. In 1933, he published his first book of poems, *Luna silvestre* (*Wild Moon*) and directed the review *Cuadernos del Valle de México* (*Notebooks of the Valley of Mexico*), of which only four numbers appeared. The following year, the Spanish poet Rafael Alberti gave a series of conferences in Mexico that impressed Paz a great deal and, according to what he stated, were for him a great revelation. Other poets that influenced him during those early years were the Chileans Pablo Neruda and Vicente Huidobro and the Spaniard Luis Cernuda. In 1936, Paz published two poems "¡No pasarán!" ("They Shall Not Enter") and "Raíz del hombre" ("Root of Man"), the first important because it resulted in an invitation to visit Europe and the second important to his development as a poet. That same year he went to Yucatán in order to establish a school for the children of workers and peasants. His contact with Yucatán nature, the ancient Mayan culture, and the plight of the workers inspired him to write the poems collected in 1941 under the title *Entre la piedra y la flor* (*Between the Stone and the Flower*). Years later, Paz said that the subject matter of those poems was *el hombre mexicano del Sur, de Yucatán, en su paisaje* (the Mexican man of the South, of Yucatán, in his landscape).

The year 1937 was one of great activity for Paz. That year he married the writer Elena Garro, with whom he had a daughter, Elena, but it was a marriage that ended in divorce years later. That year he published "Sonetos," a collection of five sonnets, which appeared in *Taller Poético*, a literary review published from 1936 to 1938 by Paz, Rafael Solana, and Miguel N. Lira. As the result of having published "¡No pasarán!" and upon Neruda's recommendation, he was invited to attend the Second Writers Congress of Anti-Fascist Writers meeting in Paris, Barcelona, and Valencia. In Paris, he met Pablo Neruda, Louis Aragon, and César Vallejo. From Paris, accompanied by his wife, he proceeded to Barcelona and from there to Valencia, where he became acquainted with other writers who were attending the meeting, among them Vicente Huidobro, Miguel Hernández, Manuel Altolaguirre, Antonio Machado, and Alejo Carpentier. In Valencia in 1937, Altolaguirre published Paz's collection *Bajo tu clara sombra y otros poemas de España* (*Under Your Transparent Shade and Other Poems of Spain*). In his 1990 book *Pequeña crónica de grandes días* (*Small Chronicle of Great Days*), he included the essay "El lugar de la prueba" ("The Test's Place," Valencia, 1937), in which he relates that in 1987 he was invited by the city of Valencia to give the inaugural speech to celebrate the fiftieth anniversary of the 1937 meeting. After summarizing his personal impressions of the events, he says that the "deepest and most permanent impressions of that summer of 1937 were not from my association with writers. . . . I was moved by my encounter with Spain and its people: to see with my own eyes and touch with my own hands the landscape, the monuments, and the stones that since childhood I knew through my reading and my grandparent's stories."

After returning to Mexico in 1938, Paz began to write his first essays on international politics for the workers' newspaper *El Popular*. He also published the monthly literary periodical *Taller* (*Shop*, 1938–41), where he printed the first anthology of T. S. Eliot in Spanish. He had already published the poems in *Raíz del hombre* (1937), a collection that is considered to be the beginning of his mature period as a poet, for it marks a transition in his poetic development. Henceforward it would be the universal themes that would attract his attention, even though his preoccupation with the problem of language was preeminent. In 1941, he edited the influential anthology *Laurel*, in which he included international poets, among them John Donne.

Influenced by the vanguard writers he had met, Paz in 1943 was instrumental in the establishment, with the help of Octavio G. Barreda, of the first vanguard literary review in Mexico, *El Hijo Pródigo*. The following year he received a Guggenheim Fellowship, which liberated him from his job as a bank clerk. Paz spent that year in the United States, principally in San Francisco, Los Angeles, and New York. In Middlebury, Vermont, where he taught one summer, he met poets Robert Frost and Jorge Guillén. From Middlebury he went to Washington, D.C., where he met Juan Ramón Jiménez. It was during this stay in the United States that Paz took notes about the life and customs of the people, which he was to use in his book *El laberinto de la soledad* (*The Labyrinth of Solitude*), not published until 1950. In 1945, in New York, the Mexican ambassador Francisco Castillo Nájera, a friend of Paz's father, invited him to join the diplomatic service. The poet José Gorostiza, as chief of the service, sent Paz to Paris, where he started a new career, not to be abandoned until 1968, the year he resigned in protest for the events that took place in Tlatelolco, Mexico City, on October 2 of that same year. It was during this visit to Paris that he met André Breton, as a result of which his interest in the surrealist movement was strengthened, for he established an enduring friendship with Breton, who later visited Paz in Mexico. By 1949, Paz had written a quantity of poems, which he collected in *Libertad bajo palabra* (*Sworn Freedom*), the book that gave him international recognition as a poet of first rank.

The decade of the fifties was one of the most productive in Paz's life. In 1950, he came out with his seminal *The Labyrinth of Solitude,* a book that gave him recognition as a perceptive critic of the cultural, historical, and political processes. This collection of essays was followed, in 1951, by another masterpiece, *¿Águila o sol?* (*Eagle or Sun?*). That year, Paz made his first trip to the Far East, an experience that was to influence him the rest of his life. In Mexico, he continued his literary activities, publishing three additional books of poems, *Semillas para un himno* (*Seeds for an Anthem,* 1954), *Piedra de sol* (*Sunstone,* 1957), and *La estación violenta* (*Violent Season,* 1958), while collaborating in 1956 with the group Poesía en Voz Alta (Poetry Readings) in staging his only known dramatic production, *La hija de Rappaccini* (*Rappaccini's Daughter*), a one-act piece inspired by a short story by Nathaniel Hawthorne. This unique work was first published in the *Revista de Literatura Mexicana* (1955–57), a literary review founded by himself, Carlos Fuentes, and Emmanuel Carballo. While in New Dehli, Paz met Marie José Tramini, whom he married in 1964. In 1967, he became a member of the prestigious Colegio Nacional de México, whose members are appointed for life by the president of the republic.

After 1968, Octavio Paz devoted himself to writing and lecturing, offering seminars in several American and European universities such as Pittsburgh, Texas, Cornell, Cambridge, and Harvard. In October 1971, he founded the magazine *Plural,* and in 1977 *Vuelta* (*Return*), which is still being published. Being an intellectual and man of letters, Octavio Paz received several prizes, among others the Gran Premio Internacional de Poesía in 1963, the Premio Cervantes and the International Prize for Literature in 1982, the Premio Internacional Menéndez Pelayo in 1987, and the Nobel Prize in Literature in 1990.

In the intellectual and cultural environment of Mexico, Octavio Paz continued a long tradition of leading figures that goes back to the nineteenth century with men like Ignacio Manuel Altamirano, Justo Sierra, and Alfonso Reyes, a position he achieved as a result of the international recognition of his poetry and his brilliant essays, as well as from his intellectual independence and his defense of the rights of the writer.

Paz considered his juvenile poems, those that were published while still a student, as simple experiments in the art form. Since his trip to France and Spain in 1937, he developed two modes, the social and the surrealist. The first is not the axis upon which the aesthetics of Paz's poetry turns. It was soon abandoned. To the question asked by the critic Claude Couffon, "Is there no hope for social poetry?" Paz answered: "Poetry in itself is not good if it does not possess a sense of liberation. But generally, social poetry is confused with political poetry. Now then, in that sense, social poetry is not only bad poetry, which basically would not be very serious (it would be only one more bad poem), but it would be bad politics." Although he had given up writing social poetry, the political and social can be found in his essays, but always in the context of the theme of liberation. Surrealism, on the other hand, is a literary trend that affected Paz profoundly and gave his poetry a distinctive note.

To the question of Couffon, "Aren't there in *Raíz del hombre* more profound reminiscences of certain foreign trends, above all of the surrealist?" Paz gave a long response that we cite in part: "Indeed, I was more impressed by the discovery of D. H. Lawrence, of the English writers, of the German romantics, of Saint John Perse (*Anabase*) and of Breton (his *Amour fou*), than by the reading of the national poets. In the period of *Raíz del hombre* I was very concerned, as the title of my work indicates, about the problems of contemporary man. You asked me about surrealism. For me its influence has been decisive, but more as mentality, as attitude."

In an essay included in *The Siren and the Seashell* (1976), Paz observes, "Poetry continues to be a force capable of revealing to man his dreams and of inviting him to live those dreams in the light of day." This force can be found in Paz's own poems also, and especially in the books beginning with *Entre la piedra y la flor* (*Between the Stone and the Flower*, 1941), *A la orilla del mundo* (*At the World's Edge*, 1942), and *Libertad bajo palabra* (*Freedom Under Word* [*of Honor*], 1949), three books in which he

collected his best poems of that period. The idea of freedom is fundamental in Paz and it never disappeared from his writings. It is interesting that the theme of freedom, as well as that of love and rebellion, he
found in surrealistic poetry. He told Couffon that what he saw in Spain
in 1937 made him "consider with much skepticism the possibilities of
transforming the human condition. . . . A sentiment identical to the one
to be found in the poems . . . later collected in *Raíz del hombre.*"

In the collections of poems published since 1954, the publication date
of *Semillas para un himno* (*Seeds for an Anthem*), the freedom of man is
the theme that Paz develops in depth, but without giving up his poetic
vision of reality, which is cosmic and includes not only the universal
problems that confront modern man but also his human nature. This
vision is expressed in his constant search for new images, since for Paz
the image is the heart of the poem. His poetic works, and the same can
be said about his essays, are a constant effort to arrive at a synthesis of
reason and beauty as manifested in our time. One of his favorite images,
that of the bow and the arrow, could be applied to his own literary work.
The bow, according to Paz, consecrates and sings of man and thus gives
him a place in the cosmos; the arrow, on the other hand, forces him to
transcend and fulfill himself in the act.

The poetic form that Paz gave to his personal experiences can best
be observed in *La estación violenta* (*Violent Season*), a book in which he
collected nine poems written between 1946 and 1957 and published
in 1958. In "El cántaro roto" ("The Broken Jug"), the poet faces those
problems as manifested in his own country through its history. "Piedra
de sol" ("Sunstone"), a poem of 584 hendecasyllabic verses distributed
in irregular strophes, has a circular structure that reflects the concept of
circular time. The repetition of the same images and traditional symbols
(tree, water, wind), as reflected in a mirror, gives the poem a magical
tonality. To emphasize the circular nature of time, the last six verses are
identical to the first six, which allows the reader to return to the beginning, thus completing a circle, as does the sunstone. To give the form
greater continuity, capital letters and end periods are omitted. This composition is an excellent example of what Paz calls *poesía en movimiento*
(poetry in motion). He expanded the concept of poetry in motion and

applied it to poetry in general, using the phrase as the title of an anthology of Mexican verse he and others published in 1966. The term can also be applied to Paz's own poetry, which is constantly in search of new forms.

In the poetry published after *Salamandra* (1962), a new note appears, the introduction of Eastern ideas, concepts, and images, as can be observed in the collections *Viento entero* (*Total Wind*, 1965), *Blanco* (*White*, 1967), and *Ladera este* (*East Slope*, 1969), books in which the poet integrated Eastern philosophy and imagery in his verse without, of course, letting it supplant nor prevail over his own well-defined attitude toward reality. Nevertheless, it gives his poetry of this period an exotic note unknown before. In one of the poems, "Total Wind," Paz gave expression to the Eastern theme "the present is perpetual" using universal images. The book *Blanco* contains a single poem printed with black and red ink and in a long strip, as in the pre-Hispanic codices. In the collection *Poemas* (1979), Paz said about *Blanco:* "As the reading advances, the page unfolds into a space whose movement allows the text to appear and, in a certain way, creates it. . . . The typography and binding of the first edition of *Blanco* were meant to give emphasis not so much to the presence of the text as to that of the space containing it, which is what makes possible writing and reading." The subject matter of the poem, nevertheless, is as important as its form, for it deals with the confrontation of the poet with reality, which, for Paz, was to be found in *la palabra*, the word itself, and not in the senses or thought. For him, words reflect sensorial impressions, and therefore the words constitute reality, as expressed in the following verses from *Blanco:*

> the flower
> not seen nor imagined:
> heard,
> appears,
> a yellow chalice
> of consonants and vowels,
> burning.

Always in evolution, Paz in 1968 published the concrete poetry collections *Visual Disks* and *Topoemas,* and in 1971 *Renga,* with Edoardo Sanguineti, Charles Tomlinson, and Jacques Roubaud. In 1979, he collected the best of his poetic work in *Poemas (1935–75).*

Since 1950, the year he published *The Labyrinth of Solitude,* Octavio Paz has been recognized also as a brilliant prose writer and deep thinker and historian of culture. With that book, translated into the major languages of the world, Paz was accepted abroad as the principal interpreter of Mexican culture. Besides its clear style, the value of the work is to be found in the interpretation of Mexican history and its culture, an interpretation that invalidated all the previous ones, including that of Samuel Ramos as found in his book *El perfil del hombre y la cultura en México* (1934; *Profile of Man and Culture in Mexico,* 1973) which, until Paz's book, was accepted as the best analysis. The essays that Paz collected in *The Labyrinth of Solitude* present not only a lucid interpretation of Mexico, its people, its culture, and its history, from its origins to the present, but also a search for the true character of the Mexican people. In an article by Juanita Darling that appeared in the *Los Angeles Times* the day Octavio Paz received the Nobel Prize (October 12, 1990), it is stated that the Swedish Academy of Letters praised Paz's "exquisite love poetry," as well as his social and literary essays, especially the collection *The Labyrinth of Solitude,* calling it "an exploration of Mexican identity that has become a standard text in courses on Mexican history and political science since its publication in 1950." Perhaps the most significant aspect of *Labyrinth* is the fact that Paz thought that many critics had misinterpreted it. As early as 1970, the year he published *Posdata,* translated as *The Other Mexico,* he said: "Perhaps it would be worth the trouble to explain (once again) that *The Labyrinth of Solitude* was an exercise of the critical imagination: a vision and, simultaneously, a revision—something very different from an essay on Mexicanness or a search for our supposed being. The Mexican is not an essence but a history. Neither ontology nor psychology, I was and am intrigued not so much by the 'national character' as by what that character conceals; by what is behind the mask."

That the method by means of which Paz analyzed Mexico and the Mexican in 1950 had not changed in twenty years is what can be deducted from this sentence found in *The Other Mexico:* "In *The Labyrinth of Solitude* I tried hard (without wholly succeeding, of course) to avoid both the pitfalls of abstract humanism and the illusions of a philosophy of Mexicanness. . . . In those days I was not interested in a definition of Mexicanness but rather, *as now,* in criticism: that activity which consists not only in knowing ourselves but, just as much or more, in freeing ourselves. Criticism unfolds the possibility of freedom and is thus an invitation to action." Criticism is, indeed, the constant element found in all of Octavio Paz's essays. And it's this deep-seated belief in criticism and freedom, a message so needed in the contemporary world, that has kept *The Labyrinth of Solitude* alive. There are, of course, other elements besides the ideological content that have helped to keep it in the canon: its external form, its inner structure, its clear and terse style, and in general the skillful use of poetic imagery to express philosophical ideas. The work represents a conjunction of Paz the poet and Paz the essayist.

The Labyrinth of Solitude has stimulated the thinking of prominent writers. Carlos Fuentes, in his collection of essays *Myself with Others,* tells us that in 1950, the year he went to Europe to study international law, "Octavio Paz had just published two books that had changed the face of Mexican literature, *Libertad bajo palabra* and *El laberinto de la soledad.* My friends and I had read those books aloud in Mexico, dazzled by a poetics that managed simultaneously to renew our language from within and to connect it to the language of the world." In the future, this seminal book by Octavio Paz will continue to be read and to have influence on the shaping of Mexican thought and the shaping of international concepts about Mexico and its people.

In 1956, Paz began to publish a series of books on literature, art, and aesthetics, with which he became well known in these fields. In the first one, *El arco y la lira,* not translated into English until 1973 (as *The Bow and the Lyre*), he elaborated a brilliant theory of poetics which he continued to expand in *Los hijos del limo* (1974; translated that year as *Children of the Mire: Poetry from Romanticism to the Avant-Garde*); *The Siren and the Seashell and Other Essays on Poets and Poetry* (1976);

On Poets and Others (1986); and *Convergences, Selected Essays on Art and Literature* (1987). He also expressed his ideas on the subject of translation in an essay included with others in the book *Traducción: Literatura y literalidad* (1971), and wrote critical essays about Latin American literature collected in the books *Las peras del olmo* (*The Pears of the Elm*, 1957), *Cuadrivio* (*Four Essays*, 1965), and *Corriente alterna* (*Alternating Current*, 1968).

Not content with having achieved world recognition as a poet and essayist, Paz also expressed his frank opinion about world politics in his books *El ogro filantrópico, historia y política, 1971–1978* (*The Philanthropic Ogre: History and Politics, 1971–1978;* 1979), *Tiempo nublado* (*Cloudy Weather*, 1983), and *One Earth, Four or Five Worlds: Reflections on Contemporary History* (1985). In *Tiempo nublado,* he collected essays published in *Vuelta* and other periodicals between 1980 and 1983. In the foreword to *Tiempo nublado* he says, "I am not a historian. My passion is poetry and my occupation literature; and neither the one nor the other gives me the authority to express my opinions about the convulsions and agitations of our time." However, he traces with great skill and understanding the problems that afflict the world today.

Not less important are the books of poetic prose that Paz published, among which two stand out. The title of the first, *¿Águila o sol?*, refers to the two sides of a Mexican coin, which Paz uses to refer to the uncertainties of life. Eliot Weinberger called this collection "one of the most important books of Spanish prose poetry." The other collection is *El mono gramático* (*The Monkey Grammarian*, 1970). Both works were included in *Poemas* (1979). Although drama was the genre that least attracted Paz, he did publish and later staged a one-act dramatic piece, *La hija de Rappaccini* (*Rappaccini's Daughter*, 1956), inspired by a short story of the same title by Nathaniel Hawthorne.

In 1982, Paz published a most important book of literary criticism, *Sor Juana Inés de la Cruz o Las trampas de la fe* (*Sor Juana; or, The Traps of Faith*, 1988), an exhaustive study of the life, works, and times of the great seventeenth-century poet Sor Juana Inés de la Cruz. In 1971, he had been invited by Harvard University to give a series of lectures, one of which dealt with Sor Juana. In 1973, he repeated the series and, armed with all the notes he had taken, gave a series of conferences in 1974 on Sor Juana's life and works. It was not until the following year that he decided to write a book about this famous Mexican nun and intellectual. The first three parts were completed in 1976. Nothing else was written until 1980, at which time, he tells us, moved by a certain kind of remorse, he finished and published it the following year. He tells us: "My book is not the first one about Sor Juana, nor will it be the last. The bibliography about her and her works extends for three centuries and to several languages, although we still lack the forecasted study of an erudite Japanese scholar. The last to arrive were women. But they have enthusiastically made up for the time lost: Dorothy Schons, Anita Arroyo, Eunice Gates Joiner, Clara Campoamor, Elizabeth Wallace, Gabriela Mistral, Luisa Luisi, Frida Schultz, and others. This group has been recently joined by Georgina Sabat de Rivers and Margarita López Portillo."

Paz's study will be hard to surpass, since it is a definitive study enriched by the author's interpretation of seventeenth-century life in Mexico, to which he dedicates the first three parts of the book. The rest is an insightful analysis of Sor Juana's great seventeenth-century poetry as interpreted by a great contemporary poet. Toward the end of the book, Paz finds new meaning in Sor Juana's tragic end: "The lamentable end of Sor Juana does not give her work another meaning, like her censors wanted to. On the contrary, her defeat gains, thanks to her works, a different meaning, illuminated by its own light. Her writings, especially her *Respuesta* and *Primero sueño,* are the best remedy against that moral intoxication which wants to make her end and humiliation an edifying lesson."

As a poet, essayist, and critic of art and literature, Octavio Paz can be considered as one of the most brilliant figures in the Hispanic world during the twentieth century. His numerous books in all fields, but principally in poetry and literary and cultural criticism, merited the many prizes he received, crowned with the Nobel in 1990. He was a genuine representative of Latin America's authors and thinkers. As a poet he had a great sensibility, and as a thinker a profound vision and a strong belief in liberty and justice. With his death in 1998, Mexico lost one of its most respected spokespersons, inside and outside the country.

Although famous as a lucid prose writer, Octavio Paz was essentially a poet. His numerous books of poems reflect an evolution unequaled in the history of Mexican poetry. Reading them, one can easily trace the development not only of Hispanic poetry but also of the contemporary poetry of the Western world. His is *poesía en movimiento,* a constantly changing poetic expression that has served as a model to other poets since 1937; and yet, in it there is a permanent basic undertone that characterizes it and gives it an original and distinctive quality. In essence, his poetry can be said to be a search for a perfect form to give expression to transcendental themes, but without losing its Mexican identity. Octavio Paz will be long remembered not just as one more Nobel Prize winner or another Mexican poet but also as a giant in the international world of thinkers and writers.

19

JUAN RULFO

Although Juan Rulfo's literary production was meager, it has had an impact on Latin American narrative fiction that surpasses that of many prolific novelists or short story writers. His popularity, not only in Latin America but also in Europe, may be explained by the fact that his collection of short stories *El llano en llamas* (1953), translated as *The Burning Plain and Other Stories* (1967), and his novel *Pedro Páramo* (1955) capture in a powerful way the essence of rural Mexico and its people. There may be another reason for this popularity, and that is the introduction by Rulfo of a new type of fiction into Latin American letters, a fiction that was soon to explode into the so-called boom, with the novels of Carlos Fuentes, Gabriel García Márquez, Julio Cortázar, and Mario Vargas Llosa, among others.

Rulfo's two major works of fiction, his film scripts—collected in *El gallo de oro* (*The Golden Cock*, 1980)—and his photographs, many of which were published in *Juan Rulfo: Homenaje nacional* (1980), translated into English as *Inframundo* (1983), deal with the countryside of his native region, the southern, bare, arid, economically deprived part of the central Mexican state of Jalisco, where he was born on May 16, 1918, in the town of Apulco. His full name was Juan Nepomuceno Carlos Pérez Rulfo Vizcaíno. He was the son of Juan Nepomuceno Pérez, a civil servant, and María Vizcaíno Arias de Pérez, both also born in the

First published in *Latin American Writers,* vol. 3, ed. Carlos A. Solé and María Isabel Abreu (New York: Charles Scribner's Sons, 1989), 1215–27.

same region. Soon after Rulfo's birth, his family moved to nearby San Gabriel, the city that left an indelible image in his mind and was later to be integrated into his fiction.

In San Gabriel, Rulfo attended elementary school with his two brothers and experienced the Cristero revolt (1926–27), a religious war that broke out in central Mexico against the federal government. His father was assassinated in 1925, which left a profound emotional wound in the young boy, and two years later his mother died of a heart attack. In 1928, Rulfo and his brothers were sent to Guadalajara and were placed in the Luis Silva School for Orphans, where Rulfo remained until 1932.

Wishing to continue his education, he registered at the Universidad de Guadalajara, but on the same day he entered school, a strike was declared by the students and the university was closed. Because of the strike, he went to Mexico City early in 1934, where he attended the national university to study law. As soon as his financial aid provided by an uncle stopped, Rulfo abandoned the university and began to seek employment. From 1935 to 1945, he worked in the Department of the Interior as an immigration agent.

In Mexico City, Rulfo soon wrote a novel, of which little is known except the title, *El hijo del desaliento* (*Son of Affliction*), and a short fragment, "Un pedazo de noche" ("A Piece of Night"), dated January 1940 but not published until 1959 in the *Revista Mexicana de Literatura*, later collected in *Antología personal* (1978). Although this fragment seems to be a chapter of a longer work—perhaps the unpublished novel—it has the structure of a short story. The fragment reflects the style and narrative technique of later stories by Rulfo, such as the aura of vagueness that hovers over the identification of people and things, as well as the indecisiveness of the characters, who are surrounded by a sense of mystery. Also present in the story is the stylistic device of personifying the emotions, which Rulfo was later to bring to a high degree of perfection. No less conspicuous in this early prose work is Rulfo's keenness in character descriptions. Unlike his predecessors, he seems to remove himself completely from the scene and allow the personages to characterize themselves. Pilar, the protagonist, does not need to say she is a prostitute; her profession is revealed by her words and actions.

In the story, Rulfo makes use of certain narrative techniques that were to become his trademarks. The first-person narrator (Pilar) tells the story in the present about an incident that occurred long ago, but she relates it as if it has just happened or is happening. The narration gives the reader the sense that the action is taking place in the present, and therefore interest in the development of the plot is heightened.

Rulfo had the fortune to have as an immigration coworker Efrén Hernández, an accomplished short story writer from whom he learned a great deal about the art of writing. Hernández introduced Rulfo to Marco Antonio Millán, the editor of the literary periodical *América,* where in 1945 Rulfo published his first story, "La vida no es muy seria en sus cosas" ("Life Is Not Very Serious About Things"; collected in *Antología personal*). The story is about an expectant mother who has lost her husband and therefore puts all her hope of happiness on her future child, whom she is sure will be a boy. However, her concern for her dead husband leads her to a second tragedy, the death of the unborn baby. The story is of interest because the main preoccupation is with death.

Rejected by Rulfo as unworthy of his ability, this story can only be considered inferior when compared with the two others he published the same year, 1945, while visiting Guadalajara. There he joined Juan José Arreola and Antonio Alatorre in the publication of the literary periodical *Pan,* where two of Rulfo's best stories, "Macario" and "Nos han dado la tierra" ("They Gave Us the Land"), appeared in July and November of that year. Both stories were collected in *El llano en llamas.* In these two stories, Rulfo demonstrates a mastery of technique and style not present in his earlier efforts. These two *Pan* stories are his first significant works.

"Macario" reflects the assuredness of the master storyteller, well versed in the psychology of his characters, especially the eponymous protagonist, whose mentality is limited. Rulfo presents in depth the experiences of a young boy (or perhaps a young man, since his age is never revealed) whose world is very confined. Macario characterizes himself by means of a long interior monologue; through Macario's limited perspective, the reader becomes acquainted with his world. The technique is the same as that used by William Faulkner in *The Sound and the Fury* (1929), where

Benjy describes his world. In "Macario," Rulfo has created a unity of impression that has a powerful impact on the reader.

In "Nos han dado la tierra," Rulfo approaches a sociopolitical subject, the distribution of land by the revolutionary government of Mexico. The story tells of a simple incident regarding the delivery of land to the heads of families of a small rural community. The campesinos leave their homes at daybreak in order to receive the promised land parcels. It is a very hot day, and the group begins to dwindle. By early afternoon, only the narrator and three others are left. Finally the government representative appears to deliver the deeds. The campesinos want the land near the river, but they are given the llano, more like a desert than farmland. They protest but to no avail. The desperate situation is made all the more dramatic by the description of the desolated plains, the first description by Rulfo of his native region. As is characteristic of Rulfo's work, the social content in the story is not stated explicitly, as was done by most of the writers of the revolution. His stories are usually expressed by the actions of the characters and not by any editorializing on the part of the author.

In 1947, Rulfo married Clara Aparicio, with whom he had three sons, Francisco, Pablo, and Juan Carlos, and a daughter, Claudia. Back in Mexico City that same year, he began to work in the publicity department of F. G. Goodrich, a position he held until 1954. Meanwhile, in 1952, he had received a fellowship from the Centro de Escritores Mexicanos, which made it possible for him to dedicate more time to writing. He decided to collect his stories, published and unpublished. This first book, which was an immediate success, was published the following year under the title of one of the stories, *El llano en llamas*. The Centro fellowship was extended for another year, and it is assumed that during this period he wrote the novel *Pedro Páramo*. In 1954, he had already published its first chapter in the January–March issue of the periodical *Las Letras Patrias* under the title "Un cuento" ("A Short Story"). In 1955, the year the novel *Pedro Páramo* appeared, he accepted a position with the government to develop the Papaloapan River basin in southern Mexico. The project was discontinued in 1956, and Rulfo was back in Mexico City. Two years later he returned to office work, this time in charge of the archives of the Sociedad Mexicana de Geografía y Estadística. He apparently liked this type of work, which was suitable for his rather quiet, withdrawn nature.

Dissatisfied, though, with life in metropolitan Mexico City, in 1959, he went back to Guadalajara with his family in search of peace and tranquillity. However, in the state capital, things went from bad to worse, his life being complicated by his heavy drinking and ill health. While working at Televicentro, he found time to write a short novel, *El gallero* (*The Cockfighter*), which he did not publish, and the script for a short film, *El despojo* (*The Plunder*). But in 1962, he went back to Mexico City, this time to stay for the rest of his life.

By this time Rulfo had become quite popular outside of Mexico, since his fiction was being translated into many languages. In spite of this fame, he had to go back to work at another archive, this time at the Instituto Nacional Indigenista, where he was also in charge of publishing the periodical *México Indígena*. It was about this time that he began writing a new novel, to be called *La cordillera* (*The Packtrain*), another work that was never published.

The public had to wait until 1980 to read another new book of fiction by Rulfo: *El gallo de oro y otros textos para cine* (*The Golden Cock and Other Film Scripts*), a slender volume of only 143 pages. It is not clear whether these texts were reconstructed from the films, from the original scripts, or if they are the original versions written by Rulfo during the early 1960s.

In *El gallo de oro*, folkloric elements predominate, as in some of the stories collected in *El llano en llamas*. The characters (Dionisio the cockfighter and Bernarda the singer), the ambiance (the small towns in Jalisco during fair time), and the imagery are all related to Mexican folklore. The story is rather common. By raising and gambling on fighting cocks, and with the help of his wife, Bernarda, who brings him good luck, Dionisio is able to amass a fortune. When Bernarda dies, though, he loses everything. Suicide is the only way out for Dionisio, who blames Bernarda for not having warned him that she was mortally ill. Bernarda's tragedy is that her magic powers bring success to others but not to her: she is desired by men for her powers and not for the love she desires. Although this work does not compare to *Pedro Páramo*, Rulfo's personal style still enlivens the world created in the story.

Even though Rulfo published only three books, his skill as a fiction writer has been recognized throughout the world. In 1970, the Mexican government awarded him the Premio Nacional de Letras. Ten years later, Mexico again recognized Rulfo with additional ceremonies. In September 1980, he was admitted to the Academia Mexicana de la Lengua, and, the same year, the Instituto Nacional de Bellas Artes held conferences in his honor and published deluxe editions of his works. In 1986, the Museum of the National University of Mexico in San Antonio, Texas, held an exhibit of his photographs.

Rulfo was extremely well read. His favorite authors were, of course, novelists, especially the leading Russians, Scandinavians, Italians, Americans, and Brazilians. His interest in literature, and above all fiction, dates back to his early years in San Gabriel. The local priest had left Rulfo's grandmother a small library that Rulfo utilized. The first novels he read were those of the Italian Emilio Salgari and the Frenchman Alexandre Dumas, books of adventure liked by most boys. Then he became interested in English, American, and northern European novelists. The novel *Hunger*, by Knut Hamsun, left a deep impression on him. Later he went on to read more sophisticated novels, by James Joyce, William Faulkner, John Dos Passos, Ernest Hemingway, and others. Among the contemporary French writers, one of his favorites was Jean Giono; among the Germans, Günter Grass; and among the Italians, Vasco Pratolini. Rulfo also acknowledged that he learned a great deal about writing from Efrén Hernández. Among the many writers influenced by Hernández three stand out: José Revueltas, Juan José Arreola, and Juan Rulfo.

Arreola began to publish his short stories in Guadalajara in the 1940s and represents another trend in the Mexican short story of the period, the fantastic. His fiction, like that of Jorge Luis Borges, does not normally reflect the national milieu. When Rulfo's stories appeared, critics immediately contrasted his fiction with that of Arreola. The two writers became the representatives of the two trends predominating at the time in Mexican literature: the national and the cosmopolitan. One year after

Rulfo's first book was published, the critic Emmanuel Carballo published a lengthy article comparing the two writers. He observed that while Arreola universalizes his experiences, Rulfo introduces personal subject matter: "Arreola proposes problems that could occur anywhere, while Rulfo, starting from a localized place and digging deeply, gives what is national, and even regional, a universal tone."

Two of the stories that appear in *El llano en llamas* foreshadow Rulfo's novel *Pedro Páramo*. "En la madrugada" ("At Daybreak") and "Luvina" have the same locale as the novel, a region Rulfo described as depopulated, the people having gone either to the Pacific coast, the high plains, or the United States. As Ricardo Estrada has pointed out, "Luvina" can be considered "the strongest evidence available regarding the gestation of the ambience of *Pedro Páramo*, and perhaps it could be stated that it contains the germ from which the novel grew." The description of the ghost town named Luvina, for example, anticipates, to a certain extent, that of the novel's Comala, after the cacique has died and the community has become a dead town.

In "En la madrugada," the town appears with its original, actual name, San Gabriel, while in the novel it is called Comala. Rulfo explained the reason for the change: "The name does not exist, no. . . . But the derivation of comal—an earthenware utensil that is placed over the embers for the purpose of heating the tortillas—and the heat that prevails in that town was what gave me the idea of the name. Comala: the place over the embers." Although there is no Comala in Jalisco, where the action of the novel takes place, there is one in the neighboring state of Colima, situated at the foot of the Volcán de Fuego. The selection of the name Comala was appropriate, as it underscores the fiery nature of Pedro Páramo, the protagonist. This change in the name of the town, however, came much later, perhaps after the novel was completed. The year before it was published, the first chapter appeared in a periodical, and there the town is called Tuxcacuexco, a real town not far from San Gabriel.

Rulfo said that the idea of writing a novel about San Gabriel, the town where he had spent his boyhood, came to him "from an earlier period. It was, it can be said, almost planned about ten years before. I had not written a single line when it was already turning in my mind." The setting, the characters, the tone, and the narrative devices found in his short stories appear in the novel. The great difference is that in the novel all the people are dead. The idea of creating a ghost town where the inhabitants continue living after they have died came to Rulfo after a visit he made to San Gabriel, where, instead of finding the idealized town he had carried in his mind for years, he found a ghost town. The novel is the result of a desire to bring this town back to life.

In *Pedro Páramo*, the presence of death predominates. This preoccupation with death as a theme is also characteristic of most of Rulfo's short stories. The stories serve as a prelude for the novel, which is an orchestration of the theme of death. It begins when Juan Preciado arrives at Comala in search of his father, Pedro Páramo, the cacique who has disinherited him, and ends with the death of Pedro, killed by another of his sons, Abundio. In the town, the dead talk about killings and death, and in their graves they continue their conversations about death. The novel ends with the following description of Pedro Páramo's death: "He leaned against Damiana and tried to walk. After a few steps he fell down, pleading within but not speaking a single word. He struck a feeble blow against the ground and then crumbled to pieces as if he were a heap of stones." Rulfo's preoccupation with death and violence was perhaps due to the many encounters he himself had with death—the revolution, the Cristero revolt of the late 1920s, and the violent deaths of some of his relatives: his father and his uncle were assassinated; his grandfather was strung up by his thumbs and lost them.

Critics are in agreement that with the publication of *Pedro Páramo*, the Mexican novel reached a high degree of perfection. In his essay "Landscape and the Novel in Mexico," Octavio Paz says, "Juan Rulfo is the only Mexican novelist to have provided us an image—rather than a mere description—of our physical surroundings. Like [D. H.] Lawrence and [Malcolm] Lowry, what he has given us is not photographic documentation or an impressionist painting; he has incarnated his intuitions and his personal obsessions in stone, in dust, in desert sand. His vision of this world is really a vision of *another world*." In *La nueva novela hispanoamericana* (*The New Spanish-American Novel*),

Carlos Fuentes writes, "The work of Juan Rulfo is not only the highest expression which the Mexican novel has attained until now: through *Pedro Páramo* we can find the thread that leads us to the new Latin-American novel."

Juan Rulfo died on January 7, 1986, of lung cancer, which had been diagnosed in October 1985. One of his friends, the writer Fernando Benítez, successfully recommended to the president of Mexico that Rulfo be buried in the Rotunda de Hombres Ilustres, the resting place of most famous Mexican writers and artists. Rulfo, then Mexico's most widely read writer, had revitalized prose style, had introduced complex narrative structures, and had revealed to the world Mexico's other side, such as the strength of the rural people in spite of their suffering, their attachment to the land, and their tragic sense of life. In short, Rulfo can be considered as the representative, par excellence, of Mexican fiction writing.

20

CARLOS FUENTES

"I believe profoundly in societies that don't kill their own past."

—CARLOS FUENTES

Carlos Fuentes has stated that fiction can be useful in looking at history from new perspectives, and this is precisely what he has done in most of his novels, wherein he has presented a vision of history that cannot be gathered from the reading of history books. And, even more, he has reinterpreted history to present a new version of its development, a version reflected by a mind keenly conscious of the significance of past events in the shaping of the contemporary course of human events. In most of his novels, he has gone one step further, to the re-creation of history by the combination of realistic and mythical structures. The purpose of this essay is to trace the intrusion of history and myth upon Fuentes's narrative and to observe how he has solved the technical problems involved and yet has managed to produce novels that are aesthetically satisfying.

The interaction between history and myth is a topic that has aroused the interest of the philosopher, the historian, and the literary critic since ancient times. Among contemporary historians, Arnold Toynbee has stated, "History, like the drama and the novel, grew out of mythology, a primitive form of apprehension and expression in which . . . the line between fact and fiction is left undrawn." And if it is true, as he says, that "history cannot entirely dispense with the fictional elements," it is also

First published in *Carlos Fuentes: A Critical View,* ed. Robert Brody and Charles Rossman (Austin: University of Texas Press, 1982), 3–17.

true that fiction cannot entirely dispense with the historical elements and technique. "Lastly," says Toynbee, "the drama and the novel do not present fictions, complete fictions and nothing but fictions regarding personal relationships. If they did, the product, instead of deserving Aristotle's commendation that it was 'truer and more philosophical than history,' would consist of nonsensical and intolerable fantasies."

One of the characteristics of the writers of the new Spanish American novel, however, is the tendency to create pure fiction. One of the leaders of this trend has been Carlos Fuentes. He, like other new novelists (García Márquez, Cortázar, Rulfo, etc.), has moved in this direction by combining two narrative modes, the realistic (historical) and the mythical. Northrop Frye has discussed these two modes at length, and he differentiates between them by saying that realism is the art of verisimilitude, the art of implied similarity, and myth the art of implied metaphorical identity. However, he says that the presence of a mythical structure in realistic fiction "poses certain technical problems for making it plausible, and the devices used in solving these problems may be given the general name of *displacement*."

The realistic-naturalistic fiction of the late nineteenth century degenerated into a documentary narrative in which the emphasis fell more upon historical documentation than on aesthetic elements. Novelists were more interested in giving historical facts than in creating reliable characters through whom they could present an artistic view of society. Carlos Fuentes, among others, acidly criticized the Spanish American realistic novel for the reliance it placed upon documenting the social life and describing the physical environment rather than presenting an integrated vision of that society. "Closer to geography than to literature," Fuentes said of those novels.

In the novel of the Mexican Revolution, Fuentes finds a change but not yet a complete break with the earlier fiction. He praises its authors for having introduced ambiguity in characterization but deplores their dependence on historical fact, on documentation: "*Los de abajo, La sombra del caudillo,* and *Si me han de matar mañana,* over and above their possible defects in technique, and in spite of their documentary ballast, introduce an original note in the Spanish American novel: they introduce ambiguity. Because in the dynamics of the Revolution the heroes can be villains, and the villains can be heroes."

More important than the introduction of ambiguity is the introduction of myth. This innovation Fuentes finds in Juan Rulfo's novel *Pedro Páramo:*

> There is in the Mexican novel of the Revolution, nevertheless, a forced lack of perspective. The subject matter found at close range burned the novelists' hands and forced them to use a documentary technique which, to a large extent, prevented them from penetrating into their own discoveries. It was necessary to wait until 1947 for Agustin Yáñez to write the first modern vision of Mexico's immediate past, in *Al filo del agua,* and finally, in 195[5], for Juan Rulfo to proceed, in *Pedro Páramo,* with the mythification of the situations, the characters, and the language of the Mexican countryside, thus ending forever the tendency, in the fiction of the Revolution, of using documentary materials.

In *Pedro Páramo,* Fuentes finds the thread that leads to the new Spanish American novel and, of course, to his own novels, which for the first time in Mexican letters mark the creation of a fiction that gives a mystified vision of history without sacrificing the aesthetic elements so essential in the new novel and utilizing the most recent techniques of fiction writing. This he has done without abandoning realistic themes, for, aside from some fantastic elements in some of his works ("Chac Mool," *Aura, Cumpleaños* [*Birthday*]), his fiction is essentially realistic. He has, however, abandoned traditional realism, a realism that was expressed by psychological introspection or by the illustration of class relations, and has embraced the new realism based on the utilization of mythical structures and themes.

This change has not been abrupt. The title of his first book, *Los días enmascarados* (*The Days of Masks*), already referred to the Aztec myth of the five days at the end of the year when time stopped in readiness for the new life, the rebirth, the eternal return. One of the stories, "Chac Mool," was inspired by a historical event, the 1952 Mexican exhibit in

Europe which included the pre-Hispanic god of rain, the god whose mere presence brought on the rains, according to the Mexican newspaper account read by Fuentes: "The data from the sensational, journalistic account of the art exhibit focused my attention on a fact evident to all Mexicans: the living presence of old cosmological forms from a Mexico lost forever but which, nevertheless, refuses to die and manifests itself from time to time through a mystery, an apparition, a reflection."

In "Chac Mool," Fuentes solves the problems of displacement by the use of realistic motifs: the action takes place in Mexico City and Acapulco; the two characters are clerks in a government office; and Filiberto, the protagonist, purchases a statue in a well-known market. To introduce historical fact, the technique of the diary, in which conversations are recorded, is used. The fictitious Filiberto writes about historical events in his diary, such as the introduction of Christianity after the conquest and the effect it had on the conquered people. In the other aspect of the story, Fuentes re-creates the myth of the eternal return by the illusory transformation of the statue of the god, which Filiberto had placed in the basement of his home. Chac Mool comes back to life with the coming of the rains and takes control of Filiberto's life, finally driving him to suicide. Thus, Fuentes skillfully blends the historical and the mythical into a continuous narrative form, which derives its structure from the tension created by the interaction between two different cultures, that of ancient Mexico, represented by Chac Mool, and the contemporary, represented by Filiberto.

The technique used in this early story was soon perfected and expanded in the novel, and it has become the distinguishing mark of Fuentes's fiction. The models that he followed for this mode of fiction he found principally in the works of William Faulkner, Malcolm Lowry, and Miguel Ángel Asturias. From them, he learned the art of utilizing myth, either as form or theme, in the context of the realistic novel. "In Faulkner, by means of the tragic search of everything left unsaid (of impossible writing) the myth of man unconquered in defeat, violence, and pain is born. In Lowry, it's not the class relations between Yvonne and the Consul that are important, but the myth of paradise lost and its tragic and fleeting representation in love." The fiction of Asturias is important to Fuentes because it did not stop "with insignificant documentation, but found significance in myth and language. His method of giving a personality to the anonymous Guatemalan men was by endowing them with their myths and magic language, a language substantially related to that of the surrealists."

The novels of Fuentes, with some exceptions, can be considered as mythical approaches to history or creative history. The success of his novels is due in great part to this use of myth to interpret history; for history, as Ernst Cassirer has observed, is determined by the mythology of a people. "In the relation between myth and history myth proves to be the primary, history the secondary and derived, factor. It's not by its history that the mythology of a nation is determined but, conversely, its history is determined by its mythology—or rather, the mythology of a people does not *determine* but *is* its fate, its destiny as decreed from the very beginning." In his first major work, *Where the Air Is Clear*, Fuentes presents a mythical history of Mexico City and its four million (as of 1958) inhabitants. The characters who represent the historical aspects of the novel are products of the Mexican Revolution and, at the same time, representative of Mexican society during the 1950s: Robles, the revolutionary turned into a conservative banker; his wife, Norma, the social climber who marries for money; Zamacona, the brooding intellectual who becomes one of the sacrificial victims; the decadent Bobó, from the new upper middle class; Gabriel and Beto, the displaced braceros back from California; and the Ovando family, the impoverished representatives of the dethroned *porfiristas*.

In the novel, the representatives of its mythological counterpart are found in the old lady Teódula Moctezuma and Ixca Cienfuegos. They symbolize Mexico's past, a mythical Mexico that still survives and believes in ritual, in sacrifice as the only way for man to redeem himself. The Mexican people have been chosen by the gods to feed the sun and keep it moving so that mankind can survive. Without sacrifices this would be impossible. Displacement in the novel takes the form of parallel action in the fictional world representing history. Both Norma and Zamacona are sacrificed to modern gods. This revelation of the mythical nature of Mexican history is accomplished by the use of image and metaphor. The characters, the description of the city, the action, and the plot are all expressed by uniting two worlds, that of the remote past and that of the present. The interaction between the characters representing both cultures becomes the central technique of displacement. Mythical episodes are used by Fuentes to give his work a pure, literary quality. History and myth balance each other to give the novel equilibrium. The introduction, spoken by Ixca, offers the key to the structure of the novel. Mexico City, as the modern version of ancient Tenochtitlán, is the center of the world, "el ombligo del mundo," the umbilical cord of the world, a sacred city. "The center, then," states Mircea Eliade, "is pre-eminently the zone of the sacred, the zone of absolute reality." In his introductory speech, Ixca says, in reference to Mexico City, "City of the three umbilical cords. . . . Incandescent prickly pear. Eagle without wings. Serpent of star." The image of the eagle and the serpent, related to the myth of the founding of the city, is repeated in the first chapter. Ixca also tells about the myth of the creation of the sun, which can be found in Sahagún. The god that became the sun was a humble god, a leprous god, "a leper, yes, the one who threw himself into the furnace of original creation to feed it. He reappeared transformed into a star—a motionless star. A single sacrifice, even if exemplary, was not enough. It was necessary to have a daily sacrifice, a daily feeding of the god, in order for him to shine, to keep moving, to feed others." This passage prepares the reader for the sacrifices in the historical world that are to follow.

Ixca Cienfuegos also questions whether the historical present is better than the mythical past. In a confrontation between Ixca and Zamacona, who represent the past and the present-future, Ixca asks the latter, "Is this cheap, petty power, bereft of greatness, better than that power which had, at least, the imagination of allying itself with the sun and the real, permanent, and inviolable cosmic powers?" Like Tolstoy's *War and Peace,* the novel ends with an essay (one of many in the book) in which Fuentes recapitulates the history of Mexico City from its foundation to the present, neatly balancing the mythical introduction; the technique of opposing two antagonistic elements (historical fact and myth), similar to that used in "Chac Mool," gives the novel tension. Irony, of course, cannot be ruled out. Fuentes himself has stated that the novel reflects "the excessive and somewhat mythical preoccupation [of the members of the Mexicanist movement] over nationality, ancestry, and patrimony rampant at the time in Mexico."

La muerte de Artemio Cruz (*The Death of Artemio Cruz*) and *Aura* were published the same year, 1962. While in the latter work the mythical predominates, historical elements surface in *The Death of Artemio Cruz*, but even here mythical aspects are evident in the structure of the subject matter and the characterization of the hero. After writing the social history of Mexico City in *Where the Air Is Clear*, Fuentes continued and re-created the history of modern Mexico in *The Death of Artemio Cruz*, approximately from the era of Santa Anna to the 1950s, with the period of the revolution receiving the most attention. Historical personages are freely mentioned, as are historical facts and events. However, this is not a novel of the revolution, as are those by Azuela or Guzmán. On the contrary, it is a mystified novel similar to Rulfo's *Pedro Páramo* or García Márquez's *Cien años de soledad* (*One Hundred Years of Solitude*). It is also a history, as seen through the eyes of Artemio Cruz, an unreliable character. The mythical structure is found in the use of the myth of the descent into hell to depict the career of the hero, who re-creates in his mind, just before he dies in the hospital, the twelve most important moments of his life. These twelve days represent the twelve months of the year. This motif is repeated in the temporal structure of the novel, in which the narrative time covers the last twelve days in the life of Artemio. Comparing *Pedro Páramo* and *The Death of Artemio Cruz*, Djelal Kadir has said: "Insofar as these works transcend to ritual and oracular image, they synchronize rhythm and pattern, thus becoming *myth* and archetype. The archetype re-enacted by these works is Mexican history become myth."

In the novels published after *The Death of Artemio Cruz* and *Aura*— *Zona sagrada* (*Sacred Zone*, 1967), *Cambio de piel* (*A Change of Skin*, 1967), *Cumpleaños* (*Birthday*, 1969), *Terra Nostra* (1975), *La cabeza de la hidra* (*The Hydra Head*, 1978), and *Una familia lejana* (*A Distant Family*, 1980)—Fuentes has given more emphasis to the mythical than to the historical, but he never forgets history or the social condition, which underlies all his fiction.

In *Aura,* he gives expression to the historical and the mythical by creating characters symbolic of both forms of thought. Two male characters—Llorente, a general of the period of Maximilian's empire, and Felipe Montero, a young contemporary historian who later turns out to be the general's double—represent the historical component in the novel. For balance, there are two additional archetypes, both female—Consuelo (Llorente's wife and a sorceress), who conquers time by recovering her youth, and Aura, her counterpart as a young girl. Consuelo accomplishes her transformation by performing an ancient rite, the sacrifice of a goat. "Through the paradox of rite, profane time and duration are suspended." The creation of the mythical characters sprang from history. Fuentes has said that the inspiration for this short novel came to him in the Chapultepec Castle Museum, where he saw a picture of Carlota, the young and beautiful wife of Maximilian. Later he found another picture of her in her coffin, "wearing the nightcap of a little girl: the Carlota who died insane, in a castle the same year that I was born, the two Carlotas: Aura and Consuelo." As in an earlier story, "Tlactocatzine, del Jardín de Flandes" (in *Los días enmascarados*), the sacred place in *Aura* is reduced to a mansion in Mexico City. In the short story, the mansion, dating from the time of Maximilian, was located on Puente de Alvarado, a street associated with the Conquest of Mexico. In *Aura,* the mansion is on Donceles Street, in the old part of town that dates from the colonial period.

If the myth of the city or mansion as a sacred center is presented unconsciously in *Where the Air Is Clear* and *Aura* (the author has never mentioned this myth in referring to these novels), it is indeed intentional in *Zona sagrada,* beginning with the obvious title. To leave no doubt in the mind of the critic, Fuentes has said regarding this novel, "I am very much interested in the mythical zone, and when I speak about a sacred zone, of course, I am establishing a territory, an enclosure. It's the very old idea of the temple, the temple as a defense against epidemics, against sieges. . . . It's the place that is all places and in which myth has its seat." More significantly, he adds: "*Zona sagrada* interests me a great deal as an experiment. The point of departure of the novel lies in the relations of a great movie star, a charmer who is at the same time a mother, with her son. The importance of living myths . . . is that they really never end. . . . I found an equivalent in Apollodorus, for example, in the *Greek Myths* of Robert Graves: the true conclusion of the myth of Ulysses, the one that Homer does not relate."

The mythical elements are to be found not only in the external structure but also in the thematic content, the relation between Claudia Nervo, the mother, and Guillermo (Guillermito, Mito), the son. The first chapter, titled "Happily Ever After," narrates the myth of the sirens in the story of Ulysses, but in a present-day context—a football game that is played in a sacred zone, the staked field. In the last chapter, "Zona sagrada," Mito is transformed into a dog. While in *Where the Air Is Clear*, the beginning and the ending of the novel are in opposition (mythical introduction, historical epilogue), in *Zona sagrada* they are parallel. The novel ends with the episode of Circe, the sorceress who changes men into animals. Since Claudia Nervo is associated with Circe, the transformation of Mito into a dog becomes a part of the myth. As a theme, the myth of Ulysses has also been re-created, for the characters represent Penelope and her son Telemachus. Even Telegonus, the son of Ulysses and Circe, is there, under the name of Giancarlo. The historical part of the novel is based on the life story of a famous Mexican movie star.

A Change of Skin signals a change of attitude in Fuentes as a novelist. Here for the first time he builds a purely fictional construct. He has said, "The only way to understand this novel is to accept its absolute fictitiousness. . . . It's a total fiction. It never pretends to reflect reality. It pretends to be a radical fiction, up to its last consequences." By *radical fiction*, Fuentes means that some of the action is not realistic, that is, carried out by the fictitious personages, but rather invented or imagined by them and presented as if they had actually lived through the experiences. Also, the narrator could be a character imagined by one of the personages, such as Javier. Displacement is achieved by introducing numerous realistic motifs, starting with the date when the events in the novel begin—Palm Sunday, April 11, 1965. On that precise, historical day, two couples leave Mexico City in a Volkswagen on their way to Veracruz, taking the old road and stopping at Cholula, where the rest of the action takes place, at a second-rate hotel and inside the great pyramid. This, however, is preceded by a prologue with a displacement function and in which the destruction of Cholula by Cortés and his men is re-created. Fuentes has said that in the novel there is an intention to fictionalize: "Therefore, the scenes in Prague or in New York, which in appearance are presented in a realistic manner, are some of the fictitious scenes of the novel. In the same way the narration about events in the past, which I also include, convert the history into fiction, into pure imaginative narration."

Regarding his intention to present the empirical facts as fiction and the imaginative elements as real, Fuentes adds, "I believe that this is what gives unity to the novel, a novel that at times appears to have no unity . . . : History [*la historia*] is fiction, reality is apocryphal, the New Testament was written by Jules Verne." Therefore, the theme of the novel is the mythification of history. In history there is no progress, time has been abolished, as in myth. This explains why the violent acts occurring at the end of the novel—the death of Franz and Elizabeth in the center of the pyramid, the killing of Isabel by Javier in the hotel—are structured in parallel trajectories with some of the most violent events in history: the destruction of Cholula by Cortés, the massacre of the Jewish people. "There is," Fuentes has said, "a paralyzed history [in the novel]. There is a history converted into a Statue of History referring to itself, returned to itself. There is no historical progress, that is what the novel is trying to say: there is no eschatology, there is only pure perpetual present." History, therefore, becomes myth when its events are repeated and become a rite. "The gesture acquires meaning, reality, solely to the extent to which it repeats a primordial act." In the novel, a number of ceremonial acts are repeated.

The myth of the sacrifice to feed the gods found in *Where the Air Is Clear* appears in *A Change of Skin* also. Two of the four principal characters, Franz and Elizabeth (the two foreigners) are sacrificed to the gods at Cholula by being buried alive as a result of an earth tremor. This sacrifice occurs inside the old pyramid, precisely in the "center of the pyramid, the navel, the cord from which the labyrinthine beehive of the *Gran Cu* [Great Temple] of Cholula is born." The importance of the use of the pyramid as a motif has been pointed out by Fernando Benítez, who wrote, "Outside of Octavio Paz, no other writer has meditated about the fact that the pyramid is the geographical form of our country, from the coast to the volcanoes; that it has been the highest expression of the sacred for the last two thousand years." In spite of its mythical nature, the novel has a social message. Fuentes himself has said, "The creative process of *Cambia de piel* was born with the intention of documenting all the vulgarity, the excesses, and the impurity of our world."

Cumpleaños (1969) is the first novel by Carlos Fuentes in which the action takes place outside of Mexico. It is also the first that transcends his preoccupation with Mexican history and myth, being based, instead, on European history and myth. However, there are, as in his first novels, both historical and fictitious personages. Also, in *Cumpleaños,* as in previous novels, there is a sacred place, where the theologian, accused of heresy, takes refuge to escape his enemies. This place becomes a bedroom in a contemporary London house, where the old man, Nuncia, and the boy live. Both places merge into one labyrinthine residence symbolic of the universe. In the bedroom, the old man remembers his past life, which extends back to the thirteenth century, since he is the reincarnation of Siger de Brabant, a theologian from the University of Paris persecuted for his ideas by Étienne Tempier and Thomas Aquinas. In the present he is George, an architect in London, husband of Emily and father of Georgie, whose tenth birthday they are celebrating that day. This novel is the least realistic of those written by Carlos Fuentes; yet, even here, there are historical elements in the plot, in the artistic motifs, and in the description of the milieu: books read by the boy (*Treasure Island, Black Beauty,* etc.); realistic descriptions of London; the life story of Siger de Brabant (1235–81/84?), the French philosopher who came into conflict with his colleagues at the University of Paris, was accused of heresy, and fled to Italy, where he built a refuge at Orvieto but was, nevertheless, killed by an insane servant or secretary. He had accepted Averroism in its entirety, which drew the opposition of Albertus Magnus and Aquinas, and the condemnation of Bishop Tempier of Paris in 1270 and 1277. His ideas, especially his rejection of the real distinction between essence and existence, form the theme of *Cumpleaños,* although, here again, irony could very well play a part. The myth of immortality in the novel takes place through ceremony. The pact carried out between successors, from Siger to George, is sealed in blood. The distinguishing mark is a wound on the arm. This ceremony, like all mythical ceremonies, is repeated each time that the reincarnation takes place. The idea of a center or lack of a center as symbolic of order and chaos is also present: "I never imagined that the dinner was to be served in the garden without a roof, in the center of that hexagon that could be an imitation of the patio of the great Romanesque castle of Capodimonte. But Emperor Frederick conceived it as an absolute center; it could be possible to lose oneself in the circular chambers, but finally one would end up in that pivot of the building. Here, on the other hand, nothing can persuade me that the garden, like the whole building, is not eccentric: no one could find the point of its formal equilibrium."

In this passage, ceremony and sacred place come together, giving the novel a mythical tone. As Eliade has said, "Just as profane space is abolished by the symbolism of the Center, which projects any temple, palace, or building into the same central point of mythical space, so any meaningful act performed by archaic man, any real act, i.e., any repetition of an archetypal gesture, suspends duration, abolishes profane time, and participates in mythical time."

In *Cumpleaños,* all traces of Mexican history have disappeared, but the same is not true of *Terra Nostra, The Hydra Head,* and *Una familia lejana. Terra Nostra* deals with the history of Spain during the Renaissance period, but in the second of its three parts, "The New World," the subject is pre-Hispanic Mexican myth and the conquest of the land. By the use of history and myth, Fuentes attempts to apprehend the meaning of the age of Philip II and, therefore, the destiny of the Hispanic people, both in the Old World and in the New World, and even in the other world, also the title of the last part of the novel. As a technique, he superimposes several historical periods, going back to the age of Tiberius and pre-Hispanic Mexico and forward to the end of the century. By this means, he creates a new historical reality, which, although it is purely fictional, is based on empirical fact and real historical personages. The figure of Philip II, however, becomes an archetype, since he is a composite of several Spanish rulers who have exercised absolute power, and it is this obsession with power on the part of Philip II that gives universality to the novel.

Terra Nostra opens with a scene in Paris on a precise day, July 14, 1999, and ends there on the last day of the same year, the end of the millennium. Thus, the entire narrative partakes of the apocalyptic myth. In the second part, Fuentes creates a space in the New World where historical, fictional, and mythical characters act their roles in a purely mythical time. But even here are found the ever-present historical references, presented with the techniques of fiction. "In *Terra Nostra* Hispanic culture is thereby viewed in terms of universal myth and history, for which it becomes the exemplary case." Fuentes, himself, in his long essay "Cervantes o la crítica de la lectura" ("Cervantes, or the Critique of Reading"), has given the key to the historical background that structures the novel. "Surely," he says, "the present essay is a branch of the novel, *Terra Nostra*, that has kept me busy during the last six years. The three dates that constitute the temporal references in the novel can very well serve to establish the historical background of Cervantes and *Don Quijote:* 1492, 1521, 1598." These dates, which appear in the novel's last chapter, are related to both the New World and Philip II. Since the mythical elements are just as important as the historical, the novel becomes a summa that attempts to give the reader a total view of Hispanic culture, a view that only a novel can convey, for as Fuentes has said recently, "Many things history does not see, or reason, logic, science do not see, are perhaps seen by novelists. There are things only Dostoevski sees. You do not find it in the history books." And there are things that only Fuentes has seen.

In the two novels, *The Hydra Head* and *Una familia lejana*, history plays a secondary role to fiction. A current event, the struggle for the control of Mexican oil deposits, is the subject of the first, a detective novel. The protagonist, Félix Maldonado, is patterned after a present-day mythical archetype, James Bond. In *Una familia lejana*, Fuentes tries to establish, in a minor way, the cultural relations between Mexico and France, as he had done with Spain in *Terra Nostra*, but in a more personal way. The protagonist, Mexican archeologist Hugo Heredia, husband of a French girl, Lucie, and father of two sons, Víctor and Antonio, delivers a long, historical essay in the first part of chapter 20. At the same time, the author identifies himself with the protagonist, thus becoming the hero of his own novel. Branly, fictitious friend of the narrator, tells him, "Tomorrow is November 11, Fuentes. It's your birthday." (Fuentes *was* born on that day.) Then, on the last page of the novel, the reader discovers what he had already suspected. The narrator says to himself, "Heredia. You are Heredia."

Mythical elements in this novel, which predominate, are given expression by means of several devices: the association of the characters with the mythical past of Mexico (Lucie as La Llorona); the use of the double (Heredia and "Heredia"); the use of motifs related to Día de los Muertos, which is November 2; and, especially, the use of fiction itself as myth. Mexico is a country, says the narrator, "which has not resigned itself to banish death from the realm of the living." Above all, there is the myth of the cycle life-death-life. The action takes place in November, symbolic of the autumnal period of life when there is a brief pause before death; the title of the last chapter is "Verano de San Martín" ("Indian Summer"). Branly says, "For your other life, Fuentes, for your adjacent life. Think what it could have been and celebrate with me your anniversary and the arrival of Indian Summer with a wine that postpones death and offers us a second vintage." In this novel, Fuentes also treats a topic at the center of his thinking: the past, history, must be preserved, for it is only by knowing the past that the present and the future can be understood. Hugo Heredia has chosen the profession of archeologist in order to preserve the past. "You had a past and you can't remember it. Try to identify it in the little time you have left or you shall lose your future." In a recent interview, Fuentes said that "man is responsible for his history, including the past. He's also responsible for his past. It wasn't made by God, it was made by him. He must understand it. And I think that you can only have a present and a future if you have a past, if you remember your past, if you understand your past. Historical amnesia, I think, leads society to the greatest blunders of not understanding itself and not understanding others."

In general, then, it can be said that the narrative of Carlos Fuentes swerved strongly at the beginning toward the historical, and strongly after

1969 toward the mythical, but never in a pure form. His idea of history, however, is not that of the empirical historian, but goes beyond fact to a reality that includes myth and legend, so important in the shaping of the Mexican mind. Quite often, he fills the lacuna of the historical record with oral history, legend, or myth. His fiction reveals that history itself often becomes myth; and although it is based on a collection of facts, the mythical consciousness of the author is ever present before the facts are verbalized. Certainly, in Mexico, the most famous historians have been mythmakers; their works are composed of fact and fiction, as are novels. This is true from the early chronicles of Bernal Díaz del Castillo, which, in spite of their title, are a combination of fact and myth. The same can be said of works by Fray Servando Teresa de Mier, Vicente Riva Palacio, and José Vasconcelos. Their authors are, more than true historians, true verbal artists, as is Carlos Fuentes, who said to Bill Moyers, "Beyond the knowledge of science, of logic and politics, there is the knowledge we call imagination. And it's only achieved through a verbal structure we call a poem or a novel. This is an important thing to keep alive in order to compensate for many of the voids of history."

"The knowledge we call imagination" is greatly nurtured by myth. And although the employment of myth and history in the same work of fiction, as pointed out by Frye, poses a problem for the novelist, that problem has been solved by Fuentes by the use of displacement, that is, the balancing of history with myth to prevent the novel from becoming a social document, as is common with some of the novels of the revolution, or, on the other hand, from losing verisimilitude. By fusing history and myth in his novels (and the same can be said of his play, *Todos los gatos son pardos* [*All Cats Are Black*]), Fuentes has been able not only to reveal important aspects of the mind and character of the Mexican people, but also to project his own hopes and aspirations, one of which is not to kill the past.

21

JOSÉ A. MONTOYA

José Montoya, poet and artist born in 1932, began to write early in life, but it was not until 1969 that his first poems appeared in print. As reported by Bruce-Novoa in his book *Chicano Authors: Inquiry by Interview,* Montoya met Octavio Romano, the editor of *El Grito,* in 1968 at a Chicano art exhibit in San Francisco. There Romano mentioned that he "had heard that I wrote poetry, and he asked me for some for *El Grito.* He liked it and decided to hold it for *El Espejo,* the anthology. That's how I first got into print. *El Espejo/The Mirror* came out and I started to be known, give readings and all that. But I had been writing for a long time before then."

Montoya has said that mostly American authors have influenced his writing. When he was in the navy, he read *Tortilla Flat,* a novel that left him in anger. But later, while at San Diego City College, he discovered some of Steinbeck's other works and was attracted by his style. The *El Espejo* poems, however, were written under the influence of Walt Whitman. In an interview that Wolfgang Binder included in his book *Partial Autobiographies* (1985), Montoya said that Whitman was the first poet "to show me that you did not have to rhyme and meter, and I really, really liked him." The poem he dedicated to him, "Pobre viejo Walt Whitman" ("Poor Old Walt Whitman"), the first of the nine appearing in *El Espejo* in 1969, was written at a time when Montoya was disillusioned with

First published in *Reference Guide to American Literature,* 3rd ed., ed. Jim Kamp (Detroit: St. James Press, 1994), 613–15.

Whitman the man, and his ideology, and therefore the poem reflects not admiration for Whitman, but "[a] lot of anger, a lot of anger."

At that time, Montoya was also very much attracted by another American poet, William Carlos Williams, whose works he had read at Berkeley. He told Bruce-Novoa: "The one I could relate to most was William Carlos Williams. I liked the way he wrote, so I made an effort to find his work." He also read the poetry of the beat poets, with whom he sympathized. However, he says, "they were so far out that it took the works of Eliot and Pound as well as Whitman and Williams to get me to accept their stuff early on. Now I consider them to have been an influence—especially Snyder and Ginsberg." At that time, he also read French authors, among them Rimbaud, who impressed him by his rebelliousness, and Camus' *The Myth of Sisyphus*, which to him became a symbol for the struggle of the Chicanos. "I thought that the Chicano really knew how to push that rock up there and let it roll down and enjoy the trip. The dealing with the search became, at that time in my life, very real."

Also included in *El Espejo* was one of Montoya's best-known poems, "La Jefita" ("My Mother"; also, literally, "The Little Boss"), in which he re-creates the image of a representative Chicana mother as the master in her own house, striving to keep the household going and the family together. This image is vividly rendered by the use of onomatopoeic verses reflecting the never-ending activities of the hardworking *jefita*. The use of English and Spanish in the same verse, a technique at which Montoya is a master, is quite effective in this poem:

> When I remember the *campos* [fields]
> *Y las noches* [and the nights] and the sounds
> . . . I remember I remember my *jefita's*
> > *Palote* [rolling pin]
> > Click-clok; clak click-clak

In "Los vatos" ("The Dudes"), also appearing in *El Espejo*, Montoya for the first time introduces a pachuco, a popular character in Chicano society of the late 1930s, 1940s, and 1950s, later the subject of his most famous poem, "El Louie." The most striking formal characteristics of the poem "Los vatos" are the longer verse form, the prose introduction ("Back in the early 1950s el Chonito and I were on the way to the *bote* [jail] when we heard the following dialogue"), and the dramatic narrative structure: "Below I sing of an unfortunate act of that epoch."

"El Louie," Montoya's most successful poem, appeared in 1970, a year after "Los vatos," in an obscure Oakland, California, periodical, *Rascatripas,* but it was popularized in 1972 by Antonia Castaneda Shular, Tomás Ybarra-Frausto, and Joseph Sommers in their anthology *Chicano Literature: Text and Context.* Since that year, it has been widely anthologized and analyzed. When Binden asked Montoya, "How can you write about *pachucos,* you were too young?" he replied, "Well, I was not writing about *pachucos.* I was writing about 'Louie', and I was writing about 'Los vatos'." That statement underlines the main characteristic of Montoya's poetry: he writes about what he has experienced. "I can only write what I feel and have lived," he said in the Binder interview. He had known Louie, who was a *vato* from Fowler, California, named Louie Rodríguez.

> *Era de Fowler el vato* [dude]
> *Carnal* [brother] *del Andi y el*
> Ponchi—los Rodríguez
>
> His death was an insult
> *Porque no murió en acción*
> [Because he did not die in action]
>
> Rented room—perhaps like in a
> Bogart movie.
>
> The end was a cruel hoax
> But his life had been
>   Remarkable!
>
> *Vato de atole* [maize drink], *el Louie Rodríguez*

In the late 1960s, Montoya, as a poet, underwent a change. He decided to abandon models offered by Whitman and other learned poets and write in a popular vein, more like the beat poets, making a more extensive use of Spanish and the language of the Chicano people and giving more importance to social issues. The result was the poetry included in his first published book, *El sol y los de abajo* (*The Sun and the Underdogs*), a collection of twenty-four poems (three of them entirely in Spanish). The title poem, in seven parts, is characteristic of the rest of the poems in this collection, in which Montoya re-creates a Chicano world from the perspective of an underdog, a person trying to find a way out of his miserable condition.

Twenty years were to pass before Montoya could collect all the poems he had written and publish them in a single volume, *InFormatioN: Twenty Years of Joda* (1992), a book also containing three portfolios of his own drawings. For the first time, the reader has the opportunity to observe Montoya's development as a poet, since the compositions appear in chronological order according to the date of publication or composition, from 1969 to 1989. Outstanding are those poems in which Montoya gives a voice to the downtrodden, presenting their plight in their own *caló* but without forgetting to express an underlying ray of hope.

The Mexican engraver José Guadalupe Posada as well as the muralists Diego Rivera, José Clemente Orozco, and Alfaro Siqueiros have influenced Montoya as a graphic artist. In 1975, with the collaboration of John M. Carrillo, Montoya wrote an unpublished paper about Posada in which he includes a comparative analysis of his work and that of the Chicano art movement, as well as some notes about the influence of Posada's *calaveras* on Chicano art. In the poems and drawings collected in *InFormatioN*, however, it can be seen that Montoya is not a slavish imitator of the Mexican masters. In the poem "I paint because," he states his desire to innovate when he says:

> I paint because I love Orozco and Shan.
> I paint to destroy Orozco and Shan.

In his paintings, as in his poetry, Montoya's subject matter is drawn from life in the barrio and from the experiences of the Chicano people in their struggle for a better life. His close association with the community has not only inspired him to express with pen and brush the sufferings and aspirations of the people he loves and knows so well, but also to transform this expression into action through his humanitarian service to the community.

The reception of Montoya's poetry and art by the public and critics alike has been favorable. Although his poetic production so far is rather limited, he has been able to impress the critics with his rich depicting of life in the barrio and, especially, with his vindication of the pachuco and his culture, a theme that was to be later adapted to other media (film, theater, novel) by Luis Valdez and others. As Charles M. Tatum says in his reference to *El sol y los de abajo,* Montoya's heroes are "the *vatos locos . . .* who are rejected by many of their own people and harassed by Anglos who do not understand their rebelliousness." Tatum also points out that one of the techniques utilized by Montoya to achieve his aim is the use of humor and satire: "The poet takes a humorously irreverent swipe at different aspects of what he considers to be a society that alienates the individual."

Montoya's best-known composition, the poem "El Louie," has been highly praised by most critics, since they find in it the essence of the personality of the pachuco. Shirley considers it "one of the most famous poems about the zoot-suiter," since its "muted comic tone doesn't undermine the tragedy. . . . Bruce-Novoa calls this work an excellent paradigm of Chicano literature because the poem rescues the dead protagonist from oblivion by preserving his memory." Ignacio Orlando Trujillo, in his extensive study of the linguistic aspects of this poem, observes that "El Louie," along with other poetic works of the 1960s, "is a key composition in the revival of mass interest in Chicano poetry and the resurgence of its writers. Not only has it been anthologized in various collections, but it has also been recited and dramatized because of its popular oral and visual quality." "El Louie" is not, of course, the only poem by Montoya worthy of study; that it has attracted the attention of the critics is due, perhaps, to its subject matter, the life of a pachuco, as well as the masterfully integrated use of the two languages, English and Spanish.

"El Louie" and the rest of the poetic and artistic works of José Montoya are representative of the nature of Chicano literature and art that emerged during the first decade of the Chicano renaissance (1965–75). Montoya, as other writers and artists of that period, was both a man of letters and an activist. His main interest was to place art and literature at the service of the people. For him, the function of art is social, and therefore it should be used to help the people and to vindicate their history and their cultural values. In this sense, it is very much like the art and literature that appeared in Mexico as an aftermath of the revolution. Montoya, along with Alurista, Rodolfo "Corky" Gonzales, Sergio Elizondo, Ricardo Sánchez, Luis Omar Salinas, and others, formed part of a group of writers that pioneered the renaissance of Chicano poetry. Their contributions to Chicano culture constitute a high point in the development of Chicano intellectual and artistic life during that most important decade.

22

TOMÁS RIVERA

Besides his public life as an administrator of the University of California, Riverside, Tomás Rivera was well known in literary circles as a writer of prose and poetry. Although he published only two books and some scattered poems, short stories, and literary essays and left parts of an unpublished second novel, he was able to influence greatly the trend that Chicano literature was to take during the 1970s and into the 1980s. His most important work, . . . *Y no se lo tragó la tierra* (. . . *And the Earth Did Not Part*), a novel composed of short narratives, was awarded the Premio Quinto Sol in 1970 and published in 1971. Critics have praised the novel for its original structure, its terse style, and its faithful presentation of life among Chicano migrant workers. Less well known is his collection *Always and Other Poems* (1973), in which there is the same faith in the future of the Chicano community.

Born in 1935 in Crystal City, Texas, the son of Florencio Rivera and Josefa Hernández, Rivera spoke Spanish at home since both his parents had emigrated from Mexico to Texas. His father had come to El Paso from the central state of Aguascalientes at the age of fifteen. He migrated to the Midwest, where he had several jobs, mostly on the railroad. On his way back to Mexico during the Depression, he stopped in

First published in *Dictionary of Literary Biography: Chicano Writers,* vol. 82, 1st ser., ed. Francisco A. Lomelí and Carl R. Shirley (Detroit: A Bruccoli Clark Layman Book, Gale Research, 1989: 206–13.

Crystal City, where he met his future wife, whom he married there in 1930. As a young woman she had come to Texas with her family from the state of Coahuila and had lived in several cities in Texas. Her father had been an officer during the Mexican Revolution.

Before attending public school in his hometown, Rivera learned to read and write Spanish in the barrio school. Although his family had to travel yearly to the Midwest to work in the fields, he was able to graduate from high school. However, in order for him to be able to continue his studies at Southwest Texas Junior College, Rivera's parents let him work only three months so that he could come home in September. As he told Juan Bruce-Novoa in a 1980 interview, "My parents were still working in Iowa, but I would only work three months and then I had to return to complete the year at the college."

From junior college Rivera went on to Southwest Texas State University, where he majored in English and received a B.A. degree in 1958. That same year he began to teach art in elementary schools. He married Concepción Garza in the late 1950s. He also continued his studies at Southwest Texas State, where he received an M.Ed. in administration in 1964. In 1969, Rivera earned an M.A. in Spanish literature and a Ph.D. in romance languages and literature from the University of Oklahoma. At Oklahoma, he specialized in Spanish literature and for his dissertation wrote about León Felipe, a Spanish poet who lived in exile in Mexico from the end of the Spanish civil war in 1939 until his death in 1954. In 1967, Rivera's poem "Me lo enterraron" ("They Buried Him"), in which he remembered the death of his father in 1959, was published. Immediately after receiving his doctorate from Oklahoma, Rivera returned to Texas to accept a position at Sam Houston University, in Huntsville, where he remained until 1971.

Rivera moved to the University of Texas, San Antonio, as a professor of Spanish in 1971. Two years later he was appointed dean, and in 1976 he was appointed vice chancellor for administration. He discovered that he could benefit the Chicano people more as a university administrator than as a professor. It was for that reason that Rivera later accepted the position of executive vice president of academic affairs at the University of Texas, El Paso. In 1979, he was appointed chancellor at the University of California, Riverside, where he remained until his death in 1984. In a special issue of *Revista Chicano-Riqueña* dedicated to Rivera (Fall–Winter 1985), Rolando Hinojosa-Smith said that perhaps too much has been made of the fact that Rivera was the first Mexican American to serve as chancellor in the University of California system. "It's a fact and undeniable, and it may also be a reflection upon the State of California. But look at these facts: Tomás Rivera won his Ph.D. from the University of Oklahoma in 1969, and he was named Chancellor less than ten years later. Now *that* was an accomplishment."

Rivera's administrative ability and his great concern for the educational problems of students earned him several honors. He was named, in 1976, a member of the board of the Carnegie Foundation for the Advancement of Teaching; he received a presidential appointment to the Board of Foreign Scholarships (which directs and administers the Fulbright program); and he was named member of the board of the National Chicano Council on Higher Education. In 1980, he served on the presidential commission established with the purpose of identifying the educational problems that the nation was to face during the 1980s. He was also a corporate officer of the Times-Mirror Corporation and a member of the board of directors of the Ford Foundation.

Rivera's success as a writer and administrator was due to his personal qualities. He had a great reserve of physical energy, a well-defined objective in life, and an unusual sense of human and social values. Most important, he was unfailingly optimistic. His poem "The Searchers" reveals his hopeful sentiments:

> We were not alone
> after many centuries
> How could we be alone
> We searched together
> We were searchers
> And we will continue
> to search
> because our eyes

still have

the passion of prophesy.

Hinojosa-Smith observed that "a careful reading of 'The Searchers' will illustrate those strong, enduring human values which he [Rivera] possessed and which all of us admire, if not exactly follow and set for ourselves."

Rivera's desire to write came from the advice of his maternal grandfather, who told him that writing and art were the most important things in life. Although he wrote stories and poems, Rivera did not publish any until the late 1960s, when they began to appear in Chicano periodicals. In 1969, the editors of a Berkeley, California, periodical, *El Grito*, decided to establish an editorial house—which they called Quinto Sol Publications —and to offer prizes to the best works submitted by Chicano writers. Rivera had not published some of his early poems and stories because, as he told Burt A. Folkart in the *Los Angeles Times* (May 17, 1984), they were written in English, and he felt they did not reach into his subconscious. "But when I learned that Quinto Sol accepted manuscripts in Spanish, it liberated me. I knew that I could express myself as I wanted." He completed . . . *Y no se lo tragó la tierra* and sent it to Quinto Sol. The novel received the first prize in 1970. It was translated into English by Herminio Ríos C. and published in a bilingual edition in 1971.

Rivera's essay "Chicano Literature: Fiesta of the Living" (1979) is preceded by a quotation from Octavio Paz's book *The Labyrinth of Solitude*, which reads, "Every poem we read is a recreation, that is, a ceremonial ritual, a fiesta." Rivera's essay focuses on Chicano literature "as a ritual, a fiesta of the living." For him the most important characteristic of Chicano literature is the striving on the part of the writer to conserve past experiences, real or imagined, in "a ritual of cleansing and a prophecy." The ritual of remembering is based on two common images, the house and the barrio, and on the concept of struggle. With the three elements Rivera presents a unique view of the Chicano world: "The ritual is simple yet complex. The bond is there and so is the cleansing, both for the Chicano writer and for his reader. These effects of the ritual are produced through simple forms as *la casa* and *el barrio* and by the transgressive and ingressive concept of *la lucha*," or struggle. It is relatively easy to find examples of the narrative technique of remembering in Rivera's work. In "Me lo enterraron," the speaker establishes the relationship between dead father and living son by remembering recurrent, and therefore ritual, actions carried out by the father. The poem is structured around the assumption that the persons who buried the father did not know about the intimate relationship that had existed between father and son, while the son did and could therefore remember:

> They did not know
> that he taught me
> how to cry
> and how to love

> They did not know it
>   that is why
> they buried him.

The boy regrets his father's death; the burial is a ritual action that he wanted to prevent, but could not:

> Not I, they
> they buried him.

> I refused to do it
> I didn't bury him.

In the issue of the journal *El Grito* that appeared during the fall of 1969, Rivera published, besides "Me lo enterraron," six other poems. One of them is "The Rooster Crows en Iowa y en Texas," a composition that can be traced to the days when, with his family, the author was a migrant worker making the yearly journey from southern Texas to the Midwest during the early summer and returning in the fall. In an article in *Atisbos: Journal of Chicano Research* (1975), he remembered that during those days,

There was always someone who knew the old traditional stories "el gigante moro," "el negrito guerin," etc. Then there were always those who acted out movies, told about different parts of the world and about Aladdin and his magic lamp. An oral literature was, in that way, developed in migrant camps. People find refuge not only in the Church or with their brothers but also by sitting in a circle, listening, telling stories and, through words, escaping to other worlds as well as inventing them. It was natural that a type of narrative world developed in the children and worlds were crystallized because of the tedium of every-day work.

He did not forget those stories, and in his fiction, as well as in his poetry, Rivera makes reference to them.

> The rooster crows.
> The alarm rings.
> They eat and go to work.
> "Aladín y su lámpara maravillosa."
> The snow falls.
> The truck runs full of people.
> And we return . . . . home.

The use of English and Spanish in this poem places the composition in the popular trend of the late 1960s among Chicano poets, who tried to create a new means of expression by combining the two languages, thus reflecting more accurately a Chicano vision of the world. The use of motifs common among the rural people, in this case the rooster, was also common at that time. In Rivera's poem, the rooster symbolizes the monotony of life in the fields, where the only entertainment is the telling of stories around the bonfire after the day is done.

In Rivera's collection *Always and Other Poems,* there is a brief poem, "Past Possessions," which is significant for the simplicity with which the poetic voice remembers and gives expression to childhood days through the listing of toys associated with a boy in the barrio or rural environment:

A piece
of string
A broken top
A crooked kite
A wooden gun
A mop ...
Quiet ... noise
A long thin weed a lance
A few large cans a dance
Boxes
For cars and houses
Such trivial things.

The poem "The Overalls," which again makes use of a common image, expresses the void and the emptiness felt as a result of the death of a member of the family and, at the same time, shows how the experience of remembering the ritual of the burial leads to personal discovery:

Frightening
as the attic hole
the overalls in the garage, hanging and the vapor from the train
swung to my face
as the cross that
shouted the lump
in the cemetery
and the sounds of clods
of earth hitting the coffin reminded me of something
I knew nothing about
the glancing of tearful eyes embracing
as I sensed
that I had been born
the crushing vapor
and the overalls, hanging
in the garage,
never to be filled again.

Rivera best succeeds in giving form to the life of migrant workers in his novel . . . *Y no se lo tragó la tierra*. As he told Bruce-Novoa:

> In *tierra* and those stories, I wrote about the migrant worker in that period of ten years [1945–55]. During that period I became very conscious, in my own life, about the suffering and the strength and the beauty of these people. I was more conscious of their strength when I was living with them. Later, 1967–68, I'm writing. The Chicano Movement was a complete power already in the university and so forth. I wanted to document, somehow, the strength of those people that I had known. And I was only concerned about the migrant worker, the people I had known best. . . . So I began to see that my role—if I want to call it that—would be to document that period of time, but giving it some kind of spiritual strength or spiritual history. Not just this and this happened, but to give a spiritual dimension to the people of that time. I see my role more as a chronicler of that period of time when the migrant worker was living without any kind of protection. There was no legal protection, and without legal protection, there is nothing. I saw a lot of suffering and much isolation of the people. Yet they lived through the whole thing, perhaps because they had no choice. I saw a lot of heroic people and I wanted to capture their feelings.

In the novel, Rivera exalts the values of the Chicano family (*la casa*), the community (*el barrio*), and the struggle to obtain justice. As he said in his *Atisbos* article, "the political and economic structures which surrounded the lives of these families will always appear in history as something brutal, outrageous and inhuman. . . . Migrant workers still exist today [1975], but in fewer numbers and now have some protection by the law. But, in the long run, the migrant worker was and always will be exploited." In the novel he tries to re-create those conditions under which the migrant worker was living during the 1940s and 1950s, and this is what gives the work a sense of tragedy, found especially in such episodes as "The Children Were Victims," "Little Children Burned," and "When We Arrive." What saved the Chicano from being dehumanized was, according to Rivera, his relationship with his own people, with the land he cultivated, and his rejection of the system that exploited him, since he realized that the system did not offer any rewards "for acting human or for loving his neighbor unselfishly. This is the type of character I tried to portray in my novel."

The Chicano novel published before the 1970s was, as a rule, a work of social protest or based upon personal experiences somewhat fictionalized. No attempt was made to present the realistic materials in an innovative form. Rivera, following the example of previous Chicano novelists, develops in . . . *Y no se lo tragó la tierra* the theme of social protest, but, unlike his precursors and following in the steps of contemporary Mexican and Latin American novelists, he uses a fragmented structure. At the same time, the action is observed from a limited point of view, that of a young boy who does not completely understand the meaning of what he observes.

The technique of remembering used by Rivera is best exemplified in the last chapter of the novel, titled "Under the House," where the boy hides and remembers. Rhetorically, the ritual of remembering on the part of the boy under the house serves to recapitulate and give structural unity to the episodes that form the novel, the experiences that have been remembered in the previous twelve central chapters, symbolic of the twelve months of the year. The boy thinks, "I needed to isolate myself in order to understand many things. From here on all I have to do is come back here in the dark and think about them. And I have so much to think about, and so many years to catch up on. I think that today I wanted to remember this past year. But that's just one year. I'll have to come here to remember all the others." The fragmented structure of Rivera's novel has led some critics (Daniel P. Testa and Juan Rodríguez, for example) to consider the work as a collection of short stories, yet there are unifying elements. A frame unites the stories. Short introductions to each chapter function to set the mood for the story that follows. For example, "The Prayer," in which the mother implores the Virgin Mary to protect her son who is fighting in Korea, is preceded by an anecdote about a visit by several mothers to a medium to find out the fate of their sons in Korea, some of whom have been lost in action. Interrelated motifs make . . . *Y no se lo tragó la tierra* an organic work composed of integrated stories preceded by related anecdotes or comments and framed by encompassing chapters at the beginning and the end.

The criticism of Rivera's work has been extensive and very favorable. Most of it, however, deals with his novel. Herminio Ríos C., who translated the work in 1971, places ... *Y no se lo tragó la tierra* in a historical context and says that the novel "reflects the multiple experiences of the Mexican-American and explores a multiplicity of Mexican-American themes." Rivera's work is examined from different perspectives in the special issue of *Revista Chicano-Riqueña* dedicated to him. His narrative techniques have been studied by Lauro Flores (the discourse of silence), myself (the ritual of remembering), and Eliud Martínez (Rivera as witness and storyteller). The use of language and dialogue is examined by Nicolas Kanellos, while Julián Olivares traces the characters' search for identities. All this is complemented by Patricia de la Fuente's study of the presence of women in Rivera's narrative and Sylvia S. Lizarraga's thematic study of patriarchal ideology in one of the chapters of Rivera's unpublished novel, *La noche que se apagaron las luces* (*The Night of the Blackout*). Other critics have undertaken comparative studies of ... *Y no se lo tragó la tierra*. Representative of this critical method is the study of Erlinda Gonzales-Berry and Tey Diana Rebolledo, who compare the novel to Sandra Cisneros's *The House on Mango Street* (1983), from the perspective of growing up Chicano. John C. Akers includes ... *Y no se lo tragó la tierra* in a study of fragmentation in the Chicano novel.

Rivera transcended the political. He had a deep sympathy and respect for humanity, especially for the migrant workers from whom he drew his inspiration to write and to work building a better society in the Americas. As he told Bruce-Novoa, "To me they [the migrant workers] were people who searched, and that's an important metaphor in the Americas. . . . I hope I can also be a searcher." His search, unfortunately, ended with his early death. His life has been commemorated in many ways. The main library at the University of California, Riverside, now bears his name, as does the Tomás Rivera Center at Claremont, California, and the elementary school that he first attended in Crystal City, Texas. The University of California, Riverside, has established the

Rivera Archives in order to preserve and make available to researchers his papers as a writer and an administrator.

Rivera would have been honored by the poem that a native of his hometown in Texas, Isidra H. Ríos, read during the ceremony when Airport Elementary School was named the Dr. Tomás Rivera Elementary School, which says in part:

> *En las escuelas del pueblo*
> *él estudió desde niño*
> *por eso lo recordamos*
> *lo hacemos con gran cariño.*

> In the schools of this town
> he studied as a boy
> that's why we remember him
> we remember him with love.

Rivera died in 1984, at the age of fifty-four.

23

AMÉRICO PAREDES

It is indeed an honor for me to have been invited by Professor Joseph Nagy to participate in this conference dedicated to Don Américo, which gives us an opportunity to remember his *ricas contribuciones* not only to the study of Chicano-*mexicano* folklore, but to a number of related anthropological fields, from both theoretical and historical perspectives. I had the good fortune of having met Américo Paredes in Austin during the summer of 1963, on the occasion of the annual meeting of the Instituto Internacional de Literatura Iberoamericana. It was there that I first heard him play the guitar and sing corridos and traditional Mexican songs. I had the pleasure of hearing him again in Urbana, Illinois, where he published his *Texas-Mexican Cancionero: Folksongs of the Lower Border*. In 1987, I had the honor of delivering the first presentation at the Américo Paredes Distinguished Lecture Series at the University of Texas in Austin. It is for these reasons that I am very pleased to participate in this conference today.

In this paper, I limit myself to the study of Américo Paredes's evaluation of former Chicano folklore research and end with his own contributions, which represent the culmination of studies in this field. It is often stated that Chicano folklore studies are of very recent origin. Naturally,

A paper presented June 8, 2000, at the conference dedicated to Américo Paredes held at the University of California in Los Angeles. First published in *Western Folklore* 64, nos. 1 and 2 (2005): 83–92.

we cannot talk about the history of such studies if that history has not been written. For instance, as of today, we have very little information regarding the contributions of early Chicano scholars, with the exception of those by Professor Aurelio Macedonio Espinosa and his contemporaries.

I will briefly explore the accomplishments of those early scholars, not with the idea of establishing the roots of Chicano folklore scholarship, but only to document the state of Chicano folklore studies before 1942, the year Dr. Paredes published in the *Southwest Review* his first article, "The Mexico-Texan Corrido." Then I will end by enumerating the contributions that he made to a new type of folklore scholarship. I will not mention his contributions to other fields, since I have done that already in an earlier study. By *Chicano folklore scholarship*, I mean the research carried out by scholars of Mexican descent living or having lived in the United States any time after 1848. As far as 1 know, no effort has been made to write the history of their contributions, although there are studies about individual scholars. The earliest Chicano folklorists were not so much scholars as they were aficionados interested in preserving the history of the Mexican American people. Unfortunately, their efforts have remained in the form of manuscripts. Most of them are kept in the libraries of the Southwest, among them Bancroft Library in Berkeley, California; the University of Texas Library at Austin; the University of New Mexico Library at Albuquerque; and others.

It is for this reason that we must consider Aurelio Macedonio Espinosa as the founder of modern Mexican American folklore studies. He opened two new fields of investigation, linguistics and folklore, both essential to the humanistic study of Chicano culture. Espinosa began by studying the folklore of New Mexico and then went on to include that of Spain and California. His Hispanist theory of the origin of Mexican American culture is well known, as is its rejection by Américo Paredes. Espinosa's great contribution is not to be found in his theoretical assumptions, but in the fact that he was the first professional scholar who dedicated his whole life to the study of folklore among residents of Mexican origin in the Southwest. His studies of the folktale, the *romance*, and the *décima* are still consulted today. He is also remembered for the discovery of important manuscripts, such as the popular plays *Los comanches* (1907) and *The Texans* (1943). No less important are his teaching and his training of a number of students to continue his work, among them Arthur Campa, Juan B. Rael, and his own son, José Manuel Espinosa. Américo Paredes, in the introduction to his book *Folktales of Mexico,* states that Espinosa's study, "New-Mexican Spanish Folklore," which appeared in the *Journal of American Folklore* in 1910–11, represents "the first truly scholarly work on Mexican folklore" and is "the first real collection of Mexican folk narrative." Although Espinosa's book *Cuentos populares españoles* (*Spanish Folktales*) is a collection of folktales from Spain, "the notes accompanying them," as stated by Paredes, "are a standard reference for the folktale in Latin America."

Aurelio Espinosa published his most important work during the first two decades of the twentieth century, which he dominated as a scholar. There were, during the 1920s, however, other researchers that followed Espinosa's example. Among them, in Texas, Jovita González, whose studies appeared in the annuals of the Texas Folklore Society. Américo Paredes tells us that she was "one of the first Mexican-Americans to write in English about her own culture."

During the 1930s, the work of Espinosa was continued by his son José Manuel, whose collection of 114 Mexican folktales from the southwestern United States, which appeared in 1937, was considered by Américo Paredes as "a scholarly and well documented work." This collection was surpassed only by one of his father's own students, Juan B. Rael, whose book *Cuentos españoles de Colorado y Nuevo Méjico* (*Spanish Stories from Colorado and New Mexico*), was considered by Paredes as "the best collection of Mexican folk narrative published to date."

In 1930, Arthur Campa opened a new field in Chicano folklore studies with his pioneer book *A Bibliography of Spanish Folklore in New Mexico.* He continued to do extensive research during the 1940s and published studies dealing with several aspects of popular literature in New Mexico. In 1946, he published *Spanish Folk-Poetry in New Mexico* and included several chapters on folklore in *Hispanic Culture in the Southwest,* which appeared in 1979, although it had been in press in 1978, the year of Campa's death.

Chicano scholarship began to diversify in the 1950s. Scholars interested in other fields besides folklore began to appear, especially in the political sciences, anthropology, sociology, literature, and the arts. To this generation belongs Américo Paredes. Although he had published three articles before 1958, it was that year that his seminal book *With His Pistol in His Hand* appeared. With this and subsequent studies, Paredes created a new Chicano folklore scholarship. The main characteristics of this new scholarship can be summarized as follows: foremost, by his special way of carrying out research, which combines the scientific method with a humanistic approach. In his introduction to the book *The Urban Experience and Folk Tradition*, a collection of essays by several authors that he edited in collaboration with Ellen Stekert, Paredes states that some field-workers suffer from a communication problem, which becomes worse in situations "where the informant's basic personality and innermost values are framed on the basis of a language other than English." The researcher never bothers to find out how the informant feels about the result of the investigation. Paredes adds, "When the field worker is attempting to generalize on such matters as values, worldview, and unconscious motivations, it's critical for him to know whether he has really communicated or not." This preoccupation with the informant, whose feelings, ideas, and values must be respected, gives uniqueness to Don Américo's contributions. Young Chicano scholars have incorporated this legacy into their methodologies.

In addition, folklore research must be carried out in a historical or social context, keeping in mind the nature of the group or community being studied. In his own research, Paredes took this approach, thus becoming a pioneer in cultural studies. In this respect, he was inspired by Dan Ben-Amos's ideas as expressed in his article "Towards a Definition of Folklore in Context," which Paredes often quotes. In the introduction to the book *Towards New Perspectives in Folklore*, which Don Américo edited in 1972, he says that folklore is "an organic phenomenon in the sense that it's an integral part of culture. Any divorce of tales, songs, or sculptures from their indigenous locale, time, and society inevitably introduces qualitative changes into them."

Complementing Paredes's coherent new folklore scholarship is his insisting upon keeping in mind the importance of border areas. He set an example of this awareness in many of his studies, a fact that was observed by his colleagues Richard Bauman and Roger D. Abrahams, who said, "In Américo Paredes's work recognition of the generative power of borders and other contact zones assumes really central importance." Recognition of this generative power of borders is already present in Paredes's first book, *With His Pistol in His Hand*, and reappears in his *A Texas-Mexican "Cancionero": Folksongs of the Lower Border* (1976). The first one is not only the story of a ballad and its hero, but also a history of the border region, of the people who produced the ballad, and of the hero, Gregorio Cortez. We do not know if Paredes was influenced by the life of another Southwest popular hero, Billy the Kid, as written by an early Mexican American, Miguel Antonio Otero Jr. (1859–1944), first Hispanic governor of the territory of New Mexico (1897–1907), who in 1936 published a book entitled *The Real Billy the Kid*. John-Michael Rivera reprinted this rare book in 1998, with an introduction. This work is of interest because Otero relates the life of the Kid in a social and cultural context, just like Paredes would have done. In his introduction, the young Chicano critic Michael Rivera states that "Otero's recreation of the life and history of Billy the Kid not only reexamines and exposes the colonial past of New Mexico, it also deflates and undermines the dominant Anglo American Western narratives about Billy the Kid that helped shape the popular imagination of America as being only Anglo-American in culture and history." And this is precisely what Paredes did in *With His Pistol in His Hand*. I mention this work as an example of what kind of research is still to be accomplished in order to write the history of Chicano folklore scholarship.

In 1964, Dr. Paredes published in Spanish in the periodical *Folklore Americano* (Lima, Peru), the study "El folklore de los grupos de origen mexicano en Estados Unidos" ("Folklore Among People of Mexican Origin in the United States"), which was translated into English by Kathleen Lamb and published by Joseph Sommers in 1979 under the title "The Folk Base of Chicano Literature." This seminal study was reprinted in Paredes's 1993 collection of articles, *Folklore and Culture on the Texas-Mexican Border*, as the leading article under the title "The Folklore of Groups of Mexican Origin in the United States," thus restoring the original Spanish title, although the date of publication given is that of Sommers's book, 1979, and not that of the original Spanish version, 1964. It is in this article that Paredes first puts to rest both forms of the Hispanist interpretation of folklore. The first form, the extreme form, considers Mexican American folklore superior to Mexican folklore, since it came directly from Spain. The less extreme view, which relies on chronology, is considered inferior by the Hispanists, since it "is mixed with indigenous elements which have diluted its grace and elegance." Unfortunately, Paredes laments, this latter form has influenced serious scholars like Espinosa, about whom Paredes says: "The renowned scholar Aurelio M. Espinosa, for instance, made admirable discoveries of remnants of Spanish folklore in the Southwestern United States, but in general he was rarely concerned with the purely Mexican elements, which were decidedly in the majority. . . . Among his materials were Mexican corridos of very recent creation, like 'De Ignacio Parra,' yet he did not recognize them as Mexican because he was convinced of the purely Hispanic character of New Mexico folklore. His prestige, in fact, made a sort of dogma of the supposed peninsular origin of New Mexican folklore."

Don Américo, being an honest scholar, gives credit to Arthur L. Campa for having first demythified this Hispanist theory. He wrote in the same study: "When in 1933 Arthur L. Campa affirmed its basically Mexican character, his observations seemed almost revolutionary, though they merely indicated what was evident to those who wished to see."

Not satisfied with having rejected the direct Spanish origin of Southwest Hispanic folklore, Paredes goes farther and rejects the myth of the Spanish nature of the people itself. In his second book, *A Texas-Mexican "Cancionero": Folksongs of the Lower Border*, he rejects the pure Castilian origins of the early inhabitants of the Southwest and concludes by reaffirming his mestizo theory: "The Spanish-speaking people in the United States whose ancestors came from what is now the Republic of Mexico are all one people, as far as any people may claim to be a single whole. Their origins, from the very beginning, were anything but pure Castilian. . . . Genetically, we are mestizos; culturally, we belong to a generalized Mexican culture."

In 1971, he was to return to this topic in his study "Mexican Legendry and the Rise of the Mestizo." After disposing of the Hispanist theory, Paredes goes on to tackle Vicente T. Mendoza's diffusionist theory, a theory based on the idea that the Chicano folklore of the Southwest was brought here by immigrants from Michoacán. This theory, Paredes observed, is the opposite of the Hispanist, since it considers Chicano folk "the detritus of Mexican folklore, without any originality. It may consist of a few variants of texts well-known in Mexico, variants that would serve as footnotes to Mexican folklore." Paredes rejects this theory by pointing out that the earliest modern corrido mentioned by Mendoza is "The Corrido of Kiansis," definitely a product of the Southwest. In his *Cancionero,* Paredes observes that this corrido "is the oldest Texas-Mexican corrido that we have in complete form." We now know about the existence of earlier complete corridos produced in northern Mexico, one of them being "El corrido de Leandro Rivera," from Rayones, Nuevo León, which dates from 1841.

The third theory applied to the interpretation of Chicano folklore, the regionalist theory, used mostly by non-Chicano folklorists, Dr. Paredes easily discards by arguing that other ethnic groups are cut off from their roots, while there is a constant exchange "between endemic Mexican folklore and that of the México de Afuera, a continuous mutual influence moving in both directions, which is not typical of other regional cultures in the United States. This is the result of a simple geographical fact: the Atlantic Ocean divides Pennsylvania from Germany, and Louisiana from France, but only an imaginary line divides México de Adentro (Mexico as a territorial unit) from México de Afuera. The line is easy to cross, legally or illegally."

Although Don Américo conceded that "none of the three ways of seeing Mexican American folklore is entirely wrong," he did propose his own theory. He argued that the corrido, the popular legend, and other narrative forms were the result of cultural conflict. In his 1964 study, he says that his intention was "not only to present a rapid overview of the genesis and development of Mexican American folklore but to demonstrate the importance of cultural conflict in its formation." What led him to search for a new theory to look at Chicano folklore was the fact that the three in existence did not explain its nature satisfactorily, especially, as already said in this study, its historical and social contexts. For him, history and folklore are intimately related. In his article "Folklore e historia: Dos cantares de la frontera del norte" ("Folklore and History: Two Songs of the U.S.–Mexico Border"), he states that historians need to be versed in folklore, which can be useful to them. At the same time, folklorists must know history, for it is essential that research be historically oriented. Speaking about his own studies, he said, "Much of my work has been on culture conflict, and one way of expressing such conflict is by moral judgments about the other side."

This new Chicano folklore scholarship, the bases of which were laid by Américo Paredes, is also characterized by a desire on the part of scholars to correct erroneous interpretations of the Chicano experience arrived at by those who apply theories that do not take into account the psychology and values of the Chicano, due perhaps to the fact that they are superficially acquainted with Chicano culture and language.

In his essay "On Ethnographic Work Among Minority Groups: A Folklorist's Perspective," Don Américo examines this problem thoroughly, taking into consideration the objections and criticisms that more recent Chicano scholars have made against the studies of certain non-Chicano anthropologists. On the basis of those objections, he set forth a methodology that has had a significant impact on young Chicano folklorists. In the first place, he observed, techniques must be changed when moving from the study of rural groups to that of urban societies, especially ethnic groups. "Sampling techniques used for Chicano groups," he pointed out, "have often been modeled on those used for 'simple' societies, without regard to the fact that Chicanos, as Americans, are part of the varied fabric of modern life." In the same essay, which we consider to be one of the most important ever written by a Chicano scholar, Américo Paredes touches upon the complex problem of objectivity. Anthropologists, and therefore folklorists, are trained to be objective. Such efforts, according to Don Américo, "have led towards a greater and greater tendency to make of anthropology a computerized science, to think of raw anthropological data in terms of mathematical formulas." This is unfortunate because that method ignores human interaction, which is a key concept in Américo Paredes's method and a prime legacy for young scholars. Human interaction is essential if the researcher wants to apply the performance-oriented approach, where the informant is considered "not only as a more-or-less representative member of a group but as a potential artist, and an individual person as well, with interests and goals of his own."

Related to the problem of objectivity is the problem of what Don Américo calls "expected behavior" in contrast to observed behavior. Expected behavior, according to him, is often embodied in stereotypes. Since it is easy to fall into this stereotype trap, the scholar must be constantly on the alert to avoid it. This warning is, without question, one of Américo Paredes's most important contributions to the new scholarship, for he perceives reality as neither subjective nor objective, but as an interaction between the two.

The numerous publications of Don Américo have inspired young Chicano scholars to continue doing high-quality research in the field of Mexican American folklore. His legacy has been especially fruitful not only in folklore, the area to which he dedicated his life, but also in related fields. Historians have learned from him the value of folklore studies; critics of literature have learned from him the value of popular literature, such as the corrido, the *décima,* and the folktale. His book *With His Pistol in His Hand* has served since its publication as a model for the study of a poem in its historical and social contexts. His *Texas-Mexican "Cancionero"* has served as a model for the type of research that takes into consideration a humane approach to the study of the artistic productions of a social group.

Américo Paredes deserves the highest honor, for he dedicated his life to the study of the popular culture of his own people, who for too long had been deprived of a voice to make known its human and aesthetic values. They could not have found a better voice than that of Don Américo Paredes, whose academic activities did not separate him from his roots. He was a man worthy of the greatest tributes that his colleagues, students, and followers could offer him. As Teresa McKenna said of Don Américo in the special issue of *Aztlán* dedicated to him that she edited in 1982: "In the needs of our daily lives we are linked to the greater struggle of the survival of our community. That we can accomplish this struggle in an academic setting is his personal legacy."

24

ROLANDO HINOJOSA-SMITH

I wish to thank David Montejano for his invitation to participate in this important *homenaje* dedicated to Rolando Hinojosa-Smith, a friend of many years, that is, since the early 1960s, when he came to the Spanish Department at the University of Illinois, Urbana-Champaign, to work for his doctorate. Since that time we have kept in touch with each other as friends and colleagues. And, since that time, he has become a respected professor, a dedicated scholar, and a prolific and renowned writer. So, it is a great honor for me to be here today to express my respect and admiration on the occasion of his *homenaje*.

The task of speaking about Rolando is facilitated by the numerous references, in his own essays and interviews, about himself, his family, and the community where he was born and grew up, the lower Rio Grande region, especially that space known as the valley, to which he has dedicated all his novels.

Hinojosa-Smith, we know, is the descendant of a Mexican family who has resided in the valley since the eighteenth century. He traces the origin of his forebears to a family that came, with the explorer and settler José de Escandón, to a place that he considers to be his place. Between 1746 and 1755, Escandón explored what today is the Mexican state of Tamaulipas and the region between the rivers Nueces and Grande, or Bravo. Most of the towns and communities he founded have

Speech delivered at the University of Texas at Austin, February 21, 1997.

kept the names he gave them. In his novels, Rolando has documented extremely well life in the valley, providing it with a metahistory.

In the lecture presented to the Texas Library Association at the Convention held in San Antonio in April 1983, Hinojosa-Smith asked himself the question, "What do I write about?" and gave the following answer: "I write about what I assume other writers write about: that which they know. I happen to know something about people and about how some of us are. I happen to know some history about the Valley, the county, the state."

In the same lecture, he referred to "a place called Belken County, of which I'm the sole owner and proprietor, as Faulkner once said when he spoke of his county." Although fictitious, the history of the county and its people, in his novels, is based on empirical facts recollected from oral accounts, written documents, and the history of his own family, as the history of the people of the valley is the history of his own people. For himself and his family, "history began in 1749 when the first colonists began moving into the southern and northern banks of the Río Grande." By the time the Americans had taken possession of the valley, "the border had its own history, its own culture, and its own sense of place: it was Nuevo Santander, named for old Santander in the Spanish Peninsula." In his essay "The Sense of Place," published in 1983, he tells us that that year marks the one-hundredth anniversary of the birth of his father, Manuel Guzmán Hinojosa, "born in the Campacuás Ranch, some three miles north of Mercedes, down the Valley." The border is, therefore, Hinojosa-Smith's space, and, more precisely, that space along the Rio Grande known as the valley.

Born in the valley, in Mercedes, he was nurtured and educated there in both Mexican and American schools, where one language supplanted the other for a while, but they eventually balanced each other out. As a result of that education he developed an awareness of differences and similarities among people. Most important, the personal voice he developed became his public voice.

That process began at age fifteen, in high school, when he contributed with his first writing to the annual literary event called *Creative Bits*. Among the principal activities that prepared him to become a well-tempered writer were his two years in the army after graduating from high school; his service in Korea during the early 1950s as an officer, and then in the Caribbean as director of the army's newspaper; his studies at the University of Texas; and his teaching in the Browns-ville high schools.

His first paid publication, however, did not appear until 1972. The years in between were not lost years; on the contrary, his varied activi-ties prepared him very well to become the writer we admire and honor today.

Rolando's life in the valley was interrupted for a second time in 1960, when he left the state to go to New Mexico to study for a master's degree at Highlands University. It was there that he met Professor Ralph McWilliams, who had been my fellow student at the University of Chicago. As Rolando said, "And so, to my good fortune at the advice of Ralph McWilliams, a mutual friend, I enrolled at Illinois, and this formed the basis of our friendship." That friendship developed through home visits, scheduled monthly literary discussions, and coffee *tertulias* at the Vatican—our name for the Newman Club cafeteria on campus. I remember that during his third year as a teaching assistant and sponsor of Sigma Delta Pi, Rolando and I shared the same office.

After leaving Illinois, our *amistad* continued through an exchange of letters in which Rolando informed me of his activities. In a letter dated March 19, 1973, he refers to my comments about his first paid publica-tion, *Por esas cosas que pasan*, published in *El Grito*, translated by José R. Reyna "en la cual yo [Rolando] colaboré algo"; he also says that he will go to the library to read Salado Álvarez, since I had mentioned him in my letter. He informs me about some yet-unpublished works: *Una vida de Rafa Buenrostro* and *The Mexican American Devil's Dictionary*. He also writes that he has signed a contract with Quinto Sol to publish *Estampas del Valle*, and that *Vidas y milagros* "está en manos de la casa Quinto Sol" pero que "no hay contrato aún." He comments about his academic du-ties at Texas A&M at Kingsville: "El trabajo acá es de rigor (comités, conferencias, reuniones, clases, el departamento, en fin, lo de siempre)."

Rolando's second absence from the valley had ended in 1969, when, after nine years of peregrination in New Mexico and the Midwest, he returned home as a professor to teach first at Trinity University in San Antonio and then at Texas A&M at Kingsville, where he held several administrative positions. Then, in 1977, he accepted the position of chair in the Department of Chicano Studies at the University of Minnesota, where he remained until 1981, the year he was promoted to the rank of full professor. That same year he came to the University of Texas at Austin as full professor in the English Department. Since 1985, he has been the E. C. Garwood Professor.

In his essay "Chicano Literature: The Establishment of Community," Tomás Rivera tells us that one of the fundamental principles of Chicano writers is their interest in the community. According to Rivera, in the Chicano literary works that have been published since the Chicano social movement (El Movimiento) began in 1964, interest in the community has predominated, shadowing all other narrative elements, such as action and thematic contents.

And, according to Rivera, the concept community—in the mind of the Chicano writer—is formed not only by the physical aspect of the barrio, but also by the values held by its people, by the existing personal relations among them, and by the presence of their own culture, manifested in the conversations among members of the community. Rivera affirms: "What better description than this is there to define a work by such a distinguished Chicano writer as Rolando Hinojosa-Smith, where we find *lugar, modales, relaciones personales, conversación* as constant motifs?"

Around these motifs Rolando has organized his narrative, the Klail City Death Trip series, giving emphasis in the early *entregas* to life in the barrio—as observed by Chicanos—from the early beginnings to the contemporary scene. In some of them he expands the space by setting the action in Korea, where Chicanos participated in that conflict during the fifties.

Early in his life, I am sure, Rolando had decided to write a revisionist history of his own people. When he began to write it, after his graduate work was completed, he chose a metahistorical form, which included the social history of the community and the *vidas* of the people. As he told José David Saldívar: "I don't think I could write a novel without referring to some form of history. That much is evident when I first used a supposed diary from the Mexican Revolution as early as *Estampas*. . . . I also think that my work would be lacking without the presence of the historian, critic, an essayist in there."

Regarding the content of his novels, he decided to write about the border and the life of its people, a subject he knew best. "For me, then," he wrote, "part of the sense of the Border came from sharing names, of places, of a common history, and of belonging to the place; one attended funerals, was taken to cemeteries, and one saw names that corresponded to one's own or to one's friends and neighbors, and relatives." What kind of common history did the valley have? we may ask. Hinojosa-Smith himself has given us the answer: "The history one learned there was an oral one and . . . we learned the ballads of the Border little knowing that it was a true native art form. And one was also raised and steeped in the stories and exploits of Juan Nepomuceno Cortina, in the nineteenth century, and with stories of the Texas Rangers in that century and then . . . as always, names, familiar patronymics: Jacinto Treviño, Aniceto Pizaña, the Seditionists of 1915, who had camped in Mercedes."

Rolando's concept of the history of the Southwest is that of Américo Paredes, who conceived of it as including northern Mexico. That is why in his novels, Rolando always has scenes that take place on both sides of the Border. In the novel *Klail City* the following incident is introduced, in which the two spaces, the valley and Puebla, are associated by means of a letter.

> Sergeant Leonides Buitrón looked at the return address: PO Box 245, Klail City, Texas, U.S.A. He handed the letter to Pvt. Manuel Guzmán on May 10, 1920 at Aljibes, Puebla.
>
> Guzmán, an American citizen as his father and his father's father before him, formed part of a cavalry troop chasing President Venustiano Carranza's trains on their way to Veracruz. The detachment was led by General Sánchez, an Obregón backer.

Don Manuel had been in the armies of Villa first and then, after Villa's defeat, in those of Obregón. When the latter was killed at La

Bombilla, he returned to Klail. He became a revolutionary for a second time, having joined "the Constitutionalist Army in the Papantla, Veracruz, Military District. This, in great part, explains his long friendship with Don Víctor Peláez. The experiences of these revolutionaries are interwoven, by means of letters and other techniques, with the lives of people in the valley, as are the lives of all the others who act outside of that world.

Rolando's life and works have been exemplary. His contributions to Chicano literature are outstanding. He is the only Chicano novelist who has consistently added to his narrative saga, always offering new materials, new approaches, new techniques, and new narrative structures. His use of fragmented plots, his ironic sense of life and customs, his humor, his creation of unforgettable characters, his historical insights, and his rich and fluent use of both English and Spanish give his novels a unique quality. As a critic has said, "Hinojosa-Smith's work shows every sign of long life."

Although, as has been observed by some critics, the years spent living in the valley form the substance of most of Rolando's novels, that substance has been enriched and given a broader meaning by presenting it in the context of world history and by considering Mexican society along the border as one unit. More than a series of *episodios regionales,* Klail City Death Trip is a multidimensional postmodern innovative metahistorical series.

What Robert Houston said in the *New York Times Book Review* about Hinojosa-Smith in his review of *Dear Rafe* is true of the whole series: "Although his sharp eye and accurate ear capture a place, its people and a time in a masterly way, his work goes far beyond regionalism. He is a writer for all readers."

25

RUDOLFO ANAYA

The deserved recognition that Rudolfo Anaya has received as a novelist has detracted from the study of his short fiction. Although his novels have been thoroughly analyzed, his short stories have received little notice. This is unfortunate, for his short stories are excellent illustrations of his mastery of the art of fiction, as well as added examples of his magical interpretation of his native land and the people who have inhabited it for generations. At the same time, they reflect the writer's sense of life, which is representative of that of the people with whom he grew up and whom he knows so well. He has said that he feels fortunate to have been born on the llano. "The wild, nomadic vaquero was my father, sheepherders were my old *abuelos,* and a woman from the river valley was my mother." This *apego a la tierra* explains Anaya's ability to write about universal themes as they are interpreted through the perspective of a Chicano who sees reality as it has been seen by the people whose culture he has inherited. His is an interpretation that is not different from that found in the novels and short stories of some of the most famous Latin American writers, such as Miguel Ángel Asturias (Nobel Prize in Literature in 1967), Alejo Carpentier, Juan Rulfo, and Gabriel García Márquez (Nobel Prize in Literature in 1982). Anaya, like them, has been able to create new visions out of old realities.

First published in *Rudolfo A. Anaya: Focus on Criticism,* ed. César A. González-T. (La Jolla, Calif.: Lalo Press, 1990), 335–48.

And yet, Anaya, like his Latin American contemporaries, speaks with a voice that has reached out beyond his immediate environment. The attraction that his works have had for European readers and critics attests to that fact. Alan Chase has observed that although Rudolfo Anaya may be the "dean" of Chicano fiction writers, his collection of short stories *The Silence of the Llano* makes clear "he speaks in a firmly accented voice to questions that lie far beyond the boundaries of the American Southwest."

In a brief essay, "The Writer's Inscape," written for the special number that the *South Dakota Review* dedicated to the subject of the writer's sense of place, Anaya defended the regional perspective but recognized that those who utilize this literary mode have to be skillful, otherwise they fail, especially if they let the materials "become more important than the human element behind them." And that is precisely what Anaya never allows to happen in his own stories, for he is careful not to let them remain simple anecdotes. In this aspect, he resembles the New Mexico traditional *cuenteros* (storytellers), with whose art as oral raconteurs he is very well acquainted. Like them, he re-creates in story form the lore of his own people, for, as he says, their stories, representing the voice of the past, are "bright, piercing commentaries on life. The language of the people is alive in them. And each one speaks across the centuries as to the conditions of our contemporary life." In a way, in his short stories, Anaya has assumed the role of *cuentero*. As he tells us, these popular stories, although very old, are alive today. "We hear them," he says, "in the wind which sweeps across our mountains and deserts. We sense them in the work of the people, [for] the stories are in the people as they work and dance. They are in the vision of beauty and art which has been kept alive in the craft of the *santeros*, the colors of the painters, in the songs the native poets sing, and in the *colchas* and rugs that women weave!"

There is strong evidence showing that Anaya has been greatly influenced by the legendary *cuentos* of the people of Mexico and Spain, which have survived in the Southwest, especially in New Mexico. The importance that he attaches to them is present in all his fiction. In *Heart of Aztlán,* he tells us, "I created Crispín, the old poet of the barrio, and around him the younger men gathered to listen to his cuentos." His own childhood was much more "magical and mysterious and imaginative because of people like Ultima," and it was certainly enriched by his grandfather, who "told marvelous *cuentos* and side-splitting *chistes.*"

The words quoted apply also to the *cuentos* collected by Professor Juan B. Rael in southern Colorado and northern New Mexico, some of which were adapted by José Griego y Maestas and published in 1980, with Anaya's English versions, under the title *Cuentos: Tales from the Hispanic Southwest.* While translating these folktales in 1979, Anaya was struck, as he was as a child, "by their deep sense of the human condition." In one of his own stories, "B. Traven Is Alive and Well in Cuernavaca," of the same year, he introduces a character, Justino, who has the characteristics of the *cuentero.* The narrator, who has gone to Mexico in search of short story materials and a place to write them, hears from Justino a *cuento,* "El pozo de Mendoza," about a very popular subject, the buried treasure. While telling the story, Justino makes reference to a popular legend, that of La Llorona, which Anaya later turned into a short novel, *The Legend of La Llorona* (1984). Traven, according to Anaya's imagined story, had also heard from Justino the story about the buried treasure, and remarks that "people like Justino are the writer's source." In Justino, Anaya has created a character overflowing with humanity, doubtless inspired by some of the *cuenteros* he knows personally. Besides the human content that Anaya so much admires, the *cuentos* have another important quality, the traditional form, which has become, since it has been repeated throughout the centuries, a classic structure. "The short story, when presented in the oral tradition," Anaya says, "can be a simple but compelling form."

Contrary to what may be thought, the use of these traditional forms does not limit the scope of the story or its universal appeal. Anaya knows this well, as revealed by what he had to say about this type of story, that is, that it "can also be made to move beyond its regional arena to engage language form in the expression of a vision which reflects the writer's sense of life." And that is precisely what the reader finds in Anaya's own stories: his own sense of life, a sense of life that is manifested, as it is in his novels, by his sense of place and by the recreation of ancient native myths. In one of Anaya's stories, "The Place of the Swallows," written, he says, "under the strong influence of *Bless Me, Ultima,* but not published until 1976 in the anthology *Voices from the Río Grande,* and included in *The Silence of the Llano,* a group of boys go hunting in the valley. At the end of the day they sit around the fire, and one of them, the storyteller, must recount the group's exploits. This simple anecdote has a universal theme, for, according to the author, it is "really about the art of storytelling and the role and function of the storyteller within the tribe, his social group. The tribe of boys reflects mankind."

By recounting the activities of the group, the *cuentero,* to paraphrase Tomás Rivera's words, is giving *forma a la vida.* Anaya himself has said that whatever suddenly rings with the tone and pitch that he has come to sense as a story is "the germ of the story." Once that small seed or germ is deposited, he has to write the story. "Life provides us with the seed; the writer as artisan must give it form." The narrator in "The Place of the Swallows" says, "All day I have known that someone will have to tell the story of today's exploration; someone will be chosen to give form to our exploits. It's always like this." The internal story, of course, goes beyond the simple description of the events of the day and becomes a work of art by means of the rhetorical use of language:

> There is a special time which the telling of the story creates, a time and place which become more important than the adventure lived. Why? I ask myself. What do the words create? In the story the small marsh becomes a swamp, slipping into mud becomes a near-fatal fall into the quagmire, and the stoning of a harmless garter snake becomes the killing of a poisonous viper. In the shadows of the river I make them see great monsters, unknown enemies which I know are only reflections of the words I use. I choose details fully and weave them all into the image; they see themselves as heroes and nod their approval.

This self-reflecting storyteller has not yet, at this point, reached the "germ of the story," which has to do with the senseless killing of innocent swallows. In this case, the function of the narrator of the internal story goes beyond that of being a mere storyteller, for his real purpose is to make the boys who are listening to him feel their guilt. And the same can be said of the function of Anaya as a fiction writer, since many of his stories make the reader reflect about his own actions. In the story, the boys do not like to hear about their senseless action, and when it is over they walk away, one by one. The storyteller, however, must speak the truth, even if he has to walk alone. "Perhaps modern society has placed the storyteller in conflict with his social group. Now, to tell a lie is to live; to tell the truth is to die. For the storyteller it means a perversion of his original role." Thus, the storyteller's function is, in Anaya's fiction, universalized: he becomes humanity's consciousness. In the context of Chicano culture, the writer has become the conscience of the people. The storyteller, according to Anaya, "tells stories for the community as well as for himself. The story goes to the people to heal and reestablish balance and harmony, but the process of the story is also working the same magic on the storyteller. He must be free and honest, and a critic of things as they are, and so he must remain independent of the whims of groups."

In "The Place of the Swallows," as in most of Anaya's stories, the characters are always in close contact with nature. The voice of nature, indeed, seems to inspire Anaya more than any other factor. This is one of the characteristics to be found in his fiction that join it to the poetry of pre-Hispanic Mexico, as well as to the contemporary Native American writers, who, like their ancestors, consider themselves to be not the creators but the interpreters of the poetry to be found in nature.

In the story "The Silence of the Llano," it is not only the author who hears stories in the wind, but all the people of the llano. And more important, the stories are an antidote to the oppressive silence: "When a man heard voices in the wind of the llano, he knew it was time to ride to the village just to listen to the voices of other men."

What gives form to this powerful short story is precisely the depicting of the loneliness of the people, which is the result of the silence of the llano, that is, the absence of the poet or storyteller. The life of the protagonist, the rancher Rafael, is presented as a case exemplifying the consequences of living in total isolation, both external and internal. In Rafael's solitary life there is but a short respite from loneliness, when he marries Rita. After a brief period of happiness—Rita soon dies giving birth to a daughter—Rafael returns to silence, a silence not to be broken for sixteen years. This is accomplished when he identifies his daughter with Rita, his dead wife. The simple anecdote serves Anaya to portray the relationship between human beings and their environment. Just like the silent llano, the two characters, Rafael and his daughter, are silent persons. This lack of communication, this absence of a storyteller, leads to tragedy.

The story, Anaya tells us, was inspired by the image of a silent girl in a ranch house: "The llano is a lonely place. One comes upon lonely, isolated ranch houses. . . . I had seen the face of the young girl in the story peer at me, so many times. . . . One day the face of the young girl appeared again, and I sat down and wrote the story. . . . The story is about silence, what it can do to people . . . and it's also about the vast gulfs which can separate people when the word is not present between them."

The underpinnings of the story—and the same can be said of the other stories in this collection—are to be found in the magic description of the landscape and in the close relationship between *la tierra* and the characters.

The author has said that "The Silence of the Llano" is a story "which creates its own aura and ambiance." Its composition was not, apparently, done while Anaya was in the llano, for he adds, "When I wrote that story I felt myself returning to the *llano*, I saw and felt it again as I knew when I was young and growing up. The aura became very real for me. It became palpable." This is understandable, for Anaya has also stated that he composes from memory. In his essay "The Writer's Landscape: Epiphany in Landscape," he says, "The relationship I feel with the earth fuses with time and memory and imagination and creates the scenes, characters, images, symbols and themes that are woven into the story. Sitting quietly behind the typewriter I evoke the epiphanies sleeping in memory and the flood begins."

This evocation of the llano is, of course, highly colored by the writer's imagination, and the result is a landscape that can be considered to be the product of an artist observing nature through the perspective known in Latin American literary criticism as magic realism. This can be demonstrated by comparing the descriptions of the llano in New Mexico done by Anaya with those of the Mexican novelist and short story writer Juan Rulfo, who has described another llano in central Mexico, in the state of Jalisco. The landscapes found in the stories of both writers are similar. Anaya writes:

> The people of this country knew the loneliness of the llano; they realized that sometimes the silence of the endless plain grew so heavy and oppressive it became unbearable. . . . They knew that after many days of riding alone under the burning sun and listening only to the moaning wind, a man could begin to talk to himself. When a man heard the sound of his voice in the silence, he sensed the danger in his lonely existence. Then he would ride to his ranch, saddle a fresh horse, explain to his wife that he needed something in the village, a plug of tobacco, perhaps a new knife, or a jar of salve for deworming the cattle. It was a pretense, in his heart each man knew he went to break the hold of the silence.

In Juan Rulfo's masterful story "Luvina," from the collection *The Burning Plain and Other Stories,* the protagonist, who has just left the village of Luvina, located in the llano, describes the desolated community with these words: "San Juan Luvina. That name sounded to me like a name in the heavens. But it's purgatory. A dying place where even the dogs have died off, so there's not a creature to bark at the silence; for as soon as you get used to the strong wind that blows there all you hear is the silence that reigns in these lonely parts. And that gets you down. Just look at me. What it did to me."

Solitude is the theme of another of Anaya's stories, "Iliana of the Pleasure Dreams" (1985), in which the protagonist, a beautiful girl, lives in psychological isolation due to the character of her husband, Onofre, who neglects her because he "believed in his heart that a man should take pleasure in providing a home, in watching his fields grow, in the blessing of the summer rains which made the crops grow, in the increase of his flocks. Sex was the simple act of nature which he knew as a farmer." Unlike Anaya's other stories about solitude, "Iliana of the Pleasure Dreams" ends on a happy note, with the husband and wife reaching an understanding and confessing their love for each other. But it takes a miracle to bring about the change.

Anaya's deep sense of place is matched only by his strong reliance on legend and myth, which he has used to advantage in his short fiction. To exemplify this trend we shall examine his short story "The Road to Platero." In this story, the setting is the same as in "The Silence of the Llano," but the theme is that of the popular Spanish *romance* (ballad) "Delgadina," which often appears in Mexico and the Southwest in the form of a corrido. "Some years ago," Anaya has said, "while reading through old Mexican corridos, the ballads of the people, I came across the Ballad of Delgadina." As is well known, the *romance*-corrido "Delgadina" deals with the theme of incest, a theme that is, Anaya observes, "as old as mankind . . . the subject of many literary works, but the subject is still taboo, and it's a theme which is difficult to treat."

"Delgadina" is one of the best-known *romances* in the Spanish-speaking world and in the Southwest among Hispanics. The Mexican folklorist Vicente T. Mendoza, in his classic study *El romance español y el corrido mexicano,* collected no fewer than twenty-one versions, from both Spain and Mexico. Professor Aurelio Espinosa added nine texts, and Arthur Campa three more. These two Mexican American scholars included versions found in both California and New Mexico.

Anaya's short story "The Road to Platero" is entirely original. Of the *romance* "Delgadina" he only utilizes the theme of incest between father and daughter. He enriches the anecdote so much that it becomes a truly contemporary story unrelated to the old *romance*-corrido. If it were not because the author himself has told us that he was inspired by the theme of "Delgadina," no critic would have seen the relation between the *romance* and the short story. The theme, however, has been developed by Anaya in a play, *Rosa Linda.* "I have been writing and revising that drama for a number of years, and so it's natural for the theme of the father/daughter relationship I am exploring in that drama to find its way into some of the stories I was writing at the same time. The theme begins to appear in "The Road to Platero." In a sense, the story is almost

a warming-up exercise for the bigger and more challenging story in
the play." In the *romance,* of early origin, the father is a king, while in
Anaya's short story he is a caballero of the llano. Delgadina is, of course,
a princess in the romance, while in New Mexico she is a *llanera,* a girl
of the plains.

In the Spanish poem the incest is not consummated, as Delgadina
is a virtuous girl who would not submit to her father's advances. As a
consequence, she is placed in a cell, where she dies.

> When they came back from Mass, he embraced her in her hall; "Del-
> gadina, daughter of mine, I want you to be my mistress."
>
> "Don't let it happen, my mother, nor you, all-powerful Virgin, for
> it's a sin against God and the perdition of my soul."
>
> "Come together, my eleven servants, and put Delgadina in prison;
> see that she is well locked up," said the king in great anger.

In the *romance* the king is not punished. In Anaya's story, on the other
hand, the father is killed by his son-in-law. His daughter Carmelita—
one of Anaya's most humane characters—unlike Delgadina, admires
and loves her father, and the incest is consummated. Her son, who is the
narrator, remembers the tragedy vividly: the death of his grandfather
at the hands of his half-insane father; the daily outbursts of anger on
the part of his father, who wants to avenge his disgrace; and finally the
death of both parents, who kill each other in his presence. Carmelita
wants to forget the past but is unable to do so because her husband will
not let her forget:

> "Your father made sure that we could never forget the past. . . ."
>
> "Forgive? Oh no, your sin is too dark to be forgiven. . . . Your sin is
> the sin of hell, and you will do penance by serving me forever."

The husband, however, is afraid of the grandfather's ghost, who haunts
the road to Platero and terrifies him. He, of course, blames Carmelita
for the ghost's appearance: "It's you whose sin brings the ghost of hell
to our doorstep. You will be happy with that devil!" In life Carmelita

and her husband were separated by the presence of the ghost, symbolic of the transgression, but in death they are finally able to be together. In front of their bodies, which lie still, their son thinks, in a final internal monologue:

> It's done, the torment is done. . . . I feel death enter the room.
>
> Strangely, a peace seems to settle over them as they lie in each other's arms. Outside, the wind dies and the streets of the village are quiet. The women of Platero sleep, a restless sleep. In the corral the mares shift uneasily and cry in the dark. The horseman who haunted the road is gone, and only the gentle moonlight shimmers on the road to Platero.

Throughout the story, the imagery that predominates is that which elicits in the reader the concept of machismo. As in Juan Rulfo's novel *Pedro Páramo*, in "The Road to Platero," the presence of symbols associated with the macho predominates, especially those of the horse and the spurs. In the last scene, when Carmelita is killed, the instrument used by the husband is the spur: "'Witch!' he groans and lifts his sharp spurs and slashes at her. My mother cries out in pain as the spurs cut a deep gash along her throat." The spurs also announced the arrival of the husband and their jingle had put fear in the boy's heart: "On the portal I hear his sharp spurs jingle, then the door opens and he fills the house like a howling wind, his harsh laughter echoes in the room."

The other symbol that reappears throughout the story is that of the horse. The macho dominates his women as he does his horses. "My father rides with the vaqueros. For him the road is haunted, and every day I hear him curse God and torment his horse with whip and spur." Carmelita believes that women are the slaves of men, and that even her own son will grow up to be a macho. Anaya very skillfully combines the two images to give expression to the theme of the story. Carmelita asks her son: "Will you, too, raise your spurs and rake your mother's flanks when you are grown? . . . Yes, we are the slaves of our fathers, our husbands, our sons . . . and you, my little one, my life, you will grow to be a man."

The stories selected here for analysis are representative of Rudolfo Anaya's short fiction. An extended treatment would reveal that his art as a short story writer is based on the principles pointed out in this brief study. Other interpretations are possible, as that is a characteristic of literary criticism. Anaya may even change his technique in the future, for he is a dedicated short story writer, and will undoubtedly write and publish many more *cuentos*. As he tells us, he is constantly in search for inspiration for his stories. "But a writer just doesn't sit and wait for the story to begin. One learns to think continuously about stories. In fact, one's thought process becomes that of reinterpreting life as story. I call this process 'story-thinking.' . . . 'Story-thinking' is part of the creative process, the dialogue with the world. It's an exhilarating process."

Life as story. Indeed, Anaya has provided the reading public with an original interpretation of reality, especially of his environment and his people in New Mexico, as seen by a gifted short story writer. He and his works are as much a part of New Mexico as are the *cuenteros,* the *santeros,* and the many popular artists who have contributed with their distinctive and unique works to enrich our vision of that region, and, by extension, of the world.

26

SANDRA CISNEROS

With her first novel, *The House on Mango Street* (1985), Sandra Cisneros joined those writers who have documented community life among Chicanos. Her book contributes to the portrayal of Chicano urban life, in this case in the city of Chicago. Mango Street, where Esperanza Cordero, the protagonist and narrator of the novel lives, becomes a metaphor for the Chicano experience in a metropolitan city. In her second book, *Woman Hollering Creek and Other Stories* (1991), Cisneros transcends the relatively limited space of the Chicago Mango Street community to paint, on a larger canvas, life among Chicanos not only in the Midwest and other cities in the United States, but also in Mexico City and other Mexican communities.

In *Mango*, Esperanza identifies herself with her house, which is, for her, the center of the universe. As she grows up, she becomes attached to a larger space, the community where she spent her childhood, in one of Chicago's run-down neighborhoods. In *Woman,* this center, this microcosm, becomes a macrocosm, encompassing a space that extends from Chicago to Tepeyac. The spatial unity found in *Mango* is replaced with the presence of complex characters, a variety of rich anecdotes, and ironic ambiguity.

The forty-four short sketches found in *Mango* are given unity by the presence of the house and the protagonist. From the first sketch,

First published in *No Longer Voiceless*, by Luis Leal (San Diego: Marín Publications, 1995), 127–34.

describing the house from the outside, to the last, something is added to the history of the family and the character of Esperanza. The narrative progresses from the external to the internal aspects of both the environment and the characters. On the other hand, in *Woman,* although some of the characters reappear (Lucy, Rachel), the twenty-two stories are independent of one another. Cisneros here abandons the popular fragmented novelette format, replacing it with that of the true short story.

In *Mango,* what Esperanza remembers most is the need of a house with which she can identify. It is not until the family have grown to six that finally they own a house on Mango Street. Although it is not the ideal house Esperanza had in mind, it is a home where they do not have to pay rent, or share the yard with other people, "or be careful not to make too much noise and there isn't a landlord banging on the ceiling with a broom." For the first time, a certain degree of privacy is attained here by Esperanza, even if the house is not the one she thought her family would get. "You live right here, 4006 Mango, Alicia says and points to the house I am ashamed of."

Yet it was better than the houses in which they had lived before. "We had to leave the flat on Loomis quick. The water pipes broke and the landlord wouldn't fix them because the house was too old. We had to leave fast. We were using the washroom next door and carrying water over in empty milk gallons."

For Esperanza, a real house was one with running water and pipes that worked; a house with real stairs, like houses on television; a house with a basement and at least three washrooms; a house painted white and with trees around it; a great big yard and grass growing without a fence. "This was the house Papa talked about when he held a lottery ticket and this was the house Mama dreamed up in the stories she told us before we went to bed."

But the house on Mango Street was not like that. It was small, painted red and not white, "with tight little steps in front and windows so small you'd think they were holding their breath . . . there is no front yard . . . a small garage for the car we don't own yet and a small yard."

Esperanza identifies her name with things Mexican, like the records her father played on Sunday morning; and with her relatives, especially her grandmother, who had the same name. "'Esperanza.' I have inherited her name, but I don't want to inherit her place by the window." At the same time, her name is a source of embarrassment at school, where non-Spanish-speaking students mispronounce it. "They say my name funny as if the syllables were made out of tin and hurt the roof of your mouth. But in Spanish my name is made out of a softer something like silver." Esperanza's acquaintance with Mexican culture is not only the result of her being of Mexican descent. She had been to Mexico or had lived there, and the architecture of some of the houses in her Chicago neighborhood reminds her of Mexico: "One day we were passing a house that looked, in my mind, like houses I had seen in Mexico. I don't know why. There was nothing about the houses that looked exactly like the houses I remembered. I'm not even sure why I thought it, but it seemed to feel right. Look at that house, I said, it looks like Mexico. Rachel and Lucy look at me like I'm crazy, but before they can let out a laugh, Nenny says: Yes, that's Mexico all right."

This identification with Mexican culture is kept by Esperanza—as it is by most Chicanos—through the presence, at home and in the barrio, of Mexican images provided by songs, food, dress, movies, television, and other mass-media forms of communication, and, of course, by the use of the Spanish language and by participating in Mexican religious and cultural rites and ceremonies. This process is continued in the first stories of *Woman*. In "My Lucy Friend Who Smells of Corn" and "Eleven," the action takes place in a barrio very much like that found in the stories of *Mango*, and the protagonists are the same, Lucy in the first and Rachel in the second; also, characterization and structure are obtained by the use of Mexican images: "Lucy Anguiano, a Texas girl who smells like corn, like Frito Bandito chips, like tortillas, something like that warm smell of nixtamal." In the story "Mexican Movies," the heroes are the old screen idols Pedro Armendáriz and Pedro Infante, who sing the favorite Mexican *ranchera* songs. In the movie house, they sell churros and tortas.

In other stories collected in *Woman*, however, this transplanted Mexican popular culture materializes into direct images, since the action takes place in Mexico. The imagined Mexico of Esperanza becomes a reality in the stories "Mericans" and "Tepeyac," both about the cultural conflicts that Chicanos encounter when they visit their relatives in Mexico. Although both stories take place in the Villa de Guadalupe, the Anglo-American images of popular heroes (Flash Gordon, the Lone Ranger, Tonto) do not disappear entirely. However, Mexican images predominate: the Basílica de Nuestra Señora de Guadalupe, Juan Diego, Tepeyac, flying feather dancers, the *tlapalería, la tortillería, la sopa de fideo, el café con leche, la ofrenda* box, and a number of others.

In Chicago, Esperanza's friends are young people from the neighborhood very much like herself, although not all of them are Chicanos. There is Cathy Queen of Cats, of French descent, whose family moves away from Mango Street to make room for more recent immigrants to this neighborhood in transition. "They'll just have to move a little farther north from Mango Street, a little farther away every time people like us keep moving in."

Then there are the sisters Lucy and Rachel Guerrero, who have moved to Chicago from Texas. Esperanza, apparently, has had a better education. "'We come from Texas,' Lucy says and grins. 'Her was born here, but me I'm Texas.' 'You mean she,' I say. 'No, I'm from Texas, and doesn't get it.'"

Then there is Meme Ortiz, whose real name is Juan, the owner of a dog with two names, one in English and one in Spanish. Juan is a recent arrival whose family moved into Cathy's house, a wooden house whose floors slant, with no closets and with lopsided front steps.

Alicia is another person living in a one-parent household, in a house infected with mice. Her father's old-country ideas regarding women do not stop her from going to the university to study. A woman's place, according to him, "is sleeping so she can wake up early with the tortilla star. . . . Alicia, whose mama died, is sorry there is no one older to rise and make the lunchbox tortillas. Alicia, who inherited her mama's rolling pin and sleepiness, is young and smart and studies for the first time at the university."

Growing up on Mango Street is an experience that swings from the playful to the disagreeable, and sometimes to the tragic. Esperanza's world is a world of young people, and she lives all the experiences common to those living in the crowded neighborhoods of large cities. The only exception among her friends is Ruthie, the tall skinny lady who likes to play with them. "She is Edna's daughter, the lady who owns the big building next door, three apartments front and back. Every week Edna is screaming at somebody, and every week somebody has to move away." From Ruthie, Esperanza learns how to see beauty in ordinary things, for "Ruthie sees lovely things everywhere."

Out on the streets, Esperanza learns about life, first from her close friends, then from outsiders, and begins to learn about love from her neighbors: Earl, the jukebox repairman who brings women to his apartment; Sire, the boy who keeps looking at her, but who already has a girlfriend, who, according to Esperanza's mother, is the kind that goes into alleys. Then there was the boy who held Esperanza once so hard that she felt the weight of his arm, but it was only a dream. The only encounter she had with a strange boy left her disillusioned. "They all lied. All the books and magazines, everything that told it wrong."

As Esperanza's awareness of life develops, she learns many things: the restrictions that society places upon young women; and that marriage can be a way of escaping from the drab life of the neighborhood. Her friend Sally, who is very beautiful and who dreams about loving and being loved, has to abide by the strict rules of her father. Sally marries before eighth grade. "She has her husband and her house now, her pillowcases and her plates. She says she is in love, but I think she did it to escape." There is Mamacita, whose husband cannot make her happy in the third-floor front flat across the street because she is always thinking about the beautiful house she had in Mexico. Then there is Rafaela, whose husband keeps her locked indoors because he is afraid she "will run away since she is too beautiful to look at." Minerva, who is a little older than Esperanza, with two children and abandoned by her husband, cries a lot but consoles herself by writing poems, and she and Esperanza exchange their poetry.

Esperanza's first encounter with death occurs when her grandfather, who lived in Mexico, dies and she realizes that the same thing could happen to her father. She experiences death even closer when her aunt Lupe, who is blind, dies alone in her apartment after much suffering from a crippling disease. By that time, Esperanza is already writing poetry, which she often reads to her aunt. It was her aunt Lupe who encouraged her to keep on writing, as writing would set her free. After Lupe's death, Esperanza becomes a dreamer. "And then she died, my aunt who listened to my poems. And then we began to dream the dream." Esperanza was also encouraged by her mother, who had dropped out of school and abandoned her career as an opera singer. She advises Esperanza to go to school and study hard so that she can someday be somebody.

Esperanza continued to write poetry and, to a certain degree, lived in the world of the imagination. Although this helped, she could not entirely escape the sordid life around her. She felt that she did not belong, that she was an outcast. Her friend Alicia is from Guadalajara and will one day return there. Esperanza, on the other hand, has no place to call her own. "No, this isn't my house I say and shake my head as if shaking could undo the years I've lived here. You have a home, Alicia, and one day you'll go there, to a little town you remember, but me I never had a house, not even a photograph ... only one I dream of."

Esperanza's real home is not on Mango Street, but in her dreams, as it is for many who live in these poor neighborhoods, feeling trapped, with no way to escape. Esperanza dreams of a house as a space for herself to go. "Not a flat. Not an apartment in back. Not a man's home. A house all my own. Only a house quiet as snow, a space for myself to go, clean as paper before the poem." She dreams of leaving the house on Mango Street, but she knows that her ties to the community and to her many friends and neighbors will one day draw her back. "They will not know that I have gone away to come back. For the ones I left behind. For the ones who cannot get away."

Although the setting for some of the stories found in *Woman*, as we have seen, is still Chicago's West Side, less emphasis is given to the influence of the multicultural environment and more to character development, the development of well-rounded anecdotes, and the presence of Mexican culture. Although the action of the story "One Holy Night" takes place in Chicago, the setting could not be identified unless it was known that South Loomis is the name of a street in that city. The emphasis here falls upon the anecdote, which deals with the rape of an adolescent girl (the narrator) by a Mexican Blue Beard, an impostor who calls himself Chaq Uxmal Palenquín and pretends to be a descendant of Mayan princes. The story is rich in Maya myth and imagery. In fact, Chaq Uxmal impersonates the famous protagonist of the well-known Maya legend "El enano de Uxmal" ("Uxmal's Dwarf"), a legend also utilized by Rudolfo Anaya in his short story "The Village Which the Gods Painted Yellow."

Not less important is the fact that in the stories collected in *Woman*, Cisneros is able to establish much more authorial detachment than in *Mango*. In "One Holy Night," she lets the nameless protagonist tell her own story from her own psychological perspective. In "My Tocaya," which takes place in San Antonio, Texas (although the reader knows this only because the newspaper *San Antonio Light* is mentioned), distance is attained by giving the anecdote—dealing with the experiences of Trish—a mythical structure, that of death and rebirth. The same thing is done in the title story, "Woman Hollering Creek," based on the well-known legend of La Llorona but adapted to reflect life among Chicanos in contemporary society. On the other hand, in the stories "*La Fabulosa*, a Texas Operetta" and "Remember the Alamo," distance is established by the use of parody.

The transition from *Mango* to *Woman* has been accomplished smoothly, the stories in the two books being integrated by means of the reappearance in *Woman* of characters with whom the reader of *Mango* was already acquainted and backgrounds already familiar. By introducing well-known Mexican icons (the Virgin of Guadalupe, Zapata, etc.), Cisneros has given the stories in *Woman* greater depth and, at the same time, she has broadened the space. This new space, which is the patrimony of all Chicanos, is much more satisfactory and gives the stories of *Woman* a culturally realistic tone not found in *Mango*. Sandra Cisneros's pilgrimage from Mango Street to Tepeyac symbolizes a growing-up, not only culturally and spiritually but also as a writer.

NORTH = SOUTH

27

LA MALINCHE

La Malinche studies have a long and distinguished history, one that began with the earliest chroniclers of the Conquest of Mexico, among them Bernal Díaz del Castillo, whose book *Historia verdadera de la conquista de México* (*A True History of the Conquest of Mexico*) is that from which comes most of the biographical information about Doña Marina, also known as La Malinche. Always referring to her as Doña Marina, Díaz del Castillo writes about her family life, her service as an interpreter to Hernán Cortés, her marriage to Juan Jaramillo, her children with both, and other facts about her life.

Although La Malinche's presence in histories of the conquest was common, in fiction (novels, stories), drama, and poetry, she does not appear until the early part of the nineteenth century. A novel in Spanish under the title *Jicoténcal,* a work in which Doña Marina plays a prominent although negative part, appeared in Philadelphia in 1826. In this historical novel, she represents the forces of evil and is characterized as wily, perfidious, and treacherous. When Diego de Ordaz hears that Jicoténcal is to be married to Doña Marina, he exclaims: "¡Dios mío! ¡Jicoténcal, el bravo, el honrado, el virtuoso Jicoténcal unido a Marina! No permitáis, señor, una unión tan monstruosa. ¡La perfidia unida a la franqueza, el vicio a la virtud, el envilecimiento a la nobleza!" ("My God! Jicoténcal, brave, honest, virtuous Jicoténcal married to Marina! Do not

Not previously published.

allow, sir, such a monstrous union. Perfidiousness united to frankness, vice to virtue, debasement to nobility!"). Later, numerous literary works included her as a character. However, in most of them, following in the tradition initiated by *Jicoténcal*, she is presented as an evil person, and as a traitor for having sided with Cortés against her own people. As a result, the stereotype of a traitorous Malinche took root in popular Mexican culture, and the term *malinchistas* was coined to refer to people who give preference to foreign cultures, products, and values, considering them inherently superior to what they have at home. The concept of *malinchismo* became a popular subject among Mexican essayists and historians.

As Sandra Cypess has observed, "Very few Mexicans before the modern period were willing to accept her [Malinche] as anything other than a prostitute or a traitor." However, beginning in the 1930s, when nationalism in Mexico reached a high point, Doña Marina is presented in a new, positive light by a few historians, among them Federico Gómez de Orozco in *Doña Marina, la dama de la conquista* (1942); and Guadalupe Fernández de Velasco in his article "La importancia de doña Marina en la Conquista de México" (1949). Others, like Gustavo A. Rodríguez in *Doña Marina* (1935), however, associate her with La Llorona and list all her shortcomings. Octavio Paz's seminal analysis of La Malinche in *The Labyrinth of Solitude* initiated a new trend in La Malinche studies. His negative interpretation of her as the violated mother, as the mythical La Chingada has prevailed, especially outside of Mexico. In his chapter "The Sons of La Malinche," Paz says, "Who is the *Chingada*? Above all, she is the Mother. Not a Mother of flesh and blood but a mythical mother. The *Chingada* is one of the Mexican representations of Maternity, like *La Llorona* or the 'long-suffering Mexican mother' we celebrate on the tenth of May." Paz's interpretation of La Malinche has been criticized by Beth Miller in *Mujeres en la literatura* and Jorge Aguilar Mora in *La divina pareja: Historia y mito en Octavio Paz*.

However, after 1950, some historians have presented affirmative views, as was done by J. Jesús Figueroa in *Doña Marina, una india ejemplar* (1957). Alfonso León de Garay, in 1956, had considered her as "the first mother of Mexican nationality." In literature, Rosario Castellanos was the first who really initiated the revisionist trend among Mexican and Chicano writers. Rosario Castellanos's poem, "La Malinche" (1972), reviews the paradigm from a point in the history of the figure itself, initiating an approach developed by Chicana women. This revisionist trend can be found in the writings of such Chicana scholars as Norma Alarcón, Antonia Castañeda, María Herrera-Sobek, Cecilia Álvarez, Erlinda Gonzales-Berry, Sylvia Alicia González, Cordelia Candelaria, Shirlene Ann Soto, Marta E. Sánchez, Yvonne Yarbro-Bejarano, Gloria Anzaldúa, and Adelaida R. del Castillo.

Less abundant are the studies concerned with the presence of La Malinche as a subject in Chicano literature. As far as I know the only studies in the United States about La Malinche in Chicano literature available at the present time are those of Sandra Messinger Cypess, who, in her book *La Malinche in Mexican Literature: From History to Myth* includes a chapter "Re/formation of the Tradition by Chicana Writers" in which she discusses poems dedicated to La Malinche by Lucha Corpi and Carmen Tafolla and refers briefly to other authors (Lorna Dee Cervantes, Inés Hernández, and Lorenza Cabrillo Schmidt) and some of the scholars mentioned above. Other studies are those of Elba D. Birmingham-Pokorny, Vicki L. Ruíz, Judy Salinas, and Elizabeth Ordóñez. Also, at the recent conference (August 26 to 28, 1999) organized by Professor Rolando Romero at the University of Illinois under the title "U.S. Latina/Latino Perspective on La Malinche," the following papers were dedicated to La Malinche in Chicano literature: Norma Alarcón, "Postmodern Malinches: The Making of a Chicana Political Imagery"; Guisella Latorre, "Theoretical Analysis of Chicana Icons: La Soldadera and La Malinche"; Debra Castillo, "Coagulated Words: Gaspar de Alba's Malinche"; and Alicia Gaspar de Alba, "Los derechos de la Malinche."

It is our purpose in this study to examine the appearance of Doña Marina as a subject in Chicano creative writings and literary criticism in order to document the attitude toward her taken by the authors. Among the questions to be answered are the existence, or absence, of a difference in the characterization of La Malinche in Mexican and Chicano literature; also, if the attitude of the critics is a reflection of her characterization in creative literature or based on historical evidence. Not less important is the presence of different attitudes among Chicanas and Chicanos. When does the change in attitude toward La Malinche take place, presenting her as the archetypal mother rather than as a symbol of evil? Was it the result of the renewal of an interest in the study of the origins of Chicano culture, which were found in Mexican culture, especially in the creation of a Mexican nation after the conquest? Or was it because she was credited as being the mother of *la raza*, the mother of the prototype Martín Cortés, the first "historical" mestizo, and his descendants?

It must be kept in mind that among Chicanos, the writers of fiction and poetry were those who first became interested in La Malinche, beginning with the generation of El Movimiento, the name given to the social movement begun in the middle of the 1960s by César Chávez and the campesinos who fought for better working conditions in the fields of California. Their Malinche, however, reflects the stereotypical Mexican figure inherited from the nineteenth century. These poets and fiction writers were followed by the critics and historians, who in turn were influenced by what Octavio Paz said in his book *The Labyrinth of Solitude*. Another influential work by a Mexican author was Carlos Fuentes's play *Todos los gatos son pardos* (1970), in which Doña Marina appears not only as the translator and lover of Cortés but also as his wise adviser. For Fray Bartolomé de Olmedo, however, she is a demon, not for being Cortés's mistress, but for advising Cortés to revolt against the king of Spain in order to become the emperor of Mexico, and also to give up his religion. She tells Cortés: "dale la espalda a tu rey y a tu dios" ("turn your back on your king and your god"). She wants to govern alongside him: "You can be the king; you and I together." On the other hand, one of Moctezuma's tax collectors calls her a traitor. But even Cortés, when Marina complains to him about the killings in Cholula, calls her *bruja* (witch) and threatens to send her back to the slavery from which, he believes, he rescued her or to give her to the lowest of his soldiers. In spite of this, Marina gives him good advice and reiterates her love for him. Upon giving birth to their son, Marina, in a long monologue, addresses the newborn as the mestizo son who will inherit the land, thus becoming the mother of future Mexicans. Although a chorus in the play curses the new mestizo, for Marina, the baby signifies the triumph of women. A selection from this monologue, translated into English, was included in the anthology of Chicano literature edited by Antonia Castañeda Shuler, Joseph Sommers, and Tomás Ybarra-Frausto in 1972. Merlin H. Forster has observed that, in this play by Fuentes, Marina "is the only one of the three principal characters [the other two being Cortés and Moctezuma] who really senses the importance of the event in which they are all taking part. Marina is at first only the object of Cortés's sexual desire, but after a time they develop a genuine affection for each other."

Toward the end of her mostly historical article "Marina/Malinche: Masks and Shadows," Rachel Phillips, commenting upon Fuentes's play, states that "Marina does not help Cortés in his conquest in order to betray her Indian people but in order to replace the tyrant Moctezuma with Cortés, who she considers will rule with justice." It is surprising that one year after he published his play, Fuentes, in his collection of essays *Tiempo mexicano* (1971), writing about recurrent myth in Mexican history, would say: "Recurrent and triple myth of Moctezuma-Malinche-Cortés: the sacred promise is violated, Cortés is a false Quetzalcóatl, the woman generates treason and corruption, and Moctezuma, simple-minded and defeated, is the father of suspicion. . . . As a follow up, corrupted and violated femininity has to be redeemed in the myth of the Virgin of Guadalupe, an Indian like Malinche." How can we explain Fuentes's early positive opinion of Malinche as expressed in the play and its reversal a year later? Could it be that the essay about the triple myth was conceived before Fuentes wrote his play? In a recent story, "Malintzin de las maquilas," one of the nine that make up the novel *La frontera de cristal* (1995), by Carlos Fuentes, the protagonist, named Marina by her parents, who live in the desert and have never seen the ocean, works in a factory manufacturing color televisions. Although the *maquila* belongs to Mexicans and foreigners, the title of the story implies that Marina is manufacturing goods to be exported and not consumed by her own people.

In 1972, Rosario Castellanos published in Mexico her significant poem "Malinche," whose themes, according to Sandra Cypess, "provide both a context and a conceptual springboard from which to study the Chicanas' re-formation of the Malinche paradigm." In this influential poem, the poetic voice gives Marina a self-expressed identity and history. She blames her mother for having sold her into slavery, for having accepted a lover immediately after her father's death, and for having substituted the body of a dead child to make the community believe that she had died. The poem, having been translated and included in the *Rosario Castellanos Reader*, had repercussions in Chicano poetry and essays.

During the period before the mid-1960s, Chicana and Chicano writers who mention La Malinche reflect the prevalent attitude in Mexico during the nineteenth century; that is, they present her as a traitor of her people, and even as a *chingada*. This attitude also appears in some Chicano Movimiento writers such as Luis Valdez and others. In "La Conquista de México (A Puppet Show)," which Valdez first presented at El Centro Campesino Cultural, in Del Rey, California, in 1968, and later included in the *Actos del Teatro Campesino* (1971), La Malinche is one of the ten characters, some of the others being Cortés, here called Herman, and Pedro de Alvarado, called Pete. The narrator is La Piedra del Sol, that is, the Aztec calendar, who says about Malinche: "This woman was to become infamous in the history of Mexico. Not only did she turn her back on her own people, she joined the white men and became assimilated, serving as their guide and interpreter and generally assisting in the conquest. She was the first Mexican-American." Using satire to better convince his audience, the striking campesinos, Valdez presents La Malinche as the ancestor of the Chicano. When the play was written, however, the word *Chicano* was not yet used as self-identification, so La Piedra calls her Mexican American, implying that she had accepted the culture of the Spaniards, just like some Mexican American women had accepted American culture.

An early study of Malinche by a Chicana is that of Adelaida R. del Castillo, who, in 1974, published in *Encuentro Femenil* her seminal article "Malintzin Tenépal: A Preliminary Look into a New Perspective," which can be considered as the first revisionist study of Doña Marina from a historical perspective by a Chicana critic. The writer gives an account not only of the conquest, but also of the Aztec empire and of the situation of the Indian population under the rule of the *tatuanes*. She speculated regarding the problem of Marina's help to the Spaniards. Her actions, she tells us, "were contingent upon the historical events of her time." To Del Castillo, Doña Marina is important because she "syncretized two conflicting worlds causing the emergence of a new one—our own. Here, woman acts not as a goddess in some mythology, but as an actual force in the making of history." She rebukes Carlos Fuentes's statements in his *Tiempo mexicano* concerning Marina and regrets Margaret Shedd's concept of her as a lustful whore. To Del Castillo, Marina should be praised, for she represents the beginning of the mestizo nation; she was also the first Indian to be baptized. Therefore, when she is denigrated, "the character of the mexicana/chicana" is indirectly defamed. She concludes her study by giving an extended analysis of Paz's ideas about La Malinche and Mexican women in general. According to her, Paz submerges the female character in negativism and does it by demeaning the character of La Malinche.

In 1978, William P. English and Graciela Domínguez de English published a twenty-six-page paper titled *Research on Malinche: Including the Other "Doña Marina,"* which is a defense of La Malinche, believing that her negative reputation is a case of mistaken identity. Although they are wrong in believing that there were two Marinas, one good and the other bad, they do present her as "a truly honorable lady . . . the first person to preach Christianity to the natives of the continent of America." She is also considered to have been the liberator of Mexico from Aztec tyranny, an idea already found in Fuentes's play.

Besides Cypess, Elba D. Birmingham-Pokorny speaks extensively about the influence of Rosario Castellanos's works upon Chicana writers. She says that the purpose of her paper is "to demonstrate and/or illustrate through the examination of works such as: Rosario Castellanos' 'Malinche,' 'Otra vez Sor Juana' ["Once Again, Sor Juana"], and *El eterno femenino*, Carmen Tafolla's poem 'La Malinche,' Naomi Quiñónez's 'Trilogy,' and Lorna Dee Cervantes' 'Baby You Cramp My Style,' the ways through which all these writers appropriate the misogynist symbolizations of the figure of Malinche." The second part of her study is dedicated to an analysis, from a feminist perspective, of the poems "La Malinche," by Carmen Tafolla; "You Cramp My Style, Baby," by Lorna Dee Cervantes; and "Trilogy," by Naomi Quiñónez.

In her study "Sexual Politics and the Theme of Sexuality in Chicana Poetry" (1983), Elizabeth Ordóñez, like Rosario Castellanos, makes a strong defense of Malinche. "Rosario Castellanos," she wrote, "provides a possible model for numerous vindications of the Malinche figure by Chicana poets by restoring to this indigenous foremother her power of speech and self-definition." In a footnote she adds: "Octavio Paz shapes her into a symbol of the violated native woman, 'la chingada' or the passive woman open to sexual violence. To another Mexican writer, Carlos Fuentes, Malinche generates betrayal and corruption in woman." Since she believes that it is "left to the Mexicana-Chicana to restore la Malinche's good name and to reveal to the world the truth about this important woman in history," she cites examples of this vindication of Marina, quoting from poems by Lorna Dee Cervantes, who, in "You Cramp My Style, Baby," "angrily denounces the sexual exploitation of women—glorified by tradition and disguised by political rhetoric." She also observes that even poets like Adaljiza Sosa Riddell and Lorenza Calvillo Schmidt, who move freely between two worlds, identify with La Malinche, who also moved freely between two worlds. According to Ordóñez, another Chicana critic, Marcela Trujillo Gaitán, in "The Dilemma of the Modern Chicana Artist and Critic," analyzes an un-published poem, "Chicana Evolution," by Sylvia González, in which La Malinche is portrayed "as a Messiah who must return to redeem her forsaken daughters; she becomes transformed into a spiritual mother of the Mexicana/Chicana." The Chicana poet Inés Hernández Tovar also approaches La Malinche from a spiritual perspective. In her poem "Rezo," she "stresses la Malinche's unselfish capacity to love" and shows "how her virtue was transformed into vice by the perverted perspective of history. Nevertheless, for Ordóñez, Carmen Tafolla's is "the most extensive and dramatic reworking of the Malinche figure." Although not dedi-cated entirely to a study of La Malinche in Chicana poetry, this study by Ordóñez is one of the most important, for she summarizes the attitudes toward Marina prevalent among the most important Chicana poets.

Critics agree that in creative literature, Tafolla's poem "La Malinche" is perhaps the one that best represents the revisionist attitude of Chicanas. All of them trace the origin of the poem to Castellanos's "Malinche." However, the similarities between these two short poems are reduced to an aspect of the form: the narrative voice in both poems is that of Marina. She remembers: "I was sold/to the merchants, on my way as a slave,/a nobody, into exile" (Castellanos). And Tafolla: "I was sold into slavery/by MY ROYAL FAMILY." But here the similarities stop. Castellanos mentions the substitution of her body for that of a dead girl to make the town believe she had died. Tafolla, on the other hand, gives a reason for her having been sold; they sold her "so that my brother could get my inheritance." Castellanos's poem is limited to narrating the relationship between Marina and her mother; Tafolla continues the story in her poem by introducing the fall of Tenochtitlán, Marina's relations to Cortés, and, most important for Chicanas and Chicanos, her dream. She became Cortés's interpreter and lover and helped him conquer Moctezuma because in her prophetic dream she saw another world, "a world yet to be born," symbolized by her mestizo child. She reproaches Cortés for taking her "sweet mestizo new world child to raise him in your world" and finally exonerates herself:

> But Chingada I was not.
> Not tricked, not screwed, not traitor.
> For I was not traitor to myself.
> I saw a dream
> and *I reached* it.
> Another world....
> la raza
> la raaaaaaaa-zaaa.

In Mexico, the identification of La Malinche with Eve is an early one. However, it was not until the revolutionary days when José Clemente Orozco revived this association in his murals. Octavio Paz appropriated this association of Marina with Eve in his essay "The Sons of La Malinche": "When he repudiates La Malinche—the Mexican Eve,

279

as she was represented by José Clemente Orozco in his mural in the National Preparatory School—the Mexican breaks his ties with the past, renounces his origins, and lives in isolation and solitude." As María Herrera-Sobek has stated, "Eve and La Malinche became inexorably intertwined, reinforcing each other in the Mexican national consciousness." This attitude prevails also among Chicano writers. Some of them, however, still maintain the prevailing Mexican attitude of Doña Marina as a traitor.

In 1974, Carlos Morton, Chicano playwright, published the allegorical drama *El jardín*, where Eva is one of the players. In a confrontation, the serpent, another of the players, tells her that one day Spain will conquer Mexico, "And you will be there and your name will be Malinche and you will betray the Aztec people, *tu raza!* You will interpret for the bearded ones and divulge all our secrets and you will even mate with their leader, Hernán Cortés, and the first of a bastard race will be born in Méjico."

Although La Malinche first appeared in the novel, her presence in Chicano contemporary fiction is not as prevalent as it is in poetry. Not so in the Mexican novel, where works about her are numerous. However, as the *Diccionario Porrúa* states, "the novels that have arisen from the shade of this legend [Marina's] are always empty of historical content." In Chicano literature, the only novel in which she is the protagonist is Rudolfo Anaya's *The Legend of La Llorona* (1984), wherein Malinche is identified with that popular legendary character. In Aztec lore, La Llorona was associated with the goddess Cihuacóatl, but after the conquest, she was identified in some versions with La Malinche. Rudolfo Anaya has reconstructed her legend from that particular perspective in his novelette, in which the Conquest of Mexico is re-created summarily in order to give the plot a historical background. As directed by the war god, La Malinche sacrifices her twin sons, Olin and Tizoc, rather than see them leave the country with their father, Cortés, who had been requested by the king to return to Spain. After the sacrifice, on the shores of Lake Texcoco, La Malinche becomes La Llorona, the wailing woman, in constant search for her dead children.

The novelette offers much more than just the legend of La Llorona. Anaya tells the story of the arrival of the Spaniards in Mexico under the leadership of Cortés, their conquest of Tenochtitlán, and the story of La Malinche. Although the historical past has been elaborated to fit the popular legend, Anaya has been able to blend the two elements well in order to present a rapid, flowing narrative. The presence of historical characters like Cortés (called the Captain), La Malinche, and Captain Alvarado lends verisimilitude to the story, thus lifting the popular legend from the realm of folklore into that of historical fiction, as seen in the creation of the two fictitious sons of Malinche, Olin and Tizoc, two names common in Aztec history.

Anaya's Malinche is an exceptional person: "She was truly a gifted woman, a noble person, and full of kindness when she went to heal the old and the infirm. An aura of light seemed to glow around her." In the fictitious part of the novel, Malinche has two sons by Cortés, Olin and Tizoc. Why the Nahuatlan names, when Malinche had sided with Cortés against the Aztecs? It is explained that she had come to know the Aztecs well, and that they, in turn, admired and respected her power. "Her sons had been born in the Aztec city, and she gave them Aztec names." So, why did she sacrifice them? The killing of her sons is necessary in order to transform her into La Llorona. When she sacrifices them, they do not protest: "She looked at her sons. For a moment her resolve left her and she felt weak and empty. But the boys did not move, they looked at her as if they understood what had to be done, like warriors who do not fear death. Malinche understood, and this filled her with an inner peace." However, she does repent, and from that moment on she searches the shores of Lake Texcoco for them. Here Anaya attributes to her a feature that characterizes La Llorona, her white gown. When Cortés, who is looking for his boys, meets Malinche on the shores of the lake and is informed that they are dead, he does not blame her. On the contrary, he says: "Our wrongs have led you to this terrible deed." Malinche, who had earlier blamed the gods for her deed, now blames him: "'Yes, I have been wronged,'" Malinche answered, standing tall and noble before him. 'My sons were to be made slaves, and I paid for their liberation dearly. Now they are dead . . . but other sons of Mexico will rise against you and avenge this deed. The future will not forgive any of us.'"

In the short story, the best-known composition about Malinche is that of Alicia Gaspar de Alba, "Los derechos de la Malinche" ("Malinche's Rights," 1993), in which the characters, except for Malinche, are unnamed prototypes. In a long interior monologue, the narrator gives vent to her resentment against her dead father and her boyfriends, who become symbols of the male dominance over women. In a flashback to Malinche's world, this dominance is traced back to the time of the arrival of the conquerors. The function of this interpolation, which interrupts the story of the father-daughter relationship in the present time, is to give historical depth to the struggle of the contemporary Chicana in her quest to obtain her rights, *sus derechos,* just like Malinche was able to do. In Mexico, as told in the interpolated story, this dominance began with the arrival of *el hombre blanco y barbudo* (the bearded white man). However, even during the first meeting of Malinche and her new master, Cortés, Gaspar de Alba depicts her as a shrewd person who knows how to defend herself from the sexual attack of *el hombre blanco y barbudo* and not as the stereotyped Marina created by earlier writers, a Marina that is submissive and obedient.

Even when Malinche is mentioned in other novels, she is not the central concern of the writer. Although Margarita Cota-Cárdenas, in her novel *Puppet* (1985), dedicates a short chapter to her titled "El discurso de la Malinche" ("Malinche's Discourse"), her name serves only as a takeoff for a Joycean type of prose, more like an essay than fiction: "Eres tú Malinche malinchi? Quién eres tú (quien soy yo malinchi?)/ vendedor o comprador? vendido o comprado y a qué precio? Qué es ser lo que tantos gritan dicen vendido-a malinchie" ("Are you Malinche malinchi? Who are you [who am I malinchi?] /seller or buyer? sold-out or bought-out and at what price? What does it mean to be what so many shout, saying he is a sell-out she is a sell-out malinchi?") And later: "Aló, sí, soy yo, Malin . . . Pat, Petra . . . sí, fue ayer el funeral pero yo no pude sí, eso ha de ser, una crisis de . . . *nervios* . . . (es lo que te hace falta ahora, no crees ja ja Malinceech' Mah-leehncheeh)" ("Hello, yes, it's me,

Malin . . . Pat, Petra . . . yes, the funeral took place yesterday, but I could not go, yes, that must be it, a nervous breakdown [that's all you need now, don't you think so, ha ha Malinceech' Mah-leehncheeh]").

In her novel *Paletitas de guayaba* (1991), Erlinda Gonzales-Berry attributes to Doña Marina a strong character, one that has a great influence on her own heroine, Mari, who, being Marina's *tocaya* (namesake), identifies with her and learns from her about her Mexican roots. Of great interest is the dream that Mari has about Doña Marina, who predicts the fall of Tenochtitlán.

In Chicanao popular literature, La Malinche is given different interpretations in legends, stories, folktales, and corridos. In the legend "*La Llorona*, la Malinche, and la Infeliz María," found in Elaine K. Miller's collection of folk narratives from the Los Angeles area, the three characters "were linked together by a ring passed on from one to the other, which automatically condemned the wearer to death." Here La Malinche has three sons whose fathers are three different lovers. A fantastic motif is introduced when La Malinche, after having drowned her three sons, discovers that they have become a doctor, a priest, and a lawyer. After she herself has died, she sets out to search for them along the rivers, calling out and crying like La Llorona.

Upon initiating this study, which was done at the request of Professor Sandra Cypess, I did not realize the importance and the extent of the presence of Doña Marina in Chicano literature. It is true that before the beginning of the feminist Chicana movement, Doña Marina did appear in Chicano texts in which the attitude toward her was an echo of that held in Mexico in both literature and popular thought since the nineteenth century; that is, that La Malinche was considered to be a traitor to her race and her culture and the archetype of the *malinchistas*, those who, like La Malinche, take the side of the foreigner and his culture, which they consider superior to their own. They are the *vendidos*—that is, sellouts. Others, especially those portrayed in popular literature, identify La Malinche with La Llorona, the crying woman in search of her lost children, children who are metaphorically transformed into the Aztec people murdered by the Spanish conquistadores.

Beginning during the 1970s, and as a result of Mexican writers like Rosario Castellanos, a complete reversal of attitude toward Doña Marina took place among Chicanas. From being a traitor and a *vendida*, she became the archetype of the mother, the mother of *la raza*, since she gave birth to the first historical mestizos, her children by the Spanish conqueror Hernán Cortés. She became the symbol of the woman who sacrifices herself in order to save her own people, who otherwise would have been exterminated. This new vision of Doña Marina is the one that the reader of Chicana texts will find. It is a vision created by Chicana poets, novelists, short story writers, essayists, and historians, among whom the names of the most distinguished Chicana writers can be found. There are, of course, texts by non-Chicanas about La Malinche, but most of them follow the vision so well established by Chicana writers in such a short period of time.

28

OTHER FEMALE ARCHETYPES

The characterization of women throughout Mexican literature has been profoundly influenced by two archetypes present in the Mexican psyche: that of the woman who has kept her virginity and that of the one who has lost it. The violated woman emerged in literature during the conquest. Doña Marina, interpreter and lover of Cortés, became the prototype of this character. Her mythical nature was strengthened by the association that the anonymous author of the novel *Jicoténcal* (1826) made between Marina and the serpent, which placed her under the light of two feminine archetypes, one European and the other Mexican; that is, Eve and Coatlicue. Of the statue of the Aztec goddess, Father Ángel María Garibay says, "un sentido de maternidad mana de este monstruo monolito, pero hay un dejo de guerra y de muerte, a través de aquellos corazones y de aquellas serpientes" ("although a maternal sentiment flows from this monster, there is a taste in her of war and death, both of which manifest themselves in the necklaces of hearts and serpents"). And Fray Juan de Torquemada, the early-seventeenth-century historian, dramatically, in his *Monarquía indiana,* has Coatlicue speak in these terms: "Si vosotros me conocéis por Quilaztli, yo tengo otros cuatro nombres, con que me conozco. El uno es Cuacihuatl, que quiere decir 'mujer culebra'; el otro Cuahuicihuatl, que quiere decir 'mujer águila'; el otro Yaocihuatl, 'mujer guerrera'; el cuarto Tzitzimicihuatl,

First published in *Women in Hispanic Literature: Icons and Fallen Idols,* ed. Beth Miller (Berkeley: University of California Press, 1983), 227–42.

que quiere decir 'mujer infernal' ("You know me as Quilaztli, but I have four other names by which I am known. One of them is Cuacihuatl, which means 'woman-serpent'; another is Cuahuicihuatl, which means 'woman-eagle'; another is Yaocihuatl, 'warrior woman'; and the fourth is Tzitzimicihuatl, which means 'infernal woman.'"

Octavio Paz has identified La Malinche with the mythical La Chingada, and José Clemente Orozco, in another medium, painting, with Eve. In 1885, Manuel Martínez de Castro published the novel *Eva,* in which the protagonist is a woman raped by a group of soldiers. To avenge herself, she turns her hatred against all men. She, therefore, antecedes Doña Bárbara, Rómulo Gallegos's heroine, and La Negra Angustias, the leading character in the novel of the same name by the Mexican Francisco Rojas González. The violated figure reappears a few years later in another Mexican novel, *Toña Machetes* (1956), where Toña (Antonia), the offspring of the patron's weak daughter, has been seduced by a common but strong horse trainer. Toña wishes to vindicate her mother's honor and to avenge herself for the humiliation she has suffered.

Rosario Castellanos, in the essay "Mujer que sabe latín" ("Woman Who Knows Latin," 1973), observes that "la concubina india fue tratada como un animal doméstico y como él desechada al llegar al punto de la inutilidad" ("the Indian mistress was treated like a domestic animal, and, like it, discarded when she was no longer useful"). Before publishing that collection of essays, Castellanos dramatized the problem of the Indian woman in her novel *Balún-Canán* (1957), in which we find a character, Don César, who is a direct descendant of the conquistadores; he honors the Indian women by favoring them. The Indian males always saw in them the virtue that had attracted the *patrón.*

The violated woman has her opposite, the pure woman, whose symbol in Mexican literature is the image of the Virgin of Guadalupe. She is associated with Tonantzin, the Aztec goddess-mother, thus uniting two myths, one European, the other native. The Virgin of Guadalupe is an Indian symbol, represented as dark complexioned and as having manifested herself to the Indian Juan Diego. She is identified with what is truly Mexican as opposed to what is foreign. If La Malinche sided with the foreign invader and helped him conquer her own people, the

Virgin of Guadalupe protects the Indian, the mestizo, and the criollos, that is, the representatives of the new Mexican nation. She is also the shield behind which the poor, the humble, and the helpless take refuge.

In a more restricted manner, she represents women confronted by the opposite sex. When the woman in Rojas González's *La Negra Angustias* (1944) (*Angustias, the Black Woman*) dons the uniform of one of her lieutenants as a symbol of her superiority over men, she discovers the image of the Lord of Chalma attached to the hat. "Con la punta de los dedos desprendió la estampa del Señor de Chalma y dijo al Guitlacoche: —Éste se lo pones a tu sombrero; yo no necesito machos que me cuiden. . . . Búscame una estampita de la Virgen de Guadalupe" ("With the tip of her fingers she dislodged the image of the Lord of Chalma and said to Guitlacoche: 'This you can wear on your hat. I do not need machos to defend me. . . . Find me an image of the Virgin of Guadalupe'").

The Virgin appears in Mexican literature during the colonial period as well. In the pastoral novel *Los sirgueros de la Virgen* (*Songs to the Virgin*), published in Mexico City in 1620 by Fray Francisco Bramón, the feminine characters (Marcilda, Florinarda, Arminda, etc.) are idealized shepherdesses who are as pure and chaste as the Virgin they worship and to whom they sing. The Virgin Mary appears in a dream to Palmerio, one of the male characters, in the guise of a huntress, like Diana, and she wounds him with an arrow in a scene reminiscent of the myth of the killing of Orion by Diana (Artemis), who slew him with her arrow because he made an attempt upon her chastity. A parallel is also drawn between some of the feminine characters and Diana's maids. On their way to celebrate a feast in honor of the Virgin, Menandro and Anfriso, the two principal male characters, meet "cuatro hermosísimas zagalas . . . como . . . las doncellas que a la casta Diana acompañaban" ("four beautiful shepherdesses, worthy of accompanying the chaste Diana"). The novel ends with an allegorical play, *Auto del triunfo de la Virgen y gozo mexicano* (*Play of the Triumph of the Virgin and Mexican Praise*), in which we already find the association of the myth of the founding of the Aztec empire to the cult of the Virgin. Among the allegorical characters in this short play, the most original is the Mexican kingdom, who appears "riquísimamente vestido con una tilma de plumería y oro, costosamente guarnecida" ("opulently dressed, with a cloak fastened by a knot made of feathers and gold, richly embroidered.") On his left arm he carries a shield decorated with the emblem of the Mexican empire, an eagle over a nopal. The association between that symbol, which represents the founding of the Aztec nation, and the cult of the Virgin is to be found in the inscription under the emblem on the shield, which reads:

Pues tal luz le da María,
renovárela en su día.

For Mary gives it such light,
I shall renew it on her day.

Bramón's Virgin is still the Virgen de los Remedios, the Virgin brought to Mexico by Hernán Cortés. Soon, however, her cult is substituted by that of the Virgin of Guadalupe. In the work of another seventeenth-century writer, Carlos de Sigüenza y Góngora, we already find the Virgin of Guadalupe as the protectress of the inhabitants of New Spain. In his novel *Infortunios de Alonso Ramírez* (*Misfortunes of Alonso Ramírez*), published in Mexico City in 1690, whenever the narrator is in danger he appeals to the Virgin of Guadalupe. During the period of independence, the Virgin of Guadalupe becomes associated with the national spirit. Father Hidalgo uses her image as a banner during the struggle for independence from Spain. The cult of the Virgin flows from her divine and religious aspects into the worship of human beings such as the mother, the sweetheart, and, in general, all pure and good women.

Thus, we arrive at two contrasting types, the good woman and the bad woman, which have their origins in antiquity. In Mexican literature, recalling again the novel *Jicoténcal*, we find Teutila, an angelical Indian woman who is virtuous, honest, and faithful as a wife, as opposed to La Malinche. The former is called "ángel bajado del cielo" ("an angel descended from heaven"), is characterized as the innocent victim of the tyrant Cortés, and is contrasted with Marina, "una astuta serpiente" ("an astute serpent"). Dedicated to help the unfortunate, she becomes, like the Virgin of Guadalupe, the refuge of the helpless.

The Virgin, in her role as mother, also symbolizes the earth. Here, again, we detect the survival of pre-Hispanic myths. For the Aztecs, one of the symbols of the goddess Coatlicue, the obsidian butterfly, according to Father Garibay, "es la tierra en su personificada maternidad, que en su regazo abarca a vivos y a muertos" ("is the earth in its maternal personification, who in her bosom embraces the dead and the living"). In the poems collected by Fray Bernardino de Sahagún in Tepepulco during the middle of the sixteenth century, we find the following verses:

Amarillas flores abrieron la corola.
¡Es Nuestra Madre, la del rostro con máscara!

Blancas flores abrieron la corola.
¡Es Nuestra Madre, la del rostro con máscara!

¡La deidad sobre los cactus redondos;
Nuestra Madre, Mariposa de obsidiana!

The yellow flowers opened their corolla.
It is Our Mother, the one with the masked face!

The white flowers opened their corolla.
It is Our Mother, the one with the masked face!

The deity over the round cacti:
Our Mother, the obsidian butterfly!

The transition from the adoration of the Virgin to the adoration of the mother is an easy one. In Mexico, the mother is always characterized as suffering, humble, and passive. In literature, no better example can be found than La Luciérnaga (the Firefly), the protagonist in Azuela's novel of the same name. Conchita, as she is called, symbolizes the exemplary mother and dedicated wife by refusing to leave her husband, Dionisio, despite his profligacy. The narrator describes her as "la esposa cristiana que sigue a su compañero, así esté lacrado por las enfermedades, por la miseria, por el vicio, o por el crimen mismo. Si la misión de la luciérnaga es hacer mas negra la noche can su lucecilla, la luciérnaga, cintilando, cumple con su misión" ("the Christian wife who follows her companion, even if he is marked by illness, or by poverty, or by vices, or even crime. It the mission of the firefly is to make the night darker with her little light, by glowing she fulfills her mission"). Conchita is humble, obedient, unpretentious, quiet, faithful, and submissive. Torres-Ríoseco calls her "alma humilde y grande, épica en su sencillez y en su silencio" ("a humble and great soul, epic in her simplicity and her silence").

In the novel *El desierto mágico* (*The Magic Desert*), published in 1961 by Concha de Villarreal, we find, as in *Jicoténcal*, the two opposed types, the good and the evil woman. The pure, humble, dedicated, and shy Engracia, as well as the provocative, aggressive, and bold Paula are both in love with Ventura, the local schoolteacher. Engracia wins when Ventura realizes that his illicit relations with Paula are unworthy since they degrade his character. The good woman, however, does not always triumph. In *Fruto de sangre* (*Blood Harvest*), a novel published in 1958 by Rosa de Castaño, the husband, Martín, abandons his suffering, humble wife to live with a woman whose husband is away. And in *Yo como pobre* (*Someday the Dream*, 1944), a novel by Magdalena Mondragón, Julia, the good, passive wife, dedicates herself to helping the poor people of the slum where she lives after losing her husband and son.

Variants of the virginal female are the innocent and pure sweetheart, the untouchable nun, and the dedicated schoolteacher, whereas the violated woman emerges as the accessible girlfriend and the prostitute. The first group is made up of women who are respected, the second by those who can be reviled. An intermediate group between these two extremes includes the spinster and the flirt.

The relationship of mother-sweetheart is obvious in the romantic poem "Nocturno a Rosario" ("Nocturne to Rosario"), by the nineteenth-century poet Manuel Acuña, where the following verses appear:

> *Camino mucho, mucho, y al fin de la jornada*
> *la forma de mi madre se pierde en la nada*
> *y tú de nuevo vuelves en mi alma a aparecer.*
> *¡Qué hermoso hubiera sido vivir bajo aquel techo,*

los dos una sola alma, los dos un solo pecho,
y en medio de nosotros, mi madre como un dios!

I walk, walk, and at the end of the journey
My mother's silhouette vanishes into nothingness
And you again and again, in my soul appear.
How beautiful it would have been to live under that roof,
The two of us as a single soul, the two of us a single self,
And between us, my mother like a god!

In other poets, the pure sweetheart, whose prototype is the mythical Sleeping Beauty, is untouchable. Ramón López Velarde is inspired by a pure, detached woman. The association of virgin-mother-sweetheart appears in his poem "Elogio a Fuensanta" ("In Praise of Fuensanta"):

Humilde te he rezado mi tristeza
como en los pobres templos parroquiales
el campesino ante la Virgen reza.

Antífona es tu voz, y en los corales
de tu mística boca he descubierto
el sabor de los besos maternales.

Humbly I have prayed my sadness to you
as in the poor country churches
the farmer to the Virgin prays.

Antiphony is your voice, and in the chorals
of your mystical mouth I have discovered
the taste of maternal kisses.

Upon marriage, the sweetheart who is pure becomes a faithful wife and unassuming mother. If she remains single, she becomes a *solterona* (old maid), a nun, a *beata* (overly religious woman), or a schoolteacher. The *solterona* is a common character in Mexican literature. She appears in *Polvos de arroz* (*Rice Powder*, 1958), a novelette by Sergio Galindo, and in several short stories by Raquel Banda Farfán, Elena Garro, and Carlos Fuentes. Galindo's character combines the problem of the *solterona* with that of the virgin and the violated woman. Camerina becomes a *solterona* as a result of her fiancé's seduction of her sister Augusta, but the emotional problems of Camerina, as a *solterona*, are what Galindo is interested in exploring.

The *solterona* usually appears as a simple stereotype of homeliness. Galindo presents Camerina as an extremely fat woman. Raquel Banda Farfán, in her numerous short stories, often attributes to her *solteronas* the single physical characteristic of ugliness. Jova, in the story "Una extraña enfermedad" ("A Rare Disease"), is representative of this stereotype:

> *Jova era la solterona del rancho, esa solterona que hay en todas partes, sin amigas con quienes comentar su desgracia, porque una doncella que ha llegado a cierta edad, ni puede hacer ronda con las jóvenes ni tampoco con las mujeres casadas. . . . Se recordaba bien que Jova nunca fue bonita, ni siquiera a los quince, cuando se dice que no hay muchacha fea. Era una guera pizque que no podía mirar la luz del día sin hacer gestos, y para colmo, tenía la dentadura de fuera y le era imposible juntar los labios.*

> Jova was the ranch's *solterona*, that *solterona* found everywhere, without friends with whom to share her misfortune because a maid that has reached a certain age can neither join the young nor the married women. . . . They remembered that Jova was never pretty, not even when she was fifteen, when, they say, there is no ugly girl. She was a squinty-eyed ash blonde who could not look at the light of day, and to make it worse she had protruding teeth and could not close her lips.

Another of Banda Farfán's characters is the twenty-three-year-old heroine of her story "Por un piropo" ("For a Compliment"). Dionisia is a *solterona* so ugly that "los hombres la veían con la indiferencia con que puede verse a una vaca" ("men looked at her with the indifference with which they looked at a cow"). However, Herculano is attracted to her. Why? Because "nunca antes hombre alguno la tentó ni con los ojos" ("she had not been touched by any man, not even with the eyes"). He makes love to her, though he says, "Es fea la indina, fea como un zopilote, por eso de día ni siquiera la miro" ("The unworthy girl is ugly, ugly as a buzzard, which is why in the daylight I won't even look at her"). Banda Farfán's *solteronas* are ugly, but they finally get married, even if they have to marry a dying man, as does Chona in another of her stories, "La cita" ("The Date").

This is not so with the stories of Carlos Fuentes, as we can see in "A la víbora de la mar" ("Sea Serpent"), in which a *solterona* is deceived and robbed of her savings during a boat trip from Acapulco to Miami. Isabel, from Mexico City, is in her forties and rather good-looking. "¿*Cuál sería la palabra* [*para describirla*]? Dowdy, I guess" ("How would you describe her? Dowdy, I guess"). In spite of her shyness, she falls in love with the North American Harrison Beatie, who marries her in a mock ceremony and then steals her money. Three days before reaching Miami, where Harrison and his male lover plan to leave the boat, Harrison says, "De todas maneras, pobrecita. Empezaba a quererla, como a una tía vieja. Pensar que tenemos que hacer la comedia tres días más, ¡ooooooh!" ("Poor thing. I was beginning to like her, like an old aunt. And to think that we have to act out this comedy for three more days, ooooooh!"). If Galindo and Banda Farfán see their *solteronas* with sympathy, Fuentes sees them with sarcasm, without pity.

The *beata*, or overly religious woman, is very close to the nun, a familiar character in Hispanic literature since its origins. Both appear frequently in Mexican literature, the nun especially in romantic fiction, in such extravagant novels as *Monja y casada, virgen y mártir* (*Nun and Married, Virgin and Martyr*, 1868), by Vicente Riva Palacio. His heroine, Sor Blanca, is placed by her brother in a convent, from which she escapes, marries, is tortured by the Inquisition, escapes again, is captured by a bandit, and, finally, falls to her death from a precipice, still a virgin.

In modern fiction, the *beata* is characterized by Agustín Yáñez. In his novel *Al filo del agua* (*The Edge of the Storm*, 1947), the *beatas* appear as a group, as members of the religious association Hijas de María (Mary's Daughters). All women joining this association must forego marriage. In the novel, Maclovia Ledesma disobeys this rule, marries, and leaves the association, producing difficulties for her and her husband. He loses money in every business he undertakes; she has two miscarriages; and finally she loses her mind. "Maclovia; desde recién casada fue víctima de una tristeza mortal, que nada ni nadie podía disiparle; tras la primera frustración dio en sentirse perseguida, ya por sus parientes políticos, luego por su marido, finalmente por el diablo en persona" ("Maclovia, from the day she married, was a victim of a mortal sadness which no one could dispel. After the first frustration she believed she was persecuted, first by her relatives, then by her husband, and finally by the devil in person"). But the daily life of the other members of the association (Teófila, Elvira, Maximina) is just as unbalanced. Yáñez sympathizes with the *beata,* connecting her sufferings to those of other people rather than ridiculing her celibacy.

Not so Juan Rulfo, who, in his short story "Anacleto Morones" presents a biting characterization of the *beata.* The story opens with the description by the male narrator, Lucas, of a group of ten *beatas:*

> *¡Viejas, hijas del demonio! Las vi venir a todas juntas, en procesión. Vestidas de negro, sudando como mulas, bajo el mero rayo del sol. Las vi desde lejos como si fuera una recua levantando polvo. Negras todas ellas. Venían por el camino de Amula, cantando entre rezos, entre el calor, con sus negros escapularios grandotes y renegridos sobre los que caían en goterones el sudor de su cara.*

> Old hags, daughters of the devil! I saw them coming all together, like a procession. Dressed in black, sweating like mules under the rays of the sun. I saw them from afar, like a pack of mules throwing up dust. Black all over. They came from the direction of Amula, singing and praying, in the heat of the day, with their large, fat, blacker-than-black scapularies, over which the perspiration from their faces was falling in large, thick drops.

Lucas is cynical, as he had been deceived by his wife, daughter of the holy man Anacleto, whom the *beatas* seek to canonize. The ten women who have come to persuade Lucas to testify as to the holiness of

Anacleto Morones are misguided *beatas* who worship the memory of a fake, a fact known to Lucas. In Rulfo's story some of the *beatas* are even willing to make love, and one of them stays with Lucas all night. She ends the story with this remark, which proves that Lucas is not lying: "—Eres una calamidad, Lucas Lucatero. No eres nada cariñoso. ¡Sabes quién si era amoroso con una? —¡Quién? —El Niño Anacleto. El sí que sabía hacer el amor" ("'You are a calamity, Lucas Lucatero. You are not at all affectionate. You know who was really loving with one?' 'Who?' 'El Niño Anacleto. He really knew how to make love.'")

The *beata,* however, is traditionally averse toward sex, as Mariana, a *solterona beata* who appears in the novel *La vida y yo* (*Life and I,* 1954), by Blanca B. Mauries, succinctly tells us. She has a profound horror for the sins of love. As a rule, the nun, the *solterona,* and the *beata* are not pursued by men. On the other hand, the man considers it a normal activity to try to seduce a flirt, who is characterized as loose and fickle, easily becoming a mistress or a prostitute. In the 1948 novel *Senderos de pasión* (*Paths of Passion*), by Dina Rico, one of the leading characters, Conchita, finally succumbs to Armando's demands, an act condemned by the closed society in which she lives. This leads to her tragic suicide. Another feminine character, Leonor, makes this observation:

> *Yo no podía comprender por qué, cuando delinquía una mujer, en lugar de ofrecerle una mano amiga, un hogar honesto—aun contra su propia volun-tad—donde pudiera olvidar su pecado y redimirse, se la lanzaba al arroyo, obligándola, las más de las veces, a seguir rodando por la pendiente iniciada por amor.*

> I could not understand why, when a woman breaks the rigid sexual rules, instead of being offered a helping hand, providing her with a decent home—even against her own will—where she could forget her sin and redeem herself, she is cast into the gutter, forcing her, most of the time, to keep on falling down the road initiated by love.

A variant of the flirt is the girl who risks her virginity, often with the intention of losing it. The best examples of this type are the girls

preserve, but do not [create] the values and energies entrusted to them by nature or society." Paz adds: "In a world made in man's image, women are only a reflection of masculine will and desire."

In *Mujer que sabe latín,* Rosario Castellanos blames not only men, as Sor Juana had done in the seventeenth century, but also society. She says:

> *Por eso desde que nace una mujer la educación trabaja sobre el material dado para adaptarlo a su destino y cultivarlo en un ente moralmente aceptable, es decir, socialmente útil. Asi se le despoja de la espontaneidad para actuar; se le prohíbe la iniciativa de decidir; se le enseña a obedecer los mandamientos de una ética que le es absolutamente ajena y que no tiene más justificación ni fundamentación que la de servir a los intereses, a los propósitos y a los fines de los demás.*

> From the very moment that a woman is born, the educational system works on the material at hand to make it adapt to its destiny and turn out a being morally acceptable, that is to say, socially useful. Thus she is dispossessed of her spontaneity to act; she is denied the initiative to decide; she is taught to obey the commandments of an ethic that is absolutely strange to her, that has no justification or foundation other than that of serving the interests, purposes, and ends of others.

There is no doubt that Mexican literature, like all other literature, reflects the prejudices of the ages and creates types that are within the limits of these prejudices, most of them derived from the past. Feminine archetypes, therefore, reflect the characteristics, good or bad, that have been attributed to women throughout the years; because of this long literary tradition, it is a monumental task to rid literature of these archetypes. Considering the fact that society changes, it is to be supposed that literary types will also change. The Mexican sociologist Francisco González Pineda has said that

> [*En la sociedad mexicana*] *la reclusión de la mujer va desapaciendo, y con ello la posibilidad de preservar a las hijas con medio externo de barrotes y chaperones; las jóvenes van cediendo, cada vez con mayor frecuencia, a*

*experimentar lo sexual con mayor o menor libertad. . . . Las clases medias
se están quedando cada vez con menos vírgenes para los casamientos ideal-
izados de las novias de estas clases, y el hombre mexicano, a tanto agredir
mujeres, está comprobando que ya no hay mucho que agredir y se está quedando sin oportunidades para probar su masculinidad.*

In Mexican society the seclusion of women is disappearing, and with
it the possibility of keeping young women confined by means of bars
or chaperons. Young women, more and more, tend to experiment
with a greater sexual liberty. . . . The middle class is being left with
fewer and fewer virgins for the idealized marriages, and the Mexican
man, as a result of his many sexual aggressions, is realizing that there
is not much left to violate, and has fewer opportunities to prove his
manhood.

The social changes referred to by González Pineda can be verified
in the new Mexican literature by young writers such as José Agustín,
Gustavo Sáenz, José Emilio Pacheco, Juan García Ponce, Juan Tovar,
René Avilés Fabila, Margarita Dalton, Esther Seligson, Carmen Rubín
de Celis, and others in whose works we can discover the image of a
new Mexican woman, a woman that is finally breaking away from the
stereotyped characterization based on traditional archetypes.

29

MEXICO'S CENTRIFUGAL CULTURE

The critic Ignacio Trejo Fuentes argues that the Instituto Nacional de Bellas Artes founded the journal *Tierra Adentro* "to attenuate, if not eradicate, the dreadful cultural centralization of the country." The institute's laudable attempt to limit Mexico City's literary hegemony highlights the powerful centrifugal force operating in every aspect of Mexico's life and culture. Ironically, as Trejo Fuentes laments, the Instituto Nacional published the journal through the auspices of the cultural organization Bellas Artes and "its distribution did not receive adequate support."

Leobardo Saravia Quiroz had already contended that in the northern part of Mexico, "centralism has been a reality that defines groups, lines of behavior and specific realities." He also argues that this political-cultural phenomenon explains why people from other parts of the country do not read the literature of northern Mexico. According to Saravia Quiroz, "the current rigid centralism has allowed the absence of opportunities for its extraregional diffusion. . . . A decisive factor is the absence of a publishing infrastructure that could serve as a springboard for the writers of this area."

Roberto Villarino, who edited the anthology *Primer encuentro de poetas y narradores jóvenes de la frontera norte*, complains that in Mexico, "where centralization affects culture dramatically, one wonders how many generations of poets are now lost or forgotten because their works

Translated by M. Estrella Sotomayor. First published in *Discourse* 18, nos. 1 and 2 (Fall and Winter, 1995–96): 111–21.

were not properly edited, distributed, and evaluated." And, as significant proof of the current centralization in recent years, Villarino's anthology was published by the Secretariat of Public Education and the Border Cultural Program (with its headquarters in Mexico City).

A simple glance at Federico Patán's *Los nuevos territorios* (*The New Territories*, 1992) confirms the absence of opportunities highlighted by Saravia Quiroz. The text compiles Patán's reviews published, with one exception, by the *Sábado* literary supplement between 1980 and 1990. Of the 110 books reviewed, only 8 were written by border authors, some of whom reside or had resided in Mexico City.

Historically, Mexico City has dictated the rules that organize the population. The idea of Mexico City as "ombligo del mundo" (the belly-button of the world) has mythical origins, as can be seen in the well-known legend of the foundation of Tenochtitlán "at the place where the eagle," writes Antonio Caso, "representing Huitzilopochtli, perches over the stoned cactus at the center of the island in the lake of the moon . . . luring the tribe away from the white land, Aztlán." From those mythical origins, the Aztecs extended "the domain of the city-state Tenochtitlán," Caso continues to say, "[until] the king of Mexico became the king of the world, *Cen-Anáhuac tlatoani*, and Mexico/Tenochtitlán became the capital of the Empire." Carlos Fuentes has pointed out that the central-ization of power has not changed much since then. In his *Tiempo mexi-cano*, Fuentes states that the revolution of 1910–20 "has accomplished an eclectic equilibrium; Moctezuma, not a divine autocrat anymore, becomes the Señor Presidente who sits on the golden Aztec throne for only six years and is only respected if he rules with all the malice and energy of a conqueror." René Avilés Fabila's irony has been even more drastic: each new president is the same person, only transformed. The grand recluse of the palace becomes "a Caudillo with a long life: he has been in power for fifty years. . . . Every six years he transforms physi-cally and mentally and once again runs for reelection, because he is a democrat. And a revolutionary." Of course, such person cannot be either Villa or Zapata, representatives of popular sentiment in the North and South. "When in 1915," writes Fuentes, "the popular armies of Pancho Villa and Emiliano Zapata entered Mexico City—which had not yet recovered its breath, its troops, and its peoples . . . they, for the first time, stepped on the sacred zones of the capital." However, they did not remain; the center expelled them.

After the chroniclers, especially Hernán Cortés in his "Segunda carta de relación" and Bernal Díaz del Castillo in his *True History*, wrote such marvelous descriptions of the great Tenochtitlán, the conqueror decided to rebuild the city to establish the center of New Spain and carry on the Aztec traditions. The center drew the praise of the poets, among them Bernardo de Balbuena, who in *Grandeza mexicana* (*Mexican Greatness*, 1604), calls it the "center of perfection, pivot of the world." "Regarding the *Grandeza mexicana*," Francisco Monterde wrote, "its title reveals its purpose: to promote the magnificence of the city, in opposition to the insignificance of the small towns; the grandeur of the court has made them despise the miseries of the country." Moreover, was not Sor Juana born in the country? Yes, but the power of the viceroy attracted her at an early age. And the attraction still holds. Numerous authors from the provinces cannot resist the attraction of the center.

While during colonial times the author of *Grandeza mexicana* stood out as the one who praised Mexico City the most, in the twentieth century the philosopher Antonio Caso has followed suit. In his 1943 *Geografía intelectual de México* (*Intellectual Geography of Mexico*), Caso lauds Mexico City over all the other capitals of the Hispanic world: "In our country various cities have served as the foundation of Mexican culture. Naturally, perhaps over any other, Mexico City served as the center of Colonial Mexico and the base of the Aztec culture. A famous city in the history of the world. Old Tenochtitlán, colonial and republican Mexico that, because of the lineage of its moral and intellectual tradition, excels among all its sisters, the other cities of the Spanish American continent, until it reaches, according to the opinion of natives and foreigners, a preferred place among all the great cultural empires of America."

After praising the metropolis, Caso enumerates the regions of the country that have contributed the most to Mexican literature. The North is not included, although three of its capitals (Saltillo, Monterrey, and Chihuahua) deserve honorable mention. "Saltillo is honored by the names of the poet Acuña and the great historian Carlos Pereyra.

Monterrey remembers Fray Servando Teresa de Mier and Alfonso Reyes. Chihuahua is the birthplace of don José Fernando Ramírez, don Porfirio Parra, and don Jesús Urueta." This canon, incidentally, reveals the political and literary preferences of the author. Though writing in 1943, Caso does not mention the writers of the revolution, who undoubtedly placed northern Mexico on the literary map. Among others, Martín Luis Guzmán, Rafael Muñoz, and Edmundo Valadés strengthened the North's regional, cultural, and literary identity by writing about their native region and its people. Of course, the writers of the revolution were not the first to open a literary space in the North.

The conquistadores-chroniclers who waged war against the so-called barbarians (the warlike Chichimecas, Yaquis, Apaches, and Comanches who never accepted Spanish domination, as did the Aztecs, Mayans, Tarascos, and others in the central and southern part) engaged the North first. Thus, the narratives of the northern border resulted from the Crown's expansion of New Spain, first in search of wealth and later to defend the colonized territory. The idea that those provinces are culturally inferior has not totally disappeared. Moreover, it has been difficult to eliminate the chroniclers' stereotype of an uncivilized northern border, in opposition to the mythical center of the Valley of Mexico, where the air is clear. Just as Cortés, Bernal Díaz, and Balbuena praised the center, Cabeza de Vaca, Castañeda de Nájera, Vázquez Coronado, and others defiled the North. When Cabeza de Vaca mentions the Indians who sympathize with his and his companions' misfortunes, characterizing them as "Others," he does not feel the empathy the Indians show them: "The Indians, understanding our full plight, sat down and lamented for half an hour so loudly they could have been heard a long way off. It was amazing to see these wild, untaught savages howling like brutes in compassion for us. It intensified my own grief at our calamity and had the same effect on the other victims." Later on, in reference to another tribe, he writes: "From that point North uninhabited to the Northern Sea [the Atlantic Ocean] . . . those who inhabit and walk that land are the cruelest people with bad inclination and costumes."

Cabeza de Vaca, however, does not generalize; not all the natives are barbarians. Of others he writes that they are people "much better conditioned . . . and willing than those from Méjico." The sixteenth-century conquistador Francisco Vázquez Coronado, who considered all the inhabitants from the North barbarians, wrote a letter to the Crown on October 20, 1541, in which he states: "After sixty-seven days of walking through the desert I arrived at the province called Quivira. . . . Its people are as barbaric as all the others I have seen." Coronado, of course, was not Las Casas, to whom Todorov attributed the following idea—strange for that period—about racial equality: "People will be called 'barbarians' when compared to others if they are hard to understand or if they do not speak well the language of the other. According to Strabo, Book XIV, Greeks called other people barbarians because they mispronounced their language. However, from this perspective, every person or race is barbaric in relation to another. . . . The same way we considered people from the Indies barbarians, they judge us accordingly because they do not understand us."

This attitude of Las Casas did not prevail in New Spain, especially in the North; Las Casas does not talk about those cultures. His viewpoint, radical at the time, is not expressed by the writers who speak about the Chichimecas and Apaches, with the possible exception of Fray Marcos de Niza, who explored New Mexico before Vázquez de Coronado. In his chronicle *Descubrimiento de las siete ciudades* (*Discovery of the Seven Cities*), he wrote that the region was inhabited by "men of great civility." He first mythologized the northern border by comparing its towns to the seven mythical cities. "In this first province there are seven major cities, all of them under the power of one ruler." The dwellers of the first city of Cíbola, located in the center, built their large houses from "stone and lime." On a 1541 map where Cíbola first appears, the cartographer marked the geographical location with the facade of a Spanish-style palace.

Niza's wonderful characterization did not last long. Pedro Castañeda de Nájera, Coronado's chronicler, labeled Niza as a liar. According to Castañeda de Nájera's *Relación,* when the soldiers of Coronado's expedition arrived at Cíbola, "they put so many curses on Fray Marcos, that God may have wished not to understand them." The view of the barbaric Indian predominated also in the later chroniclers and in other writers, in spite of Palafox de Mendoza's efforts in his *Virtudes del indio* (*Indian Virtues*) and Francisco Javier Clavijero, whose eighteenth-century *Historia antigua de México* (*Ancient History of Mexico*) defended the culture of the Mexican Indians in general.

A center commonly increases its hegemony by denigrating the peripheral and the marginal spaces. Mexico City's disdain of the North can also be traced to a mythical origin. Barbaric tribes would swarm from the north destroying the cities of Anáhuac. The Chichimecas (whose dog totem protected them, according to some anthropologists) were some of the last invaders. Clavijero nonetheless defends them, writing that "their customs were sweeter than one would expect from a society of hunters," footnoting that according to Torquemada, the Chichimecas dwelled in caves, and that the most important city of their kingdom was called Amaquemecan. Clavijero questions Torquemada: "Who has ever seen a city without houses? Who has ever called the caves of the forests a city?" He also denied the traditional association made between the Chichimecas and the dog. He footnoted: "Betancourt believed their name derived from Chichime, which means, he says, 'dogs,' a slur used by other tribes. But if this were the case, they would not take pride as they did in the label. The name probably derives from a place called Chichiman, as Acolman derives from Acolmecatl." The image, nevertheless, remains, as the short story "People of the Dog," by the Chicana writer Alma Luz Villanueva, demonstrates.

The stereotyping of the northern Indians as barbarians predominated until the decline of the Porfirio Díaz administration. The nineteenth-century writer Manuel Payno, who was born in Mexico City, had lived in the city of Matamoros, and had traveled to other northern cities, wrote a romantic description of Monterrey that ends with a reference to the Indians similar to those of the early chroniclers. "Monterrey would undoubtedly improve rapidly if it were completely free of the terrible Indian plague that devastates its surroundings every winter, and it would be one of the most pleasant countries in which to spend a quiet and relaxing life." Payno focuses on one of those raids in his short story "La víspera y el día de una boda" ("The Vespers and the Wedding Day"), of which Francisco Monterde wrote: "Fear and hatred towards the Comanche Indians—not absorbed by civilization—is very much alive in this narrative."

Nevertheless, during the first decade of the twentieth century, changes occur. Alfonso Reyes and other northern writers who directed literary and cultural activities changed the stereotyped image of the North as a region of barbarians. But, it seems, stereotypes never die. In 1963, Ignacio Bernal still titles one of the chapters of his *Tenochtitlán en una isla* (*Tenochtitlán on an Island*) "Los nuevos bárbaros" ("The New Barbarians").

When we examine the literature of the North we are confronted with the difficult question of defining the geographical space. Geographers do not agree about the borders of the region. The region could easily be limited to northern states that border the United States. But we know that this border, as a recent political creation, emerged from the 1836 and 1846 conflicts between Mexico and the United States. If those wars had not fragmented the North, readers could easily imagine a northern literature made up of regional subdivisions, including those of Alta California, New Mexico, and Arizona.

Ideally, if we could forget the geographical problem, we could argue that northern Mexico shares only one border with the United States. Although an argument could be made regarding the political borders of the country, it could not be made regarding the region's literary history, since pre-1848 authors who identified themselves with New Spain and Mexico lived in a region that extended beyond the Rio Grande/Río Bravo. The literature of northern Mexico originated precisely in the territories that Mexico lost to the United States. The chronicles of the Spanish conquistadores and criollos first described the peoples and attributes of the area. The literature that critics have not incorporated into the canon of Mexican literature has been claimed by Chicanos and Chicanas as their own.

Establishing the limits between the North and the rest of the country emerges as a much more difficult geographical problem. Does the literature of Baja California Sur, Sinaloa, Durango, Zacatecas, San Luis Potosí, and the northern part of Nayarit belong to northeast Mexico as classified by Ángel Bassols Batalla? Hernán Solís Garza's *Los mexicanos del norte* (*Northern Mexicans*) argues that because the boundaries of the region defined by Bassols Batalla include "more than half of Mexico, we could not label all of its population as 'northern Mexicans.'" In this study we are considering as border writers only those from the six states that border the United States, along with those of Baja California Sur, since it forms a geographical unit with Baja California Norte. For this definition of northern literature, we take as an important literary antecedent Roberto Villarino's anthology, which includes writers from those seven states.

This geographical limitation to the northern states that have a common border with the United States is, of course, arbitrary. It would be much more logical to analyze this literature based on literary tropes, but that is not our purpose in this study; rather, we are concerned with the literary relations between the North and the center, keeping in mind, as Saravia Quiroz points out, traits common to the border literature, such as the "geographical isolation, the bicultural coexistence, the center's precarious traditional assimilations, . . . the presence of a limited cultural system and sometimes a marginality that in the 1980s—experiences a relative 'eclosion.'" Those who wish to analyze this literature must keep in mind these characteristics. It will also be necessary to take into account those elements that have contributed to its formation, such as the influence of the environment, confrontation with the native inhabitants, racial and cultural conflicts, intertextuality, and linguistic background, as well as the cultural and literary influence of the United States.

Northern literature differs from that of central and southern Mexico simply by theme, due to the cultural substratum of each region, to the dialectical differences (especially vocabulary) resulting from the different languages and native dialects, and to the landscape's influence, most significantly the desert. San Luis Potosí's Manuel José Othón, who lived several years in southern Coahuila, beautifully captures the landscape in his poetry. In *Poemas rústicos* (*Country Poems*), Alfonso Reyes believes that Othón possesses the "special faculty to feel the poetic aspect of things, more the true than the fantastic, more the immediate reality than the dreamt or imagined." One has to remember that Othón has been one of the few writers who resisted the attraction of the center.

With the exception of a few trips to Mexico City, he spent his life in the North, working as a lawyer, contemplating the landscape, and writing poetry. Those writers who abandoned the region and reached their creative maturity away from the border tend to write about universal themes, as in the case of Artemio de Valle Arizpe and Julio Torri. Others (Alfonso Reyes, Martín Luis Guzmán, Rafael Muñoz) leave the North but do not forget it.

Then there are those writers who leave the North for a period of time, but who, like the prodigal son, eventually return to their native states. José Alvarado, among others, is a good example. After teaching for more than twenty years at the Escuela Nacional Preparatoria and writing essays with universal themes for major Mexico City journals, he returned to Nuevo León, where popular literature suggested themes for some of his best essays and short stories. Frequently writers like Amparo Ruíz de Burton, in the nineteenth century, leave the region for the United States. She moved from Baja California to San Francisco, where she published two novels and a play. Josefina Niggli, born in Monterrey, wrote two novels in English set in the state of Nuevo León: *Mexican Village* (1945), set in Sabinas, Hidalgo, and *Step Down, Elder Brother* (1947), set in Monterrey. The same is true of Chicano writers such as Abelardo Delgado and Aristeo Brito, from Chihuahua, and Ángela de Hoyos, from Coahuila.

Some critics insist that recent northern literature is a result of the region's proximity to the United States. Poor North, so far away from the capital and so close to Texas, Arizona, and California! Saravia Quiroz observes that this proximity "results in the sharing of myths and observations about the characteristics of the American way of life." Nonetheless, Saravia Quiroz does not accept, but rather denies, the existence of a binational culture. "It would be tempting to suggest that border writers have a binational character in terms of literary influences. It's not the case, although they reveal, especially in northwestern Mexico, a significant closeness and knowledge of United States literature." He also observes that knowledge of United States literature does not extend to Chicanos, since he observes: "In the sphere of regional influences, northern Mexican writers have not interacted with Chicano writers."

Saravia Quiroz reasons that "the border between the two countries has deterred communication between Mexican border writers and Chicano writers." Why, we must ask, does United States literature cross the frontier without difficulty, but not Chicano and Chicana literature?

Like a wave, the influence of United States literature moves southward, piercing the center's supremacy. Carlos Monsiváis has made use of this, gathering material for several of his articles. Saravia Quiroz alludes, in passing, to the fact that the marginal languages of the border have influenced the "Onda" writers. "We must not forget that the 'Onda' writers in the 1960s creatively adapted the underworld jargon of the border." Since he had already mentioned that border literature also makes use of "marginal languages," we do not know if this is a direct influence from those languages or an imitation of the Onda style. But already in 1981, Carlos Monsiváis, who focuses on border culture and Mexican literature, talked about the recent strength of border culture and provided as an example "the movement known in Mexico as the Onda (which lasted approximately from 1966 to 1972 and which is, in a way, a variety of the hippie movement), derived its slang and its first demonstrations from drug culture and rock music produced by Tijuana and Ciudad Juárez musical groups."

With the emergence of new political ideas, new nations, and new postmodern critical theories, the concept of a dominant center declines for those who believe in the primacy of margins, peripheries, borders, and geographical and cultural equalities. Villarino's anthology introduces more than ninety young northern border writers. Villarino's list of authors does not include well-recognized national figures like Jesús Gardea, Carlos Montemayor, Edmundo Valadés, and others. We can better appreciate Villarino's anthology when we take into account that the *Diccionario de escritores mexicanos*, edited by Aurora Ocampo de Gómez and Ernesto Prado Velázquez, only includes twenty-nine border authors in the history of Mexican literature from colonial times to 1967.

Finally, Rosina Conde's 1994 anthology of Mexican writers, published by Fiction International, includes sixteen border writers in the list of thirty-four. Central Mexico's growing interest in the border could of course explain the phenomenon. In "Turn-of-the-Century Mexican Narrative: A Tourist Guide," Gabriel Trujillo Muñoz observes the following: "A new element for Mexican fiction through the 1980s is the rise of regional tales and the appearance of authors who did not want to go on glossing life in Mexico City and other cosmopolitan centers, but rather to rescue the equally contradictory worlds of the country's interior. . . . The first to declare themselves in public defense of their respective regions were Jesús Gardea, Ignacio Betancourt, Daniel Sada, and Severino Salazar at the beginning of the 1980s. The north is peopled with narrative voices."

Trujillo Muñoz then includes a list of representative border writers. We have to keep in mind that Trujillo Muñoz prepared his anthology not for Mexican readers but for an English-speaking public. Nevertheless, the presence of those northern writers demonstrates that cultural decentralization has opened new avenues for border literature. We can only hope that such a strengthening tendency will benefit the national literature of Mexico.

30

ASPECTS OF THE MEXICAN NOVEL

During the long colonial period, no novels were published in Mexico, or as far as it is known, even written. All forms of fiction were considered by the Spanish government as detrimental to the morals of the Indians, and therefore banished from the New World. It was necessary, for this and other reasons, to wait until the years of the struggle for independence for the novel to be born.

Six years after Miguel Hidalgo began his fight to make Mexico independent from Spain, a criollo, José Joaquín Fernández de Lizardi, writing under the pen name of "El Pensador Mexicano," published the first Latin American novel, *El periquillo sarniento,* with the purpose of criticizing the Spanish institutions under which Mexico was ruled during the period. The novel was prohibited after the government discovered that it was anti-Spanish in tone. The last of its four parts did not come off the press until Mexico had obtained its independence in 1821.

While Lizardi's novel uses a picaresque form, it is written in a style that can be considered Mexican, as it is entirely different from that of the Spanish novelists of the period. Lizardi dared to use the language of the people, and especially that of the *léperos,* the lowest social class in Mexico City. His novel is the best picture of Mexican society at the end of the colonial period. It is still read, and its popularity is attested to by

First published in *Arizona Quarterly* 24, no. 1 (1968): 53–64.

the many translations. As late as 1941, Katherine Ann Porter published a translation in English under the title of *The Itching Parrot*.

Lizardi's example, unfortunately, was not followed by the novelists of the romantic period, who fell back upon Spanish narrative forms, styles, and techniques, especially those of the *costumbristas*. The only exception was the novel *Astucia* (1865), by Luis G. Inclán, written in the Spanish spoken by the rural people of central Mexico. He did not, unfortunately, set up a trend.

It was necessary to wait until Altamirano, in 1867, encouraged novelists to break away from their European models.

Political independence, obtained from Spain in 1821, had not produced an independent literature. Nor, for that matter, real social change. The first change in the structure of Mexican society was not brought about until 1857, when Juárez's government put into effect the laws of reform. The constitution of 1857 provided, for the first time, for free education, for the separation of church and state, for religious liberty, for freedom of speech, for the abolition of all titles of royalty, and for equality among all citizens, regardless of whether they were Indians, mestizos, or criollos.

The changes introduced by Juárez were not accepted without a struggle by the classes affected. A civil war that lasted three years was the result. The conservative party, unable to win on the battlefield, asked Napoleon III of France for help, and the second Mexican empire of the nineteenth century was established with Maximilian and Carlota as rulers.

But Juárez was persistent and finally conquered Maximilian in 1867 and restored the republic. The following year Ignacio Manuel Altamirano, an Indian like Juárez, published his first and now famous *Revistas literarias*, in which he advocated the creation of a national literature. "As long as we limit ourselves," he wrote," to imitating the French novel, whose form is unadaptable to our customs and our way of being, we will produce but pale and wretched imitations. . . . We do not deny the great value of studying all the literary schools of the civilized world . . . but we wish to create a literature which is absolutely our own."

Just like Lizardi's, Altamirano's example was not followed by the novelists of his day. They kept on imitating the French and Spanish writers of the period. After Juárez's death in 1872, the country soon fell under the influence of Porfirio Díaz, whose paternalistic form of government lasted from 1876 until 1910. During the years of his dictatorship, Mexican culture, and especially literature, was dominated again by European thinking. The influence came from France and Spain. The poets imitated the French, and the novelists the Spaniards. These two literary currents, modernism and traditionalism, unfolded side by side, with occasional skirmishes between the followers of the two schools. With few exceptions, the *modernistas* restricted themselves to the writing of poetry, essays, and short stories; the realists and naturalists, to the writing of novels and dramas.

The *modernistas*, at least in Mexico, did not write any novels. The only exception was Amado Nervo, who published two novelettes. But even here, the theme and techniques are those of the naturalists. The Mexican novelists of the period, as a rule, followed in the steps of Galdós and Pereda, going as far as imitating their style, techniques, themes, and forms. Some, like Gamboa, imitated the French naturalists, especially Zola. His novel *Santa* (1903) is an imitation of Zola's *Nana*, and his *Reconquista*, although with a different theme, shows striking similarities to Zola's *L'œuvre*.

The striving to imitate European culture came to an end in 1910, the year of the revolution. Although the movement was a product of the people, the ground had been prepared by a group of intellectuals who had formed, in 1906, a circuit of lecturers and founded a review to give expression to their ideas. Among these young men there were such well-known writers as Alfonso Reyes, José Vasconcelos, Antonio Caso, and the Dominican Pedro Henríquez Ureña. This new generation rejected the philosophy of the positivists and the aesthetics of the naturalists, firm believers in determinism. They declared freedom of thought and introduced the study of other philosophers besides Comte and Spencer. Bergson and William James were presented by Caso in his philosophy courses at the university. Soon the group organized itself into an *ateneo de la juventud* and was able to influence the then-powerful minister of education, Don Justo Sierra, who in 1908 made a speech rejecting positivism as an official philosophy.

Two years later, Madero and his followers were able to overthrow Díaz and to establish a democratic form of government. It must be pointed out that the writers of the *ateneo* were mostly interested in the essay as a form of expression, and not in the novel. However, their styles, especially those of Alfonso Reyes and Pedro Henríquez Ureña, had great influence in the forging of a new form of prose writing. It was neither an imitation of the French nor of the Spanish, but rather an original form of expression in which emphasis was given to clearness of presentation, to the use of native images, and to the abandonment of all exotic motifs.

Madero's assassination in 1913 resulted in a period of chaos that lasted until 1917. As a consequence of this political upheaval, great changes took place in the arts and in literature. After a new constitution was adopted in 1917 and the country was pacified, a cultural renaissance began to unfold. During the presidency of Álvaro Obregón, who governed from 1920 to 1924, José Vasconcelos, as secretary of education, called several painters, among them Diego Rivera, to decorate the walls of the principal government buildings. The murals of Rivera, Orozco, Siqueiros, and others, depicting the history of Mexico and the struggle of the people for freedom, had a tremendous influence in the development of the other arts, as well as in the creation of a national consciousness.

In the field of the novel, the first great work that is a direct result of the revolution is *Los de abajo* (*The Underdogs*), by Mariano Azuela, first published in November 1915, precisely a hundred years after the first Latin American novel, *El periquillo sarniento* (*The Itching Parrot*). If Lizardi's work revived a lost genre, the picaresque romance, Azuela's work initiated another, the novel of the Mexican Revolution. The book is significant not only for its theme, but also for its form. Azuela abandoned the technique of the European novelists and created a new form, genuinely Mexican, admirably adapted to give expression to the theme. Its creation was significant in the development of the Spanish American novel, as it set a trend toward the use of national subjects, characters, and environments.

Much more significant than *The Underdogs*, from the point of view of its form, is the short novel *La malhora*, which Azuela published in 1923.

Here he introduced into Mexican fiction techniques that foreshadow such novels as *Al filo del agua* (*At the Edge of the Storm*), by Agustín Yáñez, and *La region más transparente* (*Where the Air Is Clear*), by Carlos Fuentes. In *La malhora*, Azuela makes use of a fragmented structure, characterized by the overlapping of the time element, the fragmentary scenes, the flashback, the distorted plot, and the unfinished characterization. The most striking change in technique is the use of juxtaposed scenes, unrelated by logical links. This spatial arrangement makes this novel one of the precursors of Rulfo's *Pedro Páramo;* definitely, *La malhora* points the way to a new type of novel. But we must wait until 1943 before a new one appears.

President Lázaro Cárdenas ruled Mexico from 1934 to 1940. He was what could be called the last president of the period of the revolution. By 1940, the reforms envisioned by Madero, Zapata, and other revolutionary leaders had been accomplished. The land had been divided, the workers had been unionized, the church schools had been put under the supervision of the federal government, and the oil industry had been nationalized. Since 1940, the government has not tried to bring about radical social changes, but has rather concentrated on increasing the material wealth of the nation by establishing industries and by improving agriculture. Their efforts have been rewarded, and although much remains to be done, the living conditions of the people are becoming increasingly better.

In literature, and especially in the novel, a similar change took place in the year 1940. The young men who began to write in that year were, as a rule, born after 1910. Therefore, they knew about the revolution only through books and through what their parents told them. For them, the revolution, as a motivating force, and as a theme, had ceased to have any meaning. They were, and still are, very much interested in the results of the movement. Some look upon it as a success and others as a failure. These attitudes can be observed mostly in the novel and the essay, as poetry becomes once more universal in theme and interested in giving expression to problems and emotions common to all mankind.

After 1940, the Mexican novel also attained maturity. Since the theme of the revolution had been overworked, new avenues of expression had to be found. The techniques of the novel of the revolution, based on the simple device of putting together disconnected scenes, had to be discarded for new structures in order to renew interest in this art form.

The new novel, that is, the novel produced during the forties and fifties, reflects the tendencies of the European and North American novel. At the same time, it is a novel that does not lose its Mexican identity, since it does not break entirely with tradition. The influence of the novelists of the revolution—Azuela, Guzmán, Romero—is evident in the selection of themes, in the creation of backgrounds, and in the techniques of characterization. But the influence of the European and North American novel is also evident in the treatment of the national themes, in the form, and in the introduction of new points of view. Of the North American novelists the most obvious influence has been that of Faulkner, Dos Passos, and Hemingway; of the English, that of Joyce, Woolf, and Huxley; and of the French, that of Robbe-Grillet and Sarraute. The application of new techniques to the development of Mexican subject matter has produced an original novel that without losing its national identity has become universal. The novelists who have contributed most to the development of this new novel are José Revueltas, Agustín Yáñez, Juan Rulfo, Carlos Fuentes, and Salvador Elizondo.

In 1943, Revueltas published *El luto humano,* translated into English under the title *The Stone Knife,* the first novel written by a Mexican author in which an attempt is made to apply modern novelistic techniques. Although in some respects it shows the influence of Azuela, Guzmán, and Gregorio López y Fuentes, in others that of William Faulkner predominates. This novel represents a contribution to the development of Mexican fiction because Revueltas, without abandoning Mexican subject matter, tries to solve the problems of narrative technique. If he failed to solve them satisfactorily, his lesson was not lost, and soon after there were novelists who produced works of a high quality.

Revueltas's novel unfolds in a reduced space, in a very hostile, desolated environment. The characters, as in the great Latin American novels, have to fight against nature and, at the same time, against their fellow men. This struggle against nature is not, however, the central theme; the central unifying theme is death, which results from the tragic conflict among the characters. To give the novel dramatic tension, the author creates a very reduced space, Úrsulo's hut, where the principal characters meet. The occasion is the wake of Chonita, Úrsulo's young daughter. The raging storm and the presence of the dead girl combine to give the story a sense of inevitable tragedy. All the characters—Úrsulo and his wife, his friend Adán, Calixto and his wife, the drunkard Jerónimo and his wife—are common people. The only exception is the parish priest. They have all gone through the horrible experiences of the revolution. After having fought and suffered, they still live in poverty, working hard to wrest a living from a hostile land, without any motivation to keep on going except hatred for one another and an irrational love of the barren land. Before death overtakes them, they relate their life stories, all of them in tragic terms, depicting their fight against destiny, symbolic of a Mexico that was struggling to get on its feet after a long and merciless revolution. But the most important aspect of this novel is the emphasis the author gives to psychological insights into the behavior of the characters, rather than stressing their actions, as was done by the novelists of the revolution. All the action takes place in one night.

The following year, 1944, Rubén Salazar Mallén published a short novel, *Soledad* (*Loneliness*), in which he carries the psychological process farther than Revueltas had done. If in *El luto humano* we still find social preaching, in *Soledad* nothing remains but the interest in the psychological presentation of the central character, Aquiles Alcázar, a government worker in Mexico City haunted by a persecution complex. Alcázar is a symbol of the man whose life is a vacuum; a symbol of modern man, isolated from his fellow men by his own fear, incapable of carrying out any constructive action, without any will power to conquer, always thinking about the negative significance of the most inconsequential actions and words of his fellow workers. In order to present the psychological aspect of Alcázar's life, the author makes use of the stream of consciousness technique, thus giving the reader a direct insight into the character's mind.

Some critics may object that Salazar Mallén's novel is too short, that it lacks depth and complexity. This could not be said of Agustín Yáñez's novel *Al filo del agua* (*At the Edge of the Storm*), which appeared in 1947 and represents perhaps the most ambitious undertaking in the field of the novel by a Mexican writer. It brings together several trends that had been present in Mexican fiction: it is a work of art that is, at the same time, national and universal, artistic and social. If some critics consider *Al filo del agua* as a novel of the revolution, it is because in it we find the best explanation of why the revolution took place. The novelist selected a dramatic moment not only in the life of his characters, but also in the history of Mexico. The Mexican people, so well represented in this novel, were in 1909 at the brink of an explosion; the unfolding of the novel is parallel to the unfolding of Mexican history. The causes to which the author attributes the revolution are not stated explicitly in the novel, but the reader can easily reach the conclusions from the actions of the characters. Yáñez has created a community that is completely isolated from the main cultural currents, not by its own will, but by a severe censorship emanating from civil and religious authorities. It is a community where free thinking is unknown, where repressed sexual desires drive both men and women to insanity, where reading a daily newspaper is considered a major sin. No wonder, then, that there is an explosion of gigantic proportions. Yáñez obtains depth by using a dense, almost baroque style, very appropriate for telling about the nature of these tormented souls, of their spiritual conflicts, of their motivations (sex, greed, ambition). No less important is the structure of the novel, divided, like a symphony, into four parts, and each in turn into four chapters. To obtain density, the novelist presents simultaneous scenes. The first four chapters, which take place during the same night at four different places, reveal to us what is going on in the souls of four of the town's important persons at the same time. The tempo lento in which the narrative unfolds adds to the effectiveness of the novel, ending appropriately with an explosion in the characters' souls, synchronized with the national explosion of 1910. Better than anyone else, Yáñez has brought to life that world of the last years of Díaz's regime, at the precise moment when that stagnant society was ready for a change.

Another aspect of life in a small town is found in Juan Rulfo's novel *Pedro Páramo* (1955), a unique work in many respects. Through a poetic style, Rulfo is able to give life to a dead town, a town that has been choked to death by the local cacique, Pedro Páramo. The novel has also a poetic structure; that is, the transitions from scene to scene are not carried out by introducing formal linking elements; they are, like the stanzas in a poem, juxtaposed, united only by the central theme. The reader passes from one place to another, from one time to another, from one world to another (most of the characters are dead), as in a poem, by means of the introduction of lyrical motifs, which Rulfo can use with great effectiveness.

But *Pedro Páramo* is also a novel of unforgettable characters. There we find people tormented by overpowering passions: Susana San Juan by a great love; Pedro Páramo by a desire to dominate his fellow men; Father Renteria by remorse; Miguel Páramo by sexual desire. Although they are dead, this fact does not make them less real. Rulfo has been able to make his characters seem alive by using the first-person narrative and letting them tell their own stories from their own points of view, much like Dante in his *Inferno*.

The novel is a mixture of realism and fantasy. From the very first page, when the reader goes into the town of Comala with the narrator, he enters a world of fantasy. Yet the scenes described are realistic. The style, which may be called magic realism, has been created by Rulfo through the use of images that, although poetic, are structured in a language that is characteristic of the Mexican countryside. As Yáñez did in *Al filo del agua*, Rulfo, in *Pedro Páramo*, makes death the central unifying theme. The difference between the two novels is that Yáñez looks at death from the outside, while Rulfo goes beyond, to an imaginary point of view after death.

Three years after the publication of *Pedro Páramo*, that is, in 1958, Carlos Fuentes (born in 1928) published *Where the Air Is Clear*, an experimental novel in which the author tries to give expression to the spirit of Mexico City, the region where the air is clear, a metaphor used ironically. The structure of the novel is built up through the accumulation of scenes in Mexico City; but instead of passing, as in *Al filo del agua* and *Pedro Páramo*, from the mind of one character to that of another, the reader is transported from one social group to another.

We may find ourselves in the streets with a prostitute; in the home of a pseudoaristocratic family; in the home of an old revolutionary leader now turned capitalist and owner of a bank and large real estate holdings; in the primitive hut of Teódula, a symbol of the Indian past; or with Zamacona, representative of the new intellectuals. In order to integrate these diverse elements, Fuentes makes use of a mythical character, Ixca Cienfuegos, who moves from group to group with great ease. But it is the city that really comes to life, leaving in the reader a sense of it being the real protagonist.

In *The Death of Artemio Cruz*, Fuentes integrates the elements of the novel much better by creating a central character, Artemio Cruz, who on his deathbed at the age of seventy-one, reviews his entire life. The novel includes a long period of Mexican history, from the age of Santa Anna to the present. Each chapter is dedicated to an important historical event, but also to an incident that has changed the protagonist's life. Cruz is a man whose only preoccupation is survival and material well-being. To accomplish this, Cruz tramples upon his fellow men, even his friends and his own family. All the scenes in the novel have one purpose: to show how this self-made man has survived, how he has become selfish, arrogant, and hard even to the point of despising his own family, his best friends, and his own country.

After a long silence, in 1967 Fuentes finally published two more novels, *Zona sagrada* and *A Change of Skin*, the last one just off the press. He is, doubtless, Mexico's most vigorous novelist. Among the young men, that is, those novelists born after 1930, the most promising are Vicente Leñero (1933), Salvador Elizondo (1932), and Fernando del Paso (1935). Leñero became famous with his novel *Los albañiles* (*The Bricklayers*, 1964), the story of a crime that is never really solved. The reader has to infer who the criminal might have been. In this novel, Leñero is able to re-create effectively the dialogues of the construction workers in Mexico City, where the action takes place.

Much more important is the novel *Farabeuf* (1965), by Salvador Elizondo, the first attempt in Mexican fiction to write an antinovel like those of Sarraute and Robbe-Grillet. The subtitle, "Chronicle of an Instant," reveals its structure, which is based on the minute reconstruction, in the minds of the characters, of a significant moment in their lives. More than the narrative element, the minute descriptions of the scenery create interest. The theme is the torment given to a Chinese prisoner, a torment that is associated with sex drives and desires. The book is illustrated with a picture of a Chinese man being dismembered, an image that is central in the novel and that leaves the reader with a sense of horror.

Farabeuf was published in 1965 and won the Xavier Villaurrutia Prize in literature. In 1966, this coveted prize was won by a novel called *José Trigo,* the first work of Fernando del Paso, a poet born in Mexico City in 1935. This, his first novel, is an ambitious work that can only be compared to James Joyce's *Ulysses.* It has the same structure, a style that is similar to that of Joyce, and the subject matter is the journey of a man, José Trigo, in search of his soul. The novel unfolds in the old railroad station of Nonoalco-Tlatelolco in Mexico City, and through the use of the trains as motifs, Del Paso reconstructs the history of Mexico and the life of the protagonist.

Elizondo and Del Paso are not the only novelists of the younger generation. There are also Gustavo Sáenz, José Agustín, and many others. But the novels I have mentioned are, perhaps, the most significant among those written recently. These novels are equal to those of other Spanish-speaking countries and are representative not only of Mexican fiction but also of world narrative trends in general.

In the last twenty years, the Mexican novel has achieved a truly universal outlook, without giving up its national character. Mexican novelists have been able to adapt the techniques of world fiction to Mexican themes and subject matter. The result has been a novel that is at the same time national and universal; a novel that has meaning for the native reader but also for the reader who is not acquainted with Mexico.

31

MAGIC REALISM

In his article "Magical Realism in Spanish American Fiction," Professor Ángel Flores proposes the year 1935 as marking the birth of magic realism. For Flores, Jorge Luis Borges's book *A Universal History of Infamy*, which appeared that year, marks the new trend in Latin narrative. According to Flores, Borges's work reflects the influence of Kafka, whose stories the author of the *Aleph* had translated and published two years earlier. "In his laboriously precisionist way," says Flores, "Kafka had mastered from his earliest short stories—'The Judgment' (1912), 'Metamorphosis' (1916)—the difficult art of mingling his drab reality with the phantasmal world of his nightmares. . . . The novelty therefore consisted in the amalgamation of realism and fantasy. Each of these, separately and by devious ways, made its appearance in Latin America: realism, since the Colonial Period but especially during the 1880s; the magical, writ large from the earliest—in the letters of Columbus, in the chroniclers, in the sagas of Cabeza de Vaca."

Flores also considers the works of the Argentines Bioy Casares, Silvina Ocampo, Mallea, Sábato, Bianco, and Cortázar, the Chilean María Luisa Bombal, the Cubans Novás Calvo and Labrador Ruiz, the Mexicans Arreola and Rulfo, and the Uruguayan Onetti as belonging to magic realism. Flores finds in these writers the following distinguishing

First published in English in *Magic Realism: Theory, History, Community*, ed. Lois Parkinson Zamora and Wendy B. Faris (Durham, N.C.: Duke University Press, 1995), 119–24. First published in Spanish in *Cuadernos Americanos* 26 (1967): 230–35.

characteristics: a preoccupation with style and an interest in transforming "the common and the everyday into the awesome and the unreal."
And he adds: "Time exists in a kind of timeless fluidity and the unreal
happens as part of reality." He cites as an example the case of Gregor
Samsa, whose transformation into a cockroach or a bedbug is accepted
as an almost normal event.

Professor Flores does not offer a formal definition of magic realism in his study but he does say that its practitioners "cling to reality
as if to prevent 'literature' from getting in their way, as if to prevent
their myth from flying off, as in fairy tales, to supernatural realms. The
narrative proceeds in well-prepared, increasingly intense steps, which
ultimately may lead to one great ambiguity or confusion. . . . All the
magical realists have this in common, as well as their repudiation of
that mawkish sentimentalism which pervades so many of the Latin
American classics: *María, Cumandá, Aves sin nido* (*Birds Without a
Nest*)." And then he adds: "Often their writings approach closely the art
Ortega y Gasset called 'dehumanized.' . . . Besides, their plots are logi-
cally conceived. . . . This concern of the magical realists for the well-knit
plot probably stems from their familiarity with detective stories, which
Borges, Bioy Casares, Peyrou, and other magical realists have written,
translated, or anthologized."

I have cited Professor Flores's essay at length because, incredible as
it may seem, this is until now the only study of magic realism in Latin
American literature. His was a voice in the desert, though since then the
term has been used repeatedly without being precisely defined.

I do not agree with Professor Flores's definition of magic realism because it seems to me that he includes authors who do not belong to the
movement. Neither do I agree that the movement was started by Borges
in 1935 and flowered between 1940 and 1950. I will explain why.

The term *magic realism* was first used by the art critic Franz Roh to
designate the pictorial output of the postexpressionist period, beginning around 1925. Roh explains the origin of the term by saying that
with the word *magical*, as opposed to *mystical*, he wished to emphasize
that "the mystery does not descend to the represented world but rather
hides and palpitates behind it." In Latin America, it seems to have been

Arturo Uslar Pietri who first used the term in his book *Letras y hom-bres de Venezuela* (*Letters and Men of Venezuela,* 1948), where he says: "What became prominent in the short story and left an indelible mark there was the consideration of man as a mystery surrounded by realistic facts. A poetic prediction or a poetic denial of reality. What for lack of another name could be called a magical realism." After Uslar Pietri, Alejo Carpentier has paid this phenomenon the most attention. In the prologue to his magic realist novel *El reino de este mundo* (*The Kingdom of This World,* 1949), he makes this interesting observation: "the mar-velous—he says—begins to be unmistakably marvelous when it arises from an unexpected alteration of reality (the miracle) from a privileged revelation of reality, an unusual insight that particularly favors the unex-pected richness of reality or an amplification of the scale and categories of reality, reality thus perceived with special intensity by virtue of an exaltation of the spirit that leads it to a kind of extreme state."

So we see that magic realism cannot be identified either with fan-tastic literature or with psychological literature, or with the surrealist or hermetic literature that Ortega describes. Unlike superrealism, magic realism does not use dream motifs; neither does it distort reality or cre-ate imagined worlds, as writers of fantastic literature or science fiction do; nor does it emphasize psychological analysis of characters, since it does not try to find reasons for their actions or their inability to express themselves. Magic realism is not an aesthetic movement either, as was modernism, which was interested in creating works dominated by a re-fined style; neither is it interested in the creation of complex structures per se.

Magic realism is not magic literature either. Its aim, unlike that of magic, is to express emotions, not to evoke them. Magic realism is, more than anything else, an attitude toward reality that can be expressed in popular or cultured forms, in elaborate or rustic styles, in closed or open structures. What is the attitude of the magic realist toward reality? I have already said that he does not create imaginary worlds in which we can hide from everyday reality. In magic realism, the writer con-fronts reality and tries to untangle it, to discover what is mysterious in things, in life, in human acts. This is what Arturo Uslar Pietri, Miguel

Ángel Asturias, Alejo Carpentier, Lino Novás Calvo, Juan Rulfo, Félix Pita Rodríguez, Nicolás Guillén, and other short story writers, novelists, and poets do in their works. In his story "Secret Weapons" ("Las armas secretas"), Julio Cortázar has the narrator say, "strange how people are under the impression that making a bed is exactly the same as making a bed, that to shake hands is always the same as shaking hands, that opening a can of sardines is to open the same can of sardines ad infinitum. 'But if everything's an exception,' Pierre is thinking."

Magic realism does not derive, as Professor Flores claims, from Kafka's work. In the prologue to a Spanish translation of *The Metamorphosis*, Borges makes the astute observation that the basic characteristic of Kafka's stories is "the invention of intolerable situations." And we might add: if, as Professor Flores notices, in Kafka's story the characters accept the transformation of a man into a cockroach, their attitude toward reality is not magic; they find the situation intolerable and they do not accept it. In the stories of Borges, as in those by other writers of fantastic literature, the principal trait is the creation of infinite hierarchies. Neither of those two tendencies permeates works of magic realism, where the principal thing is not the creation of imaginary beings or worlds, but the discovery of the mysterious relationship between man and his circumstances. The existence of the marvelous real is what started magic realist literature, which some critics claim is the truly American literature!

In contrast to avant-garde literature, magic realism is not escapist. The English critic Collingwood, in speaking of art as magic in his book *The Principles of Art*, says:

> What is important to the aesthetician is the re-emergence of a very old kind of aesthetic consciousness: one which reverses the painfully taught lesson of nineteenth-century criticism, and instead of saying never mind about the subject, the subject is only a *corpus vile* on which the artist has exercised his powers, and what concerns you is the artist's powers, and the way in which he has here displayed them. The artist's powers can be displayed only when he uses them upon a subject that is worthy of them. This new aesthetic consciousness involves a dual vision. It regards the subject as an integral element in the work of art;

it maintains that in order to appreciate any given work of art one must be interested in its subject for its own sake, as well as in the artist's handling of it.

This interest in theme, a central characteristic of magic realism, is what unifies the works in this movement, whether they be popular or more elite examples. In Rómulo Gallegos's novel *Cantaclaro* (1934), we find a young man from Caracas who is attracted to the plains and who soon becomes disillusioned. During one significant scene, he confronts the old plainsman Crisanto, whom he considers his inferior, and dares to insult him. The plainsman says to him with great dignity: "Look, young man. I don't know how to explain myself very well, but you'll manage to get my point. . . . You keep trying to understand what is beyond your grasp. . . . You hear the buzzing of the bees—since you mentioned them—and, moving up the social scale, you hear us too, but you will never listen to the prayer of the Lonely Soul because your intelligence suppresses it." For Don Crisanto, the unreal seems to be part of reality, and he accepts it. And the same thing happens with the characters in the novel *Pedro Páramo,* where none of them "suppresses" the existence of suffering souls. But Rulfo goes even further than that, capturing reality from the dead narrator's point of view. His poetic vision of reality, expressed in verbal forms taken from popular language, gives his work a magical tone.

In magic realism, key events have no logical or psychological explanation. The magic realist does not try to copy the surrounding reality (as realists did) or to wound it (as the surrealists did), but to seize the mystery that breathes behind things. In Pita Rodríguez's story "Alarico the Potter," the belongings of the mysterious character who wears an enigmatic ring disintegrate when he dies; in Carpentier's "Journey to the Seed," time flows backward at the exact moment when the old black gardener twirls his staff; in Carpentier's *The Lost Steps,* the protagonist, returning to the jungle, is unable to find the arm of the river through which he had gone from the present to the past, from modern civilization, where life has its meaning, to a primitive American paradise. Let us keep in mind that in these magic realist works, the author does not need to justify the mystery of events, as the fantastic writer has to. In fantastic literature, the supernatural invades a world ruled by reason. In magic realism, "the mystery does not descend to the represented world, but rather hides and palpitates behind it." In order to seize reality's mysteries, the magic realist writer heightens his senses until he reaches an extreme state (*estado límite*) that allows him to intuit the imperceptible subtleties of the external world, the multifarious world in which we live.

32

AFRICAN INFLUENCES

The influence of blacks upon the development of life and culture in Mexico is a topic seldom discussed, due perhaps to the fact that their presence is numerically much less than it is in regions like the Caribbean or nations such as Brazil or the United States.

When speaking about the cosmic race, the concept invented by the Mexican philosopher José Vasconcelos to designate the Latino people, including, of course, the Mexicans, we usually think of the mestizo, the new race formed as the result of the union of Spaniards and Indians.

And although the black population also mixed with the other two, this aspect of the composition of *la raza* is usually overlooked; but it is there. As Howard F. Cline stated, "Contemporary Mexican culture is a cosmopolitan mixture of elements drawn from many sources. . . . Very early the African Negro made an appearance and contribution."

Blacks became, in Mexico, the invisible people. If, however, we look for their influence, we discover how important it has been in the formation of Mexican culture: "In the Hispanic-Indian culture that the colonial melting pot produced," the historian Cline also says, "the native Indian and the imported Negro emerged vastly more changed than did the intrusive Spaniard. These centuries and elements forged the modern Mexican template." But not only did the Africans forge the new race,

First published in *Memorias del I simposium internacional sobre etnicidad y pobreza*, ed. María del Carmen Barragán Mendoza and Roberto Cañedo Villareal (Acapulco, Mexico: Universidad Autónoma de Guerrero, 2001), 154–60.

they also helped to create an original culture, as observed by Professor Irving A. Leonard, who wrote that the black's "gifts enriched the arts of music, dance, folklore, sculpture, and carving." The presence of black people in Mexico, however, did not originate with the imported slaves brought by the Spaniards; it predates the colonial period. It goes back, apparently, to the earliest of periods, as their presence, according to some historians, is already found among the Olmecs of Veracruz and Tabasco, whose civilization flourished several centuries before the Christian era. That the Olmecs had an African origin is the impression the visitor to the Museum in Xalapa, Veracruz, gets by observing the features of the many statues, figurines, as well as by examining other Olmec artifacts.

The first black person to arrive in Mexico was a slave of the conqueror himself, Hernán Cortés. His name was Juan Cortés.

During the period of exploration of that region which is now part of the United States, the first black man to appear in its history is Estevanico, a companion of Álvar Núñez Cabeza de Vaca in his long and perilous journey on foot across the continent from Florida to Sonora, Mexico. Estevanico was one of the four survivors of the tragic shipwreck of Pánfilo de Narváez in Florida. The other three were Cabeza de Vaca, Diego Dorantes, and Alonso del Castillo. Cabeza de Vaca, in his *Relación*, refers to Estevanico as "the Black man." He became the intermediary between the three Spaniards and the natives.

"The Black man," Cabeza de Vaca relates, "always spoke to them, ascertaining which way to go and what villages we would find and all the other things we wanted to know." Soon he becomes an experienced guide. At the end of the *Relación*, Cabeza de Vaca gives us a brief account of the survivors, ending with these words: "The fourth is Estevanico; he is a Black Arab and a native of Azamor [a town in Morocco]." Estevanico, apparently, became a slave of Dorantes, for upon reaching Mexico City he was sold to Viceroy Antonio de Mendoza. He later served as guide in the 1539 expedition of Fray Marcos de Niza to New Mexico, where he died.

The first African to appear in Mexican history is Yanga, a slave brought in 1579. He escaped and took refuge in the area of Pico de Orizaba, where he became the leader of a guerrilla group made up of runaway slaves, mestizos, and even Spanish fugitives. In 1609, Viceroy Velasco sent an army to subdue them. Father Juan Laurencio, a Jesuit priest, left an account of the expedition. When Yanga and his followers finally made peace with the government, they were confined to the town of San Lorenzo de los Negros, near Córdoba, in the state of Veracruz. It is not known how Yanga's life ended.

The first black man of letters in Mexico was El Negrito Poeta, famous in Mexican and New Mexican folklore as a very creative popular versifier or *pueta,* as he was called in New Mexico, whose name, coincidentally, was the same as that of the contemporary philosopher José Vasconcelos.

His life was studied in Mexico by the historian Nicolás León and the man of letters and folklorist Rubén M. Campos, and in New Mexico he is mentioned by Aurelio M. Espinosa in his study "Los trovos del viejo Vilmas" ("The Verses of Old Man Vilmas"). León obtained most of his information from the several "Calendarios [Almanacs] del Negrito Poeta."

El Negrito Poeta was born in Almolonga, in the state of Puebla, during the first third of the eighteenth century, the son of Congolese parents brought to Mexico as slaves. He won fame for his ability to compose, on demand, quatrains based on a *pie* (verse) given to him. A good number of them were collected by León and Campos. In some he speaks about himself:

Aunque soy de raza conga
yo no he nacido africano,
soy, de nación, mexicano
y nacido en Almolonga.

Although I belong to the Congo race
I was not born in Africa,
I'm a Mexican national
born in Almolonga.

In another, answering a verse referring to the color of his skin, he replied:

—Negro, la color te agravia.
—No tengo la culpa yo;
una mano oculta y sabia
esta piel negra me dio
cual si naciera en Arabia.

"Black man, your color demeans you."
"I'm not to blame;
an occult and wise hand
this black skin gave me
as if I was born in Arabia."

As far as we know, the first to mention El Negrito Poeta was José Joaquín Fernández de Lizardi in his novel *El periquillo sarniento,* where, after mentioning several European poets of the people, says, "I could mention other improvisers, but why bother when everybody knows that in this kingdom flourished one known as El Negrito Poeta, about whom old people tell admirable abilities." Lizardi quotes only four quatrains, one of which is of interest because it associates El Negrito with Sor Juana Inés de la Cruz, who, in spite of her great ability to write poetry, was unable to rhyme a verse ending in a preposition, as had been done by El Negrito when someone, in a pharmacy, had offered him a peso if he could do this.

El Negrito immediately composed it:

Ya ese peso lo gané,
si mi saber no se esconde
quítese usted no sea que
una viga caiga, y donde
los cabellos penden, dé.

That peso I have already won it
if my knowledge doesn't fail me
get away, it may be that
that beam may fall and hurt you.

In the nineteenth-century Mexican novel, the presence of black characters is common, although they often appear as servants, as happens in the two 1861 novels of Nicolás Pizarro, *El monedero* (*The Coin Holder*) and *La coqueta* (*The Coquette*). In the literature dealing with the revolution, the best-known work in which a black woman is the protagonist is the novel *La Negra Angustias*, by Francisco Rojas González, which received the National Literature Prize in 1944. With the Zapatista revolt as a background, La Negra Angustias, not a simple *soldadera*, but a colonel, represents all women that took part in the revolution and defends them. There were, of course, plain *soldaderas* of the black race, as we can see in the photographs in the Casasola collection. In post-revolutionary Mexico, black people have participated actively in public life; quite a number of political figures, artists, writers, and industrialists have been recognized for their contributions to Mexican culture. Indeed, this is a subject that merits a book, not a ten-minute talk.

33

TLATELOLCO, TLATELOLCO

In 1968, Mexico was host to the Olympic Games, an event that skyrocketed the nation into the international orbit and gave it the recognition that for so long it had craved and deserved, since Mexico could now boast of being a developing country, with a population of nearly fifty million and a capital city of five million. Under President Gustavo Díaz Ordaz, Mexico had finally achieved the impossible, a 6.5 percent annual growth increase, which marked the transition from an underdeveloped to a developing country, taking its place alongside Brazil and South Korea.

To properly receive its guests, Mexico spent billions of pesos building Olympic City and the necessary sport palaces required by the Olympic Committee. Was history repeating itself? In 1910, another Díaz, the old dictator Porfirio Díaz, had embellished the city to celebrate Mexico's centenary as a free nation. Millions were spent to build El Palacio de Bellas Artes, the Monument to Independence on the Paseo de la Reforma (the famous Ángel), and other landmarks that still beautify the city. At the same time, there was restlessness among the people, especially in the countryside, where hunger was prevalent. The doctor and novelist Mariano Azuela, who was to become the revolution's conscience, said in his novel *Andrés Pérez, maderista* (1911), "The workers subsist on corn and beans. Farmhands make thirty-seven centavos a day.

First published in *Denver Quarterly* 14, no. 1 (Spring 1979): 3–14.

. . . But the government will spend twenty million to build a National Theatre [Bellas Artes]."

Porfirio Díaz was deposed soon after the celebrations were held. Díaz Ordaz, on the other hand, was able to carry out his plans and finish his term. The Olympic Games were held on time and turned out to be an international success. But at what price? The nation's trend toward an open, more democratic, and just society was aborted at Tlatelolco on October 2, 1968.

North of the city of Tenochtitlán, the site of the Aztec empire and now Mexico City, and by the waters of Lake Texcoco, sat the city-state of Tlatelolco. Over its old ruins the Spaniards built the first church and the first school. With the advent of nineteenth-century industrialization, it became the railroad center of the republic. Today, Tlatelolco has become a suburb of sprawling Mexico City, famous for its enormous housing project and as the site of the Secretariat of Foreign Affairs and the Plaza de las Tres Culturas. It was in this Square of the Three Cultures that the government, on the night of October 2, 1968, unleashed its army, killing over three hundred persons (most of them students or their friends), who were participants in a meeting to protest political repression, social conditions, and the Olympic Games. The event, like the one in 1910, changed the course of Mexico's political, social, and intellectual life. In literature, we can now speak of authors writing before or after Tlatelolco.

Tlatelolco was not, of course, an unexpected eruption, and there were writers who had the wisdom to foresee what was to happen. Among them, Carlos Fuentes, who as early as 1959, in his novel *Where the Air Is Clear* dealt with the problems faced by the city, brought to light its underlying causes, and predicted a confrontation. In 1962, in his fourth novel, *The Death of Artemio Cruz,* he went further back and traced the nation's problems to the betrayal of the revolution by pseudorevolutionaries such as Artemio Cruz, whose only aim in life was personal aggrandizement, regardless of the national consequences. With these two novels, Fuentes introduced into Mexican letters a new language, a language to be used in the fight against certain feudalistic aspects of government inherited from the colonial period that still survived in spite of the revolution.

No less visionary was another young writer, Fernando del Paso, who in 1966 published a laboriously structured novel, *José Trigo*, in which he gives us the history of Tlatelolco since its origins until 1960, as well as the history of the Mexican railroads, the government-run Ferrocarriles Nacionales. In the chapter titled "Cronología," as well as through the lives of the characters, we become acquainted with the violent development of that important suburb of Mexico City, the stage where a few years later the most tragic event in postrevolutionary Mexico was to take place. José Trigo, the central figure in the novel, like Ixca Cienfuegos in Fuentes's *Where the Air Is Clear*, is a mythical character who can be identified not only with Nonoalco-Tlatelolco, but also with the ancient Aztec gods who demanded sacrifices so that the people could fulfill their destiny, which was to prevent the sun from stopping on its journey, thus ending life on earth. Beyond the mythical element, the novel presents another level of meaning, the social, which has to do with the struggle among corrupt labor leaders and government officials. The structure of the novel is based on a pre-Hispanic archetype, the pyramid, an image that was later to be used by Octavio Paz to explain the events of 1968. Thus, in *José Trigo* we already have the basic elements that give originality to the new Mexican literature; that is, the combination of mythical and social realities expressed in a form rooted in the historical past of the nation. At the same time, Del Paso introduces the new language advocated by Fuentes. This trend in Mexican literature attains maturity in Del Paso's most recent novel, *Palinuro de México* (1977), in which he takes advantage of the latest techniques in the art of the novel to develop a social theme dealing with contemporary life in Mexico, a life whose many flaws were recently revealed at Tlatelolco.

The novels by Fuentes and Del Paso, which were published before Tlatelolco, foreshadow the event. But afterward, when writing *Palinuro de México*, Del Paso was then in possession of extensive materials about what had happened. Among those materials are some that appeared immediately after Tlatelolco, mostly of a documentary or denunciatory nature. These documents, however, are extremely important, for they were written by eyewitnesses such as Gilberto Balam, the author of *Tlatelolco, reflexiones de un testigo* (*Tlatelolco, Reflections of a Witness*, 1969), or by newspapermen who were shocked by the realization that such a massacre could take place in the Mexico of the 1960s, in a Mexico that was to host the Olympic Games. These writers, anxious to express their indignation, wrote accusatory books like *Tlatelolco, historia de una infamia* (1969), by Roberto Blanco Moheno. The two elements, the document and the accusation, were skillfully combined by one of Mexico's leading women writers, Elena Poniatowska, who felt the tragedy personally, having lost a brother. In her book *La noche de Tlatelolco, testimonios de historia oral* (published in 1971 and translated into English by Helen Lane under the title *Massacre in Mexico*, 1975), she collected eyewitness accounts of the happenings, as well as speeches, government statements, and materials published in newspapers, magazines, pamphlets, and broadsides. Because it is a passionate book, we should not expect an objective, well-reasoned account of what took place. All the documents she collected form an impassioned accusation of the persons responsible. The declarations of the members of the student movement, although quite subjective, are still very useful to determine the motives of the protest. It is quite obvious from these accounts that the conflict had other elements besides the political clash between the students and the government. The soldiers who attacked the students, although following orders, apparently felt that they were fighting not only a leftist group of young people composed of students, professors, teachers, and their friends, but also a social group distinct from their own, since the protesters were mostly members of the middle class. It also appears that the conflict was generational; the youth, who were representative of the new world trends and who felt solidarity with other students in revolt both in Europe and the United States, versus the representatives of the Partido Revolucionario Institucional (PRI), the party made up of older politicians which had been in power since the 1920s. It was not the intention of Poniatowska in this book to establish the causes of the massacre or to answer the question, Why? That task, as we shall see, was reserved for Octavio Paz and Carlos Fuentes. However, her book threw light on the nature of the conflict and registered the indignation felt by the participants, their relatives, and their friends.

In Poniatowska's book, we also find Rosario Castellanos's now-famous poem "Memorial de Tlatelolco," which begins by pointing out that the perpetrators of the assault waited until darkness to avoid being identified:

Por eso el dos de octubre aguardó hasta la noche
para que nadie viera la mano que empuñaba
el arma, sino sólo su efecto de relámpago.

¿Y a esa luz, breve y lívida, quién? ¿Quién es el que mata?
¿Quiénes los que agonizan, los que mueren?
¿Los que huyen sin zapatos?
¿Los que van a caer al pozo de una cárcel?
¿Los que se pudren en el hospital?
¿Los que se quedan mudos, para siempre, de espanato?

¿Quién? ¿Quiénes? Nadie. Al día siguiente, nadie.
La plaza amaneció barrida; los periódicos
dieron como noticia principal
el estado del tiempo.
Y en la televisión, en el radio, en el cine
no hubo ningún cambio de programa,
ningun anuncio intercalado ni un
minuto de silencio en el banquete.
(Pues prosiguió el banquete.)

That's why October second waited until dark
so that no one could see the hand
that wielded the weapon,
but only its lightning effect.

And she asks,
Who is the one who kills?
Who are those that agonize,
those that die?

And the answer:
No one, no one. Next day
the square woke up duly swept.
The newspapers?
They talked about the weather;
and the TV, the radio, the cinema
did not change their programs:
not even interrupted them
to flash the news.
Not a moment of silence,
the show must go on.

Castellanos interprets the tragedy as a sacrifice to the Aztec deities:

No busques lo que no hay: huellas, cadáveres
que todo se le ha dado como ofrenda a una diosa,
a la Devoradora de Excrementos.

Don't look for what there is not: footprints, dead bodies.
All was but an offering to the goddess,
to the Devoradora de Excrementos.

Nor should the inquiring person, she continues, look for information in the archives of the city, for there were no minutes taken. But there is an open wound that remains in the memory. And since it hurts, it must be true.

I remember. Let us remember
until justice takes its place
among us.

At the same time that Castellanos's poem appeared, another poet, Jesús Arellano, was also publishing a poem, written in October 1969, in his book *Clamor* (1970), under the title "Mordaza" ("Gag"), in which, in a style reminiscent of Quevedo, he strongly protests the prevailing conditions.

Rosario Castellanos chose poetry to express her grief, although in 1968 she was already famous as a novelist and short story writer. José Emilio Pacheco, a young writer representing the new generation, the generation that was active during the late 1960s, opted for the same medium, although in 1967 he had published his important novel *Morirás lejos* (*You Shall Die Far Away*), in which he treats the theme of the destruction of Jerusalem by the Romans and the destruction of the Warsaw ghetto by Hitler's men. In his book of poems *No me preguntes cómo pasa el tiempo* (*Don't Ask Me How The Time Goes By*), published in August of 1969, we find three poems dealing with the theme of Tlatelolco, the most important of them being "Lectura de los 'Cantares mexicanos': Manuscrito de Tlatelolco" ("A Reading of 'Mexican Songs': A Manuscript of Tlatelolco" [October 1968]), in which he uses the same technique he had utilized in the novel, the juxtaposition of two actions separated in time which repeat the theme of the assault and slaughter of innocent and defenseless people. He very skillfully makes use of an incident recorded in pre-Hispanic Mexico as a metaphor for a contemporary event occurring in the same place but separated by centuries. As stated in the codex "Manuscript of Tlatelolco," after the people had assembled the armored soldiers closed all the exits and the killing began:

> Then the uproar was heard
> then rose the shouting.
> Many husbands looked for their wives
> some with their children in arms.
> Treacherously they were slain
> without knowing it they died.
> And the stench of blood saturated the air.

The similarity between the two events makes the contemporary inhabitants of Mexico feel a strong kinship with their ancestors and at the same time awakens in them a sense of a common faith.

> I am a Mexican
> I suffer, my heart fills with sorrow

says the anonymous singer of the past, and the words reflect the poet's feelings also. The meaning of the poem is felt by the reader when he, being conscious of the events of 1968, interprets the faith of the ancient Mexicans in the light of contemporary history.

Castellanos and Pacheco give vent to their emotions in verse, although both are excellent prose writers. On the other hand, Octavio Paz, a great poet, preferred to express his ideas in prose. His book is the first that thoroughly analyzes the significance of the tragedy of October 2, pointing out the causes and examining the consequences. His *Posdata* (1970), translated into English under the title *The Other Mexico: Critique of the Pyramid* (1972), is a slender volume, written in 1969 in Austin, Texas, and consisting of three essays. In the first, "Olimpiada y Tlatelolco" ("Tlatelolco and the Olympic Games"), he brings to light the fact that the student revolt in Mexico was not isolated, but an aspect of an international protest initiated and carried out by the youth of the world. In Mexico, it represented a manifestation against government repression, its aim being, according to Paz, reform and not revolution. "No one wants a revolution, but reform; to put an end to the system of privilege imposed on the people years ago by the National Party of the Revolution." He points out that the students' meeting at Tlatelolco was just that, a meeting, and not a demonstration; that the killing began after the meeting was over, when the participants were beginning to abandon the square. "How many died?" Paz asks. He gives a figure taken from *The Guardian* and supposes that those wounded must have been in the hundreds, and those apprehended over two hundred, among them students, professors, and writers. The student movement came to an end with that tragedy.

Paz interprets Tlatelolco as a regression to pre-Hispanic ways, to a past that contemporary Mexico considers dead and buried. This thesis is the subject of the third essay, "Crítica de la pirámide" ("Criticism of the Pyramid"), for which it is necessary to interpolate the middle essay, "El desarrollo y otros espejismos" ("Development and Other Mirages"), in which he traces the political development of Mexico since the revolution of 1910 to 1917. Whether we accept or reject Paz's theory of regression is immaterial. The important thing is that he dared to criticize the government. He is a firm believer in the theory that without criticism there can be no change. And for him, the function of the writer must be precisely that, to be a critic of his contemporary world. Without criticism, says Paz, there can be no liberty, no democracy. "Without liberty to criticize, and without a plurality of opinions there can be no body politic." When Paz wrote his book he was a voluntary political exile, having resigned his post as ambassador to India to protest his government's actions. After the elections of 1970, he was able to return to Mexico, but in order to feel free to criticize the government, he has not, since then, accepted any official position. However, even before resigning he dared to criticize. Having been invited to write a poem extolling the spirit of the Olympics, he wrote a letter to the organizers of the Cultural Program from New Delhi, dated October 7, 1968, in which he refused to collaborate and, instead, sent them a short poem entitled "Mexico: The XIX Olympiad," which was translated by Mark Strand and published in the *New York Review of Books* one month later (November 7, 1968):

> Shame is anger
> Turned against oneself.
>
> (City
>   Employees wash away blood
>   In the Plaza de los Sacrificios.)
>   Look at this,
> Stained
>   Before having said anything
>   Worthwhile,
>   Clarity.

The criticism of the government advocated by Paz was continued by Carlos Fuentes, who, in 1972, published his collection of essays *Tiempo mexicano*, in which he brings us up to date on the political development of Mexico. In the last of the seven essays, "La disyuntiva mexicana" ("The Mexican Dilemma"), he puts into practice what he preached earlier about the new use of language to lash out at the inept and corrupt government officials. While Paz attributed the events of Tlatelolco to flaws in the character of the Mexican, Fuentes gives emphasis to the economic and social conditions prevalent before 1968, such as the existence of a paternalistic form of government, the mediocre nature of its presidents since 1940 (which he attributes to the method used by the National Party of the Revolution to select the official candidate), the government practice of favoring industrial interests and neglecting agriculture, the lack of real freedom of expression, and the population explosion (50 percent of the people were under thirty years of age in 1970). The government, according to Fuentes, is to blame, but the people are also to blame for tolerating it. The *disyuntiva* (dilemma) of the title in this essay refers to the choice of direction that lay before the new president, Luis Echeverría: either toward more repression or toward more democracy. Echeverría, Fuentes tells us, opted for the latter; however, the events of Tlatelolco, on a minor scale, were repeated on June 10, 1971, when the paramilitary brigade known as Los Halcones (the Hawks) attacked a group of students and killed more than thirty of them.

The June 10 incident has received less attention than Tlatelolco. There are fewer documents, books, and other sources of information about this conflict. In 1971, Orlando Ortiz published his *Jueves de Corpus* (*Thursday, Corpus Christi Day*), a title derived from the fact that June 10 was Corpus Christi Day. In his book, Ortiz documents what took place and transcribes taped reports from eyewitnesses, wounded students, and other victims, all illustrated with photographs. Fuentes, on the other hand, does not blame Echeverría for this incident, but instead blames the chief of police, whose resignation the president demanded and obtained five days after the event.

In *Tiempo mexicano,* Fuentes comes to the conclusion that in order to solve the social problems of Mexico, it is essential first to solve the economic problem, which has become definitely worse during the years since the publication of his book and reached critical proportions with the devaluation of the peso by Echeverría in December 1976, the last month of his presidency. The boycott of Mexico by American tourists, as a consequence of Echeverría's foreign policies, added fuel to the economic crisis. The new president, José López Portillo, has reversed the trend, aided somewhat by the discovery of large oil deposits in southern Mexico. But the economic problems have not been solved, as manifested by the large number of working people, most of them campesinos, who migrate to the United States in search of a better living.

The events of October 2 gave rise to what could be called the novel of Tlatelolco. The first writers to fictionalize this subject made use of the documents collected by Balam, Blanco Moheno, Poniatowska, and others. The theme attracted several novelists, among them Luis González de Alba, whose novel *Los días y los años* (*The Days and the Years,* 1971) is a well-documented work that describes the conflict between the student movement and the state, ending with the events of October 2. The narrator tells the story from the point of view of the students who were imprisoned for participating in the meetings and parades organized to protest social injustice, the Olympic Games, and political corruption.

In the same year, a young novelist and short story writer, René Avilés Fabila, published the novel *El gran solitario de Palacio* (*The Great Lonely Man in the Palace*), in which he satirizes the presidency and dictators in general. He ridicules the electoral process by suggesting that the president, who is elected every six years, is always the same man, only wearing a different mask. The novel is structured by means of interwoven scenes, some satirizing the dictator and others depicting the fate of the students imprisoned by the police. One of the results of October 2, the narrator tells us, is the destruction of the fiction that Mexico is "a pacific and calm Republic, happy and satisfied, united nationally around its leaders and its fiftyish Revolution, an image that was erased immediately after the violent confrontation between the students and the military and police forces, after the invasion of schools and universities by the army. And the climax, the tip of the pyramid, was the carnage at the Square of Culture and the imprisonment of thousands of persons."

Unlike Avilés Fabila, who made use of satire to expose the state of repression that prevailed in Mexico in 1968, María Luisa Mendoza and Luis Spota took advantage of the dramatic elements provided by the tragedy to express their indignation. Mendoza utilized two literary forms, the novel and the chronicle, and published a *cronovela* in 1971 titled

Con él, conmigo, con nosotros (*With Him, with Me, with Us*) in which she focuses on the event indirectly through what happens to the Albarrán family, originally from central Mexico but now living in Tlatelolco. Making use of the fact that the massacre took place in the Square of the Three Cultures, Mendoza divides her *cronovela* in three parts, representing three wars and three cultures. In the form of a long monologue in which the second-person singular is often used, the constant reference to Tlatelolco gives unity to what otherwise would be a simple narrative in the form of a chronicle. Although the author points her finger at the persons responsible for the killings, she never mentions them by name.

Spota, on the other hand, is more explicit, and there is no question as to who the responsible person is. As a veteran novelist skillful at presenting as fiction events that touch the public deeply, Spota forcefully dramatized Tlatelolco's tragedy in the novel *La Plaza* (*The Square*, 1972), in which he elaborates a very simple plot: the kidnapping, trial, and execution of the person responsible for Tlatelolco. This act of vengeance is done by persons directly affected by the event, those whose relatives had been either killed or imprisoned. Although the name of the person responsible is not revealed, it is assumed by the reader that it is the president himself. Those familiar with the habits of the president can easily identify him in the character created by Spota. Although the plot is very simple, the author gives depth to the novel by interpolating, in the form of interior monologues, the events of Tlatelolco and the consequences. The information was obtained from the books already mentioned, as well as from other sources, since Spota has had a long experience as an investigative newspaperman. The author's dependence on information already available is justified in the editor's note, which states that a novel on such a monumental subject could not be written by one person alone. The collaboration of many writers and many voices is necessary. And the purpose of writing the novel, Spota confesses, was to keep the memory of Tlatelolco alive.

In the same year that Spota published his novel, the dramatist Rodolfo Usigli presented the play *Buenos días, Señor Presidente* (*Good Morning, Mr. President*), in which the student revolt of 1968 is set forth by exploiting a clever parallel with a classical Spanish play, *Life Is a Dream*, by Calderón de la Barca. Compared with the novels we have mentioned, Usigli's play is rather pale, since the characters come through more as allegorical figures than as real persons. The play opens when the students are being attacked at night by the government military police. Harmodes, one of the student leaders, is struck on the head and passes out. When he regains consciousness, he discovers that he is the president of the nation. He promises to give the people a government of truth, liberty, justice, bread, and hope. However, the rivalry among the student organizations (which are symbolic of the political parties) ends in another tragedy, and the former president is returned to power. Is Usigli saying that it is necessary to have a strong, dictatorial government? Is he saying that even had the students (or the opposition political parties) triumphed in 1968, they could not have governed because of internal strife? Or is this play, in the guise of a dream and a parody of Calderón's masterpiece, just a clever way of bringing to the stage the events of 1968 while avoiding the government's censure? The audience must be the judge.

Of course, not all Mexican literature written after 1968 deals with Tlatelolco. As a matter of fact, most of it does not. There is a vast body of literary works that avoid the subject, not because, we believe, the authors are unconscious of the significance of what happened, but because they are committed to the writing of purely literary compositions. There has always existed a tradition in Mexican literature that is universal in tone and content. Such writers as Juan José Arreola, Salvador Elizondo, Juan García Ponce, José Agustín, Gustavo Sainz, Emilio Carballido, Vicente Leñero, and Agustin Yáñez continue to write about their favorite themes in their well-established styles. This does not mean, however, that they may not tomorrow surprise us with a work about Tlatelolco, or a work in which Tlatelolco figures prominently. Another group of writers not living in Mexico City were of course less affected by Tlatelolco and are, therefore, less likely to write about it. But we can be sure that all of them, as well as the whole nation, are conscious of its significance.

The most important consequence of Tlatelolco, in literature, is the deep impression it left in the minds of the intellectuals and creative writers. All of them agree that the year 1968 marks a break with the past, a break with the period characterized by changes brought about by the revolution of 1910–17. This break, which extends to other fields including politics, has been acknowledged by the most influential writers, among them Octavio Paz, who wrote in *Posdata*, "October 2, 1968, saw the ending of the student movement. An epoch in the history of Mexico also ended." The literature of Tlatelolco revealed that the ideals of the revolution, so strongly defended by the party in power, had become empty. José Emilio Pacheco reflects in his poem "1968 (III)":

> *Piensa en la tempestad para decirte*
> *que un lapso de historia ha terminado.*

> Think about the tempest and tell yourself
> that a period of history has ended.

34

THE UGLY AMERICAN

If we trace the development of the attitudes and opinions of American and Mexican authors regarding the nature of the people and the cultures of these two neighboring nations, we discover a striking difference. They start at opposite extremes, cross, and end up in each other's camp.

The general attitude of the American authors, as has been amply documented by Cecil Robinson, is most antagonistic during the early and middle years of the nineteenth century; it mellows during the years between the centuries, and becomes sympathetic after World War I, especially during the last few decades. No American author today would use such derogatory remarks as were frequent in earlier writings such as the dime novels, which gave preference to the frontier conflict with the Hispanic people of the Southwest. But even writers of world stature such as Washington Irving, James Fenimore Cooper, William Prescott, Walt Whitman, and Richard Henry Dana expressed negative opinions about Mexico and its people. Prescott, for example, considered the Mexican of his time to be a "degenerate descendant of the Aztecs." Whitman, in a perhaps unguarded moment, wrote: "What has miserable, inefficient Mexico, with her superstition, her burlesques upon freedom, her tyranny of the few over the many—what has she to do with the great mission of peopling the New World with a noble race? Be it ours, to achieve that mission!"

First published in *Melus* 5, no. 3 (1978): 16–25.

On the other hand, Mexican writers of the same period were surprisingly benevolent toward the Americans. When Prescott's *History of the Conquest of Mexico* appeared, it was immediately translated and published in Mexico City. As a matter of fact, two translations appeared one year after its original publication in English. One of the versions was published with a long commentary by historian José Fernando Ramírez, who, although conscious of Prescott's arrogant attitude toward the Mexico of his time, was moderate in his criticism. He commented:

> Here racial contempt is expressed without disguise and without duplicity, even in negligible trifles. Mr. Prescott has taken the pen to write the history of *barbarians,* a word that, alternating with *savages,* is to be found throughout his *History,* accompanied by others of the same category.... In short, it's not surprising that the great historian should descend from his majestic flight to the dust of trivial remarks ... to amuse himself measuring the melody or harshness of certain Mexican words; a point about which, be it said without offending, the ear of a man accustomed to hearing harmonies such as that of *Yankee Doodle* cannot be a very competent judge.

In contrast to American writers who pass from an extremely subjective attitude to a more balanced and objective one, writers in Mexico began with a sympathetic portrayal of Americans that was gradually transformed into a negative one in response, above all, to specific historical events. The first change occurred after 1836, the year Mexico lost Texas. But even after Mexico suffered that humiliation, there were still favorable opinions, such as that of José María Tornell, who referred to the United States as "the restless and enterprising neighbor." Texas, for most Mexicans, was a remote territory, and during its defense only Santa Anna's soldiers came in contact with the North Americans. This was not the case in 1846, when Mexico was invaded and a closer view of the Americans was experienced. This contact, unfortunately under war conditions, began to change the attitude of the Mexican toward the North American. Later, other important historical events reinforced this negative impression. The Spanish-American War of 1898, and the second and third invasions of Mexico, in 1914 and 1916, did not improve attitudes in Latin America toward the United States.

It is appropriate to observe that the interest shown by Mexican writers in their neighbors to the north was manifested in a lesser degree than that of the American writers. It is much more difficult to find Americans in Mexican literature than it is to find Mexicans in American literature, especially in the literature of the Southwest. Americans went first to Mexico (or the Southwest) as colonizers, then as soldiers in the War of 1846, and later as missionaries or tourists. It seems that almost everyone who visits Mexico writes of his or her experiences. In the United States, we can find a book on any aspect of Mexican culture, even one on Mexican *pan dulce*, not to mention Mexican jumping beans, burros, tequila, tamales, and other stereotyped images associated with Mexican culture.

Before Mexico obtained its independence in 1821, there are hardly any Americans to be found in histories, diaries, letters, chronicles, poems, or fiction. In fact, it appears that until the American colonies became independent in 1776, Americans were identified with the English, and it is difficult to determine if the term *inglés* in Spanish American texts refers to an Englishman or to a North American colonist. The word *gringo*, although first applied, according to the authoritative García Icazbalceta, to all persons not identified with the descendants of the Latin people, was especially used to refer to "ingleses y norteamericanos" (Englishmen and North Americans). As late as 1870, José María Roa Bárcena, in his collection of stories *Noche al raso (Night Outdoors)* refers to an Englishman as a "gringo." The narrator says: "I became suspicious of the Englishman, and also of the picture . . . and even of the ambience about which the gringo had just spoken." By 1895, however, Ramos y Duarte, in his *Diccionario de mejicanismos*, already confines the word *gringo* to designate "el natural de los Estados Unidos del Norte" (a native of the United States of the North).

In more recent years, other derogatory words, mild in comparison with those used by Americans to designate the Mexicans, have appeared in literature and are still common in the spoken language. The most frequent are *bolillo, gabacho, patón,* and *primo*. The term *bolillo* derives

Mariano Azuela's novel *Los caciques,* the protagonist says to a group of businessmen: "Gentlemen, your oracle is the *yanque;* you do not know, nor need to know another definition of the word business than the one the *yanque* has taught you."

To the Mexican, especially the one who has not been to the United States, these words bring to mind a particular stereotype: the Yankee is tall, blond, freckled, and often lanky (like Uncle Sam); he has big feet and chews tobacco; he is rich, Protestant, a good businessman, and unable to speak Spanish correctly. There are many remarkable occurrences of this stereotype, with occasional variants, in Mexican literature.

Historically, as far as I have been able to determine, Americans first appear in Mexican literature in a work by José Joaquín Fernández de Lizardi. In *La Quijotita y su prima,* published in 1819, one character is an American businessman, the first to appear in Mexican fiction, but the type that would become familiar. In this story, the American is Jacobo Welster, a rich, thirty-year-old bachelor from Washington who goes to Mexico, where he falls in love with Carlota, a sixteen-year-old Mexican girl. Since he is an Anabaptist, he converts to Catholicism in order to marry Carlota and also changes his first name to Agustín. Carlota's friends call her "la inglesita," the little English girl, a term Lizardi explains in a footnote: "Although he [Welster] was not an Englishman, Matilde called him thus because of his language, for, as he was Anglo-American, he spoke English." Welster marries Carlota in spite of her father's objections and remains in Mexico. In this atypical novelette, it is Carlota's father, a Mexican, who plays the villain, while the American emerges as hero. This role reversal can be explained by the intellectual atmosphere in which *La Quijotita y su prima* was written.

Fernández de Lizardi was a product of the Enlightenment and, therefore, an admirer of the American and French revolutions. He respected and idealized the men who created the first independent nation on the North American continent, an attitude representative of the men who fought for Mexico's independence from Spain. For them the United States was the model to be followed in the establishment of the new social and political order in Mexico. However, soon after its independence, Mexico began to resent the imperialism of the United

States. The proclamation of the Monroe Doctrine and especially the annexation of Texas were hard blows for Mexico while the country was struggling to consolidate its independence and establish a viable form of government. The understandably negative attitudes toward North American policies were reinforced ten years later when Mexico lost its northern provinces to the United States. But history again intervened: another invasion of Mexico, this time by the French, gave the United States the opportunity to regain some of its prestige by helping Benito Juárez defeat Maximilian. Abraham Lincoln, considered friend of Juárez and liberator of the American slaves, became a symbol of the new United States. Late in 1869, William H. Seward, seventy-four-year-old ex–secretary of state under President Andrew Johnson, made a visit to President Juárez. Ignacio Manuel Altamirano's important journal, *El Renacimiento,* expressed the hope that Seward would appreciate the great admiration that Mexicans had for his country because it served progress and helped to keep the American continent free. Seward was described as having the serious facial expression that characterizes all North Americans. He personified his country; firm, positive, progressive, powerful. At the banquet in Chapultepec, Juárez thanked Seward for the help the United States had given to his Mexican "family," and the writer Santacilia toasted to the great Monroe Doctrine, saver of the New World. However, the events of 1848 had not been entirely forgotten. In the same periodical, Julián Montiel published a poem to commemorate the twenty-second anniversary of the Battle of Churubusco. In this poem, he used the image of the Mexican eagle awakening from its peaceful sleep to reject the barbaric invasion of a sister nation, where force had conquered right and reason.

In the novel of the period of the reform, Americans are to be found in Manuel Martínez de Castro's *Julia* (1868), where the hero easily subdues his American opponents, and in Nicolás Pizarro's *El monedero* (*The Money Changer*), which takes place during the War of 1846 and in which the American is represented as an ugly exploiter who disregards moral principles, a stereotype to be found frequently and as recently as 1973 in Agustín Yáñez's *Las vueltas del tiempo* (*The Turns of Time*). In the latter novel, the American, Max Goldwyn, has infiltrated the political system and works from the inside. He characterizes himself as a "gringo metiche," an intruding gringo.

The relationship between Mexico and the United States under Porfirio Díaz was cordial in spite of the War of 1898, which upset Latin America. The Americans, in fact, were helping Mexico to build its railroads and exploit its mines. At the time it was not fashionable to attack North Americans, and the first discordant incident does not occur until 1906, when miners declared a strike against the powerful Cananea Consolidated Copper Company, which was put down with the help of 275 American soldiers who, under the command of Colonel Riding, had crossed the border at the request of the governor of Sonora.

This incident was the first in a series of events that culminated in the landing of the marines at Veracruz in 1914 and with General Pershing's punitive expedition in search of Pancho Villa in 1916. These violations of Mexico's territory, especially the one of 1914, gave rise to a series of books, articles, and corridos (popular ballads) that violently criticized the United States and Americans in general. In this regard, Robert Quirk's observation is worth noting: "Mexicans, in writing their histories, have been less bitter about the war with the United States in 1846 than the intervention in Veracruz in 1914." A good example of the bitterness alluded to is found in the corrido "Del peligro de la intervención Americana" ("Of the Dangers of American Intervention"), in which we find a summary of the grievances against the United States. The novel *Don Pascual* (1920), by Alberto A. Rodríguez, contains a blow-by-blow account of the landing of the marines in Veracruz. Although the author is rather moderate in his criticism of Americans as individuals (there are even some good ones), he judges severely the nation as a whole, in these words: "It's evident that a nation like the United States, who does not lose a single opportunity to boast about how civilized, and therefore humanitarian, she is, has men in its 'best society' who are treacherous, cowardly, and despicable, who in a cowardly manner shoot citizens unaware, citizens who respect them individually because they cannot suspect treason, since their hypocritical conduct makes them appear as people of high moral principles."

A more successful novel about the same event is *Frontera junto al mar* (*Border by the Sea*, 1953) by another participant, José Mancisidor, who has also written a novel about the expropriation of oil (*El alba en las cimas* [*Sunrise at the Mountain Top*, 1953]). The novelists of the Mexican Revolution, preoccupied with their subject matter, had surprisingly little to say about Americans. However, several Americans appear in the novels of Martín Luis Guzmán, who knew the United States well. In *El águila y la serpiente* (*The Eagle and the Serpent*, 1928), there is a beautiful female spy working for the Mexican government; a revolutionary lawyer in San Antonio, Samuel Belden; and several adventurers in Villa's armies. In general, Guzmán's attitude toward Americans may be synthesized in this quotation: "We are fortunate that Yankees, with rare exceptions, are people with whom you can talk frankly. What a great country if the nation were like the individuals!"

Rafael Muñoz, on the other hand, was less favorable in his assessment than Guzmán. He also knew the United States well, especially the motion picture world of Hollywood. In his short story "Un asalto al tren" ("A Train Assault"), he satirizes several American stereotypes, among them the cowboy actor, the middle-aged tourist, the big-game huntress, the summer school student, and the foreign correspondent. The movie actor Tim Six boastfully relates his daring acts only to become paralyzed with fear when faced with a real bandit. An American tourist, in search of Mexican curios, speaks Spanish like those Americans who learn it from the dictionary; she wears an orange-colored summer dress and a parrot-green sweater. The huntress, daughter of a guide who served Theodore Roosevelt, has killed tigers and lions in India and Africa but faints at the sight of a Mexican revolutionary soldier. The newspaperman is also a stereotype; in this story he represents GADDA (Gran Alianza de Diarios Americanos), a syndicate with over 1,000 newspapers and 142 magazines. After questioning the passengers about the assault, he writes exactly the opposite of what really happened. To the question: "What did the assailant look like?" the student replies: "He was a tall, handsome man." (Actually, he was the only one who had entered the car at that time.) The correspondent writes an unintentional parody: "A torrent of men, more like cavemen, armed to the teeth with guns in hand and daggers in their mouths, rushed shouting into the car. Their unkempt hair and long beards made them look like beasts."

Muñoz's Americans are definitely caricatures, as are those of Rodolfo Usigli, the contemporary Mexican dramatist who created Oliver Bolton, the Harvard historian in search of the truth about the fate of a Mexican revolutionary. Blond, suntanned, well dressed, Bolton immediately gains the sympathy of César Rubio, the protagonist of the play *El gesticulador* (*The Gesturer*, 1937). But César's wife, Elena, is not so trusting. When César invites Bolton to spend the night in his home, since there are no hotels in the town, his wife is skeptical and says: "But we do not know who he is." To César's reply that he "seems to be a decent fellow," Elena answers: "With Americans, you never know; they all dress well, they all dress the same, they all have cars. For me, they are like Chinese: they are all alike."

Of this group of writers, José Vasconcelos is perhaps the most antagonistic. He blamed the United States for every imaginable problem that Mexico had and even coined a new word, *poinsetismo,* to designate the policy of considering Mexico as an American province, a policy initiated by Poinsett and, according to Vasconcelos, renewed by Morrow. He considered Poinsett to be the source of all evil and the person who divided the Mexican family. Vasconcelos's attitude toward the United States was strongly colored by his religious beliefs. The fact that most Americans are Protestant was in itself enough for him to reject their culture.

Although there is an amelioration in the criticism of the United States during the years of World War II—Mexico had joined the United States in the struggle against the Axis powers—the trend of depicting Americans stereotypically continued unabated. In Juan José Arreola's only drama, *La hora de todos* (*Everybody's Hour,* 1949), which takes place in New York and in which all the characters are Americans, Harrison Fish, the protagonist, epitomizes the traits that make up the stereotyped ugly American. He has seduced his secretary and other women and is responsible for the death of at least one man. Since he is from the South, he is blamed for the lynching of a black man. Arreola also satirizes the American's preoccupation with insurance. An art collector in the play insures her professional judgment for half a million dollars. If she should happen to purchase a copy instead of the original, the insurance company would pay for it.

Although the characters in Arreola's play seem to be unreal and drawn entirely within the preconception of the stereotype, the opposite is true with the few Americans we find in his famous short stories, in which he satirizes, among others, the inventor of useless gadgets or absurd machines. In "Baby H. P.," we discover that mothers can buy a little machine to be attached to a child's back that will convert its activities into a supply of energy, a most appropriate invention in today's energy-conscious world. Another invention is a woman made of plastic, advertised as the perfect wife. Arreola satirizes other contemporary Americans as well, such as the doctoral candidate in search of materials for a dissertation; in the story "De balística," a graduate student from the University of Minnesota travels to Spain looking for materials for a two-hundred-page thesis about catapults. Arreola's American characters, in general, illustrate Octavio Paz's contention that North Americans are credulous; optimistic; trusting; enjoy inventions; believe in hygiene, health, work, and contentment.

Robinson's assertion that "beyond a doubt the deep attachment for Mexico among a number of American intellectuals is generally unrequited by their Mexican opposite numbers" could be extended to refer to the whole of Latin America. It is important to bear in mind that since 1898 very few Latin American intellectuals have praised the United States or set it up as a model to be followed. Nevertheless, in the same period, Mexican intellectuals have admired American writers, but these American writers are generally those who have been alienated from their own culture, or at least have criticized the United States.

One of many Mexican intellectuals who have admired such American writers is the novelist Carlos Fuentes. Fuentes quotes the works of American writers and has dedicated studies to C. Wright Mills, Ernest Hemingway, Oscar Lewis, William Styron, and others. Although we find Americans in most of the novels of Carlos Fuentes, they are not of the type that he admires. I shall mention only two stock characters

not mention any literary works written by Chicanos, although he says he has read some. To Armas's question, "Do you know the literature of the Chicanos?" Paz responded: "I know it very little. I have read some poems that I have liked: also some prose works: but I do not know it well."

In this interview with Armas, Paz touched upon an important subject in contemporary Chicano thought. Armas begins by asking Paz how he, being a cosmopolitan man of letters, came to write *The Labyrinth of Solitude*. Paz defends himself by saying that not all his works treat of universal themes. He added that he has written extensively, in prose and poetry, about Mexico. "I have written," he says, "many poems with Mexican themes. I have written *Posdata*. I believe that, besides, I have written extensively about Mexican literature and art." He further states that a good writer writes about all themes in which he is interested. "I consider," he says, "that a good national writer is a good universal writer. And that a universal writer has to be national. Both things are related." Armas goes on to say that he had asked him that question because here in the United States the moment in the political development of the Chicano has arrived when it is thought that *la raza* should stop being nationalistic and become more universal. Paz inquires, "Do you mean more Anglo-American?" and Armas says, "In some ways." Paz rejects the idea and goes on to advise the Chicanos to preserve their identity. This does not mean, of course, that they should ignore the external world. "It's very difficult," he says, "to maintain this equilibrium, but you must do it. You have to be, on the one hand, Chicanos, and on the other, members of the North American world. Because you live here. You belong here. . . . You have done it before, and you can keep on doing it."

Paz sees no problem in the fact that the Chicano is standing between two worlds. For him, the interrelationship of cultures is an essential historical process. To understand a national group, it is necessary to understand its relationship to other national or international groups. "The history of Mexico," he says, "cannot be understood without the history of Spain," and the Chicanos and the *mexicanos* cannot understand each other without knowing both the history of Mexico and the history of the Chicanos. At the same time, Chicano history cannot be understood without understanding the history of the United States, any more than the Mexican can understand himself without understanding pre-Hispanic history and the history of Spain; and the history of Spain cannot be understood without understanding Arab history, any more than the history of the United States can be understood apart from the history of England. He ends by saying, "Without world history, you do not know what you are, nor do I know who I am. In this sense you and I are universalists. But we are universalists in a point in space and in a determined time. After that you are the Chicano and I am the *Mexicano*. We belong to a nation, to a family, to a barrio, to an epoch."

The dialogue between Armas and Paz had been initiated precisely with a question about the differences between the Chicano and the Mexican. To the question, "Do you see any differences between the Mexican and the Chicano?" Paz answered, "It's obvious that there are differences. There is a great difference, of course, between a Mexican and a Chicano." To the question, "Are these differences cultural, social, political, or national?" Paz said:

> We both have the same origin. We are fundamentally the same, but have had an independent history. The War with the United States, and then a series of catastrophes that have taken place in Mexico have forced part of the Mexican population to immigrate to the United States. As a result a large Mexican community was created, and little by little it has been transformed into the Chicano movement. Then we can say that although the origins are the same, we have lived un- der different environments and have had a different evolution. This is what characterizes us: a common origin, a common culture, and at the same time, social, economic, and some cultural differences.

The most surprising revelation in this interview is the discovery that Paz is in favor of some aspects of Chicanismo. To him, the Chicanos have maintained their cultural traditions much more faithfully than the large city dwellers of Mexico. He finds this traditional strain of the Chicano in the maintenance of certain provincial values, especially in the keeping of strong family ties. For Paz, the family is the depository of traditional values that is necessary to keep. The family has been the vehicle through which these values have been transmitted; that is to say, certain fundamental attitudes toward life, such as good and evil, ugliness and beauty, sex, death, life beyond, the value of time, the value of pleasure, the community. "For example," he says, "I believe that among Chicanos there is something very important and that is communication. You represent a society much less lonely than the North American society. I believe that communal values are much more important among Chicanos than they are in the Anglo-American society."

Do Chicanos accept or reject what Paz has to say about them? Not a great deal has been written about the first chapter of *The Labyrinth of Solitude* dealing with the pachuco. There is no question, however, that Paz's name is mentioned by Chicano writers in superlative terms, sometimes even with reverence. Hilario Contreras, in his article "The Chicanos' Search for Identity," calls him "the great Mexican poet and thinker," and Sylvia Alicia Gonzáles, in her study "National Character vs. Universality in Chicano Poetry," refers to him as "the eminent writer and philosopher," to mention only recent references.

This fascination with Paz goes beyond the writer. As José Armas points out in his introductory remarks to the interview, "Octavio is the most widely read Latin American writer among the Chicanos. Probably every Chicano Studies Program at the college level has made *The Labyrinth of Solitude* required reading." The reason for this popularity, according to Armas, is because the book "came at a time when Chicanos were beginning to reassert themselves and make themselves heard and seen as a people." About this time, *The Labyrinth of Solitude* was discovered by Chicanos. In it they found "insights into the make-up of the Mexicano." The groping Chicano, according to Armas, embraced Paz because he "gave their identity some reassurance, and offered some guidance from which to build their movement."

This is not to say, he continues, "that the Chicano movement is the result of Octavio Paz.... But Paz provided some framework from which to begin to determine for themselves, in an intellectual sense, what were some of the things that made a Chicano a Chicano." Another reason given by Armas to explain Paz's popularity among the Chicanos has to do with his stature and the interest that he has shown in the Chicano. "Paz, as a Mexican," says Armas, "presents another picture of ourselves. We, as Chicanos, seldom get that feedback. Paz represents our roots, cultural base, and our history as a people." An excellent example to il-. lustrate what Armas says would be the book *Pensamientos en los chicanos,* by Eliú Carranza, who accepts Paz's ideas as expressed in *The Labyrinth of Solitude,* in total and at face value. Another one would be Luis Dávila's unpublished article "On the Nature of Chicano Literature: *En los extremos del laberinto,*" in which he makes use of Paz's idea of the pachuco as a solitary being.

On the other hand, the ideas presented by Paz in his book have been criticized both here and in Mexico. Rubén Salazar Mallén, in Mexico, wrote several articles critical of the ideas presented by Paz. In reference to chapter 1, he says, "El Pachuco resulta anacrónico personaje episódico que ha desaparecido" (The pachuco turns out to be an anachronistic episodic individual who has disappeared). But it is Carlos Blanco Aguinaga's article "El laberinto fabricado por Octavio Paz" ("The Labyrinth Built by Octavio Paz"), published in *Aztlán* in 1972, that really brings out Paz's untenable generalizations about the character of the Mexican, his inconsistencies in his interpretation of history, and the subjective nature of many of his observations about culture. Although this study does not refer only to chapter 1 on the pachuco, but deals with the book in its totality, one of the reasons it was written was to warn the Chicano about the deceptive nature of Paz's ideas.

More specifically, Don Porath, in his article "Chicanos and Existentialism," addresses himself to Paz's study of the pachuco and finds it wanting. He blames Paz's analysis for the misinterpretation of the importance of the pachuco "by suggesting that everything he does is masochistic, and he is redeemed when he is finally put upon by the dominant society." At the same time, he says, Paz "fails to recognize the 'true' Mexican in the *Pachuco* since the *Pachuco* evinces a different reaction to a different environment. . . . Unfortunately, rather than give him credit for the uniqueness he exhibits, Paz sees him only as a clownish aberrancy caught in limbo between two cultures." On the other hand, he agrees with Paz about the pachuco being the precursor of the

Chicano. But, he states, "there are a number of intervening variables, such as World War II, and the G.I. Bill which offered an opportunity for Chicanos to enter college in relatively greater numbers." More to the point, Porath states, his conclusions have nothing to do with the Chicano, and do not parallel Chicano thought. However, he praises Paz for supporting the rights of the Chicano to develop his differences, for his existentialist approach to the problem, and for being cognizant of the differences in character between the Anglo-American and the Mexican. But we must keep in mind that for Paz the pachuco and the Chicano are, in character, also Mexican. "Whether we like it or not," he says in *Labyrinth,* "these persons are Mexican, are one of the extremes at which the Mexican can arrive."

Two years before, Arturo Madrid, in his essay on the pachuco, rejected Paz's central thesis; that is, that the pachuco had voluntarily, and for masochistic reasons, isolated himself from society. He says, "Are we to believe the *Pachuco,* or any other Mexican, sought out that 'painful satisfaction' in the curbside clubbings, the stationhouse beatings he regularly received? Does anyone really think redemption was to be had in the solitude of the cellblocks of Chino, San Quentin, or Folsom?"

In order to give perspective to this statement by Madrid, it must be pointed out that Paz's book is an analysis of the character of the Mexican, and the pachuco represents one of the extremes at which that character can arrive. For this reason, the essay on the pachuco takes on national meaning when read in context with the rest of the book. Armando Rendón, in his *Chicano Manifesto,* for instance, makes use of the idea presented by Paz in chapter 5 of *The Labyrinth of Solitude,* "Conquista y colonia" ("The Conquest and Colonialism"), to better explain the Chicanos' religious experience.

Summarizing, we may say that the ideas of Octavio Paz regarding the pachuco and the Chicano have had more influence upon Chicano thought than those of any other contemporary Mexican thinker. Discussion of the nature of the Chicano cannot be complete without taking into consideration his ideas on the subject. Whether we agree with them or not, there is no question that they have stimulated discussion about the true nature of the Chicano, as well as his relationship to the pachuco, the Mexicano, and the Anglo-American. They have served also as a foundation upon which to build a Chicano existentialist philosophy, a philosophy not yet completely formulated, although the basis for it already exists, thanks to Paz's interest in the Chicano and his destiny.

The main contribution of Octavio Paz toward the quest for unity is that he has helped Chicanos to identify with a Mexican heritage. And it is here that we find the great difference between the pachuco and the Chicano. The pachuco, according to Paz, rejected his Mexican background and at the same time refused to accept the Anglo-American culture. On the other hand, the Chicano, by identifying with Mexican traditions and history, has been able to rediscover his cultural heritage, which has become an important base in his quest for identity.

36

MIRROR, MIRROR

Volumes have been written from every conceivable point of view on the political relations between the United States and Latin America. But the same, unfortunately, cannot be said about their literatures. Latin American literature is, of course, read and studied in the United States, and Anglo-American literature is certainly not neglected in Latin America. But there still remains the fact that there are scarcely any comparative studies focusing upon the interrelationships of the literature of Latin America and the literature of the United States. In the following pages, we examine briefly an aspect of that relationship, the attitude of Spanish American writers, and especially that of the Mexican writers, toward Anglo-American literature.

Although Latin American writers of the early nineteenth century admired Franklin, Jefferson, Thomas Paine, and other leaders who had worked to obtain independence from England and who had a part in writing the Constitution and the Bill of Rights, which were to become models for every country south of the border, the interest was political and not literary. Paine's *Common Sense* was paraphrased and used to advance the cause of Chile's independence by the writer Camilo Henríquez as early as 1812. However, it was not until the middle of the century that the Argentine Domingo Faustino Sarmiento discovered Anglo-American literature in the novels of James Fenimore Cooper. He was

First published in *Revista Canadiense de Estudios Hispánicos* 5, no. 1 (1980): 61–73.

the first to harbor the idea that the literatures of the Americas have much in common. In his classic book *Facundo,* published in 1845, we find the first effort to express the nature of Spanish American literature. As a romantic, it was Sarmiento's belief that literature is molded by nature. During his trip to the United States he met Ralph Waldo Emerson. He tells us that when he returned from Lexington, Massachusetts, he spent another day conversing with Emerson "in that dialogue that comes so naturally and is prolonged, between men who represent different countries, literatures, civilizations, and customs, and are nevertheless alike." Here we see that Sarmiento was conscious of the fact that the literatures of the two Americas, although divergent, had much in common. He was especially fascinated by the novels of Fenimore Cooper, for they proved his theory of the relationship between literature and nature. Similar natures, he wrote, produce similar types of men. The gaucho and the cowboy are alike because they live in similar environments, the gaucho in the pampas and the cowboy in the western plains.

Sarmiento saw American culture as the result of man's struggle against nature, as the struggle between civilization and barbarism, the first represented by the city, the latter by the countryside. For Sarmiento, the literatures of the Americas reflect that struggle. No better example can be given than his own *Facundo,* whose subtitle is *Civilization and Barbarism.* It is fitting that this book was the first Latin American literary work translated into English and published in the United States. It was done by Mrs. Horace Mann and appeared in 1868.

Sarmiento himself had the autobiography of Benjamin Franklin, the American he most admired, translated into Spanish and published in Chile. As a young man he had read Franklin and, he tells us, "his kind of glory always attracted me more than that of Washington, and as a boy I tried many times to imitate him."

Cooper, in spite of Sarmiento's efforts, has never been popular in Latin America. This cannot be said of Poe and Whitman. Sarmiento was, more than a literary critic, a statesman and *pensador.* But he was insensitive to the works of Anglo-American poets. On the other hand, José Martí, a poet and prose writer of the highest rank, was aware of the contributions of Anglo-American men of letters. He was the first

Spanish American to praise the virtues of such writers as Emerson and Whitman. Although he thought that the United States and Latin America had two irreconcilable ways of life, he admired Anglo-American literature and praised the contributions of its greatest authors. His essays on Emerson, Whitman, Longfellow, Whittier, and others, collected in his book *Nuestra América,* are memorable not only for their style, but also for the penetrating analysis of the characteristics of these writers, whom he so admired. Octavio Paz, in one of his Charles Eliot Norton lectures at Harvard in 1972, made this statement, "Whitman is the grandfather of the European and Latin American avant-garde. He makes an early appearance among us: José Martí presented him to the Spanish-American public in an article written in 1887. Rubén Darío was immediately tempted to emulate him—a fatal temptation. Since then he has continued to excite many of our poets: emulation, admiration, enthusiasm, empty clatter."

Looking at Anglo-American literature through the eyes of a Spanish American, Martí could see relationships that would not be lost to an Anglo-American critic. He noticed that Longfellow wrote about the struggle between "civilization and barbarism" when he said that the poet "supo . . . de la América salvaje" ("knew . . . about the savage America"). Acquainted with the *indigenista* novel, Martí was attracted to Helen Hunt Jackson's romantic novel *Ramona* and translated it into Spanish. He considered it "a work that in our countries of America could mean a true resurrection." Martí was a real prophet, for the *indigenista* novel in Spanish America was to give its best fruits some four decades after he had made that observation. At the same time, he was aware of the similarity of the literatures of both Americas regarding the place of nature. The writers of both, north and south, had found in nature materials for their poetry. What Norman Foerster has said about nature in nineteenth-century Anglo-American literature can be applied to Spanish American literature. "In an age in which the American nation was adolescent, the distinguishing feature of men's thoughts and feelings—and consequently of their literature—was apparently a new gospel of nature. From Jean Jacques Rousseau to Walt Whitman and his disciples, whatever the cross-currents and back-eddies in the intellectual and emotional stream of the time, the prevailing current seems to have been a fresh enthusiasm for nature."

Three years after Martí's death, the United States declared war on Spain and took over Cuba, Puerto Rico, and the Philippine Islands. The Spanish-American War of 1898 expanded the country's territories, but the price paid for the building of a modern empire was the loss of the goodwill of Latin American intellectuals. The United States has still not yet regained their sympathies. Even the *modernista* poets, who by reputation were not interested in the affairs of the world, wrote poems condemning the United States. Rubén Darío, who in 1888 had published a sonnet to Walt Whitman, stopped for a moment from being inspired by princesses and violoncellos to speak out against President Theodore Roosevelt, the symbol of American imperialism, and the nation's motivating force, Manifest Destiny. Darío identified Roosevelt with a conquering North America:

Eres los Estados Unidos,
eres el futuro invasor
de la América ingenua que tiene sangre indigena,
que aun reza a Jesucristo y aun habla español.

You are the United States,
the future invader
of the naive America of Indian blood
the America that still prays to Christ and still speaks español.

Darío's poem "A Roosevelt" appeared in 1904, four years after another *modernista*, the Uruguayan José Enrique Rodó, had published a slender book, *Ariel* (1900), which was to become the manifesto of Latin America in its struggle for survival. Using symbols taken from *The Tempest*, the United States was identified with the materialistic, utilitarian Caliban, and Latin America with the spiritual, ethereal Ariel. In his book, however, Rodó recognized the virtues of the United States. Unlike Sarmiento, he had little use for Franklin's morality and refers to it in sarcastic terms. Speaking about John Stuart Mill's morality, Rodó says, "The very culmination of that morality is only that of Franklin; a philosophy of conduct which has for its goal a commonplace sagacity, a prudent usefulness, in whose bosom will never rise the emotions of holiness of heroism; and which, fit only to give to one's conscience in the common affairs of life a certain moral support—like the apple-tree cane with which Franklin ever walked—is but a fragile staff with which to surmount great heights." Unfortunately, Rodó did not have a firsthand knowledge of the United States or personal contact with its writers, as he had with French culture and European writers. In his *Ariel,* he makes reference, besides Franklin and the Federalists, to Poe, Emerson, Channing, and Longfellow. Of Longfellow, he mentions two poems, "Excelsior" and "A Psalm of Life," as examples of the tenacious and arrogant faith Americans have in the future. Although he does not mention Walt Whitman, it seems that he was acquainted with his poetry. Emerson is mentioned as an example of the American who rejects the leveling tendencies of utilitarian democracy and upholds self-elevation and leadership. He was acquainted with Baudelaire's essay on the life of Poe, and it is this writer who receives the greatest attention in *Ariel.* It is interesting to note that Rodó, in 1900, already advanced the theory that, in the United States, literature and the fine arts are the product of men alienated from their society. "No one will say that Edgar Poe," he wrote, "was not an anomalous individual, rebellious to the influences around him: his chosen spirit represented a particle unassimilable by the national soul." A few pages later he elaborates on this idea by saying, "Prodigal of his riches—for meanness is not his fault—the North American has learned only to acquire by them the satisfaction of his vanity and material luxury, but not the chosen note of good taste. In such a surrounding, true art can only exist as the rebellion of an individual. Emerson, Poe are as strays of a fauna expelled from their true habitat by some geological catastrophe."

Rodó's book influenced the attitude of the following generation, sometimes called the Arielistas, in their appraisal of Anglo-American literature and the United States in general. However, this new generation was composed of men of great talent and discrimination and did not follow Rodó's ideas slavishly. They were aware of Rodó's lack of knowledge regarding Anglo-American literature, as well as the weak aspect of his simplified characterization of north and south by the

antithetical symbolism of Caliban and Ariel, which in a way perpetu-
ated Sarmiento's "civilización y barbarie," only that now it was applied
on a continental basis. The most critical of Rodó's ideas were Pedro
Henríquez Ureña, Alfonso Reyes, José Vasconcelos, and Luis Alberto
Sánchez, the latter criticizing him on different terms, his blind spot regarding economic exploitation of Latin America by the United States.

Due to the influence of Pedro Henríquez Ureña, then living in Mexico, the group of new writers turned away from the exclusive study of
French literature to that written in English. American writers and philosophers, especially William James and George Santayana, were read
and discussed. Henríquez Ureña had lived in New York while a young
man, and in 1913 attended the University of Minnesota, where he received a Ph.D. He became very well acquainted with Anglo-American
literature and, in 1927, while teaching at the University of La Plata in
Argentina, published a survey article, "Twenty Years of Literature in
the United States." The essay opens by stating that during the period
between 1907 and 1927, the literature of both Americas had been transformed, the transformation having been greater in the United States
than in Latin America. He very accurately defined the main literary
trend in nineteenth-century American literature, which ended, according to him, with the psychological novels of Henry James, the regional
stories of Bret Harte, and the humorous literature of Mark Twain. The
year 1907, according to Henríquez Ureña, marks a change in the development of Anglo-American literature. That year William James published his book *Pragmatism*, which prompted Henríquez Ureña to say,
"If the world was becoming Americanized in material things, here it
could find the formula for the Americanization of the spirit." However,
he continues, "his pragmatism was not the first philosophy of the twentieth century, but the last of the nineteenth." Three years later, George
Santayana, a James colleague at Harvard, began publishing his *Life of
Reason*, in which Henríquez Ureña finds the seeds of critical realism, the
philosophical concept that was to emerge as characteristic of twentieth-
century America.

According to Henríquez Ureña, an Anglo-American writer who was
able to see the change that was taking place in philosophy and letters was

Henry Adams, who, in 1907, then seventy years old, had not yet published his two most important books, *Mont St. Michel and Chartres* and *The Education of Henry Adams*. He says, "If I were forced to say which, for me, is the most important book that has been written in the United States, I would say without hesitation: *The Education* of *Henry Adams*."

In the last part of his essay, written in La Plata, Argentina, in 1927, Henríquez Ureña discusses the most important Anglo-American authors writing after 1910, and asks himself why it is that "life in the United States, more than in any other country, dissatisfies men and women of spirit, in spite of the marvelous nature of its industry, in spite of its common honesty and its easy kindness." The answer is similar to that given by Rodó. "In the United States of the twentieth century," says Henríquez Ureña, "the thinker and the artist, if they are sincere, are rebels; instinct and reason tell them that acquiescence would sink them in mediocrity. . . . To the army of rebels the United States will owe its moral and intellectual salvation, if these rebels are not conquered by the army of philistines." And who are these rebels? Among others, H. L. Mencken, Waldo Frank, Van Wycks Brooks, Lloyd Morris, Ludwig Lewisohn, Sherwood Anderson. He examines at length the works of the principal novelists, dramatists, and poets and ends the essay with these words: "The soul of the United States, its spiritual salvation, is in the hands of its major poets, Sandburg, Masters, Lindsay, Frost, Robinson; its best novelists, Dreiser, Anderson." It is interesting to observe that although he mentions Hemingway, he does not include him among the best novelists. Of course, Hemingway had not yet published his major works. But there is another reason. In a footnote, Henríquez Ureña tells us that in a conversation he had with Joseph Warren Beach, the latter told him that he considered Waldo Frank, Dos Passos, and Hemingway as full of promise, but recognized in them certain flaws. Unfortunately, after 1927, with a new interest in Spanish American philology, Henríquez Ureña wrote less and less about Anglo-American literature.

About the same time that Henríquez Ureña was writing his essay, an interest in Mexico on the part of the rebel writers, both American and English, brought about an understanding never before seen. As a result of the Mexican Revolution and the social experiments in Mexico, which paralleled the deterioration of social conditions in the United States, Mexico became an alternative model for the faltering industrialized nations. The English writer D. H. Lawrence, with his novel *The Plumed Serpent* extolling Quetzalcoatl and Mexico's Indian past, and the American writer Waldo Frank, with his book *América hispana,* led this movement. Some of Waldo Frank's pages remind us of Rodó's *Ariel.* "The United States," he says, "is in danger of catastrophe, because although its speed is great its aim is poor because the nurture of its creative life is being weakened while the proliferation of its material life, which only the creative spirit can control, continues." To Frank, the United States and *América hispana* represent two faces of a single problem. He writes, "The problem [of *la América hispana*], seemingly so different, is the same as that of the United States. In one place, there is order that lacks life, in the other, there is life that lacks order." And according to Frank, Spanish America has something to offer not only to the United States, but to the world. Spanish America, he says, "is strong in its intuition of the nature of the real person. It also can survive only by becoming great with this truth which the world needs."

Never before had Spanish American intellectuals praised an American writer like they did Waldo Frank. As a result, Anglo-American literature became fashionable, and in Mexico such writers as Xavier Villaurrutia and Salvador Novo began to read, translate, and analyze it, as well as to stage its dramas. This newfound love, however, did not extend to the whole country, or even to all its literature. They were admirers of those writers who were dissatisfied with American culture and society, even though they themselves were critical of writers representing the literature of social content and social protest. They had more in common with Pound and Eliot than they had with Azuela and Guzmán.

Novo translated Ezra Pound, and studied the poetry of Edgar Lee Masters. Villaurrutia, the most influential member of the group called Contemporáneos, using the title of the review that they published, lived for a year in the United States and studied dramatic art at Yale University, where he was accompanied by Rodolfo Usigli. In 1928, one year after Henríquez Ureña had published his essay on American literature, Villaurrutia complemented it with his review article of Eugene Jolas's

French anthology of new American poetry. Villaurrutia demonstrated his acquaintance with the subject by pointing out Jolas's weak points, especially in the omission of certain poets, among them E. E. Cummings, whose acute sensibility he praises, considering him a fine product of the new conquests of poetry.

In 1900, Rodó had bemoaned the lack of interest in aesthetic undertakings in the United States. In 1928, Villaurrutia quoted what Enrique Díez-Canedo had said, that the United States is a country "where poetry flourishes," and added, a "country where poets flourish and proliferate. Doubtless, the large number of poets [included in the Jolas anthology] prevent us from observing it with attention."

From 1935 to 1936, Villaurrutia lived in the United States, first in New Haven, Connecticut, and then in Pasadena, California, and San Francisco. Villaurrutia wrote a series of letters to Novo in which he tells about his experiences in the United States. In New Haven, he read American authors, among them T. S. Eliot, whose drama *Murder in the Cathedral* was presented by the students at Yale, and of which he says, "The work is excellent and represents the greatest poetic effort." In New York, he attended a performance of *Winterset,* by Maxwell Anderson, whom he considered "the liveliest American author today."

The literary review *Contemporáneos,* which did so much to acquaint Mexican readers, and especially writers, with the literature of the United States, stopped publishing in 1931. The next literary review of importance, *Letras de México,* did not appear until 1937, and *El Hijo Pródigo,* the most important of all, in 1943. These were years of great political activity, especially in the relations with the United States. The Great Depression had affected life in all its aspects. Thousands of *mexicanos* left the United States, where they were no longer wanted. In 1938, President Cárdenas expropriated the British and American oil wells, but the predictions of the invasion of Mexico by the United States Marines, a common expectancy, did not take place; on the contrary, Mexico joined its neighbor a few years later in its struggle against the Axis powers.

It was during these years also that a young writer, Octavio Paz, began to publish articles and poems in the periodicals mentioned, as well as in *Taller,* which he directed. The interest of Paz in the United States was the result of his first visits to this country. In an interview with Rita Guibert, he said, "My stay in the United States [in 1944] was a great experience, no less decisive than that of Spain. On the one hand there was the amazing and terrible reality of North American civilization; on the other, my reading and discovery of a number of poets: Eliot, Pound, William Carlos Williams, Wallace Stevens, Cummings. Years later I met William Carlos Williams, who translated my poem 'Himno entre ruinas' ('Hymn Among the Ruins') and also Cummings. I saw more of Cummings, and translated some of his poems."

From San Francisco, Paz sent to a Mexican weekly some reports about the meetings of the United Nations in 1945. His stay in California was significant for his own development as a poet. "Those San Francisco days," he says, "were marvelous—a sort of physical and intellectual intoxication, a great mouthful of fresh air. That was where I embarked on my path in poetry—if there are paths in poetry." In the same interview, Paz comments about one of his books, *Eagle or Sun?*, and its similarity to one by William Carlos Williams:

> A North American friend . . . pointed out that there was an analogy between my book and one by William Carlos Williams, published years earlier: *Kora in Hell*. The similarity isn't textual but as to aim. In fact, both books are poems in prose, inspired by French poetry. However, *Kora in Hell* is a deeply American book and could only have been written by a North American. In the same way I think *Eagle or Sun?* could only have been written in Mexico. . . . Another similarity: William Carlos Williams also wrote a very beautiful book called *In the American Grain*, a collection of essays on American themes. Well, *The Labyrinth of Solitude* fulfills a corresponding purpose. I wrote *The Labyrinth of Solitude* first as a confession or to relieve my feelings, and immediately afterwards I wrote *Eagle or Sun?*

The Labyrinth of Solitude is, of course, where Paz for the first time expresses his feelings and ideas about the United States. This book, more than any other, has been influential in shaping attitudes toward the nature of life and society north and south of the border. We shall limit ourselves to comments related to his ideas about Anglo-American literature. When he wrote the first essay of the book, "The Pachuco and Other Extremes," Paz, like his intellectual precursors, believed that Anglo-American literature was written by authors alienated from the mainstream of American feeling. "The United States," he says, "is a society that wants to realize its ideals, has no wish to exchange them for others, and is confident of surviving, no matter how dark the future may appear.... It's true that this faith in the natural goodness of life, or in its infinite wealth of possibilities, cannot be found in recent North American literature, which prefers to depict a much more somber world." In a footnote appended to the second edition of the book, and also to the English translation, he clarifies his statement, not in regard to the nature of literature, but in regard to the American people: "These lines were written," he says, "before the public was clearly cognizant of the danger of universal annihilation made possible by nuclear weapons. Since then North Americans have lost their optimism but not their confidence, a confidence based on resignation and obstinacy."

In his attitude toward the future of the two cultures of the Americas, Paz is a pessimist. Like Rodó and Martí, he does not believe that they can be reconciled. After detailing the differences between the two ways of life, in Mexico and in the United States, he says, "The two attitudes are irreconcilable, I believe." He has not changed his opinion with the passing of time. In the collection of essays titled *Alternating Current*, published in 1967, he repeats: "Rodó and Darío were not mistaken in their belief that there was a fundamental incompatibility between Latin America and the United States." And more recently, in his book *Children of the Mire* (1974), explaining the nature of *modernismo*, he expresses the same idea. He says:

> The recovery of the Indian world and, later on, of the Spanish past, counterbalanced the admiration, fear, and anger evoked by the United States and its policy of domination in Latin America. Admiration for the originality and might of North American culture vied with fear and anger at the repeated intervention of the United States in the life of our nations. I have referred to the phenomenon elsewhere; here I will only emphasize that the anti-imperialism of the *modernistas* was

not exclusively based on political and economic grounds but on the idea that Latin America and Anglo-Saxon America represent two different and probably irreconcilable versions of Western civilization. The conflict was not only between classes and economics and social systems but between two visions of the world and of men.

And in this book, too, Paz expands the idea of the conflict between literature and society to include all modern literature, which, he says, "is an impassioned rejection of the modern age. This rejection is no less violent among the poets of Anglo-American 'modernism' than among the members of European and Latin American avant-gardes."

Paz's appreciation of Anglo-American literature is complemented by that of Carlos Fuentes. Paz, as a poet, has given emphasis, especially in his book *Children of the Mire*, to the development of poetry in the United States. Carlos Fuentes, a novelist, has been interested in the development of the genre in which he writes. His essays on American novelists, collected in the book *Casa con dos puertas* (*A House with Two Doors*, 1970), deal with those novelists he considers to be expatriates from their own culture. Professor Cecil Robinson's assertion, in his book *With the Ears of Strangers*, that "beyond a doubt the deep attachment for Mexico among a number of American intellectuals is generally unrequited by their Mexican opposite numbers" could be extended, as we have seen, to refer to the whole of Latin America. Nevertheless, Latin American intellectuals have admired individual Anglo-American writers; but these American writers are generally those who have been alienated from their own culture, or at least have criticized the United States. Fuentes is representative of these intellectuals. He likes to quote Anglo-American writers and has dedicated studies to C. Wright Mills, Ernest Hemingway, Oscar Lewis, William Styron, and others. At the same time, his interest in the American novel led him to write essays dealing with the works of Herman Melville and William Faulkner. His essay on Melville has the subtitle "The Novel as Symbol," and that on Faulkner, "The Novel as Tragedy."

In the latter essay, he discusses the central themes that give meaning not only to the Anglo-American novel but to Anglo-American literature in general. That central theme, according to Fuentes, is the relationship between man and nature. For Faulkner and others, original sin consists in using, and in violating, nature. Here Fuentes illustrates his point by quoting from the story *The Bear*, in which Faulkner says that man is different from God because God only contemplates nature and loves it directly, while man hunts, fishes, mutilates: in a word, utilizes. But sin contains its own punishment. Man, after he has violated nature, either loves it or denies it. Fuentes says:

> Here we face one of the central themes of North American literature, a theme that has its start in the struggle of Ahab against the whale in *Moby Dick* and reaches its climax in the struggle of the old man Santiago against the fish in Hemingway's *The Old Man and the Sea*. In Faulkner's story, the protagonists are the bear and the forest. Like Ishmael and Santiago, in the novels of Melville and Hemingway, Ike McCasslin in *The Bear* immediately loves nature and understands that the land belongs to all and that man, in order to redeem himself from original violation, can only offer confession, humility, suffering, and resistance. On the other hand, Popeye in *Sanctuary*, like Ahab in *Moby Dick*, fears nature because it reflects his own perversion.

Unfortunately, Fuentes does not pursue the treatment of this theme by Anglo-American authors to make a comparison with what we find in the Spanish American novel. In such works, for instance, as *La vorágine*, the only person to escape with his life from the jungle is the old man Silva, the only one who had not violated nature. Fuentes does compare the novel produced in the two Americas when he speaks about the theme of defeat, common to both literatures. "Defeat," he says, "is the axis of Faulkner's works, and the defeat of the South was the only one that North Americans have suffered. . . . That is why we Latin Americans feel so close to Faulkner's works; only Faulkner, in the literature of the United States, only Faulkner, in the closed world of optimism and success, offers an image that is common to both the United States and Latin America: the image of defeat, of separation, of doubt: the image of tragedy." Fuentes is not the only new Latin American novelist who has observed the affinity existing in the world of Faulkner and those worlds depicted by Latin American authors. Gabriel García Márquez has said that the writer to whom the new Latin American novelists are most indebted is William Faulkner. "Faulkner," he says, "is found in all the fiction of Latin America. . . . I believe that the great difference that there is between our precursors and us is Faulkner; he is the only thing that happened between these two generations." He further states that Faulkner's method is very effective for the description of Latin American reality: "The European method was not useful," he says, "nor was the traditional Spanish method; and suddenly we find Faulkner's method, very adequate to talk about our reality. . . . In a way, Faulkner is a writer of the Caribbean, in a way he is a Latin American writer."

The article that Fuentes dedicated to Ernest Hemingway, written in 1964, is more than anything else a review of Hemingway's book of memoirs, *A Moveable Feast.* For Fuentes, this book represents the tragedy of Hemingway in search of Hemingway, and is his best novel since *A Farewell to Arms,* comparable only to *The Sun Also Rises* and his short stories. To Fuentes it does not seem paradoxical that Hemingway, who sacrificed his literature to his personal image, ended up by finding in this lost Hemingway his best fictional character. The enigma of the memoirs can be stated as follows: Who is Ernest Hemingway? Here Fuentes tells us that some old friend of Hemingway had told him in New York that during his last years Hemingway had reached a total confusion as to his personality. "Hemingway did not know if he was one of his own characters or even the motion picture actors representing his characters." Fuentes is intrigued, more than anything else, by Hemingway's *simpatías y diferencias;* that is, his opinions about his fellow American writers living in Paris during his early years: Ford Madox Ford, Gertrude Stein, F. Scott Fitzgerald, Ezra Pound, T. S. Eliot. But behind all this, Fuentes finds that the real subject of Hemingway's book is Hemingway himself, Hemingway against Hemingway, Hemingway in Hemingway. The result is one of the most exact and moving portraits of his literary formation.

In the essay on Faulkner, Fuentes points out the contributions of these two great Anglo-American novelists to literature: Hemingway's is the search of adventure outside the frontiers of the West; Faulkner's, the discovery of a new language. Hemingway's choice of foreign locales had its origin in the fact that the characteristics of Anglo-American society—optimism, innocence, economic success, elementary Manichaeism, self-reliance, and democratic camaraderie—did not provide him with the elements necessary to write great novels, that is, a rich history and a complex social order. According to Fuentes:

> the two typical attitudes of the North American writer consist in translating environment itself, changing it into a drama thanks to the density of the naturalist reproduction and the ferocity of the critical spirit—Crane, Norris, Howells, Dreiser, Dos Passos—or in confronting the North American with the world, throwing him out of his environment to discover his dramatic dimension in his response to the unknown: Ahab and the whale in *Moby Dick*, Frederick Henry and the war in *A Farewell to Arms*, Jake Barnes and the bulls in *The Sun Also Rises*, Dick Diver and the postwar European society in *Tender Is the Night*.

If we compare Fuentes's essays on C. Wright Mills and Oscar Lewis, we discover that he, Carlos Fuentes, a Mexican intellectual, is defending the right of two American writers to criticize: the former, his own government, the latter a foreign country, a country that happens to be the Mexico of Carlos Fuentes. The arguments are the same. "The Mexican intellectual class," he says, "has defended the right of Oscar Lewis to write about Mexico and the right of our most prestigious publishing house, the Fondo de Cultura Económica, to publish his book." In the same way, he defended Mills's right to criticize his own country.

And it is here that Octavio Paz and Carlos Fuentes, however apart they may be in other respects, agree. Both believe that the most important activity a writer can undertake is the criticism of his own society and of society in general. And it is this rebellious tradition that gives the writers of the two Americas a common ground. Their writings transcend national frontiers and make the concept of the literature of the Americas a reality.

37

BEYOND MYTHS AND BORDERS

Beyond its basic moral and aesthetic values, a work of literature also entails certain social and historical functions that have been recognized by critics the world over. In his essay "Breve reseña histórica de la crítica" ("Brief Historical Review of Criticism"), Alfonso Reyes clearly states that literature must inevitably fulfill a social role "not merely by reason of its origin, but because of the essential unity of the spirit." Reyes adds that "the ancillary nature of literature is made more apparent during times of crisis when, with all the resources at its disposal, human intelligence is attempting to provide remedies; and also it's emphasized in proportion to the increase in the human transcendence of the work in question."

One of the social functions that literature fulfills is that of creating personal or social paradigms that serve as models for the reader. Whether directly or by means of translations, readers are made aware of a community's ways of living, thinking, and being; of the behavior of a nation's inhabitants, their aspirations, and ideals, their attitudes and values, as well as their myths, legends, and prejudices, even though the particular community may be physically unknown to the reader. And in cases where the reader can claim a prior knowledge, the experience of reading is often much more effective than other ways of learning and interpreting

An earlier Spanish version was first published in *Mexican Studies/Estudios Mexicanos* 9, no. 1 (Winter 1993): 95–118. Reprinted in *Common Borders, Uncommon Paths: Race, Culture, and National Identity in U.S.–Mexican Relations,* ed. Jaime E. Rodríguez O. and Kathryn Vincent (Wilmington, Del.: S. R. Books, 1997), 143–65.

the history of a nation. In the book *En tierra yankee* (*In Yankee Territory*), in which Justo Sierra gives his impressions of a trip he made to the United States and Canada in 1895, we find the following rather interesting statement: "All this pessimism of mine is 'bookish' and derives from what I have read about North American society. I didn't observe well."

Furthermore, literature recognizes no boundaries. It is not limited to verifiable facts, because it can encompass events in imaginary lives. Literature finds its characters among the most obscure beings and can give them a voice. Carlos Fuentes has observed that "there are many things that history, reason and logic don't see, but that perhaps novelists do see. There are some things that only Dostoyevsky has seen."

No less important for literature is the presence of myths, both old and new. Myths are firmly established as a way of interpreting human nature and culture. According to Mircea Eliade, myths have not disappeared. He claims that the presence of certain symbols in society may be interpreted as the persistence of collective thought, a form of thought that has not altogether disappeared and within which myths are the principal form.

The North American writer Ambrose Bierce, in his satirical book *The Devil's Dictionary* (1911), published two years before his death in Mexico, defines mythology as "the combined beliefs relating to the origin, early history, heroes, gods, and other concepts that are found among primitive peoples in contrast to the true beliefs that are invented nowadays." As we know, these "true beliefs" of modern man are of capital importance to the social groups that invent them; however, we also know that those beliefs and myths are often damaging in their effect on other communities and therefore contribute to dissolution rather than to the unity of nations. Such is the case of the myth of the racial and cultural superiority of the Anglo-American and the inferiority of Hispanic and indigenous races. These harmful concepts, negative beliefs, and historical and cultural myths are what literature helps history to overcome.

From this perspective, it seems to me that literature affords an excellent means of international exchange, because it can help to correct errors and prejudices and thereby reduce tensions and conflicts, especially between neighboring countries that have different cultures, as in the case of Mexico and the United States. In the nineteenth century, Ignacio Manuel Altamirano was aware that literature had the power to project the cultural wealth of a nation beyond its geographical borders. He tells us that the novels of Sir Walter Scott brought the attention "of the entire world to his country, which previously had been so unknown."

According to this view, literature has the power to transcend artificial national borders in order to circulate and make known in other countries a truer vision of the people and the culture that produce it and thereby to promote a better understanding among nations. By literature, we mean works of fiction such as novels, short stories, dramatic works, essays, and poetry. We also can include here the works of some historians when they refer to literature or when they express ideas related to the theme of the present discussion.

Although there are numerous historical and political studies of the relations between Mexico and the United States, the literatures of these two neighboring countries have not been studied from such a perspective, with the aim of documenting the contributions of each. The only exceptions are the books of Cecil Robinson (*Mexico and the Hispanic Southwest in American Literature*) and Stanley T. Williams (*The Spanish Background of American Literature*), which, however, do not concern themselves with the other side of the coin, which is the presence of the United States in Mexican literature.

For the purposes of the present essay, we will be able to just briefly examine the nature of some of the myths that occur most frequently in literature and that have been the source of conflicts between representatives of the two great cultures that settled in the New World. The emphasis will be on the myths that appeared among the people of the United States and Mexico, for it was these two nations that confronted each other, face-to-face, in North America.

The Roots of Euro-American Conflict

During the colonial period, the conflicts that developed between Anglos and Hispanics, whether in Europe or in the New World, were primarily the result of religious and racial antagonisms. In Europe, the wars between Protestants and Catholics were very intense. The racial struggles grew out of the pseudoscientific myth that held that America was a continent on which both nature and human beings had degenerated. According to the theories of the celebrated French naturalist Georges-Louis Leclerc, Comte de Buffon, who was the author of *Histoire naturelle* (1749–89), the climate of the New World was malignant and caused the degeneration of both plants and animals. The philosopher Corneille de Pauw, author of *Recherches philosophiques sur les Americains* (*Philosophical Research on the Americans*, 1771), extended the theory to include the native peoples of the Americas, while the Scottish historian William Robertson, author of the *History of America* (1777), accepted the idea and caused it to be spread throughout the English-speaking world. The ideas that Robertson expressed were taken up by other authors who wrote about Mexico and the Latin American countries. Stanley Williams indicates that Robertson's book was responsible for the almost century-long popularity of various types of prose and verse narratives about South America and Mexico. It also influenced romantic historians such as Washington Irving and William H. Prescott. Raymund Paredes, in his study of the origins of anti-Mexican sentiment in the United States, adds that the popularity of Robertson's work "served to bring into play the final component necessary to form an ideological prism through which Americans would view contemporary Mexicans in the nineteenth century."

The theory of the supposed inferiority of America and Americans was contested by, among others, Thomas Jefferson and Benjamin Franklin. The Italian scholar Antonello Gerbi notes that Jefferson defended the inhabitants of America, who had been slandered by De Pauw, and that he attempted to confound Buffon by ordering that a moose be sent to him from America. Gerbi also writes that Franklin invited the abbot Guillaume Raynal, who was a popularizer of the ideas of De Pauw, to a dinner attended by five very short Frenchmen and five gigantic Americans, in order to give the abbot an object lesson.

Among the Mexicans of the period who most forcefully attacked the ideas of De Pauw and Robertson were Francisco Javier Clavijero and

Fray Servando Teresa de Mier. While in Italy, Clavijero wrote an entire book (*Disertaciones,* a supplement to his *Historia antigua de México,*
1780) to rebut the theories of the degeneration of the Mexican people, but primarily to oppose the ideas of De Pauw, whose book, which
Clavijero calls a collection of blunders, attempted to convince the world
that everything in America had degenerated. According to Clavijero, his
refutation is based on direct, personal knowledge of the Mexicans; on his
extensive study of their culture; on having known and dealt intimately
with the Americans; on having personally observed their character, their
genius, their predilections, and their habits of thought; and on having
very carefully studied their ancient history, their religion, their government, the laws and customs—all of which qualified him to dispute De
Pauw's contentions. Clavijero considered the souls of the Mexicans in
no way inferior to those of Europeans, for Mexicans were capable of
mastering all the sciences, even the most abstract, if only serious attention were given to their education. "Never," he states, "have Europeans
done a greater disservice to their own reason, than when they question
the rationality of the Americans."

Fray Servando Teresa de Mier is much more aggressive in his objections than is Clavijero. Mier was firmly convinced that the Spanish had made available to De Pauw negative reports about the New
World. Therefore, in the first of his *Cartas de un americano* (*Letters of an
American,* 1811–12), Mier wields his combative style, asserting that the
Consulado (Merchants' Guild) of Mexico had sent an account to the
Cortes of Cádiz that was a compendium of the nonsense that the Spanish had communicated to De Pauw, the very same nonsense that was
carelessly repeated by Robertson, Raynal, and Juan Bautista Muñoz.

Manifest Destiny and the Myth of Anglo-American Superiority

In 1816, Fray Servando traveled from London to the United States in
the company of General Xavier Mina. They carried with them a printing press with which they planned to issue proclamations in favor of
independence for New Spain. Mier returned to the United States in

1821, and under a variety of influences, among them Thomas Paine's *Common Sense,* he wrote the *Memoria político-instructiva,* a work that favored a republic instead of the empire that Agustín de Iturbide was establishing. The six thousand copies he published and sent to Mexico became a source of republican ideals, but not of the Anglo-American belief in the mythic origin of their culture, a belief that would lead to the expansionist policies of Manifest Destiny. Animated by this myth, the North Americans undertook the territorial expansion of the United States to the south and west; they initiated a process that began with the Louisiana Purchase of 1803, continued with the annexation of Texas and the Treaty of Guadalupe Hidalgo in 1848, and culminated with the Spanish-American War of 1898, thus completing a series of historical events that revolve around a myth of origin.

Shortly after the Louisiana Purchase, the United States expanded toward the southern and western regions of the continent with the intention of establishing commercial ties and, shortly afterward, to settle the area. In 1807, Commander Zebulon Montgomery Pike, while exploring the western frontier of Louisiana, inadvertently found himself in territory of New Spain, where he was made a prisoner and taken to Santa Fe. In 1810, he published an account of his adventures, which stirred the interest of North Americans in that world, which they heretofore had ignored. After 1821, they began to invade the vast and largely undefended territory of Mexico. This gave rise to the first conflicts. Mexicans resented the new invaders and their myth of racial superiority. The historian David J. Weber observes that the stereotype of the inferior Mexican appears as a result of the arrogant sense of cultural and political superiority known in U.S. history as Manifest Destiny. It was perhaps in an effort to combat this myth that in 1823, during Mexico's first empire, the secretary of state and foreign affairs, José Cecilio del Valle, published in his newspaper *El Amigo de La Patria* an article that quotes Alexander von Humboldt. The Prussian scholar discredited those who drew "frightening portraits of this beautiful half of the earth," and he defended Mexicans against the attacks of De Pauw. In his masterpiece *Kosmos,* Humboldt would later deny the existence of superior or inferior races of human beings.

During the first decades of the nineteenth century, myths are prevalent in nearly all North American literary works that dealt with Mexico. Even in the work of Zebulon Pike, one finds a superior moral attitude (Pike being a good Puritan) that is critical of the Mexican way of life: their treatment of women; their dances, which he considers indecent; and their priests, whose conduct he finds deplorable. In the first North American novel about Mexico, *Francis Berrian; or the Mexican Patriot* (1826), by Timothy Flint, the protagonist takes the side of the insurgents and fights for the independence of Mexico in the armies of Morelos. In this work, the criticism of the Mexican is expressed through the character of Doña Martha, the daughter of the governor of Durango and Berrian's fiancée. The young woman praises the North Americans: "What a noble people! What a difference it is to compare their faces and persons with those of people here!"

One might say that Doña Martha's exclamation gives literary form to the myth of the supposed inferiority of the Mexican. Doña Martha considers the North Americans superior to the Mexicans in their physical appearance as well as in their nobility. Doña Martha is a fictional character created by a North American novelist. Her words reflect the thinking of the author. On the other hand, Lorenzo de Zavala's *Viaje a los Estados Unidos de Norte América* (*Trip to the United States of North America*, 1834) compares the character of the North Americans and the Mexicans without showing prejudice. The book gave Mexican readers an opportunity to form a clearer notion of their neighbors' way of life, which is captured well by Zavala. Justo Sierra was familiar with the book, as it was reissued in Mérida, Yucatán, in 1846, with an introduction by Sierra's father.

Not all North American writers of the period credited the myth of Mexican inferiority, however. Although Zebulon Pike and Albert Pike, another traveler of the period (author of a book entitled *Prose Sketches and Poems*, 1834), criticize the culture of the New Mexicans, they occasionally—in a very few instances—praise certain characteristics, such as the hospitality of the people. This was not the case, however, of the authors of popular novels, such as the so-called dime novels and westerns, whose central theme was border conflict. For writers of these works, no aspect of Mexican culture was worthy of praise, and their view would prevail in North American literature well into the twentieth century. In his novel *Legends of Mexico*, written in 1846 and published in 1847, George Lippard predicts the conquest of Mexico with the following words: "Just as the Spaniards conquered the Aztecs, so the mongrel race will be conquered by the northern race of steel."

Lippard and other authors of sensationalist fiction were responsible for the mythification of the historical events of 1836 through 1848. The great myth of Texas began with the dream of Moses Austin and reached its apotheosis at the Alamo, where a handful of "brave men" defended the now-sacred site against the "powerful" army of Santa Anna. Today the Alamo is a shrine that preserves the cult of William Travis, Davy Crockett, Jim Bowie, and the other heroes who, according to the myth, were sacrificed there for Texas's independence. The historian Walter Lord, who has traced the development of the Texas myth from its origins, writes that in spite of the zeal with which Texans defend the myth of the Alamo, the heroes who died there were not native Texans. Two-thirds had just recently arrived from other states, and only half a dozen of them had been in the territory more than six years. Still others claim that some had come from Europe to aid the cause of liberty. Lord's statements are supported by the inscriptions on the walls of the Alamo, which indicate the place of origin of each of the heroes. According to those plaques, the only real Texans were the Mexicans who died there.

The myth of the Alamo, which has been so widely popularized by North American novelists and filmmakers, is only one manifestation of a larger myth that is fundamental to North American nationhood, and that is the myth of the frontier. This larger myth was given great importance by Frederick Jackson Turner in his famous essay of 1893 on the significance of the frontier in American history. Turner attributed the democratic character of North Americans to their struggle to tame the frontier. The defeat of Santa Anna at San Jacinto, which resulted in the independence of Texas, gave great hope to the desires of Anglo-Americans who wished to conquer the entire Southwest and establish a nation that extended from the Atlantic to the Pacific.

In spite of efforts by historians to demythify the Alamo, the myth has persisted and has become stronger over time. Novels have had an especially corrosive effect, which at times has carried over into the historical record. Walter Lord notes that Amelia Williams, who made the first attempt to demythify the Alamo legend, built her case on one of the worst novels to depict the historic battle: *Margaret Ballantine, or the Fall of the Alamo.* Williams obtained biographical information from this novel that later was found to be false.

In Mexican literature, the demythification of the Alamo occurs in *Julia* (1868), a novel by Manuel Martínez de Castro that takes place during the Texas revolution and in which the hero easily defeats the Anglo-Americans. However, that work was published after the events of 1846–48, when Mexican attitudes toward the United States and toward North Americans had changed completely. In the United States, another version of the physical superiority myth had been created: that of the marines who defeated the Mexicans and, according to the marines' hymn, advanced to "the halls of Montezuma." The North American invasion produced a Mexican myth as well, that of the Niños Héroes (Young Heroes) of Chapultepec who uselessly gave up their lives in defense of their country.

In the poem "Los niños mártires de Chapultepec" ("The Young Martyrs of Chapultepec"), Amado Nervo composed the following verses, which present the historical event in a mythic light:

> Their death was no Phoebean conjunction
> nor Diana's melancholy setting,
> but Vesper's eclipse which re-creates
> the heavens with twinkling illumination
> and yields to the brilliance of morning.

Hilarion Frías y Soto attempted something similar in his "Discurso," an address delivered in 1874 on the occasion of the twenty-seventh anniversary of the Battle of Chapultepec, in which he decrees that "there the fighting was sublime; for it had a majesty that even Homer couldn't have imagined for his heroes." On the other hand, in 1875, Guillermo

"Fidel" Prieto published a Sunday piece about the very same battle as seen from the point of view of a student named Martín Zapatilla, undoubtedly a fictional character, whom Fidel "quotes." The student lived to write his picaresque memoirs, including an eyewitness account of the famous battle. According to Zapatilla, he is a bit of a poet and he writes the following verses to his beloved Cuca:

> The cannon explodes
> the clamor quickens
> and I scream and curse the pitiless Yankee,
> and in order to restore my valor,
> I remember the eyes of my Cuca.

Zapatilla adds a critical statement to his own composition: "But this consonant rhyme in 'uca' disturbs me, perturbs me, sets my wig to bristling, that is, if I were a wigged gentleman." Zapatilla is not a hero like the martyred youths of Chapultepec. According to Fidel, the memoirs end with the following confession: "As I had no funds, nor a gallant figure, like a deer I slipped away as soon as the general was secure."

Joaquín Murrieta: History or Myth?

One of the results of the War of 1847 was the conflict that arose for the Mexicans who remained in the territories that were ceded by Mexico to the United States. The conflict was most intense in California because of the discovery of gold there in 1849, an event that attracted new immigrants from Mexico. The injustices committed against these newcomers caused them to react violently and form small groups of armed marauders who traveled on horseback throughout the state.

These groups are represented in history and legend by Joaquín Murrieta's small band. Despite Murrieta's short life and brief career as the avenger of the wrongs suffered by the *californios,* his name has provided historians, novelists, playwrights, and poets with a subject for a good number of works. Many California historians mention his name, many poets sing of him, and many novelists have made him into a mythic hero. And although the historical record on Murrieta is scanty, he is the protagonist of many novels, as well as of other artistic forms, such as theater and films.

In the case of Murrieta, history and fiction have become so interwoven that it is impossible to separate them. As an example, in the *Breve historia de México* (*Brief History of Mexico*), José Vasconcelos contributed to spreading the North American version of the myth when he derived his information not from the historical texts, nor even from the first novel, *The Life and Adventures of Joaquín Murrieta*, by John Rollin Ridge ("Yellow Bird")—the source of all information about the hero—but from a motion picture, *The Robin Hood of El Dorado* (1936), which was based on a novel of the same name by Walter Noble Burns. Vasconcelos accepted the movie version of Murrieta's life without question, giving a step-by-step description of his adventures, while interjecting his own comments on Mexican politics. He states, for example: "But even with [the presence of] Murrieta the bandits are without a program. They are like Mexican politicians who shout slogans from this or that manifesto without either understanding what they mean or how to implement them if chance should concede them the victory."

Although Vasconcelos declares that the film is "an extraordinarily significant work of fiction," he adds, almost immediately, that Murrieta was a "historical character who was more or less modified in the film version, yet was eminently representative [of reality]." He then describes the key scenes of the film: "Murrieta was robbed of his land, his bride was raped, a generous Yankee friend offered to support his claims. . . . A short time later, Murrieta was beaten by a lynching party. Finally, a bandit came to his aid and made him the leader of a small band that terrorized the district. . . . One night, Murrieta assaulted, not the North Americans, but a group of Mexican property owners who were meeting in an attempt to save their lands from the Yankee businessmen who were usurping their properties."

The film narrated by Vasconcelos does not transform the protagonist as far as Joseph E. Badger's novel *Joaquín the Saddle King* (1881), in which Murrieta becomes a young blond Spaniard who supported the

Texas revolutionaries and later fought on the side of the North Americans in the Mexican War of 1847. When someone asks him why he loves the Americans, Joaquín says: "Oh, because they are very manly: I have lived with them, I have eaten, fought and ridden with them. I am proud that they are my friends. How I wish that they were my countrymen as well!" Thus, in Badger's novel, Murrieta becomes a hero for all North Americans by rejecting his own culture.

North American Views of Mexican Literature

Shortly after the wars of 1846–48, the North American poet William Cullen Bryant, who had shown an early interest in demythifying the pernicious belief in Mexican cultural and racial inferiority, was a guest of the Mexican government. In fact, Bryant was the first writer in his country to recognize that Mexicans possessed a culture that was capable of producing a literature of great merit. By 1827, Bryant had reviewed the novel *Jicoténcal,* which, although written by an anonymous author, dealt with the conquest of Mexico. That review was the first critical work on a literary text dealing with a Mexican subject to appear in the United States. In addition, Bryant somehow obtained José Rosas Moreno's *Fábulas (Fables),* which he adapted for the North American public. According to Stanley T. Williams, one stanza by Rosas Moreno, a poet who was hardly known outside of Mexico, affected Bryant more deeply than all of Lope de Vega's comedies. Unlike Longfellow and Lowell, Bryant was immensely interested in Mexican poetry. In 1872, at the age of seventy-eight, Bryant traveled to Mexico, where he was received with high honors and recognized as a great friend. In one of six lengthy letters that recorded his impressions and appeared in the New York *Evening Post,* Bryant referred to Mexican literature in the following terms: "Mexico has her men of science, her eloquent orators, her eminent researchers, her historians, her excellent novelists, and numerous poets who write in the melodious language spoken in this country."

It is a fact that even American literary figures of international reputation, such as Washington Irving, James Fenimore Cooper, Walt

Whitman, and Richard Henry Dana, accepted the myth of Anglo-American racial superiority. This is in contrast with what a century later the Old Gringo—the title character of Carlos Fuentes's novel *Gringo viejo* (1985), who represents the writer Ambrose Bierce—tells another American character, the schoolteacher Harriet Winslow, about what he believes to be the superiority of the Mexican *mestizaje* over the myth of racial purity advanced by the North Americans. He declares, "Now open your eyes, Miss Harriet, and recall that we killed our redskins and lacked the courage to fornicate with Indian women and thus produce at least a nation of half and half. We are trapped in this business of forever killing people of a different skin color. Mexico is the proof of what we could have been, so do keep your eyes open."

American Literature in Mexico

Professor Cecil Robinson observes that "without a doubt, the great sympathy that some American intellectuals have for Mexico is not reciprocated by their Mexican counterparts." This observation, however, cannot be applied to writers such as Alfonso Reyes, Xavier Villaurrutia, Octavio Paz, and Carlos Fuentes, among others, who have expressed favorable opinions about many aspects of North American life. The interest in North American literature is due, in part, to the influence of Pedro Henríquez Ureña, who introduced a very significant change in Mexican letters when he recommended to the members of the Ateneo de la Juventud (Athenaeum of Youth) that they read U.S. literature, with which he was quite familiar, as may be seen in his essay "Viente años de literatura de los Estados Unidos" ("Twenty Years of Literature in the United States").

The study of North American letters was one of the values that the generation of the Contemporáneos (1930s) inherited from the Ateneístas (1910s), and this influence is reflected in the work of the younger writers. I will mention only one of them, the poet Xavier Villaurrutia, who published "Guía de poetas norteamericanos" ("Guide to North American Poets") and completed studies of Elmer Rice, George Santayana, and Walt Whitman. Thus, it is understandable that the work of Villaurrutia receives more attention in the universities of the United States than anywhere else outside of Mexico.

The interest in North American literature that was first shown by the Ateneístas and the Contemporáneos has continued to the present. Octavio Paz has published translations of several poets; Carlos Fuentes has written critical studies of C. Wright Mills, Ernest Hemingway, Oscar Lewis, William Styron, and others. Salvador Elizondo, José Emilio Pacheco, and many others have continued to study the literature of the United States. And the same thing is happening in the United States, where the influence of Mexican literature has reached a peak, partly due to the popularity of the writers of the Latin American literary boom and also because of the participation of Chicano writers and readers.

Mythical Modes in Chicano Literature

Let us now examine the case of various Chicano writers, who are the product of a synthesis of the cultures of Mexico and the United States. In general, although their work is written primarily in English, it is evident that a Mexican cultural background is always present in their writing. Especially after the decade of the 1960s, as a result of the Chicano movement, they searched for their roots in the country of their ancestors. They found those roots in Indian mythology and in the heroes of the war of independence and the revolution. A profound nationalism moved them to create a myth of their origins, of Aztlán, the land abandoned by the Aztecs and reclaimed by the Chicanos. The myth of Aztlán unites Chicanos with the past, especially with the Aztecs, with the Seven Caves, and with the creative deities Coatlicue and her son, Huitzilopochtli, as well as with the mythic journey and the no-less-mythic founding of the Aztec empire in Lake Texcoco.

The Aztlán myth, whose Mexican origins go back to the sixteenth century, has evolved over time. Its recent rebirth must be attributed to Chicanos and, in particular, to the poet Alurista, although, as he himself stated in his study of three Chicano novelists, myths are not the product of individuals but of generations of people who share a common space over a considerable period of time. But it is Alurista who, in fact, identified Chicanos with the myth of Aztlán. His "El plan espiritual de Aztlán," which he presented in Denver in March 1969, declares the following: "We are a nation, we are a union of free peoples, we are AZTLÁN." The impact of the myth is clearly evident in the work of the principal Chicano writers of the 1970s, a decade in which poems, novels, and anthologies appeared with the word *Aztlán* in the title, for example, the journal *Aztlán*, which began publication in 1970; the poems "Floricanto en Aztlán" (1971), by Alurista; the novels *Peregrinos de Aztlán* (1974), by Miguel Méndez M., and *Heart of Aztlán* (1976), by Rudolfo Anaya; and the anthology *Aztlán* (1972), by the theater director Luis Valdez.

Of fundamental importance to the creation of that and other myths is the epic poem *Yo soy Joaquín* (1967), by Rodolfo "Corky" Gonzales, in which the hero is identified with a mythic Joaquín. One may ask, Who is Joaquín? The most obvious answer would be Joaquín Murrieta. But Joaquín as a historical-mythical character is transformed in the poem into a symbol of and for Chicanos. Joaquín becomes a synthesis of various popular heroes and antiheroes in Mexican and Chicano cultures. However, the poetic subject is personified by the figure of Joaquín Murrieta:

> I rode the mountains of San Joaquín.
> I rode to the East and the North
> as far as the Rocky Mountains
> And men feared the pistols
> of Joaquín Murrieta.

Joaquín, as a symbol of Chicanos, is, for the first time in the literature of his people, identified with Mexicans and their culture, which are exalted and praised for their merit and values. He is directly identified with various mythic Mexican heroes. Some are Indians from the period before the conquest; another, Juan Diego, is also an Indian who belongs to the colonial period. Finally, two are twentieth-century revolutionaries. The voice of Joaquín declares:

> I am Cuauhtémoc
> majestic and noble
> a leader of men ...
> I am Nezahualcóyotl,
> the renowned chief of the Chichimecas.
>
> I am the loyal, the humble Juan Diego
> I am ... the apostle of Democracy
> Francisco I. Madero.

However, there is never a direct identification with Pancho Villa. It is clear that Joaquín is not Villa, for he calls himself a companion of the rebel chief, who remains at a distance:

> I am Joaquín
> I rode with Pancho Villa,
> so coarse and charming.

On the other hand, there is total identification with Zapata, who had fought to reclaim the land. Joaquín allows the hero of the South to speak:

> I am Emiliano Zapata.
> "This land,
> this earth, is OURS."

This identification with popular Mexican heroes, whether direct or indirect, represents only one of Joaquín's two faces; the other is formed by antiheroes and despots like Hernán Cortés, Porfirio Díaz, and Victoriano Huerta. The connection in the case of Cortés, however, is not to the conqueror himself, but to his sword, the symbol of the destruction of the indigenous cultures:

402

> I am the sword and the flame
> of Cortés, the despot.

To counteract the shock of the identification with the conqueror, there is an immediate reference to the symbol that unites the Aztecs that Cortés conquered with the Mexicans of today:

> I am the eagle and the serpent
> of the Aztec civilization.

While the poem foregrounds the identification of Joaquín with Mexican heroes, antiheroes, and symbols, that is not the only association, for there is also a natural association with popular Chicano heroes such as Elfego Baca and the Espinoza brothers of the San Luis Valley, who, in a parallel structure, are identified with Mexican heroes. But the main association that structures the entire poem is, of course, a mythical synthesis with Murrieta:

> Hidalgo! Zapata!
> Murrieta! Espinozas!

The syncretic cultural images of the poem give form to another type of identity that involves the gods, the people, and the symbols of the nation and of nature. The antithetical images and concepts are multiplied, and Joaquín becomes a Mayan prince, but he is also Christ; he is a pagan and also a Christian; he is the sword of Cortés and also the Aztec's eagle and serpent; he is a tyrant as well as a slave; he is the Virgen de Guadalupe and also Tonantzin; he is a member of the rural police and also a revolutionary; he is Indian and also Spanish; he is a mestizo and also a criollo; he is a soldier and also a *soldadera;* he is a farm laborer and also a farm owner. But most of all, he is the Chicano people, the outcome of a racial, social, and cultural synthesis. Chicanos are the descendants of racial mixtures; they are the representatives of that mythical cosmic race of which Vasconcelos spoke. Joaquín is a Yaqui, a Tarahumara, a

Chamula, a Zapotec, a mestizo, a Spaniard, a Mexican, a Latino, an *hispano,* a Chicano, or whatever I may call myself:

> I will look the same
> I will feel the same
> I cry and I sing the same.

Of all the mythical Mexican heroes, the figure of Zapata is the one that has most influenced Chicano writers, artists, and leaders. Among the younger generation, however, there already is an apparent desire to demythify the great hero. An example of this is found in "The Eyes of Zapata," a short story by Sandra Cisneros, from her collection *Woman Hollering Creek.* In the story, Zapata appears not as the mythical hero of the corridos and the narrative literature of Mexico and Aztlán, but as he is seen by one of his numerous lovers, a woman named Inés Alfaro, with whom he had children but did not wish to marry. According to the character of Inés, Zapata is a legend, a myth, and a god to other women. But to her, Miliano (as she calls him) is the young man she met at the fair of San Lázaro; he is not a peasant who dresses in the white linen trousers and blouse of Diego Rivera's Cuernavaca murals. No, he is a horseman who wears the tight pants; the short jacket; and the large, braided sombrero of the *charro.* Although the peasants may follow him they know that he is not of their social class, that he is not one of them.

Another myth demythified by Sandra Cisneros is that of La Llorona, a story as popular among Mexicans as it is among Chicanos. Her demythification takes place in her story "Woman Hollering Creek." The demythification consists, first of all, in the name change from woman crying to woman hollering. Furthermore, the story is no longer the lament of a woman in search of her lost children, but the triumphant shout of a woman who is liberated from the man who abused her. Before Cisneros's short story, Rudolfo Anaya had tried to demythify La Llorona by identifying her with a historical character, Doña Marina, who killed her children rather than permit Hernán Cortés to take them away to Spain.

In Chicano literature, Luis Valdez demythified the Spanish conquest of Mexico in an *acto,* a play based on the historical events, in which he uses irony and satire to demythify the heroes, now seen from a Chicano perspective. The conquistadores are characterized as ordinary men who are more interested in finding gold than in the redemption of the Indians. The satiric, demythifying effect is obtained by means of various linguistic devices such as translating proper names into English (Herman Cortez, Pete Alvarado) and also by attributing modern-day negative characteristics to the principal characters: Cortez is a bearded coyote, the term used to describe a smuggler of undocumented persons; Fray Bartolo is Cortez's chief witch doctor; La Malinche (Cortez's Indian mistress) is the first traitor. The only character that is not demythified is Cuauhtémoc, who opposes the Aztec emperor Moctezuma. He attempts to convince the emperor that the Spaniards are not gods and calls on him to defend his empire. In the final speech of the *acto,* Cuauhtémoc blames the Mexicans, saying that they were defeated because they lacked unity. But he is already speaking from a contemporary perspective, given that the *acto* is directed at farmworkers who lost their fight against the owners because of the same lack of unity. Cuauhtémoc says, "We Mexicans of ancient times lost because we were not united with our *raza* brothers, because we believed that those white men were powerful gods and because we never wised up."

Luis Valdez's characterization of Doña Marina (La Malinche) is consistent with the image of her that has prevailed in Mexico, which condemns her as a woman who betrayed her people. The voice of the sunstone, which presents the historical events in the *acto,* says of La Malinche, "She was destined to be an infamous figure in the history of Mexico. Not only did she turn her back on her own people, she joined the white men and assimilated, serving them as a guide and interpreter, and generally assisting in the process of the Conquest."

The social myth of Doña Marina as a traitor to her people has been contested by Chicana writers who have created a countermyth of La Malinche as a heroine, as a feminist prototype, and as the creator of the "cosmic race."

The influence of Mayan mythology on Chicano literature is evident in two short stories, "The Village Which the Gods Painted Yellow," by Rudolfo Anaya, published in his 1982 collection *The Silent Llano,* and in "One Holy Night," by Sandra Cisneros, which is included in her previously mentioned book of short stories. Both stories are shaped by the well-known legend of the dwarf, of Uxmal. Anaya re-creates the mythical character of legend by giving him a new dimension (e.g., death and resurrection), whereas Cisneros attempts to demythify the dwarf of Uxmal by presenting him as a picaresque figure who uses the myth to seduce and deceive women. Gonzalo, a tourist guide, is the reincarnation of the dwarf of Uxmal in Anaya's story. According to the myth, the dwarf of Uxmal constructed a palace (or a pyramid) overnight. Thus, Gonzalo, a lame, hunchbacked dwarf, wants to repeat the feat, but when he fails to do so, he is sacrificed, and the same fate will await his successor. The rite, which is carried out "in honor of the dying sun," is reenacted annually on the day of the winter solstice.

Sandra Cisneros's character, on the other hand, is not a real dwarf representing Uxmal, but a vagrant who calls himself Chaq Uxmal Palenquín and says that he is a descendant of the Mayan princes. His name means "boy-child," which becomes Boy Baby in the story. Boy Baby says that when he was a child, he prayed in the Temple of Uxmal the Magician (in other words, in the Temple of the Dwarf), where his father made him promise that he would restore the ancient Mayan traditions. The reader discovers, however, that Boy Baby is actually a bluebeard who uses the Uxmal myth to deceive and seduce women. There is a suggestion that he already has killed more than seven women. The two stories are good examples of the tendency in contemporary Chicano literature to both re-create and demythify some of the traditional Mexican myths.

Mutual Understanding Through Literature

In general, it can be said that the fiction writer is able to create imaginary worlds in which history and myth work hand in hand to present a reality that transcends cultural frontiers. Yet one must also keep in mind that those works of fiction either may be the result of cultural and racial antagonisms or may represent a desire to bring peoples together. Although in the nineteenth century some fiction writers in the United States spread the myth of Mexican racial and cultural inferiority, others defended the Mexicans.

The image of Mexico current at the time—the result of a limited knowledge of Mexico's cultural values—was replaced during the twentieth century by a more balanced understanding. In some writers, this appeared as outright sympathy and admiration for Mexican culture, which previously had been considered exotic, distant, and incomprehensible. Although some critics may claim that sympathy is not mutual among Mexican writers, a more careful analysis reveals that Mexico, too, has experienced a change in the attitude of its writers toward North American culture, a change that tends to be much more favorable.

In conclusion, it is apparent that the study of literature helps to complement the historical view that the inhabitants of a given country may have of themselves and of their neighbors. Unfortunately, in the case of Mexico and the United States, critics have not taken into consideration the reciprocal influence that the two literatures have had on the development of political and cultural relations between the two countries. My hope is that this brief essay will encourage others to undertake further research, as the subject is a promising one that would undoubtedly help to improve relations between these neighboring countries, the representatives of the two great cultures of the American landscape.

Index

Luis Leal has been a member of the faculty of the University of California, Santa Barbara, since 1976. In 1991 he received the Aztec Eagle from the Mexican government and in 1997 the National Humanities Medal from President Clinton. Each year the Luis Leal Award for Distinction in Chicano/Latino Literature is presented for a landmark work in Latino literature.

Ilan Stavans is the Lewis-Sebring Professor in Latin American and Latino Culture and Five College–Fortieth Anniversary Professor at Amherst College. His books include *The Hispanic Condition, Art and Anger, The Oxford Book of Latin American Essays, The Riddle of Cantinflas, Mutual Impressions, On Borrowed Words, Spanglish: The Making of a New American Language,* and *The Essential Ilan Stavans.* His work has been translated into a dozen languages.